The Lean Sustainable
Supply Chain

The Lean Sustainable Supply Chain

How to Create a Green Infrastructure with Lean Technologies

Robert Palevich

Vice President, Publisher: Tim Moore
Associate Publisher and Director of Marketing: Amy Neidlinger
Executive Editor: Jeanne Glasser
Editorial Assistant: Pamela Boland
Operations Specialist: Jodi Kemper
Senior Marketing Manager: Julie Phifer
Assistant Marketing Manager: Megan Graue
Cover Designer: Alan Clements
Managing Editor: Kristy Hart
Project Editor: Betsy Harris
Copy Editor: Cheri Clark
Proofreader: Kathy Ruiz
Indexer: Lisa Stumpf
Compositor: Nonie Ratcliff
Manufacturing Buyer: Dan Uhrig

Pearson Education LTD.
Pearson Education Australia PTY, Limited.
Pearson Education Singapore, Pte. Ltd.
Pearson Education Asia, Ltd.
Pearson Education Canada, Ltd.
Pearson Educación de Mexico, S.A. de C.V.
Pearson Education—Japan
Pearson Education Malaysia, Pte. Ltd.

Library of Congress Cataloging-in-Publication Data

Palevich, Robert, 1945-
  The lean sustainable supply chain : how to create a green infrastructure with lean technologies / Robert Palevich.
    p. cm.
  ISBN 978-0-13-283761-3 (hardback : alk. paper)
  1. Business logistics. 2. Business logistics--Environmental aspects. 3. Technological innovations--Management--Environmental aspects. 4. Industrial management--Environmental aspects. I. Title.
  HD38.5.P348 2012
  658.7--dc23
                          2011041342

My book is dedicated to my loving parents,
Frank and Lucille Palevich,
for always believing in me.

Contents

Foreword xi

Preface xvii

Part I: **Applied Savings to the Collaborative Supply Chain**

Chapter 1   Lean Sustainable Technologies. 1

Putting It All Together 2

Creating the World-Class Company 3

Lean and Green Savings Using EDI 18

Certification Program and Scorecarding 24

References. 26

Chapter 2   Warehouse Management System (WMS). . .27

System Integration with the WMS. 28

The Functionality of the WMS. 28

Metrics Used in a WMS .31

Improve Inventory Management 34

The Improved Warehouse Worker
Productivity. 34

Improved Transportation Performance 35

Radio Frequency (RF) as a Warehouse
Management System—An Introduction into
RF Systems Used in the Distribution Centers . . .38

The Importance of the Voluntary Interindustry
Commerce Solutions Association to the Industry   42

The Applied RF Analysis: Receiving,
Directed Putaway, Stocking, and Order Filling. . .43

The Applied RF Metrics Used
in the Distribution Centers. 46

References. 47

Chapter 3   The Use of Radio Frequency Identity Tags
in Industry 49

Case Studies of Two Industries: The Medical
Environment and the Distribution Industry 60

References. 75

Chapter 4   Transportation Management
System (TMS). 77
References. 95

Chapter 5   **Savings of B2B E-commerce**. 97
The Vendor Portal. 98
The Customer Portal 101
The Distribution Portal. 107
Green IT 109
References. 119

Chapter 6   **The Introduction of Enterprise Resource**
Programs (ERP). .121
Business Processes and Analytics Features
That Can Add to the ERP Software Solution . . . 124
CRM Features. 125
Financials Features. .126
Human Resource Management Features 127
Manufacturing Features 127
Supply Chain Management (SCM) Features . . . 128
The Quantifiable Benefits of an ERP System . . . 129
ERP's Sustainable Drive to Green. 131
The Collaborative Sustainability
Scorecard or KPI. 133
References. 135

Chapter 7   **Third-Party Provider** 137
Multimodal 138
Onsite Supplier 138
Network Optimization 139
Benefits of a 3PL. 142
Lean Savings 143
Green Savings 144
References. 145

Chapter 8   **Inventory Control** .147
Pareto ABCDE Classification of Inventory. 147

Chapter 9   **Promotional Forecast System** 159
Lean Savings for Promotional Forecast
Program. 163

Chapter 10   **An Introduction to Distribution Resource**
Management. 165
Container Delivery Management. 165

Chapter 11 Joint Order Allocation **173**
           Lean Savings 177
           Green Savings 177
Chapter 12 **Variable or Fixed Reorder Periods 179**
           Fixed Period Model (FP) 179
           Fixed Order Model (FQ) 185
           Variable Period and Quantity Model (VPQ)
           with Look-Ahead. 190
Chapter 13 **Furthering Collaboration with Suppliers**
           (CPFR) 199
           The New CPFR Model. 201
           Collaborative Transportation Management 212
           References. 213
Chapter 14 **Material Handling Technology, Voice Pick,**
           and Pick to Light Technologies 215
           Batch Order Summary Sheets 217
           The Installation of the RF System 224
           The Receiving Process and the Stocking Process . . 225
           References. 237

Section I: **Introduction to an Application of Lean,**
           Green Supply Chain Management *External*
Chapter 15 **The Visual and Visible Supply Chain 239**
           The Visual Supply Chain. 239
           The Visible Supply Chain 242
Chapter 16 **Master Data Alignment and Item**
           Synchronization 245
           References. 253

Section II: **Introduction to an Application of Lean,**
           Green Supply Chain Management *Internal*
Chapter 17 **Internal Supply Chain 255**
           Environmental Facts. 255
           Designing a Paperless Environment
           with Software. 255
           Mobius Software: A Division of ASG Software 258
           System Advantages 259
           Oracle Content Management. 260
           References. 273

Part II: **Technical Sections**

Chapter 18   A Technical Explanation of Forecasting
Systems. 275
The Algebraic Model 276
Multivariate Regression Models. 278
Trigonometric Models 280
The Logistics Model 281
The Logarithmic Models 282
Exponential Smoothing. 284
Dispersion of Demand 297
Finding the Correct Forecast Model 300

Chapter 19   Forecasting Methodology and Gamma
Smoothing: A Solution to Better Accuracy
to Maintain Lean and Green 305
Introduction of Gamma Smoothing. 305
A Comparison Using Gamma Smoothing
and Exponentials Smoothing 308
The Trend Section of Gamma Smoothing
Using TI. 312

Chapter 20   The Characteristics Needed in a Forecast
Program 345

Chapter 21   The New Sustainable EOQ Formula 353
The Old Economic Order Formula 354
The New Economic Order Formula 361
The Green Effect of the New EOQ Formula . . . 366

Chapter 22   Consequences of the Industrial Revolution . .369
References. 374

Chapter 23   Different Organizations' Green Supply
Chain Management and LEED 375
References. 382

Chapter 24   Case Study: Sweetwater Sound. 383
Sweetwater Case Study. 383
References. 388

Chapter 25   Case Study: Behavioral Health 389
Case Study of the Six Sigma DMAIC
Approach in Health Care 390

Appendix A   The Summary of the Lean and Green
Technologies 407

Index. 409

Foreword

Do it Best Corporation got its start back in 1945 as the vision of Arnold Gerberding. It was known then as Hardware Wholesalers, Inc. (HWI). Gerberding set out to build an entirely new way of serving the needs of independently owned hardware stores and lumberyards. From those humble early days of the co-op and just a few hundred members in the Midwest, Do it Best Corp. has grown into a $3 billion worldwide distributor of hardware, lumber, and building materials with close to 4,000 member locations and operations in more than 50 countries around the world. That growth would not have been possible without an industry-leading supply chain.

The company's first computer was purchased in 1964: an IBM 1401 with a whopping 8K of memory! It was out-of-date almost before it was turned on. Its capabilities were certainly limited, but it was an important investment in keeping up with the company's rapidly growing base of members. Its tasks were limited to maintaining a perpetual inventory, generating billings and packing slips, and other routine tasks. With upgrades to the "next generation" of computers, an IBM 360 in 1968 and an IBM 370 in 1972, the company soon realized that the new systems could be a powerful tool in the buying and replenishment function. The ideal system would be able to track merchandise movement, vendor performance, and customer requirements. At the heart of this was the need for an effective replenishment system that factored in lead times, customer demand, promotional impact, and seasonality to help maximize inventory turns and fill rate.

Enter Rob Palevich.

Rob started with HWI in August 1970. With his undergraduate degree in industrial management and computers and a master's in business administration, he was in the perfect position to take control of the company's inventory control efforts. Rob single-handedly developed the software for a unique automated order and replenishment system called FOURTE, or Forecasting and Ordering Using Regression, Time Series, and Econometrics. In 1981, HWI was able to put the FOURTE system into service as the industry's most sophisticated inventory control system, helping the company achieve fill rates of close to 95% in its then four distribution centers. The system analyzed data for every item, vendor, and line of merchandise handled by HWI. It took into account product seasonality, regional differences, store purchase history, and more. The program could also adjust to increase an order to meet minimum dollar, weight, or cube requirements, and it could factor in manufacturing and delivery lead times as well. This extraordinary system did much more, from aiding in financial control to pinpointing problem areas and analyzing cash flow impacts. In short, Rob Palevich's development of FOURTE revolutionized the manner in which purchasing and distribution would be managed going forward and gave HWI another considerable competitive advantage in the marketplace.

The steady advancement in computer memory and processing speed provided Rob with strong, new tools and an ever-expanding canvas to further his development of the FOURTE system. As HWI became Do it Best Corp. and the company continued its rapid growth, FOURTE enabled it to maintain a fill rate in excess of 96% on more than 65,000 items in eight distribution centers with accuracy in excess of 99%. Not a bad effort for a young man who started out in the data processing department at $3.12 per hour!

Throughout his career, Rob has demonstrated a thirst for learning. Name a programming language and he's most likely studied it and used it. In 1998, he spearheaded an initial entry into e-commerce with the launch of doitbest.com. In 2001, Indiana University–Purdue University Fort Wayne (IPFW) recognized Rob with their Distinguished Service Award for his engagement with the University. He's also the only person in the company's history to have used the tuition assistance program to study two years of Chinese...not a surprise if you know Rob. But his passion all along has always been in improving the supply chain.

After 33 years of service, Rob retired from Do it Best Corporation but didn't stay idle for very long. He began a teaching career at nearby IPFW with a focus on SAP, enterprise resource management, and supply chain excellence. He quickly put his background and experience to work in the development of long-range radio-frequency identification tags. Rob is the founding director of the Business Enterprise System and Technology (BEST) Institute at the Richard T. Doermer

School of Business at IPFW, a center for knowledge management and networking in Northeast Indiana. He also serves as CEO of RP Global Technology Solutions.

Based on a considerable measure of practical hands-on experience and focused through a lens keenly trained on the future, *The Lean Sustainable Supply Chain* provides an important framework for developing a world-class supply chain that is both lean and green. It moves far beyond the basics of "inventory" management to the exceedingly more complex and content-rich environment of "information" management, and it provides a GPS map for the road to the future of the global supply chain. Even while Rob is officially retired, his talents and expertise continue to feed the success of Do it Best Corporation as they raise the bar on supply chain initiatives and strive to make the best better.

Robert N. Taylor
President & CEO
Do it Best Corp.

Acknowledgments

I am grateful for all the support I have received from so many people in writing this book. I credit Dr. Jim Moore from the Richard T. Doermer School of Business for encouraging me to participate in an International Symposium on the Green Supply Chain at Kent University. Winning the competition ultimately led to my decision to share my insights.

I want to convey many thanks to Jacqui Petersen, Bobbi Barnes, Cynthia Wilson, and Dr. Karen Moustafa Leonard for encouraging me to write a book and helping with initial editing. I also greatly appreciate the dedication of Renee Kosor, who worked tirelessly to complete the project.

I would like to give special acknowledgment to Robert N. Taylor, President and CEO of Do it Best Corp. I am humbled and sincerely appreciate the "glowing" foreword he penned for my book. I am indebted to his support and the opportunities I have enjoyed from working at Do it Best Corp. That background has enabled me to understand the intricacies of the supply chain command.

Last, but not least, I would like to recognize my wife, Bonnie, and family: Chris, Angie, Jessica, Rylee, and Maya. They have endured my long ordeal and interruptions even on vacation.

About the Author

Robert Palevich is a full-time professor at Indiana University–Purdue University Fort Wayne, Indiana (IPFW). His teaching areas are E-commerce and B2B, SAP and ERP, Lean Black Belt Six Sigma, Operation Management, Statistics, Discriminant Analysis Linear Programming, and Web Page Design. His research interests are Lean manufacturing and the Lean service industries, Six Sigma and process analysis, RFID, and the sustainable green supply chain.

He is the director of the Business Enterprise Systems and Technology Institute (BEST) at IPFW. The purpose of the BEST Institute is to inform, educate, and help existing companies attract new businesses and industries by creating a center for knowledge management and networking for all the companies in Northeast Indiana. With the cooperation of the BEST Institute and RP Global Technology Solutions, he received a $250,000 grant for the University from the Strategic Skill Initiative (SSI) for teaching the most relevant and current technologies.

Palevich is also President and CEO of RP Global Technology Solutions LLC. The company specializes in advanced technology for companies throughout the state. The technology includes RFID, Visual and Sensor Equipment, Six Sigma, ERP, Lean Manufacturing, Supply Chain, and CPFR technology.

Prior to teaching at the university, he has had 25 years of supply chain experience in logistics and enterprise resource planning at a $2.0 billion wholesaler (Do it Best Corp.) with 4,500 stores worldwide. His responsibility as CTO was to bring in all new Internet, Electronic Commerce, EDI, and Supply Chain Management (SCM) technology. He was involved with the development and integration of the Business Process Design (BPD) of the Supply Chain, Logistics, WMS systems, Knowledge Management (KM), Product Lifecycle Management (PLM), Supplier Compliance, and integrated workflow in Purchasing. He had collaborated with approximately 25 Fortune 500 companies in the process of developing certification standards between the respective companies and sharing technological innovations. He has also traveled in North America, Latin America, and Asia in consulting and educational roles.

Palevich programmed the entire Supply Chain and Inventory Control Forecasting Program, which was named FOURTE, for Do it Best Corp. FOURTE stands for Forecasting and Ordering Using Regression, Time Series, and Econometrics. The company used this program for well over 10 years to enjoy the industry-leading service levels and inventory turns.

His education and background are as detailed here:

SAS INSTITUTE CARY NC:

- Completed *all* their classes for statistics, ETS Statistical Analysis, ANOVA, MANOVA, Box and Jenkins, ARMA, ARIMA, Time Series, Correlation Analysis, Categorical Analysis, Factor Analysis, Regression Analysis, Polynomial Regression, Non Linear Regression, Neural Networks

INDIANA UNIVERSITY: MBA

PURDUE UNIVERSITY: post-graduate research in Advanced Mathematics and Statistics. Dr. David Bendixon

INDIANA UNIVERSITY: MSBA

PURDUE UNIVERSITY: BS in Industrial Management

Certified by CompTIA in 2008 as an "RFID and Supply Chain Certified Professional"

Preface

This book is a summary of the experiences I have had working with many Fortune 500 companies such as GE, 3M, National Manufacturing, Sherwin-Williams, Black & Decker, Manco, and others on collaborative processes. The rationale for this collaboration was that in today's global economy each company needed to work together to enhance corporate processes to become "Best of Breed." It is amazing what can be learned from each company during yearly technology sessions when best technologies are shared so that every company reaps the benefits. The ideas and strategies explored in this book form a compendium of those best practices and shared technology over the past 25 years.

The inspiration for writing this book began when I won the award of first place in the case study track at the International Symposium of Supply Chain Management held at Kent State University in 2010. My specialty focused on applications that clarified the newest technologies with Lean initiatives and how those technological advances affect the Green environment. The purpose of this book is to break down the processes used in creating a world-class company so that any manager interested in cutting the fat can implement the technological advances now available.

This book will demonstrate how to calculate a scorecard for the various enterprise Lean technologies introduced and will act as a Lean Savings Report and a Green Sustainability Report including environmental savings. The Lean Savings will show the increased productivity incurred from the usage of the various technologies. The Lean metrics will show how much each of these technologies saves in these areas:

- Personnel
- Paper usage
- Increased productivity
- Lessened building space, allowing for less utility usage
- Fewer miles traveled in the transportation system
- Better service levels

- Increased margins
- Lower inventory levels
- Better turns
- More efficient utilization of IT resources
- Better morale

The environmental Green Savings include the following:

- Less electrical usage due to the need for fewer employees
- Carbon savings as a result of the decreased electrical usage
- Smaller amounts of paperwork, translating into fewer trees cut down per year
- Lesser amounts of carbon dioxide being emitted and using fewer trees resulting from lean management styles and technology
- Fewer miles driven due to the use of the Transportation Management System lead to a reduction in the pounds of CO2 footprint in the environment.
- Less highway wear and tear as a result of fewer miles traveled
- Less space utilization, requiring less building expense and upkeep

Each technology is introduced so that the reader not only understands how to implement each improvement but can measure the successes through increased company performance as well as environmental Green Savings. The formulas are presented to calculate the annual decrease of carbon dioxide and conversion of gasoline from gallons to pounds of CO_2. This is shown in the introduction of each technology. At the end of the chapters, Appendix A summarizes the savings that points out each technology's effect on the company's bottom line and performance. The time has come to learn to adapt to new innovations and enhance shareowners' benefits and profitability.

1

Lean Sustainable Technologies

The supply chain is composed of all the parts of the enterprise and its associated trading partners. The Lean Green Supply Chain is made up of two major components: external and internal. There is a synergy between these two parts. The internal savings can, in some cases, be equal to the external supply chain savings. To exclude the internal improvements that supplement the productivity of the External Lean Supply Chain is to miss out on a major component of long-term sustainability.

The external side represents the suppliers and customers throughout the supply chain. Collaborative technologies and software can be used to minimize the cost of the organization and decrease the company's carbon footprint. Forecasting procedures reduce the variation in systems processes in their connection with suppliers and customers in the external supply chain. Improving forecasting methodology through the implementation of Gamma Smoothing increases accuracy in forecasting and stimulates savings.

The typical EOQ (Economic Order Quantity) considers mere receiving and carrying costs in the warehouse. The new EOQ model moves companies beyond current warehousing needs and into the external environment. Through the incorporation of inbound and outbound freight, the EOQ model increases forecasting accuracy, leading to cost reduction throughout the external supply chain.

The internal supply chain is composed of the technologies that can be used to make the corporation and its employees more productive. Implementation leads to lowering the amount of space and resources necessary to perform the job. This represents the definition of Lean and Green sustainability. The sustainability effort needs to incorporate workflow technologies and the use of software to minimize the use of paper and other costly resources.

Putting It All Together

Now it's time to enter customers and suppliers into the equation of collaboration. The most important consideration at this point is what is best for the entire supply chain. This can be emphasized only by involving the other suppliers and customers. What is good for one may not work for all. For example, 10% of the United States GDP (Gross Domestic Product), which was $14.26 in 2010, is involved with supply chain. Today's companies are realizing that the competition is not with their competitors but with competing supply chains.

According to a study by consultants A.T. Kearney, inefficiencies in supply chains can waste up to 25% of a company's operating costs. In companies with profit margins of 3% to 4%, even 5% improvements in supply chain efficiencies focusing just on material flow can double profit margins.[1] The supply chain is the greatest cost in today's industry and consequently has the best chance for the highest return if the process can be further improved.

One measure of the ability of a company to enhance its standing among the competition is the metric called Gross Margin Return on Investment (GMROI). GMROI looks at a company's quantitative ability to compete. GMROI is the gross margin percentage of a company multiplied by the inventory turns of that company. Turns are the term used to convey how well a company turns its inventory. Turns = while GMROI = GM × Turns. If two companies have the same gross margins, with one company's inventory turns being 50% better than its competitor's, the company with the higher turns is making more profit for the enterprise. For example:

> *Company A* has a gross margin of 20% and has 3 inventory turns. The GMROI throughout the year on their inventory investment is an average of 3 × 20% = 60%.
>
> *Company B* has a gross margin of 20% and has higher inventory turns of 4.5. Company B's GMROI is 4.5 × 20% = 90%.

Company B is making 90% on its inventory investment for the year. It is also making more money on opportunity cost because company B has 50% fewer inventories held as compared to Company A. This frees up capital or expenses if loans are involved. Company B can now afford to sell at a lower cost and also sell more expensive alternatives at lower prices.

Sustainability is meeting the needs of the present generation without compromising the needs of future generations. For every $1,000 spent on Lean Technologies, there is a Green payback of approximately $426, which includes savings in the environment. The greatest Green Savings is found in the transportation highway infrastructure yearly maintenance costs. Removing the cost of the transportation infrastructure from the scenario still provides for approximately $280 savings for every $1,000 spent on Green. The payback is well worth the cost, not only in dollars but also in sustainability.

Creating the World-Class Company

The following sections describe the initial components to create a world-class company. We begin with resource management, the management of resources to differentiate the company from competition. This is followed by the second part, which is forecasting the future enterprise inventory requirements. This is not just about the forecasting methodology but also integration and collaboration within the value chain. The term *value chain* is used to make notice of all the savings within the supply chain, savings that can separate your firm from the competition. The collaboration was made possible with VMI (vendor-managed inventory) and certification programs. The topics of EDI (electronic data interchange) and the various transaction sets are used for infrastructure integration and automation. At the end is a summary of the lean and green benefits.

Step One: Resource Management

The global competition is changing for the entire set of business paradigms. Today's companies need to be more competitive, flexible, innovative, and lean because of increased global competition. It is not a privilege to make a profit today, it is an expectation of stakeholders—employees, banks, government, and suppliers. The global recession has forced companies to cut costs and look for new, innovative ways to do more with fewer people. This has brought on the concept of Innovation Management, the need to think creatively and find better ways to be more productive. This differentiates a company from its competition.

How can a company remain innovative enough to separate itself from the competition? This was Steve Job's major mantra when he came back to Apple Corporation in 1997. Apple needed to catch up with the competition: IBM. At the time, people needed something different to overcome their fear of computers. Steve's comment to the team at Apple was, "Apple cannot keep trying to get one step better than their rivals. They must be innovative and make something different." This was the start of Apple's comeback with the introduction of the iMac.

The iMac was the first computer that looked friendly and came in bright, vivid colors. This simple change brought about the start of Apple's great growth pattern. The popular belief is that if Apple would have waited an additional year, they would have been doomed. Another example of Apple's innovative philosophy involved asking their employees to spend 20% of their time thinking creatively. The employees sat in a comfortable room, separate from their work area, to explore ideas that were new and innovative.

Charles Darwin said, "It's not the strongest species that survive, or the most intelligent, but the most responsive to change." Innovation Management is the concept of trying to create the most innovative atmosphere in the company that's possible. How do employers teach people to think beyond the box? One way to facilitate this is to have the managers go to one or two conferences focusing on areas where improvement is needed each year and then return to share their knowledge with the rest of the staff.

Staff training is a good time to facilitate affinity analysis. This is the concept of recording the ideas on a chart so that the information is easily seen by the group. The information flow can be categorized and prioritized by importance. An overriding theme for each innovative improvement is to improve the product by changing the playing field on the competition. Implementing an open training forum makes it harder for competitors to ramp up in a new direction. By the time they catch up, the innovative management team is already on the next playing field.

Innovation Management will not succeed without Talent Management. Creativity and innovation are viable only when the most talented people in the organization are placed into an atmosphere conducive to thinking outside the box. Google understands this concept and touts the practice on their Web site of creating "an atmosphere that, when they had hired the most talented people, they, in turn, did not want to leave. This not only refers to not leaving for another job, but also refers to wanting to spend more time at work. The employees actually enjoy being at work." Innovation Management drives talented people to companies that practice this method.

Employee retention requires a top-down attitude of Talent Management. Creating a desirable work environment might mean providing on-site health classes such as yoga, offering local gym memberships, or bringing in guest speakers to focus on personal and professional improvement. The benefit to the company includes decreased health-related absences, lower health-insurance costs, and increased camaraderie among the staff. For employees in manufacturing or distribution, injuries such as carpal tunnel syndrome are commonplace. The wellness program can help lower the incidence of medical claims.

The final piece of the Talent Management puzzle is the profit-sharing program. Profit sharing creates a personal stake in the success of the company, which increases employee productivity. Do it Best Corp. has instituted a profit-sharing program that led to one of the highest retention rates in the industry. Their profit sharing today is over 20% of employee pay, which has increased staff involvement in cost-cutting methodology.

After the talent is in place, the next necessary step is to spark the innovative talents of the staff by creating an atmosphere of Change Management. The key element in Change Management is continuous improvement through motivating employees to consider change a benefit and to embrace each one as a new challenge. This is done with the introduction of continuous improvement concepts. These improvements can be introduced to the employees in a discussion forum, which allows them to confer with others on the viability of each concept.

For example, the manager's job is to find the why and how of extra inventory problems. Employees have the answers and a good manager seeks those answers through the philosophy of Management by Walking Around (MBWA). Managers who are there to listen allow subordinates to be more open to sharing improvement ideas. Sometimes the best ideas come from informal conversations with employees. Employee objectives should be made visible through the use of scoreboards throughout the office and communicated through weekly meetings. The objectives are then used to create constant awareness in the way each step is taken in the supply chain.

Employees who are rewarded with incentives are more likely to consider corporate objectives and improved processes. Acknowledgement of critical milestones through the creation of public displays promotes the team players who can be imaginative. Companies that nurture the spirit of thinking beyond the box open communication and encourage and reward new ideas. The corporate culture of new idea generation requires constant nourishment. It also requires the right people who are self-motivated and willing to work with others.

An additional but essential part of Change Management is execution. There are too many CEOs and directors not clearly tied to their goals. Their pay and bonus structure does not reflect the performance and profitability of the company. To move with the times, execution must reflect from the top of the organization down to the production floor.

Companies have prospered through the generations with each technological advancement:

In 1910: Mass production

In 1960: Lean technologies

In 1980: Flexibility through computerization

In 1990: Reconfiguration

In 2000: Knowledge management

In the era of knowledge management, the leaders must grow creatively to unlock the potential of the personnel. The only way to perform this is through Execution Management. Steve Jobs of Apple Computers envisioned the Mac computer, iPod, iPhone, iPad, and iTunes. He knew how to execute the vision and make it happen. Allen Mulally of the Ford Motor Company turned Boeing around and then transformed Ford with its new styling and innovative models.

Execution is giving the personnel direction and a vision of what needs to be accomplished. A company can empower employees to succeed by enabling them to make the vision possible while motivating them to use their talents to execute the vision. Execution is making things happen that delight the customers and shareholders.

Technology is changing the environment, allowing companies to execute in an even more expeditious fashion. There are four trends that make this possible:

1. Development of an ERP (Enterprise Resource Planning) environment. All knowledge in real time and all from the same source. Information is more accurate and relevant, which expedites decisions and informs all interested parties of progress.

2. On-demand, which means going to the next-generation real-time management systems called SAAS, or Software as a Service. The user is billed and pays only for what is used. This software is more pervasive than the old-style ERP systems. It is assumed that the software will be downloaded from the Internet in a cloud, ASP (Application Service Provider), or App Environment. Now information analysis can be more readily available on all data realized from the ERP system above.

3. BI, or Business Intelligence, which is software that is inbred into a DSS, or Decision Support System. This expands the horizon of the two preceding steps. Analysis is achieved with the on-demand software, and the information received will translate to knowledge for the corporation through the use of Business Intelligence. It allows the intellectual capacity of the analytics system support to aid the managers in decision making and risk analysis. This difference is what separates the leaders from the followers.

4. On Device, or mobile, which means that the employee can be engaged anytime and anyplace. This has started the new generation of the always-on, always-connected world. These devices will transform the business industry. Now when decisions need to be made immediately, communication between management and staff will not be put on hold. The decisions can be made more expeditiously.

After the team is in place, the Lean Green journey can continue through the management paradigm and begin again with Innovation Management. Innovation Management works best when Talent and Change Management techniques are implemented in unison. For instance, when a new forecast system was needed to streamline the purchase of 55,000 items, innovative management sought out the most qualified employee and worked with him to allow his creativity to produce the technology necessary to create the system. He was permitted to leave the job site daily at noon and work at the location of his choosing for six months.

From a table at a local coffee shop, this employee coded the Forecasting and Ordering Using Regression, Time Series and Econometrics (FOURTE) system. When implemented, FOURTE allowed the company to differentiate itself from the competition by attaining the industry leadership in turns and service level. The system increased productivity by a factor of 16. The same employee was later offered the opportunity to design the only promotional forecast system in the industry using SAS as the analytic engine. Without an attitude of innovation, this company would have missed out on long-term sustainability and an unmatchable competitive edge.

Today's successful company involves each department in the corporation as well as customers and suppliers along the supply chain. Collaborative versions of technology software such as ERP II (Enterprise Resource Planning) and MRP II (networked closed-loop manufacturing requirement planning) are networked with accounting financials and other departments such as Human Resource, Distribution, and Marketing. The one overriding feature is that there are no more silos for independent enterprise software. The common thread in creating the world-class corporation is determining how each decision affects every point in the supply chain, as well as knowing what is best for the entire company.

Step Two: Forecasting the Future Enterprise Inventory Requirements: Best of Breed Forecast Systems and the Supply Chain

Vendor-Managed Inventory

Vendor-managed inventory (VMI) is an agreement between the supplier and the retailer of merchandise. The retailer must give the usages, on-hand and on-order information to the supplier so that they can take full responsibility for maintaining the retailer's inventory. This is usually in the form of an EDI (electronic data interchange) transaction set 852. The supplier now has the goal of balancing the demand and supply side of the equation for the retailer. A 3PL or third-party logistics provider can also be used by the retailer to augment the success of the VMI program by maintaining better control of the inbound and outbound traffic.

In the traditional relationship, the distribution centers stock their warehouse with products from the supplier and the orders are based on demand forecast from the supplier. The vendor could also stock stores in a similar fashion, in which case the supplier could bring in extra storage, displays, or promotions. The vendor may have to pay a slotting fee for storage in the retail store, but it is worth the time and expense because it increases sales and profits due to the added visibility of product. The product can also be delivered on a consignment basis, which means the product is owned by the vendor and the retailer does not have to pay for the inventory. This is great for the retailer because they garnish the sales from the additional product and pay for the items only when they are sold. The supplier, in turn, bases forecasts and inventory levels on past orders from the retailer.

In a VMI arrangement with the retailer, the supplier may take over the inventory functions that the customer managed. In this scenario, the supplier responsibilities include the following:

- Providing the racking or bins for the storage. This also includes all signage and advertising media.

- Determining how the merchandise will be displayed. Is it an end-cap or a dump bin?
- Determining the receiving schedule for inbound receipts. This needs to be approved by the retailer of the distribution site.
- Maintaining all inventory transactions. This needs to be very visible with the retailer and supplier.

In the traditional relationship, the customer has an incentive to keep inventory lean by placing small, frequent orders. This is called the just-in-time (JIT) concept. This ensures that the customer maintains an acceptable fill rate and a low inventory level. When this concept is used, it is necessary to be cognizant of the increased cost of added transportation and receiving.

With the Green variable for the supply chain, the vendor will not have to ship the product as often as the just-in-time arrangement from the retailer. This saves in mileage traveled by the manufacturer, and the extra inventory is stored in one facility, usually owned by the supplier. This facilitates smaller warehouses on the retailer's side and smaller supply chain inventories because it is not stocked heavily in many locations.

The onsite supplier (OSS) can measure the climate of each sale and get closer to the customer. This is very important when the vendor is looking for new product information or is looking for better information for a promotion. The keys to making VMI work is shared risk. Often if the inventory does not sell, under the VMI partnership the supplier will repurchase the product from the buyer (retailer). In other cases, the product may be in the possession of the retailer on consignment. This can dramatically increase the turns of the buyer's inventory. The general definition of turns is :

$$\frac{\text{Cost of Goods Sold}}{\text{Average Inventory}}$$

Let's say the average inventory is 1,000 units and sales per year equal 4,000 units. If T = 4 then there is an average of 1/4 of the year's inventory on hand:

$$\frac{1000}{4000} = \frac{1}{4}$$

When inventory is consigned, it is written in the books as sold only when the sale takes place. If a business is open 360 days a year, the item is owned only for the day it sold. The turns for the consigned inventory equal 360.

Lowes has an agreement with its suppliers on large appliances to be the marketing representative of brands such as LG. After the customer buys the product, it is shipped out of LG's warehouse and delivered to the customer by Lowes. This is a great savings in inventory because the product is not stored in two places, it is stored only at LG's facility. This is a great savings in the total aggregate supply chain.

Consigning inventory is expanding into industries such as the HVAC (Heating, Ventilation, and Air Conditioning) industry. The HVAC service companies have the parts inventoried by the parts distributors in their warehouse. If the HVAC company gets a job, their service representatives go to the appropriate distributors to pick up the product and then go the customer to fix or service their heating or air-conditioning systems. This saves the HVAC company from having to store its distributor's entire inventory in the warehouse.

If they did store the material, there would be a duplication of inventory in the supply chain. Companies may enter into an arrangement with the suppliers that 20% of the items that represent 80% of the sales could be stored with HVAC's distributors. This could represent 50% to 60% of the HVAC's inventory. The VMI partnership helps foster a closer understanding between the supplier and the manufacturer by using EDI formats. EDI software and statistical methodologies are used to forecast and maintain correct inventory in the supply chain.

Vendors benefit from more control of displays and more contact to impart knowledge to employees, thus enhancing the growth of the partnership. The retailers benefit from reduced risk, better store staff knowledge (which builds brand loyalty for both the vendor and the retailer), and reduced display maintenance outlays. Both vendor and retailer or distributor benefit by the usual once-a-year technology meeting in which both partners share their knowledge of the best-of-breed technology in the companies. The overriding theme for these conferences is that both parties realize that if they help each other the whole will become better than the sum of the parts.

Consumers benefit from knowledgeable store staff who are in frequent contact with manufacturer (vendor) representatives when parts or service are required. Employees with greater knowledge of the products offered by the entire range of vendors have the ability to help the customer choose from competing products for items most suited to them. This actually increases the manufacturer's sales because the retailer's employees are more knowledgeable about the supplier's product line. They can suggest items that they had no knowledge of in the past. In a VMI partnership, manufacturers stand to increase sales by 3% to 4%.

An additional reason to use VMI is to add compliance and optimization into the supply chain. There are a number of technologies available, but the main issue is to optimize collaboration between trading partners. Vendor Managed Inventory will also minimize the "bullwhip effect." The bullwhip effect is variation in demand caused by poor communication between the retailer and the manufacturer. Its name originated with Wal-Mart and PG's VMI program.

Do it Best Corp. has about 5,000 vendors and approximately 4,000 customers. The VMI vendors were chosen using the Pareto approach, considering which vendors had the biggest bang for the dollar: the 20% that contributed 80% to sales. These vendors are usually the most sophisticated and able to enter into long binding partnerships with the company. In most cases, an EDI network is needed to make sure that the data is sent and received in real time and accessible by all parties involved.

Certification programs will become more and more necessary when entering into these long-range contracts. They help in establishing standard operating procedures (SOP) among trading partners. This is essential to realizing the truest form of economy of scale with manufacturers. There must be a grading scale to guide future progress and maintain balance with numerous VMI trading partners. A sample document for the VMI or VMI partner response to the suppliers is shown in Table 1-1. This form is to be used in the certification process for the suppliers. It is a list of rules they must follow to be included in the certification program.

Table 1-1 The VMI Partner Document

XYZ Distributor Vendor Managed Partnership Form The Supplier Portion	
VENDOR NAME _____	RDC SHIPPED TO: _____
VENDOR NUMBER _____	VENDOR SHIP POINT: _____
EMPLOYEE NAME _____	DATE SHIPPED: _____
	CARRIER: _____
1. UTILIZE A GOOD QUALITY, SOLID HARDWOOD OR PLASTIC PALLET FOR MERCHANDISE.	
2. SHIPMENT PRESORTED AND SEGREGATED SO THE SAME SKUs REMAIN TOGETHER.	
3. MERCHANDISE SHRINK-WRAPPED.	
4. PALLET MARKED/LABELED: "DO NOT BREAK SHRINK WRAP."	
5. MIXED CARTONS ARE IDENTIFIED WITH MANUFACTURER'S NUMBER AND QUANTITIES ON THE OUTSIDE OF THE CARTON. ALL SKUs SHIPPED IN CASE PACK QUANTITIES WHEN QUANTITY ORDERED PERMITS.	
6. PALLET CONTENTS IDENTIFIED: ITEMIZED ON PACKING LIST OR PLACARD ATTACHED TO THE PALLET.	
7. PACKING LIST ATTACHED TO FREIGHT.	
8. THIS QUICK-RESPONSE COMPLIANCE FORM ATTACHED TO CARRIER DELIVERY DOCUMENTS OR PLACED INSIDE A HIGH-VISIBILITY ENVELOPE & ATTACHED TO PALLET #1.	
9. SECOND PACKING LIST PROVIDED WITH CARRIER DELIVERY DOCUMENTS OR PROVIDED TO ACE VIA EDI (ADVANCE SHIP NOTICE).	
10. CARRIER BILL OF LADING PRESENTED AS: "SO MANY PALLETS SAID TO CONTAIN SO MANY CARTONS."	
11. MERCHANDISE SHIPPED ON A PREFERRED CARRIER.	
12. PALLETS CONTAINING MIXED SKU MERCHANDISE STACKED TO A HEIGHT OF 60" OR LESS (FROM FLOOR TO TOP OF MERCHANDISE).	
13. PALLETS CONTAINING SINGLE SKU MERCHANDISE STACKED TO A HEIGHT OF 42" OR LESS (FROM FLOOR TO TOP OF MERCHANDISE).	
XYZ RETAILER PORTION	
RECEIVER I.D.: _____ _____	No. OF POs: _____
DATE RECEIVED: _____	ACE PO#: _____
NONCOMPLIANCE ISSUES:	CHECK IF LOAD WAS BROKEN DOWN BY CARRIER:

The Savings of EDI

Electronic data interchange (EDI) is used to transfer electronic documents or business data from one computer system to another computer system. In the following explanation, data is exchanged from one trading partner to another trading partner without human intervention.

The Internet provides a means for any company, without regard to size or location, to become part of a major supply chain initiative hosted by a global retailer or manufacturing company. Many companies around the world have shifted production of labor-intensive parts to low-cost, emerging regions such as Brazil, Russia, India, China, and Eastern Europe. Web-based EDI, or WebEDI, allows a company to interact with its suppliers in these regions without the worry of implementing a complex EDI infrastructure.

In its simplest form, WebEDI enables small to medium-sized businesses to receive, turn around, create, and manage electronic documents using only a Web browser. This service seamlessly transforms data into EDI format and transmits it to the trading partner. Simple prepopulated forms enable businesses to communicate and comply with the trading partners' requirements using built-in business rules. Using a friendly web-based interface, EDI transactions can be received, edited, and sent as easily as an email. No third-party software installation is necessary. The only requirement is an Internet connection. WebEDI is accessible anywhere in the world and does not require a dedicated IT person to manage software.

Some examples of the processes automated by EDI are represented by a term transaction set. The transaction set is the data formatted and sent for a particular process. The different transaction sets have a numerical name such as 810 for an invoice. Some of the examples of the common transaction sets used are the following:

- Purchase order is sent electronically with a transaction set called an 850. This will allow the sending of all purchase orders electronically to the supplier. Paperwork is minimized and employee productivity enhanced.
- Invoices are sent electronically through transaction set 810. All invoices can be sent back from the supplier electronically. These invoices are from the electronic purchase orders received at an

earlier date. The invoice is also considered a turnaround document. (A turnaround document refers to the time period after the purchase order is sent to the time the data is turned around as an invoice, the document that follows the purchase order. An invoice follows the purchase order after its receipt and the advance shipping notice is created after the purchase is loaded onto the truck for shipping.) The purchasing invoice cycle is now done electronically.

- Advance Ship Notice (ASN) is sent electronically through the transaction set 856. Receiving can be planned in advance due to the advance ship notice of what is coming in from each supplier using the ASN. Some products are hard to put away and need a specialized staff. With the ASN, it is easier to determine which trucks contain the vendor products, so staffing becomes easier. Second turnaround documents are used when a supplier receives the purchase order electronically. After a PO is received, the supplier turns around and sends the other two documents. They then ship the product and send the ASN electronically, allowing companies to reduce the paperwork requirements.

- Transportation Carrier Shipment Status Message is sent electronically through the transaction set 214. This transaction set is used to schedule a carrier into the dock. The carrier will use the 214 transaction set to notify their arrival, making arrival time approximately 90% accurate to the hour. Now a closed-looped environment has been created. Each truck is identified by the Shipment Status transaction and given a status of their location and time of delivery. Receiving is now scheduled proactively.

- Payment Order/Remittance Advice is sent electronically through the 820 transaction set. A remittance advice is a letter sent by a customer to a supplier to inform the supplier of invoice payment. If the customer is paying by check, the remittance advice often accompanies the check. Remittance advices are not mandatory; however, they are seen as a courtesy because they help the supplier's accounts-receivable department match invoices with payments. The remittance advice should therefore specify the invoice number(s) for which payment is tendered. Modern systems will often scan a paper remittance advice into a computer system, where data entry will be performed. Modern remittance advices can include dozens or hundreds of invoice numbers and other vital information. The primary purpose for the remittance advice is to let the supplier know when and how much was paid and when it will arrive. This helps greatly in the balancing of cash flow from a vendor standpoint.

- MSDS (Material Safety Data Sheet) is sent electronically through transaction set 848. The transaction set can be used to communicate chemical characteristics, hazards, and precautions for the safe handling and use of a material. The transaction set is intended to convey the information required for an MSDS as defined by the Occupational Safety and Health Administration (OSHA). The MSDS provides the receiver with detailed information concerning material identity, emergency response, chemical and physical characteristics, toxicology, and industrial hygiene procedures.

- Price Information Transaction Set is called the 879. The transaction set contains the current price or price changes to the customer for documentation or for their electronic catalog.

- Price/Sales Catalog is sent through transaction set 832. The 832 EDI document type is used to provide a trading partner with a report of vendor product data for ordering purposes while maintaining an established practice in furnishing trading partners with prices of goods or services in a catalog. The 832 Price/Sales Catalog has four major functions: catalog operation, a traditional vendor catalog, item setup and maintenance, and sales price communication. After the 832 Price/Sales Catalog is received, a 997 Functional Acknowledgment is sent back from the transportation provider indicating that the Price/Sales Catalog was successfully received.

- Traditionally Scan Based Trading programs use EDI solutions as the key component to synchronize information on store locations. Here are a few of the transaction sets:

  - Organizational Structure 816—This transaction set can be used to transmit pertinent information about a parent organization, its members, and the relationship of a member to another member and/or to the parent organization. The transaction set contains some of the following information: address, geographical location, contacts, and identity code. The identity code is the D-U-N-S numbers and the supplier company numbers, which may be internal numbers to identify the individual companies, buying units, and suppliers.

  - Items Price/Sales Catalog 832—This transaction set is used to update an electronic catalog or share pricing with the buyer or seller. It has the following components: item identification, data time reference, restrictions and conditions, product description, item physical details, pricing information, bracket pricing, currency, address information, and geographical information.

- Price Information 879—This transaction set can be used to enable a manufacturer, a supplier, a broker, or an agent to provide a trading partner with pricing information. The transaction set is also used in setting up new items in a store. When a new item is set up, Item Maintenance Transaction Set 888 is needed. The details are similar to those for the Items Price/Sales Catalog 832.

- Item Maintenance Transaction Set 888—This transaction set is used to enable a manufacturer, a supplier, a broker, or an agent to provide detailed finished goods product information to a partner. This transaction set can be used to provide information about new products or changes in existing product specifications.

- Daily Sales Product Activity Data 852—This transaction set gives the supplier or user information about the movement of the product. This transaction set is used when performing VMI or QR quick response with trading partners. It has the following fields: Item on Hand per Location, Item on Order per Location, Item Usage per Location, and Item Backorder per Location.

- Receiving's Receiving Advice 861—The transaction set can be used to provide for customary and established business and industry practice relative to the notification of receipt or formal acceptance of goods and services. It uses the following fields: Currency, Date Time, Purchase Order Reference, Carrier Details, Carrier Routing, Carrier Special Handling, Geographical Information, and F.O.B.-Related Information.

- Organizational Structure 210—The Motor Carrier Freight Invoice transaction gives the location of the delivery, and from this you can determine its approximate delivery time. This is extremely useful in planning for the receiving staff and also for customer notification of product delivery.

- Forecast Planning Schedule 830—This is one of the innovations that sets us apart from the competition. The transaction set tells the supplier what we will be selling on promotions with anticipated volume. The supplier can plan its MRP processes better, and our service levels are greatly enhanced.

Summary of the EDI Transaction Sets

Transaction set 856: Advance Ship Notice

Transaction set 810: Invoice

Transaction Set 210: Motor Carrier Freight Invoice

Transaction set 214: Transportation Carrier Shipment Status

Transaction set 820: Payment Order/Remittance Advice

Transaction set 850: Purchase Order

Transaction set 848: Material Safety Data Sheet

Transaction set 879: Price Information

Transaction set 832: Price/Sales Catalog

Transaction set 997: Functional Acknowledgment

Transaction set 816: Organizational Structure

Transaction set 888: Item Maintenance

Transaction set 852: Daily Sales Product Activity Data

Transaction set 861: Receiving's Receiving Advice

Transaction set 830: Forecast Planning Schedule

Lean and Green Savings Using EDI

This section covers the metrics and savings that can be actualized through the implementation of the Vendor Management Program and electronic data interchange. The use of these tools requires a trusting relationship between the trading partners, but the return for both is significant. When a VMI vendor is added, that vendor needs to be on the same certification program. The VMI productivity increase is composed of three parts:

1. The EDI savings on the Advance Ship Notice, Purchase Order, and Invoice
2. The VMI Reduction of Inventory
3. Productivity Increase in
   a. Sales,
   b. SKU count, and
   c. Increased Service Level for Promotional and Seasonal Items

The following is a list of some of the important EDI automation savings used in VMI.

The Advance Ship Notice (ASN) transaction set 856 offers a view of the contents of the goods arriving on the carrier in advance of the delivery date. Using this document alone has allowed Do it Best Corp. to realize a 15% increase in labor productivity in the Receiving Department and a labor savings of 7 people × .15 = 1.05 person labor hours. At $18 per hour and with additional benefits of 25%, direct labor savings is $46,800 per year. This assumes the need for one less person in receiving.

The ASN can replace the Purchase Order (PO) when the vendor is doing the planning for the customer as in VMI. The ASN shows what is coming in, and this document can be used to pay the invoice. Payment is made through the ASN. The *Supply Management Handbook* says, "It often costs organizations more than $100 in administrative expenses to generate a purchase order" and adds, "In many firms, the cost of managing and generating a purchase order can exceed $200 per transaction." The analysis conducted by Do it Best Corp. found that paper purchase orders can range from a cost of $50 per manual paper purchase order to $1.50 electronically. The solution to their success was to integrate as many transactions with the supplier as possible.

(Note: The tables in Chapter 4, "Transportation Management System (TMS)," are used in the following analysis.)

There were 1,625 × 9 = 14,625 purchase orders per month. The average PO is three pages. This is 14,625 × 3 = 43,875 pages per month or 526,500 pages per year. Normally 500 sheets weigh five pounds, which means that 5,265 pounds of paper were consumed per year. A tree produces roughly 800 pounds of paper. So performing the calculation:

$$\frac{\left(\dfrac{526,500}{500}\right) \times 5}{800} = 7$$

shows that the purchase order process consumed seven trees per year (see Table 4-4 in Chapter 4). There are 175,500 pages of invoices per year. The invoice has miscellaneous credit memos and other explanatory pages with and following the invoice statement. In estimation, the number of pages in the invoice process is about the same as in the PO process. Knowing this, we can calculate that seven additional trees are consumed in the invoice process. The total savings is 7 + 7 = 14 trees per year for automating both the PO and the invoice process.

In manufacturing paper, the wood is turned into pulp. The yield is about 50%—about half of the tree is knots, lignin, and other material not used to make paper. Therefore, a pine tree yields about 805 pounds of paper. A ream of photocopier paper weighs about 5 pounds and contains 500 sheets (paper is often seen described as "20-pound stock" or "24-pound stock"—which is the weight of 500 sheets of 17" × 22" paper). Using these measurements, a tree would produce (805 / 5 × 500) = 80,500 sheets of paper (see Table 4-4).

Lean and Green EDI Savings of the Advance Ship Notice, Purchase Order, and Invoice

Using the ASN to replace the purchase order and invoice for the VMI vendor results in Lean Savings:

- The electronic purchase order system saves $525,500 per year compared to the manual purchase order procedure.
- The electronic invoice system saves $1,228,500 per year compared to the manual invoice procedure.
- The ASN allows a 15% increase in labor productivity in the Receiving Department. This is a labor savings of 7 × .15 = 1.05 person labor hours. This means reducing the number of employees needed by one. At $18 per hour and with additional benefits of 25%, direct labor savings is 1 × 1.25 × 40 × 52 × $18 = $46,800 per year.
- The Lean Savings is ($525,500 + $1,228,500 + $46,800) = $1,800,800 per year.
- The Green Savings amounts to 14 trees per year being saved. Using Table 4-7, we can see that 14 trees equates to 910 pounds of CO_2 saved per year.
- Total savings so far is $1,800,800 per year + 14 trees + 910 pounds of CO_2 saved per year.

These savings can be used as productivity metrics for personnel or management. Visual Supply Management increases the productivity of personnel, using better and timelier information from the suppliers. For instance, in the past, it took all day for a purchase agent to review a very large vendor manually for all nine of the Do it Best Corp. warehouses. It can now be reviewed in 5 minutes. The only things to review on the VMI vendors are the turns and service levels for each warehouse. As long as the turns and service levels are increasing, they are increasing profit and sales for the company. This also shows that the supplier is doing a better job of demand forecasting if the turns are going up (more sales for less inventory) and the out of stocks are going down (more revenue with less inventory). The increase in labor efficiency is 400% using the collaborative electronic system. Employees can be deployed to more profitable jobs. Installing a VMI system does not create success by itself. Other processes are needed to enable the technology. These processes include the technologies discussed throughout this book.

Eight people are involved in the purchasing/invoice system. With a 400% increase in productivity, two are currently required. 3,060 kWh × $0.16 = $490 dollars were saved in electricity usage by reduction of computer usage for the purchasing group. Similar productivity improvements allow for the creation of a company with 50% fewer personnel than the competition.

VMI collaborative metrics for the supply chain include a 400% increase in staff productivity. There is also a 30% to 50% increase in turns. If there exists a $300 million inventory, assuming a 35% increase in turns, $78 million in inventory dollars are freed to be invested elsewhere. Using this method, Do it Best Corp. created a sales increase of 3.5% with no increase in inventory levels, a 25% increase in SKU count with no increase in warehouse space, and customer service levels of 97% or more on promotional and seasonal items, as well as significantly reduced paper-handling costs.

Do it Best Corp. originally had three turns with $300 million average inventory and $900 million in sales. At 35% increase in turns, the new number of turns, after VMI, is 4.05. With average sales of $900 million for the VMI vendors, the new inventory figure would be $900 million / 4.05 = $222 million ($78 million in reduced inventory). There was an increase of 3.5% in sales without an increase in inventory. This was possible only with a long-term partnership with suppliers who are now able to work with the customer on better selling categories, new promotions, and new items. It becomes essential for the supplier that the customer succeeds as well. The trend for DBI took approximately five years to develop. So the learning curve was five years.

The savings to Damaged and Obsolescence is 9.75% of inventory. Do it Best Corp. obtained the savings through VMI. Calculations show a 9.75% of $78 million, or $7.606 million, savings in Damaged and Obsolescence costs.

With the 400% increase in productivity and the 35% increase in turns, the calculations shown in the following section are now possible.

Lean and Green Savings of VMI Reduction of Inventory

- The Lean Savings of VMI Reduction of Inventory:
  - Starting Inventory is $300,000,000.
  - Starting Sales are $900,000,000.
  - Starting Turns are 3.00.
  - A 35% increase in turns, allowing an inventory reduction of $78,000,000.
  - The New Inventory using VMI is $300,000,000 – $78,000,000 = $222,000,000.
  - The new turns are 4.05.
  - Carrying cost of 26.66% savings yields a $20,720,000 reduction.
  - Freed-up cost of capital is .02 × $78,000,000 = $1,560,000.
- Total Lean Savings from VMI Reduction of Inventory is $22,280,000.
- The Green Savings of VMI Reduction of Inventory:
  - $490 saved in electricity usage for the Purchasing area.
  - $7.606 million per year in landfill savings.
- Total Lean and Green Savings for VMI Reduction of Inventory is $29,886,490.

The Green Savings is as shown here:

- A new warehouse (now unnecessary) would cost $14 million in inventory and $10 million in the building cost. The VMI initiative would save:
  - $3.517 million in additional infrastructure cost.
  - An additional 3 to 6.5 million with an average of 4.75 million in furnishing, equipment, racking, and automation equipment will not be needed.
  - This totals to $14 million in inventory dollars + $3.517 million + $4.75 million equals a total cost of $22,260,000.
- Without the existing improvement in technology, it would be necessary to increase the size of the warehouse by 35%. The increase would represent additional costs of 35% × $22,260,000 = $7.791 million.
- The added cost of utilities would be computed as $0.5717 a square foot annually. This is dependent on the amount of automated equipment in the warehouse. For a 450,000-square-foot warehouse the average is 450,000 × $0.57170 = $256,500 spent annually on electricity. Total savings in utility costs is .35 × $256,500 × 9 = $807,975.

The last three categories of savings are Green Savings. The savings are a 25% increase in SKU count with no increase in inventory space, a cost savings of $807,975 saved in electrical usage generation, and finally a sales increase of 3.5% without additional resource expenditures.

- The Lean Savings is the added sales = 1.035 × $900,000,000 = $931,000,000. This is a $31,000,000 increase in sales. With a profit margin of 18%, this represents an increase in profits of $5,580,000.
- The new turns are 931,000,000 / $222,000,000 = 4.19 turns.
- The Green Savings erases the need to spend an additional $7.791 million in added warehouse infrastructure costs to accommodate the 3.5% sales increase and the 25% addition in SKU count. This is considered Green Savings because raw materials for warehouse expansion are unnecessary.

- The added cost of utilities would be computed as $0.5717 a square foot annually. This is dependent on the amount of automated equipment in the warehouse. For a 450,000-square-foot warehouse, the average is 450,000 × $0.57170 = $256,500 spent annually on electricity.

The Total Lean for the three categories is the increased profits from an increase of 3.5% of sales = $5,580,000; company turns are 4.19, sales are $931 million, and inventory is $222 million.

The Total Green for the three categories is the decrease in infrastructure cost = $7,791,000; the decrease in utilities cost = $807,975; and the total Green Cost = $8,598,975.

The total savings for the entire VMI & EDI program including all the preceding steps is as shown here:

Lean Savings of $29,660,800 +

Green Savings of $16,205,465 =

Total Savings of $45,866,265

Certification Program and Scorecarding

The next area of concern is the vendor or supplier scorecard. This helps keep a dashboard view of the supplier and perhaps also the carrier's performance for eventual continuous improvement, or the Kaizen process. Development of a joint retailer/supplier scorecard is critical to success. Measurements include the following:

- Product profitability
- Inventory turns and service level
- Promotional effectiveness
- New product introduction effectiveness
- Quality/returned goods
- On-time performance

The operational issues of certification programs include these:

- Product frequency of arrival with receiving cost in mind
- Product delivery timing during the day
- Vendor minimum

- Item minimums
- Pallets
- Pallet layer stacking
- Frequency of arrivals
- Pallet or container type
- Label type to use
- Label placement
- RF collaboration with current system to make a more efficient information flow between the supplier and the distributor

Certification programs cut Do it Best Corp. lead times down by approximately one day. That one-day savings included a reduction in manufacturing lead time as well as receiving and stocking the product. Do it Best Corp. found that the certification program equates to an additional 2.2% reduction of inventory for each day saved in lead time. Therefore, the savings for the certification program is 2.2% × $222 million in inventory. This is approximately $5 million in inventory reduction, making the new inventory level $217 million.

Do it Best Corp. also mandated the use of specific labels, pallet sizes, and label placement to maximize productivity. Logistics labels are increasingly used to track containers and other logistics units through the supply chain, as recording and monitoring the movement of goods is an essential part of supply chain management. This allows the employees to scan each container or large box and know how many items are inside. These are the most successful mandates:

SCC-14 (Shipping Container Code) is a 14-digit number assigned to fixed-content shipping containers. Using the SCC-14, it is assumed that like items are in each box. When the box is scanned, the count is given without opening the container for counts. For example, the UPC number tells the system that the box holds 12 units.

SCC-18 (the Serial Shipping Container Code) is a unique serial number that is used to identify each individual pallet, assuming that various assorted products are on a pallet. Scanning the pallet gives the items contained on it. The pallet can be moved to the stocking location without the shrink-wrap being broken at this time. Employees can scan more products per hour and move products from receiving to stocking at a much faster rate.

Another part of the certification program is the use of the "funnel" program. Do it Best Corp. asked the supplier to stock like items on each pallet. This means that a pallet may have multiple purchase order numbers from multiple orders for the same item. Using the old system, manufacturers filled their orders by purchase order and any back orders were filled and palletized by PO. Having like items spread across multiple pallets hurts productivity. Do it Best Corp. also requires suppliers to have bin location numbers on their files. The suppliers place stock merchandise in the pallets with the same inventory location.

The largest part of receiving is the breakdown and sorting of product. This accounts for as much as 80% of the time spent in receiving. The bottleneck is eliminated by having the pallets go directly to the stocking location without any breakdown or sorting.

Certification Program Savings

- The Lean Savings of the Certification Program
  - Carrying cost savings $5,000,000 inventory × 26.6% = $1,330,000
  - Freed-up cost of capital is .02 × $5,000,000 inventory savings = $100,000.
- The Green Savings of the Certification Program
  - 9.75% for Damage and Obsolescence × $5,000,000 = $487,500 per year in landfill savings.
- Total Lean and Green Savings so far is $1,917,500.

To this point, after the Certification Program:

- Company turns are 4.25.
- Sales are $922 million.
- Inventory now is $217 million.

References

[1]   http://www.urenio.org/tools/en/supply_chain_management.pdf.

2

Warehouse Management System (WMS)

Warehouse management is part of Supply Chain Management and Demand Management. Supply Chain Management (SCM) is composed of two parts: Supply Chain Planning (SCP) and Supply Chain Execution (SCE). The Warehouse Management System, or WMS, is part of the SCE strategy. The execution portion of the supply chain is definitely action-oriented. Even production management is, to a great extent, dependent on warehouse management. Efficient warehouse management gives a cutting edge to a retailer or distributor. Warehouse management does not start with receipt of material. It starts with the initial planning of the container design made for a product. Warehouse design and process design within the warehouse are also part of warehouse management. Warehouse management is part of logistics and SCM.

A WMS is a key part of the supply chain and primarily aims to control the movement and storage of materials within a warehouse and process the associated transactions, including shipping, receiving, stocking, and picking. The systems can also optimize the stocking process. The optimization routine is based on real-time information of bin locations in the warehouse and the products to be put away. The system knows the cube of the product and exactly where the closest empty bin will be to place the merchandise.

The optimization programs attempt to minimize the time it takes the workers to stock the product. The system is also cognizant of the picking operations. Because it is more efficient for the picker to place the item in a particular warehouse bin in close proximity, the system navigates through the alternative locations to find the optimum bin location. The system also balances both the stocking and the picking operations by choosing product placement to minimize the time for the overall warehouse operation.

The WMS provides a computerized schedule to guide employees through their daily tasks by setting up the procedures and times for each operation performance. The system can be automated to notify suppliers electronically if product is being returned and get the authorization number e-mailed back for proper identification. It can perform the initial dialog with the Transportation Management System (TMS) to set up communication with the carriers. It won't perform the logistic functions but can notify carriers when the product will be ready to be picked up. This enhances efficiency through collaboration of both the WMS and the TMS systems. The WMS should be integrated with other systems as discussed in the next section.

System Integration with the WMS

The WMS can capture data for the ERP system. It can track employee performance, allowing managers to plan which operations the worker performs best, enabling assignments by performance ratings. This is invaluable when using an incentive system and capturing the times below the goal.

The WMS system should be linked to the Inventory Management System so that product movement is immediately visible to the ordering system. The closer the operation is to real time, the lower the inventory. Any percentage reduction of lead time has an equal reduction in average inventory. This helps in demand planning through balancing demand with real-time inventory availability. The WMS is also connected throughout the ERP system to the Accounting and Controls area of the company, allowing for a more accurate evaluation of the warehouse assets. The WMS system should be set up to communicate to the IT system with a seamless approach, synchronizing files from the WMS system to the ERP or legacy file structure.

The Functionality of the WMS

When selecting a WMS computer system, find a solution that will address as many of the following areas as possible.

Order Fulfillment—This is the process of completing the entire order transaction, including the order query, the quote, the purchase order generation, the delivery notification, and the receipt and invoicing of the purchase order. The WMS speeds up the process of receipts and picking the merchandise for the order fulfillment function.

Inventory Management—The WMS system can aid in cycle counting regardless of the type of inventory system. The faster the inventory input, the lower the receiving time. As lead times decrease, the need for extra safety stocks decreases and the more accurate the inventory count is.

Web-Based Platform—The system should have the option of a web-based program for connectivity anywhere in the company. This makes the new paradigm accessible anywhere and anytime.

Warehouse Productivity—How efficient are employee schedules? What is the best schedule to use to minimize the distance traveled by the worker? What is the optimum location needed for the system to minimize the cost of receiving and picking? This is the ABC location analysis, in which the merchandise needed the most is placed in the middle of the bin for faster picking or receiving.

Shelf Life Monitoring—The WMS can track shelf life. This is important in the stock rotation and filling orders in a FIFO (first in, first out) environment by minimizing spoilage of perishable products.

Transportation Performance—The WMS must communicate with the Transportation Management System. If the schedule is expedited, the transportation process can be enhanced. The WMS measures what TMS issues are affecting warehouse performance.

Scalability and Configurability—The system should be scaled so that it can grow easily with any future enhancement. This assumes that the system will work well in a plug-and-play environment with other software.

Receive Stock and Returns/Reverse Logistics—The system should maximize the process of receiving by creating the best schedule for labor to match incoming freight. It can match worker times and efficiency to the different types of vendors. The WMS system can facilitate a reverse logistics function. If done correctly, it will minimize the cost of the least productive part of the warehouse system. Companies can see a 10% annual savings in logistics: 20% through labor cost savings and 80% in lowered freight costs and reduced pipeline inventory.[1]

Manage Storage Facilities—The WMS can model the warehouse into multiple locations based on the best use of cube and worker productivity. This is the process of designing the warehouse and partitioning it into multiple areas such as slow pick, fast pick, heavy bulk, over stock, zone picking and receiving, mezzanine levels, and so on. The system can allow for random storage or manual storage.

Manage Stock—A simulation package can be used to minimize time and maximize employee performance by placing the goods in better locations so that they can be picked at a faster pace. Placing faster moving items in the middle of the bins or at the front of each racking location minimizes the worker's horizontal or vertical travel.

Provide Connectivity to the Enterprise—With the advent of ERP systems, the WMS system can give notification of delivery to all the departments. For instance, customer service departments need to know when an item is received. The WMS will notify customer service immediately upon receipt of the ASN. The customer support staff then notifies the customer and schedules receipt or delivery.

The WMS allows the following warehouse productivity techniques to be computerized:

Cross Docking—Cross docking is a practice in logistics of unloading materials from an incoming semitrailer truck or rail car and loading these materials directly into outbound trucks, trailers, or rail cars, with little or no storage in between. This practice can reduce overall cost of pick-to-stock and pick-to-order by 15% to 21% by eliminating unnecessary movement from receiving to stock and then back to the shipping door.

Postponement—A postponement strategy aims at delaying some supply chain activities until customer demand is revealed in order to maintain both low systemwide cost and fast response. The driving force of postponement is waiting on manufacturing, packaging, or labeling until product is needed by the customer. This is a great definition of the pull system in Lean terminology. Don't stock it until it is needed. Inventory cost is reduced and the variety of end products to the customer is increased. This process also helps to increase service levels because the interchangeable parts are stocked with a higher level of safety stock. From these parts comes the final product. Postponement cuts the total cost to delivery to the customer by 5%.[2]

Work Planning—This process organizes and coordinates the activities of an enterprise in accordance with certain policies and in achievement of clearly defined objectives. The system will plan the incoming shipments against standardized worker times to generate a schedule that uses the fewest resources. Management will be included in the decision making of production schedules, along with machines, materials, and cost.

Order Processing—This is the ability to process the order from the customer accurately and in a timely manner.

Tracking Material Flow—This involves setting metrics to analyze labor hour's efficiencies and standards. *Logistics → Logistics Execution → Information System → Warehouse → Standard Analyses → Material Flow*. By tracking material flow in the warehouse, labor costs can be cut by 20% to 40%. Management can spot the bottleneck and act immediately.

Metrics Used in a WMS

The WMS system uses several metrics to improve the order fulfillment. These are critical because the customer sees these metrics and evaluates performance based on these figures.

- Order Fill Rate—This is the average fill rate per order.
- Line Fill Rate—This is the average of all the items shipped to the items ordered. This is the average service level the customer receives and is the best indication of how quickly the customer receives the order. The service level has the normal standard distribution. The line fill rate is the center of the probability distribution of line fill rate. The normal complaints are at the left end of the curve. For instance, 50% of the customers have a service level of 97% if this is the normal line fill rate. Table 2-1 illustrates the spread of service levels when all is going well. For instance, when the service level is 97%, then 5.57% of the membership is at a service level between 90 and 97%. To be exact .76% of customers are at a 90% service level. This is why companies cannot afford to turn a blind eye on customer complaints

about service. The last example shows that .76% of the customers will have a service level of 80% or 20% out of stocks. The table assumes that the cumulative probability distribution set at .5, with a mean of .97, and the standard deviation of .5.

Table 2-1 Percentage of Customers at Specified Service Levels

Service Level	Cumulative	The Exact Service Level
96% to 97%	.8%	0.80%
95% to 97%	1.6%	0.80%
94% to 97%	2.39%	0.80%
93% to 97%	3.19%	0.79%
92% to 97%	3.98%	0.79%
91% to 97%	4.78%	0.79%
90% to 97%	5.57%	0.79%
89% to 97%	6.36%	0.79%
88% to 97%	7.14%	0.79%
87% to 97%	7.93%	0.78%
86% to 97%	8.71%	0.78%
85% to 97%	9.48%	0.78%
84% to 97%	10.26%	0.77%
83% to 97%	11.03%	0.77%
82% to 97%	11.79%	0.77%
81% to 97%	12.55%	0.76%
80% to 97%	13.31%	0.76%

- Dollar Fill Rate—This is the average of the entire dollars shipped to the dollars ordered. The indicator shows how much revenue is lost. This figure is usually lower than the line fill rate.

- Order Accuracy—This is the accuracy with which the picker picks the order to be delivered to the customer. Did the warehouse employee fill the wrong order? This is where the RF process and the WMS work well together. This combination makes it much harder to make mistakes.

- Line Accuracy—This is the accuracy of the specific SKUs in the order. Are all lines filled? Is the right product being filled?

- Orders Cycle Time—This is the time between orders. This is scheduled by the WMS to maximize the productivity of the employees.

- Number of Back Orders—This is a great metric of how well a vendor is doing in filling the order, which can cause higher outs. One of the metrics can measure the time it takes to fill an entire order, including all back orders.

- Calculated Vendor Lead Time—This is where the computer calculates the vendor lead times based on all back orders and their respective times. For example, let's say the vendor had three back orders. The first order was shipped in 15 days and was 60% complete. The second back order was shipped in 20 days and shipped 30% of the order. The last back order was shipped in 30 days and shipped the remaining 10% of the order. The new calculated vendor lead time for that distribution center is:

$$\frac{1 \times 15 + .30 \times 20 + .10 \times 10}{1 + .3 + .1} = 17.14286 \text{ days}$$

The first order weight value is 1, and it is assumed that this would be the proper lead time to use if there were no back orders. This increased lead time can be input into the system to allow for greater stock or more safety stock.

- Back Order Time to Completion—This is the total time of completion. In the preceding illustration the time would be 30 days.

- On-Time Delivery—This is usually the metric that is used to show the number of times per year the vendor shipped on time. It can also show the spread of the variance around the designated ship date.

- Vendor Lead Time—This is the normal standardized time for the vendor. The vendor lead time is calculated as Total Lead Time – Receiving to Stock Time – Transit Time.

- Individual Item Lead Time—This is the calculated average item lead time. This may not be near the vendor lead time or calculated vendor lead time of the product. In vendor negotiations, it is essential to run a vendor report and show which items have an item lead time significantly greater than the vendor lead time.

Improve Inventory Management

Improve Inventory Management is one of the greatest advances in the WMS. Service levels and turns significantly improve shortly after the WMS is introduced.

- Inventory Accuracy—This is needed when computing the perpetual inventory cycle counting system. The WMS increases accuracy in quarterly sample checks of inventory and in complete inventory counts.
- Days on Hand—This can be calculated using the WMS.
- Storage Utilization—The WMS calculates the spatial efficiency by cube in the warehouse.
- Dock to Stock Time—This is the time it takes to enter the item into inventory after receipt.
- Inventory Visibility—This can be accommodated by a real-time dashboard that shows warehouse movement and congestion. The product placement and inventory dollars can be illustrated on a CAD/CAM diagram of the warehouse.
- Simulations for Decision Making—The WMS can visually show the results of changes in the procedure and recommend a future course of action.
- Inventory Turns by Warehouse—This is an excellent metric in which to gauge the warehouse productivity. The productivity could be within the Distribution Center or it could be a function of the routing issues into the warehouse.
- Inventory Turns by Warehouse Section—The metric shows the difference in stocking levels for different sections or departments.

The Improved Warehouse Worker Productivity

The Improved Warehouse Worker Productivity can be measured with these key performance indicators:

- Orders picked per hour per worker
- Order stocked per hour per worker

- Lines picked per hour per worker
- Lines stocked per hour per worker
- Comparison of warehouse location costs
- Cost per order
- Demurrage cost by carrier
- Productivity improvement
- Comparison to standard for incentive pay by worker
- Cost as percentage of sales

Improved Transportation Performance

The WMS can also help to show the Improved Transportation Performance. This is an important metric because the transportation process is one of the more expensive segments of the supply chain. The WMS will show all the TMS key performance indicators as related to the distribution center.

- On-time deliveries
- Demurrage cost percentage
- Damage
- Missed appointments percentage
- Freight bill accuracy
- Cost per order
- Delivery date accuracy

In Management by Walking Around, problems with employee performance are discovered and potential solutions are discussed with the staff. A typical order picker can walk six miles a day through the warehouse. Order picking constitutes the highest operations cost and time, so increasing productivity through stronger talent-management techniques is a great place to start. Here is a breakdown of costs by percentage in the manufacturing sector:

- Shipping: 20%
- Receiving: 10%
- Storage: 15%
- Order picking: 55%

Order picking can be the most labor-intensive activity in the warehouse, with as much as 75% of time spent in activities related to picking. If the functions of order picking are examined with a process map using value stream mapping, the following will result:

- 10%: searching (which is non-value-added)
- 5%: writing (which is non-value-added)
- 25%: picking (which is value-added)
- 60%: walking (which is non-value-added)

When Value Stream Mapping (VSM) is used, the yield equals a 25% value-added for the picking process. Picking is a large problem for most warehouses. A dynamic scheduling program will help to optimize the efficiencies of the order pickers. A good example of making changes to the productivity of the process is to use the Pareto process.

The largest producer of non-value-added in the picking process is walking. Decreasing walking time by 30% increases efficiency from 25% to 31.25%: 25 / (10 + 5 + 25 + 40) = 31.25%. This represents a 25% increase in the total picking process, which translates to a 25% decrease in labor needs. Existing workers can be reassigned to more productive tasks.

A typical example of a worker receiving orders from the WMS is explained in this paragraph. The WMS offers the employee routing information or the warehouse location and quantity of the next pick. It offers the employee routing information or the warehouse location and quantity of the next pick. The screen can also be used in the receiving process. It tells the worker which trailers are the most important in the overall service-level needs of the company. If the receipt is being cross-docked, it will tell the employee upon receipt of the goods which items need to go to stocking and which items need to go to shipping.

Table 5-1 in Chapter 5, "Savings of B2B E-commerce," shows that the highest warehouse costs are labor and space. This can be addressed by the WMS. Use of the WMS can produce the following benefits:

- Warehouse labor hours decreased by 40% to 50%, but 50% to 60% with RF. The computer tracks the worker efficiency and flow, matching the worker to the job. The system also picks the shortest distance to travel per worker. Recall that a typical warehouse worker will walk six miles a day in filling orders. Minimizing this will significantly add to labor efficiency.

- Inventory write-off dropped by 5%. This is caused by better real-time tracking of inventory so that merchandise is not lost in the system. The system also monitors shelf life and reduces mis-ships.

- Total inventory dropped by 2.7%. The system allows better and faster tracking of inbound receipts to the stocking area. All overstock locations are minimized, so it does not take as long to split orders into stocking and overstock.

- Shipping errors dropped by 80%, caused by the double-checking of the system with the RF system (discussed in the section later in this chapter, "Radio Frequency (RF) as a Warehouse Management System—An Introduction into RF Systems Used in the Distribution Centers").

- Space utilization improved by 20% to 30%. WMS is designed to minimize the distance traveled, simulating a smaller distribution center.

- Scrap reduced by 13% to 30%. This is attributed to better real-time visibility of the inventory and process.

- Picking productivity increased by 16% to 25%. This would not be possible without the use of a fully computerized and real-time system measuring against the needed metrics. Also available:
  - Optimized picking routes
  - Labor standards to match the laborer to the task
  - Labor standards to show the need for staffing

- Customer returns reduced by 11% to 25% due to fewer picking errors.

- Cross docking saved 21% in labor cost by minimizing the distance the worker has to travel to fill orders.

WMS Savings:

- The Lean Savings
  - Warehouse labor hours dropped by 40%. A warehouse with 600,000 square feet of space would need about 200 workers.

Using 125 people with a savings of $18 per hour and benefits of 25%, the total cost is $22.50 per hour. Total savings is 250 days per year × 8 hours × $22.50 × 75 people = $3,375,000 in labor savings per year.

- Inventory reduction of 2.7% of $217 million is $6 million.
- Carrying cost savings of 26.6% × $6 million = $1.60 million.
- Freed-up cost of capital is .02 × $6 million with inventory savings = $120,000.
- Total Lean Savings is $5,095,000.
- The Green Savings
  - Improved space utilization of 25% means a warehouse designed with 25% fewer square feet. This is a savings of 600,000 square feet × 25% = 150,000 square feet.
  - Value for electric utility bill is .5717 per square foot × 150,000 square feet saved = $85,755 in utilities per year.
- Total savings so far is $5,180,755.
  - Company turns are 4.41.
  - Sales are $931 million.
  - Inventory now is $211 million.

Radio Frequency (RF) as a Warehouse Management System—An Introduction into RF Systems Used in the Distribution Centers

The RF system is used for receiving, storage, and physically counting inventory. As an extension of the WMS, it enhances the physical counting process by entering the counts in the system by the terminal, making the process of warehouse management paperless. Rather than weekly or monthly physical counts, the RF system works on a perpetual inventory cycle. Productivity is increased because inventory tracking does not require warehouse downtime due to physical count requirements. The RF makes the process of entering a number a seamless event and extends the WMS capabilities by enabling and improving the times and error rates for the following functions in distribution:

1. **Unloading and staging merchandise** on the receiving floor. This is the process of receiving and checking delivery contents against POs. Using an RF hand-held gun works extremely well in this environment. After the product is staged on the receiving floor, it can be moved to the stocking area.

2. **Sorting** the product occurs after it has been staged. It is sorted out by warehouse location number. This process takes the longest in the receiving process. Employees use the RF device to scan the item and then separate pallets by RF locations. Each pallet will go to a different location in the warehouse based on the WMS instruction. After the pallet is placed in the stocking area, the items will all be stocked in close proximity. They can be license-plated with a bar code telling the computer that the product is on the pallet. Many Warehouse Management Systems mandate the use of the RF process.

3. The RF process also helps facilitate **creating the carrier identification file.** This file keeps track of all inbound or outbound shipments by carrier.

   Track the shipments by scanning the inbound and outbound specifics:
   - Get the date of the shipment and store it.
   - Record the time of delivery. This allows management to see whether the suppliers are shipping on schedule and abiding by the shipping agreement.
   - Track the employee loading or unloading time for performance levels.

4. **Reducing paper** documentation and permission needed to perform certain tasks. The paper savings can be a great source for minimizing paperwork. Tasks can be accomplished faster without an accompanying paper trail. All the adjust inventory slips and exception **slips can be eliminated.**

5. **Minimizing errors** because less time is spent writing the adjustments on a form. The forms could also be scanned and input in the system by the RF or RFID system.

6. **Receiving multiple POs** at the same time. Depending on the WMS software, the PO and vendor number can be scanned, as well as individual boxes for receipts. In working with certified vendors, the PO, vendor number, and contents are scanned and the PO is taken off the on-order file and added to the item file simultaneously. This assumes that the product is stocked before billing starts.

7. **Improving inventory levels**. The return on investment can be anywhere from one to three years, after which the warehouse is working with improved technology and lower overhead.

8. **Improving time on return goods** or reverse logistics. Looking up the item's bin number or location is no longer required because after it's scanned the printer at the station can print the location tag to be placed on the item. If an item is damaged, a tag can be printed to throw away or repair. If the item needs to be sent to auction, the appropriate tag is printed.

9. **Cross docking** notifies the warehouse of out-of-stock merchandise. The item can be received and placed on the customer's outgoing order from receiving, eliminating the out of stock and the double trips from receiving-to-stock and stock-to-shipping.

The standardized bill of lading is used to ensure that each supplier gives the information in the same sequence. When bills of lading have fields in different positions on the form, it becomes easier to make mistakes. The standardized bill of lading will speed up the receiving process because every form looks the same. The same efficiencies will follow the product through the supply chain, from supplier to carrier to distributor to customer.

The form shown in Figure 2-1 is an illustration of the standardized bill of lading. The form was established by the Voluntary Interindustry Commerce Solutions Association.[3]

Date:	BILL OF LADING		Page _____
SHIP FROM			
Name:		**Bill of Lading Number:** _____	
Address:			
City/State/Zip:		**BAR CODE SPACE**	
SID#:	FOB: ☐		
SHIP TO		**CARRIER NAME:** _____	
Name: Location #: _____		Trailer number:	
Address:		Seal number(s):	
City/State/Zip:		**SCAC:**	
CID#:	FOB: ☐	**Pro number:**	
THIRD-PARTY FREIGHT CHARGES BILL TO:		**BAR CODE SPACE**	
Name:			
Address:			
City/State/Zip:		**Freight Charge Terms:** *(freight charges are prepaid unless marked otherwise)*	
SPECIAL INSTRUCTIONS:		**Prepaid** _____ **Collect** _____ 3rd **Party**	
		☐ Master Bill of Lading: with attached	

Figure 2-1A The standardized bill of lading (page one)

			(check box)		underlying Bills of Lading		
CUSTOMER ORDER INFORMATION							
CUSTOMER ORDER NUMBER	**# PKGS**	**WEIGHT**	**PALLET/SLIP** (CIRCLE ONE)		**ADDITIONAL SHIPPER INFO**		
			Y	N			
			Y	N			
			Y	N			
			Y	N			
			Y	N			
GRAND TOTAL							
CARRIER INFORMATION							
HANDLING UNIT		**PACKAGE**			**COMMODITY DESCRIPTION**	**LTL ONLY**	
QTY	**TYPE**	**QTY**	**TYPE**	**WEIGHT**	**H.M.** (X)	Commodities requiring special or additional care or attention in handling or stowing must be so marked and packaged as to ensure safe transportation with ordinary care. *See Section 2(e) of NMFC Item 360*	**NMFC #**	**CLASS**
					RECEIVING		
					STAMP SPACE		

Figure 2-1B The standardized bill of lading (page two)

			GRAND TOTAL		

Where the rate is dependent on value, shippers are required to state specifically in writing the agreed or declared value of the property as follows:	COD Amount: $ _____
"The agreed or declared value of the property is specifically stated by the shipper to be not exceeding	Fee Terms: Collect: ☐ Prepaid: ☐
	Customer check acceptable: ☐
_____ per _____ ."	

NOTE Liability Limitation for loss or damage in this shipment may be applicable. See 49 U.S.C.   14706(c)(1)(A) and (B).

RECEIVED, subject to individually determined rates or contracts that have been agreed upon in writing between the carrier and shipper, if applicable, otherwise to the rates, classifications and rules that have been established by the carrier and are available to the shipper, on request, and to all applicable state and federal regulations.	The carrier shall make delivery of this shipment without payment of freight and all other lawful charges.
	_____ **Shipper Signature**

SHIPPER SIGNATURE / DATE	Trailer Loaded:	Freight Counted:	CARRIER SIGNATURE / PICKUP DATE
This is to certify that the above named materials are properly classified, described, packaged, marked and labeled, and are in proper condition for transportation according to the applicable regulations of the U.S. DOT.	☐ By Shipper ☐ By Driver	☐ By Shipper ☐ By Driver/pallets said to contain	Carrier acknowledges receipt of packages and required placards. Carrier certifies emergency response information was made available and/or carrier has the U.S. DOT emergency response guidebook or equivalent documentation in the vehicle.
		☐ By Driver/Pieces	*Property described above is received in good order, except as noted.*

Figure 2-1C The standardized bill of lading (page three)

The Importance of the Voluntary Interindustry Commerce Solutions Association to the Industry

VICS, the Voluntary Interindustry Commerce Solutions Association, has worked to improve the efficiency and effectiveness of the entire supply chain. VICS pioneered the implementation of a cross-industry standard, Quick Response (QR), that simplified the flow of product and information in the retail industry for retailers and suppliers alike.[3]

A 1996 study by Kurt Salmon Associates showed that companies that implemented VICS's business replenishment processes had dramatic results: increased sales, faster turns, improved inventory control, and cost savings. Although the results were impressive, VICS continued to develop a new collaborative dimension to supply chain processes: Collaborative Planning, Forecasting, and Replenishment (CPFR®).[3]

By 2001, an AMR research study demonstrated that retailers and suppliers jointly achieved higher sales with double-digit inventory decreases and improved stock at wholesale and on the retail shelf at a lower overall logistics cost. At the same time, Kurt Salmon Associates estimated that "the benefits of CPFR for just the apparel industry alone could conservatively total $8.3 billion annually."[3] VICS's committees continue to build their legacy of supply chain excellence through continuous improvement of existing supply chain processes, development of new collaborative commerce business processes, and effective implementation of e-commerce standards.[3]

VICS is composed of the following committees:

- Collaborative Planning Committee
- CPFR Collaborative Planning Forecasting and Replenishment Committee
- Floor Ready Merchandise Committee
- Logistics Committees
  - Collaborative Transportation Management (CTM)
  - DC Bypass
  - Global Logistics Management (GLM)
- Product Image Committee

The Applied RF Analysis: Receiving, Directed Putaway, Stocking, and Order Filling

In receiving, the radio frequency (RF) process starts when merchandise arrives at the distribution center. The merchandise is unloaded and a piece-count is verified. Full pallets of merchandise are labeled with a bar-coded license plate for tracking. The scanner provides the status code for warehouse employees who are putting the merchandise into the stocking locations. The workers will have real-time information on their forklift display as to relevancy and need of the stocking items.

If this is a new item, the scanner scans the bar code from the UPC number. The new SKU number is found and entered into the scanner. This process updates the company's table for associating UPC numbers with internal numbers. The RF scanner provides a status code that will show the following results:

- Out of Stock—The forklift display shows the workers which purchase orders have the highest percentage of line outs. This can be traced to incoming shipments that have the items marked with their corresponding ASNs. The shipments can be directed to allow the most important shipments to be received first. The worker is empowered with this knowledge first and does not need to seek direction from purchasing for stocking decisions. Many times the forklift driver, rather than purchasing, knows what needs to be stocked to minimize out-of-stocks.

- On Sale—The software tells employees when each sale starts and stops. The purchase orders are rated by the timeline of receipt. If an order is being received just before the sale ends, it is given a higher priority index, which means to restock immediately.

- Central Stock to Send to Other Centers—If an item is received and the system determines that there is too much merchandise in stock, it will scan other warehouses to see whether the item is needed elsewhere. If the merchandise is needed in another warehouse, the system directs the cartons or pallet to be transshipped from the existing center to the new center. This saves the shipment from being stored and then repulled. If the item is received and is at the wrong location, the system sends a notification error indicating that it is in the incorrect distribution center. This saves any errors in receiving and stocking.

- Discontinued Items—If discontinued items are received from the manufacturer, they are redirected to the exception area. Purchasing decides whether to stock the merchandise or return it to the supplier. The message is sent to the buyer as an exception e-mail on the system software instead of a phone call from distribution, saving time for both the distribution and the purchasing centers.

- Replenishment Inventory—Material is expedited to stocking locations based on the status code provided. The license plate is scanned per pallet so that employees know what product is on a pallet and the location of each pallet. Each item, carton, or bag is labeled with the appropriate bin location number.

The second area for the WMS and RF system is the directed putaway. Material is expedited to stocking locations based on the status code. The license plate is scanned per pallet so that employees know what product is on what pallet and the location of each pallet. Each item, carton, or bag is labeled with the appropriate bin location number.

- The RF system tracks all locations within the warehouse.
- The system recognizes all empty overstock locations.
- The RF system searches for a location based on the size and weight of the pallet.
- The scanner displays the exact location of the merchandise.
- When merchandise is received, the RF system will search the warehouse for an empty location.

The third area the WMS and RF system is used is order stocking.

- The item is scanned to check the location number.
- The location is scanned to double-check the location.
- The operator places the material in the location.
- The operator verifies the quantities and keys it into the scanner.
- The receipt file is updated.
- The operator returns to the dock for the next pallet.
- The scanner will determine the sequence of stocking to reduce travel time and distance.

The fourth and final part of the WMS and RF system is the order filling.

- The scanner sequences the locations to be pulled in order by priority and for the shortest distance and time.
- The forklift operator is directed to the location from which overstock is to be pulled via display screen on the scanner.
- Member orders are filled from overstock locations.
- The RF system searches locations to do the following:
  - Avoid the need to pick a large quantity from the pick location.
  - Combine bin replenishment and order filling with one move.
  - Avoid returning partial pallets to overstock.
  - Fill orders requiring a full pallet of merchandise.

- Remove partial pallets from overstock, opening locations for the storage of full pallets.
- Sequence the locations to be pulled in the order by priority and for the shortest distance and time using the scanner.
- Direct the driver to the correct shipping door using the scanner.

The Applied RF Metrics Used in the Distribution Centers

The following represents the process improvements with the implementation of RF:

- A 28% increase in units handled per man-hour worked, showing performance and accuracy in order picking
- A 50% increase in efficiency in receiving
- An 18% reduction in cost per unit handled
- Location of each product known
- Picking accuracy of 99.95%
- Improved customer service

The Lean Savings of RF:

- The enhancements of the certification programs and the RF scanning techniques.
- The initial Lean inventory reduction is 2.4% × $211 million inventory = $5 million reduction in inventory.
- The new inventory: $206 million.
- Frees up the cost of capital which is 2% × $5 million, resulting in an inventory savings = $100,000.
- The Lean reduction of carrying cost due to the reduction in inventory. The reduced carrying cost is .266% × $5 million = $1,330,000 in additional savings.

The Green Savings of RF:

- Damaged inventory represents .75% × $5 million inventory = $37,500.
- Obsolete inventory cost reduction is 9% × inventory reduction = $450,000.
- Combined savings of $487,500 on potentially wasted merchandise.
- Inventory transfer cost of .5% to 1% in wasted movement in the system. It is moving product from one warehouse to another. The Green Savings of moving product from one warehouse to another with an average of 450 miles between the warehouses and the cost per mile for the semi truck is the variable cost of 6 miles per gallon plus wear and tear on the truck: variable cost is $3.12 per gallon × 450 / 6 = $234. The fixed cost (wear and tear) is $0.65 per mile (450 × .65 = $292). One trip has a total cost of $234 + $292 = $526.
- If a company has nine warehouses, at a pace of one trip a month for each truck to each warehouse, the total cost per year is 12 × 9 × $526 = $56,808. This does not include any round-trip costs or the wear and tear on the existing highway infrastructure.
- Total savings for RF is $1,974,308.

The savings after the RF program includes company turns at 4.52, sales at $931 million, and inventory at $206 million. The savings for the RF with a WMS program are Lean Savings of $1,430,000; Green Savings of $544,308; and a total savings of $1,974,308.

References

[1] Minahan, Tim, "Manufacturers take aim at end of supply chain," *Purchasing*, April 23, 1998.

[2] http://aisel.aisnet.org/cgi/viewcontent.cgi?article=1087&context=pacis2001&sei-redir=1#search="Postponement+metrics".

[3] "P11 VICS Voluntary Guide Lines for the Bill of Lading," February 2005, http://www.vics.org.

3

The Use of Radio Frequency Identity Tags in Industry

Radio Frequency Identity Tags (RFID) can greatly enhance a company's performance, but there must exist a definite need for this solution because it is not for all companies. RFID is an additional expense that makes sense only when the gain is greater than the cost of the technology. The expense is found in the purchase of the tags used on each item or each bin location, as well as the infrastructure expense of RFID readers and antennas at each point of read. An additional expense is the required integration of the data recorded by the readers communicating to the main computer through middleware. The cost of the installation depends on the size and complexity of the job. The larger the job, the more readers, tags, and Wi-Fi connectivity points are necessary. Issues to consider include scalability, security, inseparability, integration, administration, and managing.

Here is a generalized idea of the cost of a 900 MHz RFID implementation. Other frequencies are available but not included in this cost analysis:

- 125 to 134 kHz is classified as Low Frequency for scanning items close at hand and is used for access control, livestock, and race times, such as triathlon or marathon times for the participants.
- 13.56 MHz is classified as High Frequency. This offers more distance than the low-frequency tags and is generally used as smart tags for loyalty cards, books, and smart shelves.
- 860 to 960 MHz is classified as Ultra High Frequency. This is used in the supply chain for all the tasks discussed in this chapter.

- 2.45 GHz and 5.8 GHz are also classified as Ultra High Frequency, and 2.4 GHz is mainly used for the toll road I-Pass.

The components of an RFID system are broken down into five categories. The costs are an accumulation or a summary of the quantities used in the following groupings: RFID Tags, RFID reader, RFID printer, RFID antennas and cabling, and RFID middleware:

- RFID Tags—The passive tag is used for a license plate on a pallet, a bin location, a container load, or item-level tags. The item-level tags are relatively cheap based on volume. They can be one to five cents. The tabs for the license plate and bin tags can range from 10 cents to $1. Depending on the complexity required, environmentally protected tags are available for around $1 to $5 or more.
- RFID Reader—The reader can cost from $1,200 to $3,000 or more depending on the vendor and type used. If the reader is a hand-held it will be more expensive.
- RFID Printer—These are the devices that print a label with readable data and also have an RFID tag on them. The cost can range from $1,500 to $4,000 or more.
- RFID Antennas and Cabling—These cost $125 to $300 per antenna combination plus $50 for cabling.
- RFID Middleware—These may cost $6,000 to $300,000 or more. The cost depends on the complexity and number of jobs required by the system. This requires a talented IT staff or an external company specializing in RFID implementation.

RFID does not require line of sight as does the UPC. The RFID can read through boxes assuming that there is no metal or liquid inside. When metal or liquid is present, one layer is read, but not the entire case. This is why it is prudent to place the tag on the top of the product, so the readers can read down on the container and count the number of items, boxes, or packages inside. The container label can be read with a UPC reader, and then the RFID reader reads the carton count. The UPC tells the computer this is a box of 24 bottles, for example. The RFID read confirms that the container truly has 24 bottles. Productivity increases because no personnel are required to complete the process.

This process can also be used in the certification of suppliers. The retailer knows that the vendor accuracy is around 100%. When the items are received, they do not have to be counted. Instead, they are immediately stocked. This saves greatly in labor and in receiving-to-stock times. Lean Savings is enhanced due to greater efficiency of the operation. The Green Savings is found in fewer inventories, less spoilage, and less wasted merchandise.

The other advantage to RFID is that the tag is not a UPC but an EPC, or Electronic Product Code. The electronic product code has four fields for a 96-bit tag. The first part is the 8-bit header, indicating whether the tag is an item tag, a location tag, an asset tag, and so on. The second field is the EPC Manager with 28 bits, and it names which supplier the tag belongs to. The third field is the object class with 24 bits, and it is the item SKU or the UPC. The last field is the serial number with 36 bits, making each item unique. With 24 bottles of Dasani water, for example, each UPC will be the same but the serial numbers will be different. Having the same UPC with different serial numbers makes each bottle unique.

Every time an RFID tag is read, the time and date are recorded, which allows for tracking items throughout the supply chain. This option generates quantifiable data that can be used in the Business Intelligence system. The data from the RFID tag can be used as explored in Table 3-1.

Table 3-1 The Five Categories of Real-Time Information Used by an RFID System

Sense and Response is the name given when the system acts as an autonomous system and alerts the managers of any abnormalities when it senses them. A networked supply chain system can be built to show any abnormalities in the system, alert the appropriate personnel, and offer recommendations.

Pedigree Tracking is the term used to show that this is the right item for the delivery. As its name denotes, the item has the correct pedigree for the customer requirements.

Track and Trace makes it possible to have the Visual Supply Chain track the item through the entire supply chain. The product is traced, which allows for accurate delivery-time notification.

Chain of Custody shows who has owned the product or has had possession of it all through the supply chain. If there are damages or theft along the way, the owner knows where to look for answers.

Real-Time Location Systems are used in yard management and WMS. These systems act as an asset tracking system in either a yard or a warehouse. It gives real-time information about product, quantity, and location.

RFID technology is growing exponentially. More than 2.35 billion tags were sold globally in the year 2009: 200 million were used in the apparel industry, 105 million were used in the tagging of animals, 1.7 billion were used in factories, warehouses, hospitals, and other companies, and finally 350 million RFID tags used as tickets in transportation.[1] The RFID industry is expected to exceed $8.25 billion by the year 2014. This represents a 14% compound annual rate of growth for the 5 years 2009 to 2014.[2] The greatest growth will come from the Real Time Location Systems (RTLS) segment of the industry, representing baggage handling, animal ID, and item-level tagging in fashion apparel, library systems, consumer packaged goods supply chain, and retail systems. This segment of RTLS is forecasted to grow by 19% in the next few years.[3] When planning an RFID initiative, it is helpful to see how it has improved supply chain sustainability and competitiveness. The following paragraphs illustrate the advantage of RFID in several different industries.

The Apparel Industry—The apparel industry is expected to grow by 14% in the next few years.[4] Apparel and laundry companies globally used 200 million RFID labels in the year 2009.[4] The following is a list of the process improvements initiatives and metrics for the apparel industry:[4]

- The companies that use RFID in the apparel industry have experienced a 14% increase in sales. The biggest reason for the sales increase was the quick availability of the stock. With so many items in a retail store, a sale can be lost because the needed item is either in a different location or in the receiving room and the sales clerk cannot find it, or the customer just assumes the product is unavailable.[5]

- Their labor cost has been reduced by 30%. Fewer people are needed in the retail location because of increased accuracy and speed of the process.[1]

- Their inventory accuracy has increased by 27%.[5] This is brought about through the removal of human error. The people stocking and receiving are at the mercy of the accuracy of the tags that label the product. This is where the error can occur. Even this can be automated to a great degree.

- Inventory accuracy has increased to 98%-plus.[6]

- The system also delivers a 99% visibility to the supply chain.[1] This visibility is very important to the service level and performance of the company as described in Chapter 15, "The Visual and Visible Supply Chain."

- Visibility has also allowed the inventory to decrease by 15%. The enhanced visibility allows for faster receiving and better planning in cross-docking the received product.[1]

- On the average of all the industries sampled, the return on investments was three to four months.[1]

- Process improvement is measured by a number of metrics, as explained here:[1]

  - The system tracks every item from the time it is received until point-of-sale.

  - It facilitates stock replenishment within minutes of a sale, thereby improving inventory accuracy and maintaining available stock on the selling floor.

  - Because the RFID tags do not require line-of-sight, they can be used for cycle counting. Livingston American Apparel reported that what used to take 120 hours now takes only 15 hours.

  - Bloomingdale also confirmed this by stating that with item-level RFID scanning, the inventory counts time decreased by 96%. Item-level scanning of 100,000 items used to take 53 hours and now it is done in 2 hours. On average, 209 items could be counted in an hour with the bar coding UPC process. With the RFID process, 4,767 items are counted in one hour. Bloomingdale can count the inventory 26 times over with RFID in the time it takes to count the inventory once with the UPC system.

  - There is a definite reduction in man-hours required for restocking. This results in increased man-hours available for customer interaction.[6] The increase in efficiencies is because RFID has allowed for an increased in-stock position and shelf-level accuracy, more efficient backroom replenishment, a 50% improvement in response time to identify and resolve in-transit problems, a 20% reduction in excess product/safety stock inventory, a 20% reduction in container fleet, up to 90% improvement in reliability of delivery time windows, elimination/early detection of product theft, and elimination of the historical 10% to 15% human error rate associated with manual work processes to capture and enter data.[6]

The Animal Industry—The tagging of animals (such as pigs and sheep) is growing strongly as it becomes a legal requirement, with 105 million tags being used for this sector in 2009.[7] RFID tags will facilitate the collection of performance information following slaughter or death, a function that was far too labor-intensive and prone to error using the previous visual tags.[8] The industry as a whole will benefit from an increase in the capacity to trace sheep and lambs through the market chain and facilitate the collection of better data on characteristics such as carcass quality, superior rams, and increases in productivity.

Viewing RFID tags as an investment in tools and not strictly a cost is a key to success.[8] RFID systems can facilitate savings in labor costs by making various management chores more efficient. Improvements in flock health and productivity are made possible by applying RFID systems and flock management software. This, in turn, provides the capability to analyze production information gathered and stored electronically from individual animals.[8]

Over one-third of the calories in an ordinary American's diet come from honey bee–pollinated food—including a wide variety of fruits, vegetables, nuts, and berries.[9] RFID tags are used to monitor the beehives. By applying RFID to their processes, beekeepers, industrial buyers, and producers can get real-time visibility into the complete production chain.[9] A solution from Apitrack, for example, includes RFID tags, hand-held RFID readers, and software that allow users to collect production data from extraction rooms, fractioning rooms, and warehouses. The result is real-time data that can be used for the traceability and safety of honey, wax, and pollen.[9] Another benefit of RFID tags is tracking for diseases such as mad cow disease. When the rancher learns through the tracking system which herd the disease came from, he will not have to destroy the entire herd. The productivity of cow milk production has also been increased by the use of RFID tags. In one estimate, users claimed that their productivity was three times the national average.[10]

The Auto Industry—Misplaced or lost containers is a major problem in the automotive industry. When a container with critical parts is lost, it results in a loss of time and cost for reordering. It is estimated that the loss of parts in the auto industry costs $750,000,000 per year. To fix this problem, location, content, MSDS, and other data need to be stored. UPC does not offer this solution but RFID does. The industry might eventually phase out the UPC solution in favor of the total RFID solution for container and parts marking. The North American transmission plant, Balluff, saved $2 million per year from their automatic RFID tool management system.[11]

The Healthcare and Pharmaceutical Industry—The necessity for immediate care and medication for patients prompted the need for RFID in the healthcare and pharmaceutical industry. With RFID in the supply chain, these speedy transactions could bring a potential cost savings of $2.6 billion a year. Another benefit is the capability to keep the supply chain visible and used in a collaborative way to share demand information. This demand and supply information can be focused on medications that are critical to the activity of the clinic, pharmacy, or hospital.[12] One of the greatest benefits in the healthcare industry is the use of RFID to have better security through the Track and Trace techniques. Here are a few examples of enhanced functionalities from different perspectives:

- *Event Driven*—This is the true visible supply chain scenario in which an item may be getting close to an expiration date and still fill the shelves. The product may begin to increase or decrease in sales in the desired supply chain. These events and others will signal the supply chain operator that the questionable or bad event is about to happen. This is referred to as Opportunity Management due to the opportunity to correctly manage the supply chain.

- *Pedigree Tracking*—It is now possible to track the logistics of the supply chain to decide whether the correct item is delivered. In the pharmaceutical industry, this is very critical because it aids pharmacists in ensuring prescription accuracy.

- *Trace and Track*—This term really applies to the visible logistics network. The information here is mostly used to see where in the supply chain the product is. This improves delivery timing accuracy and ensures that receiving departments are properly staffed.

- *Chain of Custody*—This tracks ownership and location of each product. Each person who has received the product will be identified. If there was any tampering or theft of the product, each point of ownership will be identified.

The Logistics Industry—The advantages of RFID in the logistics industry is greatly enhanced through the use of sensor technology. Sensors are used to measure the following:

- Temperature within the shipping period can be measured. If the temperature has gone outside the limits set for the item, the amount of time spent outside the acceptable range is recorded. This can minimize spoilage of perishable goods.
- The humidity can be measured for items like plants that need or don't need to be in a humid environment.
- Light can be measured on the product. In certain cases, as with bacteria or film, the product will need to be in a dark environment.
- Vibration can be measured to account for certain product defects.

Warehouse Management Systems—Warehouse management systems can be greatly enhanced in the use of RFID. Not only can employees learn what is in the bins at a faster rate, but they are also notified in real time of what is in inventory. To truly automate the warehouse, RFID tags can be placed in the concrete of certain areas of the warehouse. As the forklift travels over the designated points and unloads the pallets in the location with an RFID tag on the floor, the activity is recorded. The forklift's onboard computer also knows what products are being stored or loaded at each location. Automatically assigning item, quantity, and location to all pieces in a warehouse cuts down on loss and allows for date-stamping for goods that are perishable. This aids in the creation of a true first in, first out environment.

Supply Chain Management—The supply chain and the movement of supplies can represent 50% to 80% of the cost of the procedures in the healthcare industry. Supplies are the second-leading cost to hospitals after labor in providing patient care. Managing supply chains in healthcare has been a neglected area in efforts to improve efficiency and save costs. The purchase of goods and services can account for 50% to 80% of a company's expenditure. Purchase and supply chain management has to play an important role in cost-reduction programs. This role, however, should not be restricted to obtaining price reductions from suppliers but should also be extended to more constructive areas in which the participation and involvement of purchase and supply chain management is of immense importance. This involvement of RFID extends to the technology solutions of the supply chain using VMI, CPFR, and the rest of the technologies.

The Bullwhip Effect—The level of uncertainty between demand from the retailer to the distributor to the manufacturer and to the raw material producers increases, beginning with the retailer. This also means that the level of safety stock at each stage must increase. RFID, through item level, helps minimize this effect. The bullwhip effect is significantly reduced by sharing information and collaborating with the suppliers.

Replenishment Policies—This is the decision-making policy of the company in determining the frequency of arrivals and the size of the orders. The size of the orders is also determined by the EOQ policy or the minimum inventory policies of the supplier or the distributor. RFID will improve the inventory performance by making the item-level detail more visible to the trading partners.

Asset Life Cycle Management—Asset Life Cycle Management tracks maintenance, quality issues, safety records, and the lifetime before replacement. Airbus is using RFID to track thousands of key components from the time of purchase until they are placed on the plane. The entire life cycle is tracked, including repair and maintenance records. This gives an excellent database of which vendors and which parts have the best quality records. If certified with the suppliers, this information will show them how they are doing on their partnership agreement and whether or not they are meeting the key metrics.

RFID Used in Manufacturing—The greatest success stories come from the process of labor movement in manufacturing. A good example of the RFID improvements is the system installed in Johnson Controls. It synchronized the assembly of seats with the RFID tag under each seat. The computer knows which seat is coming to each cell of operation. The operator does not have to move because, even though each seat may be unique, the computer knows exactly when the seat will hit the cell, and the appropriate material for the worker will have been previously delivered. This is true just-in-time production. The amount of time saved by Johnson controls is significant. They can produce multiple models of car and truck seats on the same line without having to worry about grouping or staging until it gets to the final ship designation. This allows them to produce on one line what would have taken multiple lines. If no modifications are required at the station, the conveyor simply passes the operator without stopping.

The Gaming Industry—RFID is being used in the form of the Progressive Table Link in Las Vegas casinos for enhancing the efficiencies of the gambling operations. The information gathered does the following:[13]

- Gives the average bet per table and per user
- Shows the high and low wagers
- Gives the casino manager an idea of the bet spreads
- Alerts the manager of a run by a customer (the customer may be counting the cards)
- Ensures that the casino will not have to invest in numerous pit clerks because the customer realizes the casino is aware of the betting strategy

The Jewelry Management Industry—The best part of the technology in this industry is the labor and asset savings of expensive inventory. Employees can use an RFID hand-held gun to scan the cases for inventory. Each piece of jewelry has an RFID tag. Inventory counting can be enhanced by 90% to 96%. The next step is to use an RFID shelf. The RFID shelf has readers in the shelf, and the employee or manager can always see the inventory count. The final design for the RFID inventory of jewelry is to have a large antenna underneath a flat surface. Each time the jewelry is placed against the flat surface, the system will read the tag. As many as 250 small pieces of jewelry can be picked up by the reader. Multiple antennas can be placed so that each time a piece of jewelry is taken from the shelf, it is recorded. The system can be hooked up to alarm or security cameras.[14]

With the integration of Business Intelligence, it is time to begin the process of Autonomic Supply Chain Management. For competitive reasons, company names are not used in the following sections. Following are some examples of process improvement efforts.

An apparel company in Mexico was taking inventory and had experienced yearly losses in the inventory count. The inventory inaccuracies were not because of theft. They had the correct procedures in place to adhere to good practices. The problem existed because the ordinary worker did not want to do extra duties to make the count perfectly accurate. The last count showed a shortage of $400,000. They were interested in an RFID system that would use apparel tags to identify the products. The system upgrade would cost $100,000 with a return on investment of three months. The system not only saves in labor, but also prevents having to mark down old merchandise because employees could not find the product quickly enough to satisfy the customer.

Another system would allow the manufacturer to track 60-pound drums of paint from the manufacturers. The product needed to be painted as it rolled off the production line. Any shortage in the paint product could stall or stop the manufacturing process. This could cost over a million dollars an hour for a production stoppage. The RFID system would track the shipment and loading of the paint drums from the supplier, creating a visible supply chain where the manufacturer can plan production on existing or all new products received. The product accuracy is practically 100%. The product can be delivered with 90% accuracy to the hour. The fact that management can plan for a contingency observed in freight is a real advantage. The cost of the system would be no more than $300,000, and this would include all the appropriate software and hardware to run the entire operation. To date, a shutdown on the line happens approximately once every 18 months. Assuming a one-hour downtime, the yearly cost would be approximately $660,000. The break-even timeframe is six months.

In the correctional system, prisoners are identified with wrist badges. When they are traveling through the court system, approximately once or twice a year a prisoner will exchange wrist badges and leave earlier than allowed. These mistakes cost the legal system about $125,000 to correct. The system necessary to avoid this in the future costs about $150,000. Considering a once- or twice-a-year incidence, the ROI would be less than a year. The system proposed would have a wristband with an RFID tag on the prisoner's wrist. This would be coupled with a 2-D biometric facial recognition system. The system is specially designed for RFID tags and to work in concert with the technology. If the prisoner takes off or swaps the wristband, it will not work through the system's scanner and will signal that something is wrong. If the tag were to be enabled on another person, the scanner would tell the guard that the prisoner has the wrong ID. This is definitely a Lean and Green Savings.

Case Studies of Two Industries: The Medical Environment and the Distribution Industry

These are case studies that talk about the benefits of using RFID in the hospital environment and a distribution environment. The names of the companies have not been disclosed for privacy considerations. The name of the consulting firm was mentioned with the permission of the owner, John Baker. The case studies were chosen because of the connection to the Lean and Green theme of using and wasting fewer resources.

Case Study: Medical Environment

This section is about a case study of the hospital system. In 2007, SIMS was created to address the problem of the inefficient use and control of costly surgical equipment. During research, it was discovered that risky surgical operations were often interrupted by the absence of the right equipment necessary to complete the procedure. It was further discovered that the reason for the absence was not due to the lack of preparation, but was instead a direct result of an antiquated inventory management system. In addition to lost time and in order to compensate for the inaccurate system, hospitals are forced to house an inflated inventory of equipment. There are even times when equipment is simply confused with loaned items and must be tracked down or replaced.

It was therefore decided that SIMS should use RFID technology to produce and implement a surgical-instrument inventory management system in order to help the healthcare industry focus more time and money on patient care. Through the use of SIMS products and services, a healthcare facility will be able to provide surgical services more efficiently and at lower costs. Currently, the use of RFID technology in the healthcare industry is limited to a few examples. If implemented properly and with the right commitment, the use of this kind of technology can provide unmatched differentiation from competitors. The ideas presented in this proposal are just the beginning of many RFID programs that can save hundreds of thousands in inventory and lost productivity cost.

It is estimated that as much as three times the necessary amount of surgical equipment is purchased and housed in a hospital in order to compensate for the lack of asset-tracking efficiency. This leads to inflated annual capital expenditures and higher monthly carrying and maintenance costs. With an average of one million dollars in inventory, this problem costs hospitals hundreds of thousands of dollars in underutilized equipment alone. Additionally, thousands are wasted each month through carrying and maintenance costs.

A much more critical problem is the unexpected delay in the operating room. It is true that surgeons are highly trained professionals who are very thorough and avoid rushing. It is also true, however, that extended delays due to unexpected equipment problems add to the risk of the procedure. This risk can manifest itself in various ways. Surgeons are human and can become distracted in these situations, which may lead to mistakes. Additionally, more medications, like anesthesia, are needed to keep patients stable, which may lead to side effects.

Operating rooms are technologically complicated environments that employ highly trained and compensated professionals. At a cost of hundreds of dollars per hour and with an estimated 1,500 operations per year in lost minutes per procedure, this can add up to tens of thousands of dollars per year.

Surgical equipment is very costly. A simple pack of drill bits may cost more than $20,000 to replace. Lost or misplaced equipment can cost a hospital hundreds of thousands in replacement capital. Even if the lost equipment is found, the time and money expended for retrieval add thousands to the bottom line.

Savings Estimation

Based on the inventory reduction assumption, the initial saving is $150,000 excess inventory × 50% reduction = $75,000. The 50% inventory replacement assumption brings $22,500 savings from the $45,000 cost for instrument replacement × 50%.

According to conversations with the hospital, employee time savings could approximate 300 hours or $12,000 per year. Surgery time saved during operating procedure is $16,875 from the 5 minutes per surgery × 1,500 surgeries per year × $2.25 per minute. The savings in sterilization is an approximate number based on the following logic in calculations.

The sterilization machine is usually filled in with four sets of instruments or 100 instruments before it is operated (per the hospital estimation). The research team assumed conservatively that currently (without RFID technology) each surgery would consume two standard sets of instruments on average. Thus, two surgeries would be necessary to fill in the sterilization machine. Hence, there are approximately 750 sterilization cycles per year from the 1,500 surgeries per year / 2. The research team assumed that RFID project implementation would reduce instrument waste per surgery by 50%. Therefore, one set of instruments instead of two would be consumed in each OR procedure. This brings down the sterilization cycles per year to 375. Based on the $50 assumption in sterilization savings, the total number is $18,750 from 75 runs per year × $50. Total savings per year is estimated to be $70,125.

ROI

During the first year of the project, total costs would be higher because of the initial investment needed. The total cost would be $208,200. This would be somewhat offset by a higher savings amount during the first year of $145,125 from the $75,000 initial savings + $70,125 yearly savings. A negative cash flow of $63,075 is expected during the initial year of the project.

After the first year there is a constant cost flow of $25,500 and a savings flow of $70,125 per year. The final result for the ROI estimate based on the assumptions in this project is 2.4 years.

Case Study: Distribution Industry

EXECUTIVE SUMMARY

The distribution company has a long history of delivering quality products to their customers. Even though the location falls within company standards, the desire is to seek a way to create more efficient movements in order to save money. Areas where this might be possible include broken, damaged, and lost inventory (BD&L), inventory knowledge, and warehouse organization.

After these possibilities were investigated, solutions were found that would reduce labor costs, carrying costs, and BD&L. The first solution is using RFID at the pallet level. This would allow a quicker and more accurate counting of the inventory on hand. The second solution would be to have RFID at the case level, which would further enhance quickness and accuracy. The third solution would be for back-stock gravity-fed shelving. This would not only help with the FIFO rotation of stock but also make everything more accessible.

The recommendation at this time is that distributor institute a pallet-level RFID solution. Other solutions could be implemented at a later date when the RFID has proven itself.

CURRENT SITUATION
Statement of Problem

Managing efficiencies within an organization is an ongoing process. Being more efficient will lead to cost savings and, in return, increased profit. Within all organizations lie certain inefficiencies that leave room for constant improvement. These inefficiencies cost companies millions of dollars each year. By implementing some relatively inexpensive processes, in relation to the current overall losses, companies can vastly improve their bottom line. In the case of the distributor, there are three such areas in which improvements can be made that could result in significant cost savings, leading to higher profits for the company as a whole:

- Broken, damaged, and lost inventory (BD&L)
- Inventory knowledge
- Warehouse organization

The first area that needs to be addressed is that of broken, damaged, and lost inventory (BD&L). Last year the distributor lost $189,400 due to BD&L.

As shown in Figure 3-1, nearly half of that loss was due to outdated products. Another 45% of total BD&L was due to reworkable or damaged inventory. The remaining 6% is due to lack of demand for a new product and inventory that has been lost.

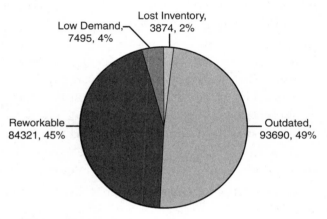

Figure 3-1 Cost associated with BD&L

The second major area in which inefficiencies exist is in the area of inventory knowledge. Currently, a daily inventory of all products in the warehouse must be taken in order to ensure that inventory is being properly tracked. If this knowledge could be gained instantly, not only would the company save on labor expenses, but also efficiency could be gained in restocking products.

The third area where efficiencies could be improved is warehouse organization. Because products are date sensitive, the company operates on a first in, first out inventory control method. (See Figures 3-2 and 3-3 for warehouse setup and product flow.)

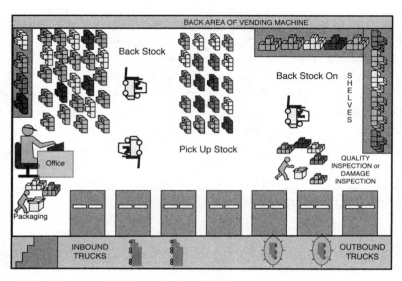

Figure 3-2 Current floor plan of the distributor

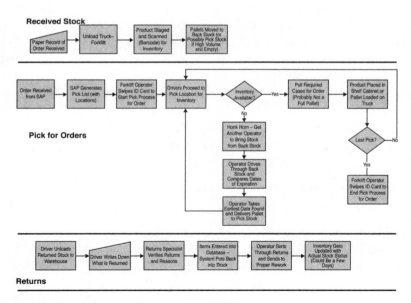

Figure 3-3 Current process map of the distributor

Currently, orders are fulfilled from the picking area in the central location of the warehouse. When the inventory in this area becomes low, a horn honk from the picking forklift operator signals to another forklift operator that more inventory is needed. The forklift operator must then go to the picking area to find out what is needed to be stocked. That driver then searches the back-stock area for the needed product with the oldest expiration date and then proceeds to refill the pick area. This is where efficiency can be created. Because none of the back stock is in a specific order, the oldest products are not always sent out first. If these older products are not used by their expiration date, they must be disposed of, resulting in BD&L.

Scope of Analysis

After the processes at the enterprise warehouse have been collected and examined, options have been compiled that could create efficiencies resulting in cost savings. One option involves implementing an RFID inventory control system on the pallet level, and another option exists in moving one step forward with RFID on the case level. In regard to warehouse organization, a complete reorganization of the warehouse to a gravity-fed inventory control system will offer one more option for increasing warehouse efficiency. These processes set forth individually or in combination will offer cost savings to the company now and into the future.

Goals

- Reduce labor-related costs by 10% by May 2010.
- Reduce the costs associated with BD&L by 25% within a one-year period.
- Reduce inventory 20% through better inventory control methods.

These goals would result in bringing the warehouse above company standards and make it the model for the enterprise across the nation. Implementing RFID would help to achieve these goals.

RFID

With properly planned cost analysis research and implementation of an RFID application system, items may be tracked automatically and without human intervention. This will minimize time involved in identification processes, and with high integrity of data capture. In today's enterprise supply chain management, this could tremendously improve the efficiency of inventory tracking and management, while reducing the cost of inventory management and property of ownership.

RFID on the pallet level offers many benefits such as its easy implementation and low-cost way to do basic inventory tracking while making it possible to send out the oldest products in the back stock first, reducing BD&L. Another benefit this solution offers is that it makes employees' tasks within the warehouse much more streamlined. Instead of having to manually receive the orders for picking, they can receive this information instantaneously from a monitor on their forklift.

The major drawback of RFID on the pallet level is rectified with the major benefit of RFID at the case level. It is a common practice to split up pallets in order to fill uneven orders. Because of this, some inventory will still have to be entered manually when RFID is done on the pallet level. If the distributor would decide to move forward with RFID in the future on the case level, the manual inventory tracking step could be eliminated. However, this step would be much more costly to implement due to the fact that the tags would have to be integrated into that packaging by the manufacture. Another drawback of this RFID solution is that when a tag is in extremely close proximity to a metal or liquid, it could possibly malfunction, causing an inaccurate inventory reading.

Gravity Flow Roller System

If the gravity flow system were implemented, it would offer several benefits. The major benefit is that this system, in combination with RFID, would streamline the distributor's FIFO inventory-control method. By guaranteeing that the oldest products are constantly being pushed to a central location near the picking area, the center could once again decrease BD&L. This option also offers added benefits to workers. Because the bulk of the inventory is on rolling racks, it can be moved with ease. This also makes the work environment much safer by reducing the probability that a pallet could be dropped by a forklift. The drawbacks of such a system include implementation costs and the need for a large amount of space. However, even with these drawbacks, this system offers the company an easy way to become more efficient.

RECOMMENDATION
RFID Implementation

The corporation could improve its operations in several ways. An RFID system needs to be implemented in the plant. Further, the company will need to install an RFID printer to print the tags it chooses to use. The distribution center will also need to supply employees with RFID hand-held readers and mobile applications so that products can be tracked instantaneously.

The company will also need to rework the current forklift process in the facility. The company currently has five forklifts that will need RFID readers installed on them. There are three single-forked units and two double-forked units; the double-forked units will need external antennas installed on them so that they can read both pallets at one time. Finally, all forklifts will need floor-facing antennas installed. It is also recommended to install two single-facing, ruggedized enclosures and four double-facing ruggedized enclosures on each dock door. Figure 3-4 shows the proposed setup of the RFID portals. Venture Research, Inc., proposed five RFID portals at the loading docks. The ruggedized enclosures will be placed at the five dock doors per the drawing in Figure 3-5. The current warehouse setup will remain the same.

The corporation will need to instruct employees about how to handle RFID tags and how to implement the process. Therefore, they should provide 1,000 floor tags and instructions for personnel. It's also recommended to provide 100 shelf tags for installation and install extra on an as-needed basis. The distributor will need to have a running server at the location, and a SAP interface will need to be written and mapped out so that the RFID software will work with the current software.

Product-flow efficiency will improve after RFID implementation. Tags will be placed on each pallet as it arrives in the warehouse. These tags will be scanned and pallets will be placed in back stock or pick locations as needed. The RFID scanner on the forklift will provide the product location with expiration date information. The forklift drivers will save a significant amount of time by not searching for product. The forklift driver will locate the product with the closest expiration date and place it in the pick line. The more efficient rotation of stock should result in a 50% reduction in outdated products cost. Labor efficiency will be improved for both the forklift operator and the person waiting for product to be restocked on the line. Figure 3-5 shows the new process map after RFID is implemented. It also gives a better indication of the flow of the process.

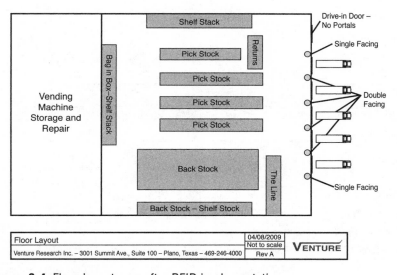

Figure 3-4 Floor layout map after RFID implementation

Information provided courtesy of Venture Research, Inc. Copyright 2003–2011

Cost Structure of RFID Implementation

Table 3-2, provided by Venture Research, Inc., is a summary report of the cost of the RFID system implementation in the warehouse. According to this table, the total cost of implementation would be about $151,909.83. This calculation is based on provided information and assumptions from 2009. The pricing is for educational purposes only and is not representative of current industry pricing. This cost includes system design, installation, equipment, software support expenses, training, RFID tags, and shipping.

Process Map after RFID Implementation

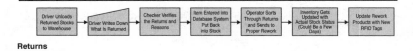

Figure 3-5 Process map after RFID implementation

Table 3-2 Cost of System Design and Installation

Post 1-Year Warranty & License Fees	Ext. Cost Nonrecurring	Unit	Qty.	Description
$0.00	$7,200.00			Design and Review
$359.40	$11,970.00			Back Stock/ Receiving
$0.00	$8,425.00			Pick Stock
$1,227.00	$35,270.00			Dock Doors
$2,166.00	$22,940.00			Forklift/Material Movement (RFID)
$4,057.88	$33,399.00			Computer/Hardware/Server/License
$0.00	$3,400.00			Integration/Shipping/Staging
$0.00	$10,800.00			On-Site installation/ Training/Support

Post 1-Year Warranty & License Fees	Ext. Cost Nonrecurring	Unit	Qty.	Description
$7,810.28	$133,404.00			
	$11,005.83	0.0825		Management/ Logistics Support
	$7,500.00	0.15	50,000	RFID Labels-4X2, Roll Stock
$7,810.28	**$151,909.83**			**Total Project**

Information provided courtesy of Venture Research, Inc. Copyright 2003-2011.

Return on Investment

The return on investment of the RFID system is based on the following assumptions:

- Outdated product loss will decrease at least 50%.
- Labor efficiency will be increased by 10% minimally.
- Inventory will reduce by 20% minimally.

Table 3-3 illustrates the savings listed in this paragraph. The warehouse had $93,690 in outdated product last year. The system would tell employees exactly which pallets to pick. In doing so, inventory rotation would be managed in a more efficient manner. This improved process for inventory rotation could result in a 50% reduction of outdated products. This reduction leads to an overall decrease of 25% of total BD&L, which would be a savings of $46,845.00 per year. The system also represents a Green Savings of $46,845 due to less waste to dump bins or salvage yards.

Table 3-3 BD&L Inventory Savings Every Year (Based on Last Year Data)

List of BD&L	Last Year Cost	Percentage Reduced Cost After RFID Implementation	Savings After RFID Implementation
Outdated	$93,690.00	50%	$46,845.00
Reworkable	$84,321.00	0%	$0.00
Low-Demand Products	$7,495.00	0%	$0.00

List of BD&L	Last Year Cost	Percentage Reduced Cost After RFID Implementation	Savings After RFID Implementation
Lost Inventory	$3,874.00	0%	$0.00
Total BD&L Cost	$189,380.00		
Total BD&L Cost Saving			**$46,845.00**

RFID, by its nature, would require less handling of the inventory. Everything would be scanned when it arrives, and the floor tags would be scanned when the product is placed in the warehouse. This would lead to a reduction of labor and less time needed to fill the orders. The daily manual inventory would also be reduced. Implementing RFID should allow for a reduction in workforce of at least one person and, at minimum, eliminate at least 50% of overtime costs. Using an average rate for warehouse salaries of $36,000 per year, labor could be reduced by $50,040 per year. This does not take into consideration the savings in employer taxes and employee benefits. This would result in a 10% reduction of labor costs within the first year after implementation. Table 3-4 shows the per-week and per-year comparisons.

Table 3-4 Labor Cost

Labor Cost Structure	Per Week	Yearly
Labor Cost/Week	$9,000.00	$468,000.00
Per Employee Labor Cost (Total 13 Floor Employee)	$692.31	$36,000.00
Overtime Charges (6% of Total Labor Cost)	$540.00	$28,080.00
Labor Cost Saving After RFID Implementation (1 Less Worker Requirement)	$692.31	$36,000.00
Overtime Labor Savings (50%)	$270.00	$14,040.00
Total Labor Savings (Lean Savings)	**$962.31**	**$50,040.00**

Savings

Industry standard for inventory carrying costs is 20% or more of total inventory. RFID could provide the opportunity to reduce inventory by at least 20%. The reasoning behind this reduction is due to increased inventory knowledge. At any given time, the system can show exactly what products are in stock. This will lead to more efficient ordering processes from the warehouse to the supplier. The warehouse typically carries a baseline inventory of one million dollars. A 20% reduction of inventory results in an inventory balance of $800,000. The $200,000 inventory no longer carried will result in a $40,000 savings in inventory handling costs using a conservative 20% savings. Table 3-5 shows the reduction in inventory after RFID, and Table 3-6 gives the total savings of RFID.

Table 3-5 Inventory Handling Cost Saving

Inventory Cost Structure	Current Inventory	Reduced Inventory after RFID (20%)	Inventory after RFID
Baseline Inventory Daily	$1,000,000.00	$200,000.00	$800,000.00
Inventory Handling Cost	$200,000.00		$160,000.00
Inventory Handling Cost Savings		**$40,000.00**	

Table 3-6 Total Return on Investment (ROI) from Direct Savings

Steps of Savings	Amount
Total BD&L Cost Savings	$46,845.00
Total Labor Savings	$50,040.00
Inventory Handling Cost Savings	$40,000.00
Total Return on Investment	**$136,885.00**

If all the savings in year one are added together, the result is a cost savings of $136,885. The total cost to implement RFID would be $151,910. The chart in Figure 3-6 shows that the timeline for the ROI would be just over one year.

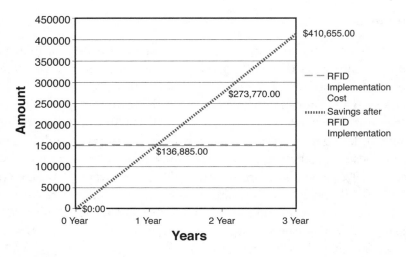

Figure 3-6 ROI chart

Indirect Cost Savings

Implementation of technology results in both direct (hard) and indirect (soft) cost savings. The RFID equipment will reduce the amount of time the office staff commits to daily inventory. It should also assist in reducing the amount of redundant paperwork that is in the system.

Future Recommendations

While the distributor should take the preceding recommendations currently, there are also steps they should look to in the future to help further improve their efficiency and product locating. First, the company should look at installing a rolling rack system. The gravity flow pallet rack is a storage system driven by gravity. The system will work particularly well with the FIFO system that the company employs. It will allow pallets to move through the warehouse on industrial shelves, which will give employees easier, faster access to products. There is an integrated braking system that slows the pallets to a stop so that they don't hit each other and ruin products.

The other recommendation is to implement RFID at the case level instead of the pallet level. This will allow the company to better track products, as pallets are often mixed with different products that the company offers. Currently, there is no way to actually tell which product is going out or coming in, but RFID at the pallet level is a great start.

References

(1) http://www.mcpressonline.com/application-software/general/have-you-looked-at-rfid-roi-lately.html.

(2) http://www.abiresearch.com/press/1618-RFID+Market+to+Reach+$5.35+Billion+This+Year.

(3) "ABI study: Some parts of RFID market will see nearly 20 percent growth through 2014," http://rfid24-7.com/rfidtalk/?p=90.

(4) http://www.idtechex.com/research/articles/rfid_market_forecasts_2009_2019_00001377.asp.

(5) http://www.adt.com/wps/wcm/connect/d2a5c98040a2914f9f78bf01a894c517/CR-ADT-101Final.pdf?MOD=AJPERES.

(6) I will talk first about the tangible benefits in apparel from RFID: http://www.apparel.averydennison.com/products/rfid.asp.

(7) http://homelandsecuritynewswire.com/rfid-market-reach-556-billion-end-2009.

(8) http://www.canadaid.com/producers/documents/RFID_Decommisioning_QA_V5.pdf.

(9) http://rfid.thingmagic.com/rfid-blog/?Tag=Agriculture.

(10) http://www.rfidjournal.com/article/print/7621.

(11) http://xerafy.com/sites/default/files/resources-files/Read%20on%20Metal%20RFID%20for%20Automotive_0.pdf.

(12) "RFID Technology: Implications for Healthcare Organizations," *American Journal of Business*, http://www.bsu.edu/mcobwin/majb/?p=627.

(13) http://homelandsecuritynewswire.com/rfid-market-reach-556-billion-end-2009.

(14) http://wn.com/Jewellery_RFID_Management_System_In_Action_Cantonese.

4

Transportation Management System (TMS)

TMS is a category of the Supply Chain Management (SCM) software. The TMS system responsibility is the routing of goods into and out of the enterprise. SCM is broken into two categories, Supply Chain Planning (SCP) and Supply Chain Execution (SCE). The TMS software is part of the SCE category. The execution portion of the supply chain requires action. This is appropriate for the TMS because its job is to move the product through the supply chain. TMS solutions can be bought as a solution within the ERP program or can be bought separately from a "Best of Breed" solution from an Independent Service Provider Vendor (ISV). The TMS approach represents the "Best of Breed" technique in which a company buys from the best-of-class software provider in the field. Real-time exchange of information or event management is essential in creating the world-class company and keeping that company ahead of the competition.

There are many ways to license the software. Some vendors offer the choice of various combinations of the licensing agreements. The four most common options are given here:

1. There's traditional purchase of the software and all modules. This works well when a company is in need of many different components of the software and requires payment for all the modules.

2. With the limited traditional model, payment is required for only the installed modules.

3. In the application service provider approach, the program is downloaded from the Internet or the vendor, which allows use as outlined in the traditional licensing agreement. The

difference here is that the software provider will take care of all maintenance and installation of software on their end. This works well when access to IT resources is limited.

4. The next form is the cloud. This is similar to software on-demand. In this format, no installation is necessary because the software is housed at the vendor's site. This format is the easiest and fastest way to implement the software solution with the least amount of IT involvement. The buyer is required to pay only for what is used and is permitted to download only a few modules from the application service provider.

Here is a partial list of some of the best-of-breed TMS vendors on the market today:

- UPS Logistics Roadnet
- Descartes Roadshow
- JDA Software Fleet Management (Manugistics)
- Supply Chain Intelligence's iSaaS and iSaaS GPS
- Red Prairie TMS
- Transworks in Fort Wayne, Indiana
- HighJump
- Oracle TMS Solution
- Microsoft Transportation Management
- HK Systems: TMS Software
- IBM Cognos software for Transportation
- SAP Transportation Management Solution

TMS usually "sits" between an ERP or legacy order processing and a warehouse/distribution module. A typical solution would include both inbound (procurement) and outbound (shipping) orders to be evaluated by the TMS for various routing solutions. After the best provider is selected, the solution can generate electronic load tendering and track/trace. This also allows for the capability of supporting freight audit and payment processes.

TMS has the potential for the greatest Green value since logistics are a large expense (sometimes the greatest) in distribution firms. TMS functions with metrics include the following:

- Order consolidation—freight cost is lower when shipments are larger and represent a savings of 2% to 6%.
- Increased utilization of fleet—fewer trucks traveling less, representing a savings of 8% to 30%.
- Most economical routing by order size (parcel, LTL, FTL, or pool)—lowers freight cost for a savings of 5% to 20%.
- Routing for multiple stops—mileage savings of 5% to 20%.
- Trend analysis—to capture changing events.
- Communication options—EDI, Web, or satellite.
- Carrier performance metrics—for carrier certification.
- Rate shopping—savings of 2% to 10%.

In-transit, visibility is one part of TMS that has a large impact on service levels and inventory with a KPI reporting function that will do the following:

- Increase service levels by .4%.
- Reduce inventory by 5% to 7%. Allocation of orders can be managed more efficiently, minimizing the bullwhip effect and allowing less variation in demand forecast.
- Reduce receiving time by 20%, allowing scheduling personnel for receipt.
- Utilize EDI 214 transaction from carriers to track to receipts, allowing accurate time to the hour of 90%.
- Prioritize each shipment by out-of-stocks, promotional goods, seasonal goods, and danger-level items.
- The effects of the TMS in inbound freight include the initial Lean inventory reduction of 5% × $206 million inventory = $10.3 million reduction. New inventory is at $196 million.

The benefits of TMS are as listed here:

- Freed-up cost of capital is .02 × $10.3 million inventory savings = $206,000.
- New turns are $931 million / $196 million = 4.78 turns.
- Lean reduction of carrying cost by 26.6% × $10.3 million for an additional $2.739 million savings.
- Average freight per ton is 12.0%.

- There are 538 routes per week with an average load of 33,000.
- Freight rate is 12%, but with a 4% discount in lieu of the TMS consolidation the new rate is 12 × 96% = 11.5% freight rate for LTL.
- Freight rate is 11.5% in lieu of consolidation, but rate shopping makes the new discount 6%.
- New freight rate is 11.5% × .94 = 10.8%.
- Yearly savings (51 weeks per year) is $0.005 × 538 routes / week × 33,000 lbs. × 51 = $4,527,270 savings in freight rate for consolidation.
- Yearly savings is $0.007 × 538 × 33,000 × 51 = $6,338,178.

The most economical routing will save in mileage and gasoline in the outbound fleet. There's a savings of 8.0% for inbound transportation:

- The fleet runs at 3.4 million gallons per year.
- The cost is approximately $3.12 per gallon.
- Yearly savings is $3.12 × 3.4 million gallons × .08 = $848,640.

The Green Savings of the TMS includes the following:

- Damaged inventory cost represents .75% of $10 million inventory = $75,000.
- Obsolete inventory cost reduction is 9% of inventory reduction = $900,000. This represents $975,000 that would have been thrown away or put into a landfill.
- Transportation savings is 8% to 12% savings per year in miles driven for outbound transportation using the route optimization techniques. Note that 3.4 million gallons × .08 = 272,000 gallons of diesel reduction per year. I used the 8% to be conservative.

One of the primary determinants of carbon dioxide (CO_2) emission from mobile sources is the amount of carbon in the fuel. Carbon content varies, but typically average carbon content values are used to estimate CO_2 emissions.[1] Diesel carbon content per gallon is 2,778 grams. For all oil and oil products, the oxidation factor used is 0.99 (99% of the carbon in the fuel is eventually oxidized, while 1% remains unoxidized). To calculate the CO_2 emissions from a gallon of fuel, the carbon emissions are multiplied by the ratio of the molecular weight of CO_2 (m.w. 44) to the molecular weight of carbon (m.w.12): 44 / 12.

Finally, CO_2 emissions from a gallon of diesel are 2,778 grams × 0.99 × (44 / 12) = 10,084 grams = 10.1 kg/gallon = 22.2 pounds/gallon. The weight in pounds of gasoline to kg is 2.2 lbs. per kg. The fleet uses 3.4 million gallons per year. This equates to 22.2 pounds × 3.4 million gallons per year = 75.48 million pounds of CO_2 extracted into the atmosphere each year. This total of 37,740 tons of CO_2 was extracted into the air for the entire fleet per year. The route optimization techniques save 3,019 tons of CO_2 from being released into the atmosphere.[1]

Another Green Savings is wear and tear of the existing highway system. Assume that one five-axle tractor semitrailer has about the same effect on concrete pavement as 9,600 passenger cars (3.83 / .0004) = 9,600.[2] Pavement is designed for a 20-year life span but there can be severe degradations to the infrastructure with an increase in semi-truck traffic. Do it Best Corp. had 258 trucks on the road and they cut their mileage by 8%, saving the use of 19 trucks. Therefore, the Green Savings was 19 trucks × 9,600 cars × 5 days × 51 weeks = 46,512,000 reduction of cars on the road per year.[3]

The average car mileage per year in 2008 was 226 billion miles.[3] The average lifetime of the highway before resurfacing was 20 years.[3] The average mileage per year driven by a passenger car is 12,000.[4] The total reduction by the TMS is 12,000 miles per year × 46,512,000 reduced cars = 558,144,000,000 miles per year. The total number of miles driven on U.S. highways in 2008 was 2,973,509,000,000.[5] The reduction of total miles driven by the TMS program is 558,144,000,000 / 2,973,509,000,000. The TMS improvements program from a large distributor can reduce the total mileage on the highways by .09%.

This may not sound like a lot, but when added to the infrastructure cost it saves .09% of the wear and tear. Federal spending on infrastructure is dominated by transportation. Although capital spending on transportation infrastructure already exceeds $100 billion annually, studies from the Federal Highway Administration and the Federal Aviation Administration suggest that it would cost roughly $20 billion more per year to keep transportation services at current levels.[4]

The TMS savings in dollars to the infrastructure per year starts with the annual highway infrastructure cost of $20,000,000,000.[4] The cost of auto traffic on new pavement is 38.5%[6] and the TMS alleviates this load by .09%. To be conservative, the weather—with changes in temperature, ice storms with de-icing, snow plowing, and heavy rains with flooding—would account for a large part of the infrastructure cost that is not included. This is a rough estimate but represents a view of the Green Savings of .09% × $20,000,000,000 × 38.5% = $6,930,000.

These numbers might not sound very large, but if all the merchants in the United States applied these changes, the benefits would definitely be green.

Most food in the United States travels an average of 1,500 miles from its point of origin to its point of consumption. It is typically transported in trucks that can each cause the same amount of roadway damage as 9,600 cars, according to American Association of State Highway and Transit Officials.[2] Pavement is designed for a 20-year life span but there can be severe degradation to the infrastructure with an increase in semi-truck traffic.[2] In 1994, U.S. residential vehicles and light trucks traveled 1,793 billion miles, as referenced in Figure 4-1.[7]

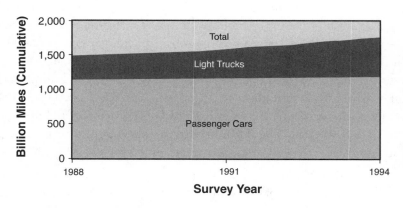

Figure 4-1 Residential vehicle miles traveled by type of vehicle

In January 2008, Americans drove a total of 226 billion miles.[3]

The graph in Figure 4-2 yields an average of 235,000 million miles per month = 2,820,000,000,000 miles per year. Figure 4-2 shows the average miles driven per month from 1970 to 2008.[8]

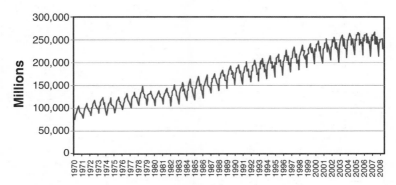

Figure 4-2 Historic monthly vehicle mileage driven per month

The number of miles driven per year is assumed to be 12,000 miles for every passenger vehicle.[9] Calculations from EPA's MOBILE6 model show an average annual mileage of roughly 10,500 miles per year for passenger cars and over 12,400 miles per year for light trucks across all vehicles in the fleet. However, these numbers include the oldest vehicles in the fleet (vehicles 25 years of age and older), which are likely not used as primary vehicles and are driven substantially less than newer vehicles. Since this calculation is for a typical vehicle including the oldest vehicles, it might not be appropriate. For all vehicles up to 10 years old, MOBILE6 shows an annual average mileage of close to 12,000 miles per year for passenger cars, and over 15,000 miles per year for light trucks.

FHWA's National Highway Statistics contains values of 11,766 miles for passenger cars and 11,140 miles for light trucks across the fleet. However, as with the MOBILE6 fleetwide estimates, these numbers include the oldest vehicles in the fleet. EPA's Commuter Model uses 1997 data from Oak Ridge Laboratories for the number of cars nationally and number of miles driven, which produces a value of just over 12,000 miles per year. Due to the wide range of estimates, 12,000 miles per vehicle is used as a rough estimate for calculating the greenhouse gas emissions from a typical passenger vehicle.[9]

Table 4-1 Miles from 1960 to 1999

					1960–1991				
	1960	1965	1970	1975	1980	1985	1990	1991
Air carrier, large certificated, domestic, all services	858	1,134	2,068	(R) 1,638	(R) 2,276	(R) 3,026	(R) 3,963	(R) 3,854
General aviation	1,769	2,562	3,207	4,238	5,204	4,673	4,548	4,400
Highway, total	718,763	887,811	1,109,724	1,327,664	1,527,295	1,774,827	2,144,362	2,172,050
Passenger car	587,012	722,696	916,700	1,033,950	1,111,596	1,246,798	1,408,266	1,358,185
Motorcycle	U	U	2,979	5,629	10,214	9,086	9,557	9,178
Other 2-axle 4-tire vehicle	U	U	123,286	200,700	290,935	390,961	574,571	649,394
Truck, single-unit 2-axle 6-tire or more	98,551	128,769	27,081	34,606	39,813	45,441	51,901	52,898
Truck, combination	28,854	31,665	35,134	46,724	68,678	78,063	94,341	96,645
Bus	4,346	4,681	4,544	6,055	6,059	4,478	5,726	5,750
Transit, total	2,143	2,008	1,883	2,176	2,287	2,791	3,242	3,306
Motor bus	1,576	1,528	1,409	1,526	1,677	1,863	2,130	2,167
Light rail	75	42	34	24	18	17	24	28
Heavy rail	391	395	407	423	385	451	537	527
Trolley bus	101	43	33	15	13	16	14	14
Commuter rail	N	N	N	173	179	183	213	215
Demand responsive	N	N	N	N	N	247	306	335

1960–1991

	1960	1965	1970	1975	1980	1985	1990	1991
Ferry boat	N	N	N	N	U	U	2	2
Other	N	N	N	15	15	15	16	19
Class I freight, train-miles	404	421	427	403	428	347	380	375
Class I freight, car-miles	28,170	29,336	29,890	27,656	29,277	24,920	26,159	25,628
Intercity/Amtrak, train-miles	209	172	93	30	30	30	33	34
Intercity/Amtrak, car-miles	2,208	1,775	690	253	235	251	301	313
Total train-miles	613	593	520	433	458	377	413	409

1992–1999

	1992	1993	1994	1995	1996	1997	1998	1999
Air carrier, large certificated, domestic, all services	(R) 3,995	(R) 4,156	(R) 4,378	(R) 4,628	(R) 4,807	(R) 4,907	(R) 5,030	(R) 5,326
General aviation	3,465	3,253	3,358	3,795	3,524	3,877	N	N
Highway, total	2,247,151	2,296,378	2,357,588	2,422,696	2,485,848	2,561,695	2,631,522	2,691,056
Passenger car	1,371,569	1,374,709	1,406,089	1,438,294	1,469,854	1,502,556	1,549,577	1,569,100
Motorcycle	9,557	9,906	10,240	9,797	9,920	10,081	10,283	10,584
Other 2-axle 4-tire vehicle	706,863	745,750	764,634	790,029	816,540	850,739	868,275	901,022
Truck, single-unit 2-axle 6-tire or more	53,874	56,772	61,284	62,705	64,072	66,893	68,021	70,304

Table 4-1 Miles from 1960 to 1999 (continued)

	1992–1999							
	1992	1993	1994	1995	1996	1997	1998	1999
Truck, combination	99,510	103,116	108,932	115,451	118,899	124,584	128,359	132,384
Bus	5,778	6,125	6,409	6,420	6,563	6,842	7,007	7,662
Transit, total	3,355	3,435	3,467	3,551	3,082	3,201	3,347	3,500
Motor bus	2,178	2,210	2,162	2,184	1,813	1,849	1,904	1,985
Light rail	29	28	34	35	37	41	43	48
Heavy rail	525	522	532	537	543	558	566	578
Trolley bus	14	13	14	14	14	14	14	14
Commuter rail	219	224	231	238	242	251	259	266
Demand responsive	364	406	464	507	363	410	469	494
Ferry boat	2	3	2	3	2	2	2	3
Other	24	30	29	34	68	77	90	112
Class I freight, train-miles	390	405	441	458	469	475	475	490
Class I freight, car-miles	26,128	26,883	28,485	30,383	31,715	31,660	32,657	33,851
Intercity/Amtrak, train-miles	34	35	34	32	30	32	33	34
Intercity/Amtrak, car-miles	307	303	304	292	276	288	312	342
Total train-miles	424	440	475	490	499	507	508	524

Table 4-2 Miles from 2000 to 2008

	2000	2001	2002	2003	2004	2005	2006	2007	2008
Air carrier, large certificated, domestic, all services	(R) 5,662	(R) 5,545	(R) 5,615	(R) 6,106	(R) 6,602	(R) 6,716	(R) 6,605	(R) 6,733	6,446
General aviation	N	N	N	N	N	N	N	N	N
Highway, total	2,746,925	2,797,287	2,855,508	2,890,450	2,964,788	2,989,430	(R) 3,014,371	(R) 3,032,399	2,973,509
Passenger car	1,600,287	1,628,332	1,658,474	1,672,079	1,699,890	1,708,421	(R) 1,690,534	(R) 1,672,467	1,615,850
Motorcycle	10,469	9,639	9,552	9,577	10,122	10,454	(R) 12,049	(R) 13,621	14,484
Other 2-axle 4-tire vehicle	923,059	943,207	966,034	984,094	1,027,164	1,041,051	(R) 1,082,490	(R) 1,112,271	1,108,603
Truck, single-unit 2-axle 6-tire or more	70,500	72,448	75,866	77,757	78,441	78,496	(R) 80,344	(R) 82,014	83,951
Truck, combination	135,020	136,584	138,737	140,160	142,370	144,028	(R) 142,169	(R) 145,046	143,507
Bus	7,590	7,077	6,845	6,783	6,801	6,980	(R) 6,783	(R) 6,980	7,114
Transit, total	3,605	3,735	3,855	3,915	3,972	4,054	4,127	4,238	4,375
Motor bus	2,041	2,104	2,156	2,177	2,169	2,192	2,214	2,241	2,272
Light rail	52	54	61	64	67	69	74	84	88
Heavy rail	595	608	621	630	642	646	652	657	674
Trolley bus	15	13	14	14	13	13	12	11	12

Table 4-2 Miles from 2000 to 2008 (continued)

	2000	2001	2002	2003	2004	2005	2006	2007	2008
Commuter rail	271	277	284	286	295	303	315	325	337
Demand responsive	532	578	613	640	651	683	708	752	803
Ferryboat	3	2	3	3	3	3	3	3	3
Other	97	100	104	101	131	144	149	163	187
Class I freight, train-miles	504	500	500	516	535	548	563	543	524
Class I freight, car-miles	34,590	34,243	34,680	35,555	37,071	37,712	38,955	38,186	37,226
Intercity/Amtrak, train-miles	35	36	38	37	37	36	36	37	38
Intercity/Amtrak, car-miles	368	378	379	332	308	265	264	267	272
Total train-miles	539	536	537	553	572	584	599	581	562

Table 4-3 Comparison of Purchase Orders Created Manually and Those Created Automatically by an ASN

The Corporation has 1,500 stocking vendors that are reviewed every three weeks. There are also sales, promotions, special orders, and nine warehouses for the orders.

Manual Orders

When a manual ordering system is used, the cost of reviewing the orders and keying in the purchase order manually is $50.00 per PO. The averages purchase orders are $1,625 \times 9 = 14,625$ purchase orders a month for all 9 warehouses. So the total monthly cost is $50 \times 14,625 \times 9 = \$731,250$ if ordered manually without any EDI or automated systems.

Automated Forecast System

When using an automated forecast system, the cost of reviewing the order before placement is $3.00 per PO. In the true VMI concept, there is no purchase order; the ASN will become the PO upon receipt. If the company has an automatic forecasting system, the actual savings is: $12 \times 1,625 \times \$3.00 \times 9$ warehouses = $525,500 per year.

Table 4-4 The Number of Pounds of Paper per Tree

A tree produces roughly 800 pounds of paper.[10] Let's perform an analysis:

526,500 pages

500 sheets = 5 lbs

The number of trees needed for the 526,500 pages is:

$$\frac{\left(\dfrac{526,500}{500}\right) \times 5}{800} = 7$$

According to the Technical Association for Pulp and Paper Industry (TAPPI) and the American Forest & Paper Association, only about one-third of the fiber used to make paper in the United States is from whole trees. Only trees smaller than 8 inches in diameter or larger trees not suitable for solid wood products are typically harvested for papermaking. The remaining two-thirds is made up of residue (wood chips and scraps left behind from forest and sawmill operations), and recovered (recycled) paper.[10]

Assume that the paper in question is typical 20-pound copy paper and it has been produced using 100% hardwood, measured in cords. A cord of wood is approximately 8 feet wide, 4 feet deep, and 4 feet high, and weighs roughly 2 tons (15% to 20% water weight). It has been estimated that one cord yields an average of 1,500 pounds of paper (300 reams).[10] If a tree produces half a cord, then one tree produces half of 1,500 pounds of paper, or 750 to 800 pounds of paper per tree.

Table 4-5 The Advance Ship Notice (ASN) Transaction Set 856

The ASN offers a view of the contents of the goods arriving on the carrier in advance of the delivery date. This is very helpful in advance planning of receipts and labor in the warehouse. Using this document alone has allowed Do it Best Corp. to realize a 15% increase in labor productivity in the Receiving Department. This gives a labor savings of 7 people × .15 = 1.05 person labor hours. At $18 per hour and with additional benefits of 25%, direct labor savings is $46,800 per year. This assumes the need for one less person in receiving.

Table 4-6 Comparison of Invoice Created Manually and One Created Automatically by ASN

- The average cost of an invoice is $7 if created manually and $0.50 if created electronically.
- The company has approximately 175,500 invoices per year. Actual values cannot be given, but this is close to the number for a company of this size.
- The annual cost to create a manual invoice is $1,228,500.
- Integration savings from allowing the ASN to become the invoice is $1,228,500.

Table 4-7 Conversion of Number of Trees to Pounds of CO_2

- A healthy tree stores about 13 pounds of carbon annually.[11]
- It might take up to 10 years before the tree can start producing at the ultimate level. Due to the CO_2 absorption, an average value of five years' loss per tree cut and replanted is necessary.
- The amount of atmospheric CO_2 savings is $13 \times 5 \times 14 = 910$ pounds per year.

Table 4-8 VMI Payback in Terms of Green Deployment

At a 400% increase in productivity, 2 people are needed for these tasks instead of 8 people.

Wattage costs:

- Desktop computers run 100–250 watts per hour.
- Laptop computers run 20–45 watts per hour.
- The typical monitor runs 80 watts per hour.
- Total watts are 200–375 watts per hour. (Watts × Hours Used) / 1,000 × Cost per Kilowatt-Hour = Total Cost.) At 8 hours a day × 250 days a year and a kWh charge of $0.16, the total cost is $255 \times 8 \times 250 \times 6 = 3,060,000$ watts per year.

Therefore, there is 3,060 kWh × $0.16 = $490 dollars saved in electricity by reducing the number of computers needed in the purchasing department.

Table 4-9 Savings of Carrying Cost

	Category Range	Value for Company	
• Cost of Goods Sold—savings			$78 million
• Cost of Goods Sold—Cost of money	2%–12%	2%	$1.56 million
• Inventory Service cost			
• Insurance	1%–3%	2%	$1.56 million
• Physical Handling	2%–5%	2%	$1.56 million
• Taxes	2%–6%	4%	$3.12 million
• Storage Space cost			
• Rented warehousing surplus	2%–4%	0.10%	$0.0 million
• Clerical & Inventory Control	3%–6%	3%	$2.39 million
• Inventory risk cost			
• Damage	.5%–1%	.75%	$0.585 million
• Depreciation	1%–2%	1.5%	$1.17 million
• Obsolescence	6%–12%	9%	$7.02 million
• Theft	1%–2%	1.5%	$1.17 million
• Inventory transfer cost	.5%–1%	.75%	$0.585 million
Total	**21%–54 avg =**	**26.6%**	**$20.72 million**

Note, the categories are given in a range. For instance, the inventory risk cost can range from .5% to 1% in the industry. The value of .75% is what the company used as its value of inventory transfer cost. The figures to the right represent the unique value for the corporation.

Table 4-10 TMS and 3PL on CO_2: The Savings in Gasoline and CO_2 Emissions

One of the primary determinants of carbon dioxide (CO_2) emission from mobile sources is the amount of carbon in the fuel. Carbon content varies, but typically the following average carbon content values are used to estimate CO_2 emissions:[12]

- Diesel carbon content per gallon: 2,778 grams.
- For all oil and oil products, the oxidation factor used is 0.99 (99% of the carbon in the fuel is eventually oxidized, while 1% remains unoxidized).
- To calculate the CO_2 emissions from a gallon of fuel, the carbon emissions are multiplied by the ratio of the molecular weight of CO_2 (m.w. 44) to the molecular weight of carbon (m.w.12): 44 / 12.
- CO_2 emissions from a gallon of diesel are 2,778 grams × 0.99 × (44 / 12) = 10,084 grams = 10.1 kg/gallon = 22.2 pounds/gallon.
- The weight in pounds of gasoline to kg is 2.2 lbs. per kg.
- If an outbound transportation fleet uses 3.4 million gallons per year, then 22.2 pounds × 3.4 million gallons per year = 75.48 million pounds of CO_2 extracted into the atmosphere each year.
- This is 37,740 tons of CO_2 extracted into the air for the entire fleet per year.
- The route optimization techniques save 3,019 tons of CO_2 from being released into the atmosphere.

Current progress from implementation of the TMS:

- Lean Savings

  Inventory reduction is 5% × $206 million inventory = $10.3 million reduction.

  Cost carrying reduction is $2.739 million.

  Freed-up capital is 2% × $10.3 million inventory savings = $206,000.

  Freight rate for consolidation savings is $4,527,270.

  Freight rate savings from rate comparisons and rate shopping is $6,338,178.

  Gasoline savings is 8% × 3.4 million gallons per year × $3.12 = $848,640.

  New turns are $931 million / $196 million = 4.75 turns.

  New inventory is at $196 million.

  The Total Lean Savings is $14,659,088.

- Green Savings

  Damaged inventory cost represents .75% of $10 million inventory = $75,000.

  Obsolete inventory cost reduction is 9% of inventory reduction = $900,000.

  Route optimization techniques save 3,019 tons of CO_2 from being released into the atmosphere.[13]

  The TMS savings in dollars to the infrastructure per year is .09% × $20,000,000,000 × 38.5[4] [6] = $6,930,000.

  Green Savings is 19 trucks × 9,600 cars × 5 days × 51 weeks = 46,512,000 reduced cars on the road per year.[2]

  The Total Green Savings is $7,905,000.

  Total savings for the TMS program is $22,564,088.

Summary Savings

- The total cumulative Lean Savings from the VMI process to the TMS process is $78,156,488. This represents 8.39% of sales saved.

- The total cumulative Green Savings from the VMI process to the TMS process is $26,296,336. This represents 2.82% of sales saved.

- The total cumulative Lean and Green Savings from the VMI process to the TMS process is $104,452,824. This represents 11.22% of sales.

- For every dollar spent on Lean, $0.34 in Green is earned. So 34% of all Lean Savings goes into Green Savings at this point. This is significant.

The total savings for the entire program is $16,025,906, as itemized here:

- Lean Savings is $14,659,088.
- Green Savings is $1,366,818.
- There are 14 trees saved per year. Using the data given in Table 4-7, 14 trees equates to 910 pounds of CO_2 saved per year.
- There are 46,512,000 fewer cars on the road per year.
- Route optimization techniques save 3,019 tons of CO_2 from being released into the atmosphere.

- The TMS savings in dollars to the infrastructure per year is .09% × $20,000,000,000 × .25[4] = $45,000,000.

The total TMS Savings Metrics in sales is $931 million, and in new inventory is $196 million. The new company turns are $931,000,000 / $196,000,000 = 4.75. The combined savings for the TMS Program is Lean Savings of $14,659,088 and Green Savings of $1,366,818.

The following is a summary of the Green Savings and corresponding references:

The Intergovernmental Panel on Climate Change (IPCC) guidelines for calculating emissions inventories require that an oxidation factor be applied to the carbon content to account for a small portion of the fuel that is not oxidized into CO_2. For all oil and oil products, the oxidation factor used is 0.99 (99% of the carbon in the fuel is eventually oxidized, while 1% remains unoxidized).[1]

Finally, to calculate the CO_2 emissions from a gallon of fuel, the carbon emissions are multiplied by the ratio of the molecular weight of CO_2 (m.w. 44) to the molecular weight of carbon (m.w.12): 44 / 12.[1]

CO_2 emissions from a gallon of gasoline are 2,421 grams × 0.99 × (44 / 12) = 8,788 grams = 8.8 kg/gallon = 19.4 pounds/gallon.[1]

CO_2 emissions from a gallon of diesel are 2,778 grams × 0.99 × (44 / 12) = 10,084 grams = 10.1 kg/gallon = 22.2 pounds/gallon.[1]

Note: These calculations and the supporting data have associated variation and uncertainty. EPA may use other values in certain circumstances, and in some cases it may be appropriate to use a range of values.[1]

References

[1] Carbon Content in Motor Vehicle Fuels" and "Calculating CO_2 Emissions," http://www.epa.gov/oms/climate/420f05001.htm.

[2] http://ftp.dot.state.tx.us/pub/txdot-info/gbe/french_fry.pdf.

[3] Source: Department of Transportation: http://www.eia.gov/emeu/rtecs/chapter3.html.

[4] http://cboblog.cbo.gov/?p=97.

(5) RITA, Table 1-32: U.S. Vehicle-Miles, http://www.bts.gov/publications/national_transportation_statistics/html/table_01_32.html.

(6) http://www.fhwa.dot.gov/policy/hcas/final/five.htm.

(7) Feb 1, 2002, http://www.eia.doe.gov/emeu/rtecs/chapter3.html.

(8) http://www.project.org/info.php?recordID=443 or http://www.fhwa.dot.gov/policyinformation/travel/tvt/history.

(9) U.S. Environmental Protection Agency, "Emission Facts: Greenhouse Gas Emissions from a Typical Passenger Vehicle," http://www.epa.gov/oms/climate/420f05004.htm.

(10) http://www.arboristsite.com/firewood-heating-wood-burning-equipment/86041.htm.

(11) http://apps.sd.gov/news/showDoc.aspx?i=4092.

(12) "Carbon Content in Motor Vehicle Fuels" and "Calculating CO_2 Emissions," http://www.epa.gov/oms/climate/420f05001.htm.

(13) http://ops.fhwa.dot.gov/freight/freight_analysis/econ_methods/lcdp_rep/index.htm, http://www.epa.gov/oms/climate/420f05001.htm.

5

Savings of B2B E-commerce

The only growth options in today's economy are through increased market share and increased internal intelligence. Both options are important, but the business-to-business (B2B) portals emphasize growth through better cash flow and merchandising planning.

Do it Best Corp. uses Microsoft SharePoint to integrate their B2B commerce initiative. A SharePoint is like a Web page. It is easily added to with a message, a link to a Web site, RSS feeds, document files, or a portal to the page. SharePoint can also be used to contact the warehouses and communicate with online blackboards or video communications. Business Intelligence (BI) on SharePoint aids in the incoming communications with the warehouse. Communications that can be utilized with Share Point include the following:

- What messages take priority?
- What are the contents of incoming shipments?
- What are the times of arrivals?
- What reminders need to be sent for meetings?
- What can we use in business intelligence for SQL?

When a portal for a company is being designed, it's important to add intelligence to the operations and retrieval of data. The data warehouse is considered a one-stop, one-shop approach to the saving and retrieval of data. The additional intelligence will allow for intelligent queries of the data.

The data warehouse is a repository (collection of resources that can be accessed to retrieve information) of an organization's electronically stored data. It is designed to facilitate reporting and analysis. More simply, a data warehouse is a collection of a large amount of data. This data is called meta data (which stands for massive data), which means a very large amount of data.

This definition of the data warehouse focuses on data storage. The main source of the data needs to be cleaned, transformed, and cataloged and is then made available for use by managers and other business professionals. Management can use the data warehouse for data mining, online analytical processing, demographics, market research, and decision making. Data must be cleansed because it comes from various sources. These sources may store the files as an Excel spreadsheet, used in an Oracle database, or stored in an SQL language, and could be stored in weekly, monthly, or quarterly periods. Data warehousing uses summary data to include business intelligence and queries to transform, load, manage, and display the data in one readable format.

The need for data warehousing comes from the absolute need for a company to differentiate itself from its competition. The only way to do this is to add intelligence into the system that the competition does not have. Information and the ability to intelligently comprehend the solutions will keep companies ahead of the competition.

The B2B initiatives can be set up as a series of portals with trading partners to add value to the supplier, the retailer, and the customer. These portals include the Vendor Portal, the Customer Portal, and the Distribution Portal.

The Vendor Portal

The Automation of the Show Market Bulletin from the Vendor Portal

The Show Market Bulletins are filled out by the manufacturers and sent electronically to the retailer. In the past, the supplier would spend approximately $275,000 in paperwork and $250,000 yearly on postage, and cost the environment 625 trees per year to send the market bulletins to partner companies. Both the supplying and the receiving end increase accuracy while decreasing the amount of internal supply chain staff needed.

If the Show Market Bulletin is filled out based on the previous year's use, then bulleting can be overlaid from year to year. The only changes the suppliers need to document are the new items for the bulletins for this year and any price and description changes. This saves the vendor time in the sale of bulletin preparation because they only enter what has been changed. In many cases, these changes represent 30% to 50% of the promotions, saving the vendor 50% to 70% of their time.

If the manufacturer has a staff of 10 people working on the project, there is now a savings of at least half the number of employees. If employees make $14 per hour, the internal supply chain stands to save $14 × 1.25 × 40 × 52 × 5 = $182,000 per year in payroll costs. This actually represents a major advance between two or more companies in the supply chain, allowing them to save in both Lean dollars and the Green carbon footprint. This is a perfect example of mutual collaboration benefiting all participants in the supply chain.

The Vendor Portal Used for the Automation of the Show Market Bulletin

- Lean
  - The supplier would save $275,000 on paper not used.
  - The supplier would save $250,000 on postage not used.
  - The supplier would save $182,000 in years on payroll savings.
  - Total Lean Savings is $707,000.

- Green
  - The show bulletin automation would save 625 trees not cut down per year.
  - Total Green Savings is 625 trees not having to be cut per year. Table 4-7 shows that 625 trees converts to 5 yrs. × 13 lbs. of CO_2 × 625 = 40,625 pounds of CO_2 saved each year in the atmosphere.
  - Total Lean and Green Savings is $707,000 plus saving 625 trees per year, yielding 40,625 pounds of CO_2 saved each year in the atmosphere.

New Items Portal from the Vendor

This gives the retailer an electronic list of all the new product listings from the manufacturer. The biggest problem with new items is the new item product introduction time. It normally takes 1.5 years for a new item to match its full-capacity sales. Shortening this cycle will increase revenue for the supplier and the retailer. New items sent electronically can be entered into the retailer's e-catalog three to six months faster. This cuts down on the 1.5-year new product introduction curve to 1 year, representing $30 million dollars in added sales per year. If profit is 18% on sales, the new profit would be $2,400,000 (see Table 5-1).

Table 5-1 Savings of B2B E-commerce

The cost of paper is around $2.50 per ream of 500 sheets. This represents one-half cent per sheet, or .005, or 50 cents per pound for a 5-pound ream of paper. If the manufacturer spent $250,000 on paper, the yearly weight is $250,000 / .50 per pound = 500,000 pounds of paper mailed per year. Table 4-4 shows that one tree represents 800 pounds of paper. Using B2BE would save 500,000 / 800 pounds per tree = 625 trees per year.

The New Items Portal from the Vendor Savings

- Lean
  - The added profit would be $2,400,000.
  - Total Lean Savings is $2,400,000.
- Green
  - No Green Savings from the New Items Portal.
  - Total Lean and Green is $2,400,000.

Information on Closeout and Discontinued Items

The vendor portal can be used to advertise for monthly specials or weekly dump-bin promotions. The closeouts are already discounted from the supplier, so the distributor can buy a significant part of the inventory to augment its product line and sell at the regular or discounted price to its retailer. This closeout merchandise can also be used by members needing to boost their sales, add to their profit margin, or increase traffic when the dealer is located near the competition.

Information on Special Events

This keeps the retailer or distributor abreast of any special events or training sessions from the supplier, drawing the retailer closer to the vendor.

Special Prices

Similar to closeouts, this can help the retailer advertise for monthly specials or weekly dump-bin promotions. The specials are already discounted from the supplier, so the distributor can buy a significant part of the inventory to augment its product line and sell at the regular price or discount the price to its retailer.

The Customer Portal

The Customer Portal tracks data better to help the customer and keep product in stock. The following are POS portal programs that can be used by the retailer. As a point of interest, Triad and Activant are leaders in this area. Activant Solutions Inc. is a technology company specializing in business management software solutions, retail solutions, and POS, retail, and wholesale distribution businesses solutions and ERP systems for wholesale distribution. Activant provides customers with tailored proprietary software, professional services, content, supply chain connectivity, and analytics. The company was also the first to provide an electronic catalog to the automotive aftermarket. Activant was formerly known as Triad Systems until it changed its name in 2003.

Lift by Category

A lift is a percentage showing the amount of increase in sales because of a promotion. The distributor can analyze the effects of sales over a very broad area and over many different demographics. With the data evaluated, the distributor can tell the retailer that if they put these items on sale they will receive a lift of 40% (which means a 40% increase in sales during the promotion period). This is a valuable tool because the distributor can analyze any of the diverse demographics for differences. It is also a very big help to retailers when planning item selection for sale circulars. The program can generally increase member sales for that category by 10% to 20%.

Variable Pricing

The variable pricing programs show the retailer which items will have the highest increase in sales for each incremental decrease in cost. These items are good candidates for sales and can be positioned around other high-price merchandise.

Lift by Item

Similar to lift by category, this shows which items should be placed in sale circulars.

Lift by Month

This will allow the retailer to plan by month, finding the best months to run promotions.

Price Optimizer

This option allows the retailer to analyze all combinations of the selling price to find the price that will maximize the sales margin of the product. This is different from maximizing the sales. The maximum margin may actually mean selling less in revenue because the profit margin may be set too low.

The Competition's Sales Choices

This gives the retailer an idea of what works best for the most successful stores in the chain. This is an excellent tool to use when planning to change merchandise selection because the retailer can see which items contribute to increased sales and profits in other stores. The report can be run by region or by similar demographics.

Merchandising Optimizer

The Merchandising Optimizer can show what other members are selling and offer a breakdown Pareto analysis by sales, margin, units, inventory-to-sales ratio, and price elasticity. It is also considered a seasonal optimizer because it starts suggesting changes in price by season, shows what other members are offering for the season, and shows the turns of the items before, during, and after the season.

Other Productivity Enhancements of the Customer Portal

The use of online invoices reduces the amount of paper used. The paper-based mailed invoices cost $250,000 per year in postage. The paper costs $275,000 per year for the paper and print. This does not include the cost of the personnel time for stuffing and sealing the envelopes.

Specifically, $250,000 of paper usage is the same as 625 trees per year. This equates to a savings of $300,000. So we can save $300,000 / $250,000 × 625 = 750 trees per year from the B2B program (refer to Table 5-1). According to Table 4-7, this equals 5 × 13 × 750 = 48,750 pounds of CO_2 saved per year in the atmosphere.

An example of online claims saving is the reduction of employees in claims from four full-time to one full-time and one part-time. It also reduces the wait time for claims posted to the requester's account from 56 days to 24 hours. In the past, the cost of postage for mailing claims was $80,000 compared to the current cost for computer processing. The Green Savings equals 225 trees per year.

The Commodities Catalog used to be printed every two months and then sent to the customer. Now, due to the electronic/digital format, a new item can be immediately introduced to the consumer. The printed Commodity Catalog costs $300,000 in paper. The cost of mailing the catalogs averaged $300,000 yearly. With the technological advances now available, that $600,000 now translates into massive savings both in the budget and for the environment.

The New Product Merchandising Portal allows companies to get the new items in front of the customer in a faster and more complete fashion. Before using the New Product Merchandising Portal, it took approximately 18 months to fully catch up to sales. This caused a rather large inventory problem because the turns would be very low for the first 18 months. Companies averaging 3,000 new items per year hold an average inventory of $450,000 due to the low turns. Using the merchandising portal, those same companies can decrease inventory to $150,000 and keep $300,000 in available capital.

Enhanced visibility of 18% × $370,000 = $66,600 increase in profit. The overall increase in member efficiency for the customer from the B2B program increased member sales by 5% or $100,000,000. The average member margin is 35% so the increase in profit for all the membership is $35,000,000. This grows current customer sales and increases customer retention. This is a supply chain savings that allows the retailer to benefit from the increase of information flow to enhance sales.

Here's the Lean and Green Savings on the $300,000 reduction in inventory for the company from the New Product Merchandising Portal:

- Lean Savings in opportunity cost is .02 × $300,000 = $6,000.
- Lean Savings on carrying cost is .266 × $300,000 = $79,800.
- Total customer Lean Savings is $35,000,000.
- The Green Savings on damaged inventory cost represents .75% of $300,000 = $2,250.
- The Green Savings on obsolete inventory cost reduction is 9% of $300,000 = $27,000.
- Total Lean and Green is $327,000, and this is not added to the landfill and dump bins.

The Customer Portal gives the following savings:

- Lean
  - Show Bulletins sent out = $275,000 in paper not used.
  - Show Bulletins sent out = $250,000 on postage not used.
  - Claims sent out = $90,000 in paper not used.

- Claims sent out = $80,000 on postage not used.
- Total Lean Savings is $695,000.

- Green
  - Show Bulletin savings is 750 trees not cut down per year.
  - Using the data from Table 4-7, this equates to $5 \times 13 \times 750$ = 48,750 pounds of CO_2 not released in the atmosphere per year.
  - Claims savings is 225 trees not cut down per year.
  - Using the data from Table 4-7, this equates to $5 \times 13 \times 225$ = 14,625 pounds of CO_2 not released in the atmosphere per year.

The Commodities Catalog Savings

- Lean
  - Bulletins sent out = $300,000 in paper not used.
  - Bulletins sent out = $300,000 on postage not used.
  - Total Lean Savings is $600,000.

The New Product Merchandising Portal

- Opportunity Cost Savings is .02 × $300,000 = $6,000.
- Carrying Cost Savings is .266 × $300,000 = $79,800.
- Sales increase experienced by the distributor of $370,000 a year because of the added visibility, and this adds $66,600 to the company's profit.
- The overall increase in member efficiency from the B2B program has allowed for an increase in member sales by 5% or $100,000,000. This adds $35,000,000 to the bottom line.
- Total Lean from the New Product Merchandising Portal = $35,152,400.
- Total Green from the New Product Merchandising Portal = $29,250.
- Total Green in tree savings from the Customer Portal and Commodity Portal = 1,725 trees saved.
- Using Table 4-7 this equates to $5 \times 13 \times 1,725 = 112,125$ pounds of CO_2 not released in the atmosphere per year.

The Operational Savings of the Customer Portal

The maintenance and reports section allows companies to change prices for their products online. They can also change the advertising circulars and descriptions electronically. The program will facilitate other miscellaneous file-maintenance procedures as well.

The maintenance and reports section allows the supplier access to the purchase history for all customers. The customers can also buy direct from the manufacturer with direct delivery to their store of choice without going to the warehouse. These direct purchases are not tracked in the purchase order history file because the orders went directly to the manufacturer. This analysis can help businesses plan inventory purchases throughout the year. With the purchase history, companies can track current demand with that of previous years. The purchase history report can also be used to budget based on historical product demand. Another benefit of the purchase history report is the capability to sort products by warehouse, state, price elasticity, month, highest margin items, suggested selling price, and price optimization point.

The Point of Sale Data Report includes warehouse stock purchases and direct ship merchandise from the manufacturer. Everything sold at the register is represented here by UPC number, stock item number, item description, price item, quantity sold, member number, time and date of the purchase, and promotion or regular stock item. The report will show the highest elasticity to demand with the largest margin. As prices change throughout the year, the system keeps track of the changes and figures the amount sold. The report can aid in determining when to do a promotion and whether everyday low pricing is an option.

The On Order Report electronically tracks orders, shipment information, delivery dates, and payment dates. Companies are better able to monitor cash flow and warehouse storage information with the use of the On Order Report.

Plan-o-grams allow companies to electronically view what other vendors have on pan-o-grams for in-store promotions. Knowing this can help in strategic product placement as well as merchandising by category throughout the store. The plan-o-gram file outlines category items similar to the NHRA (National Hardware Retailer Association) categories. All products have unique codes and subcodes for stocking and inventory.

The Distribution Portal

The distribution portal facilitates the information internally between the warehouses. Dashboards outline the relative efficiencies of each center. They can also show productivity reports so that the manager can visualize when and why each warehouse needs additional staff.

Automation

Automating the customer buying experience is another option for increased internal intelligence. For companies that offer their products at trade shows, the bulletins can be loaded online so that the member can view them with an iPad or a mobile smartphone. By using Shop Savvy, customers can scan the UPC code of the product on display and go immediately to the catalog to get the current price, full description, weight, and so on. They can scan the new Google 2-D code and go to the Web site to get a video of how to use the product. This video will play on their Apple iPhone, Android phone, or other smartphone.

The iPad Used in the Distribution Setting

Mobile technology continues to grow at a rapid rate within companies and school systems. Mobile technology includes computers, smartphones, and iPods. Executives are increasingly learning how to utilize these devices to create an engaged, dynamic connectivity, and a constant learning environment. With the release of the Apple iPod in the spring of 2010, new questions about how mobile devices can support industry have multiplied with implications for content on-the-go devices, e-books, tools for learner engagement, instruments of collaboration, videos of meetings from the CEO to the customers, retail store manager meetings with employees, and industry transformation through innovative ways to use the technology to enhance productivity.

The iPad can be used for additional savings options that increase profit margins. For instance, a company that appears at biyearly conventions can set up booth visits according to purchase history and sales tracking. Seasonal characteristics can be added into the matrix, as well as the item's sales lift or price elasticity to demand. Orders can be taken and stock overages decreased through digital access to warehousing data.

Bulletins also are offered at better pricing at the convention centers. Show content, pricing, and item information can be downloaded from the vendor portal. Visualization allows companies to see graphically how purchasing options can increase sales. Companies utilizing visualization can download On Hand from point-of-sale data and On Order from purchase history.

The concept of change management can be accelerated by the always-on, always-connected world of digital media devices. Managers can use these devices to visualize scenarios developed for advertising apps, new product introduction apps, marketing apps, target marketing apps, and even personnel appointments in lieu of new sale opportunities. Management can keep personnel updated and informed of meeting data, changes, and scheduling.

Table 4-7 demonstrates the following CO_2 savings that equate to $5 \times 13 \times 625 = 40{,}625$ pounds of CO_2 saved in the atmosphere per year. Another way to look at it is that \$250,000 of paper use is the equivalent of cutting down 625 trees per year.

The Savings of New Items Using the B2B New Item Portal

There are 3,000 new items introduced per year compared to the 65,000 SKU count. This represents 4.6% of the SKU count per year. If the time of new product introduction is reduced to 1 year from 1.5 years, there is an additional 33% increase in sales of the new items. This assumes that 66% of sales in the old system in one year compared to 100% of sales in the new system. The average increase in new item sales is 33%, which would represent a 33% × 4.6% or 1.5% increase in sales. The Lean Savings is 1.5% × \$2 billion = an increase of \$30 million dollars in sales. If the profit margin is 18%, the added profit is .18 × \$30,000,000 = \$2,400,000.

The IT Green Savings

The financial and economic downturn over the past few years has taught the business community the importance of technological advancement. From the beginning, many companies used Lean technologies to minimize the cost of operations through increased effectiveness. Companies that ignore these advances suffer as the competition moves ahead of them.

Borders bookstore had a great future in book sales. The technical and computer section offered a broad selection of books on computer languages and software. As time passed, they gained a large debt load while businesses like Amazon.com advanced through the digital generation toward the e-book, such as the Kindle or Nook. The high debt and shrinking revenue forced them into spending cuts, budget cuts, and store closings. Just as Borders faced closure, the following companies filed for bankruptcy; some recovered and some have closed permanently, and shortly after they went bankrupt.[1]

- The Conseco Inc.—December 18, 2002
- UAL Corp.—December 9, 2002
- WorldCom Inc.—July 21, 2002
- Global Crossing Ltd.—January 28, 2002
- Enron Corp.—February 12, 2001
- Pacific Gas & Electric Co.—April 6, 2001

Green IT

Energy Usage

According to the CDW Report, a typical data center consumes the same amount of energy as 25,000 households per year. Electricity consumption by data centers is about 0.5% of the world production.[2]

Energy use is a central issue for data centers. Power draw for data centers ranges from a few kW for a rack of servers to several tens of mW for large facilities. Some facilities have power densities more than 100 times that of a typical office building.[3] By 2012, the cost of power for the data center is expected to exceed the cost of the original capital investment.[4]

Greenhouse Gas Emissions

In 2007, the entire information and communication technologies or (ICT) sector was estimated to be responsible for roughly 2% of global carbon emissions, with data centers accounting for 14% of the ICT footprint.[5] The U.S. EPA estimates that servers and data centers are responsible for up to 1.5% of the total U.S. electricity consumption for 2007.[6] Given a business-as-usual scenario, greenhouse gas emissions from data centers are projected to more than double from 2007 levels by 2020.[5]

Energy Efficiency

The most commonly used metric to determine the energy efficiency of a data center is power usage effectiveness, or PUE. This simple ratio is the total power entering the data center divided by the power used by the IT equipment:

$$PUE = \frac{Total\ Facility\ Power}{IT\ Equipment\ Power}$$

Power used by support equipment, often referred to as overhead load, mainly consists of cooling systems, power delivery, and other facility infrastructure like lighting. The average data center in the U.S. has a PUE of 2.0,[5] meaning that the facility uses one watt of overhead power for every watt delivered to IT equipment. State-of-the-art data center energy efficiency is estimated to be roughly 1.2.[7]

The IT Green Initiative covers IT savings in detail. The Federal Energy Management Program's *Best Practices Guide for Energy-Efficient Data Center Design* offers a complete description of Green Initiative savings.[8] The topics presented are broken down into 13 categories for the Data Center Design:[10]

1. Using efficient servers
2. Saving with the use of rack servers

3. Using variable-speed fans

4. Using on-off power cycler devices

5. Addressing IT system redundancies

6. Sharing other IT resources

7. Using Network Attached Storage

8. Managing active energy measures for network equipment

9. Improving the power supply efficiency

10. Consolidating the hardware location

11. Introducing blade servers

12. Virtualization use of VMware

13. Using Microsoft SharePoint 2010

1. Efficient Servers

In a typical data center with a highly efficient cooling system, IT equipment loads can account for over half of the entire facility's energy use.[8] The use of efficient or sustainable servers will become a big part of the corporate decision-making process in the future. The use of efficient servers will cut the electrical usage and also decrease the size of the equipment and the room. It may also reduce the number of people needed to run and maintain the IT equipment. The added efficiency reduces the need for power to run the coolant for the IT servers.

2. Rack Servers

Rack servers tend to be the main area of wasted energy and represent the largest portion of the IT energy load in a typical data center. Servers take up most of the space and drive the entire operation. The majority of servers run at or below 20% utilization most of the time, yet still draw full power during the process. Recently, vast improvements in the internal cooling systems and processor devices of servers have been made to minimize this wasted energy.[9]

3. Variable-Speed Fans

When new servers are being purchased, it is recommended to look for products that include variable-speed fans as opposed to standard constant-speed fans for the internal cooling component. With variable-speed fans it is possible to deliver sufficient cooling while running slower, thus consuming less energy. The Energy Star program aids consumers by recognizing high-efficiency servers. Servers that meet Energy Star efficiency requirements will, on average, be 30% more efficient than standard servers.[9]

4. On-Off Power Cycler Devices

Additionally, a throttle-down drive is a device that reduces energy consumption on idle processors so that when a server is running at its typical 20% utilization, it is not drawing full power. This is also sometimes referred to as power management. Server power draw can also be modulated by installing power cycler software in servers.[9]

5. IT System Redundancies

Further energy savings can be achieved by consolidating IT system redundancies. Consider one power supply per server rack instead of providing power supplies for each server. For a given redundancy level, integrated rack-mounted power supplies will operate at a higher load factor (potentially 70%) compared to individual server power supplies (20% to 25%). This increase in power supply load factor vastly improves the power supply efficiency.[9]

6. Sharing of Other IT Resources

Sharing other IT resources such as central processing units (CPU), disk drives, and memory optimizes electrical usage as well. Short-term load shifting combined with throttling resources up and down as demand dictates is another strategy for improving long-term hardware energy efficiency.[9]

7. Storage Device

Consolidating storage drives into a Network Attached Storage or Storage Area Network are two options that take the data that does not need to be readily accessed and transport it offline. Taking superfluous data offline reduces the amount of data in the production environment, as well as all the copies. Consequently, less storage and CPU requirements on the servers are needed, which directly corresponds to lower cooling and power needs in the data center.[9]

For data that cannot be taken offline, it is recommended to upgrade from traditional storage methods to Thin Provisioning.

In traditional storage systems an application is allotted a fixed amount of anticipated storage capacity, which often results in poor utilization rates and wasted energy. Thin Provisioning technology, in contrast, is a method of maximizing storage capacity utilization by drawing from a common pool of purchased shared storage on an as-need basis. This also allows for extra physical capacity to be installed at a later date as the data approaches the capacity threshold.[9]

8. Network Equipment

As newer generations of network equipment pack more throughput per unit of power, there are active energy management measures that can also be applied to reduce energy usage as network demand varies. Such measures include idle state logic, gate count optimization, memory access algorithms, and input/output buffer reduction.[9]

9. Power Supplies

Most data center equipment uses internal or rack-mounted alternating current/direct current (AC-DC) power supplies. Historically, a typical rack server's power supply converted AC power to DC power at efficiencies of around 60% to 70%. Today, through the use of higher-quality components and advanced engineering, it is possible to find power supplies with efficiencies up to 95%. Using higher efficiency power supplies will directly lower a data center's power bills and indirectly reduce cooling system cost and rack overheating issues. At $0.12/kWh, a savings of $2,000 to $6,000 per year per rack (10 kW to 25 kW, respectively) is possible just from improving the power supply efficiency from 75% to 85%. These savings estimates include estimated secondary savings due to lower uninterruptible power supply (UPS) and cooling system loads.[9]

10. Consolidation: Hardware Location

Lower data center supply fan power and more efficient cooling system performance can be achieved when equipment with similar heat load densities and temperature requirements are grouped together. Isolating equipment by environmental requirements of temperature and humidity allow cooling systems to be controlled to the least energy-intensive set points for each location.

This concept can be expanded to data facilities in general. Consolidating underutilized data center spaces to a centralized location can ease the utilization of data center efficiency measures by condensing the implementation to one location, rather than several locations.[9]

11. Blade Servers

The two technologies that save computer time and cut the cost per operation are Virtualization (which includes blade servers) and Microsoft SharePoint.[9] There are other technological solutions through Oracle and IBM that are similar to SharePoint and Virtualization. Regardless of the technology chosen, significant strides can be made toward Green IT agenda within the IT arena.

12. Virtualization[9]

The concept of Virtualization has gained popularity within the past six years. Virtualization is allowing multiple operations or jobs on a single server. In the past, a multipartition computer hosted each job on a separate partition. Now many jobs run on a single server. In the past, computer idle time could be 75% with low computer utilization. As more jobs are run on the computer, the computer utilization increases. Virtualization will cut the number of servers needed because one can replace many servers. It will also run at lower electrical power because there is better economy to scale. For example, one server with five blades acting as individual servers replaces the previous need for five individual servers. Electrical consumption decreases by 40% because the new server requires less power.[10]

13. Microsoft SharePoint 2010

SharePoint is a tool on a collaborative platform focused on improving end-user productivity. SharePoint includes portals, document management, and records management. It is similar to building a Web page to maintain control of company data. Multiple templates are available to increase user friendliness, and various Web themes allow for different backgrounds to the page. Formatting and text type fonts are easy to use and allow for links to other pages. SharePoint also provides advances in internal communication.

All meetings can be on streaming video over SharePoint from different regions of the United States. All documents and records can be stored with content management and the rules that follow this procedure. Customers can take content from separate disparate systems with others through SharePoint. The end users' collaboration ability is radically increased. Business Intelligence and Analytics are compatible with SharePoint.

SharePoint also has the platform of services which is composed of the following:

- Sites for Collaboration—Collaboration with suppliers and customers can set companies apart as best-of-breed in the industry. It enhances the velocity of transactions and understanding.
- Communities for Portals—Savings potential is in the double digits.
- Search for More Productivity—SharePoint addresses the need for speed with the Fast Search algorithm, minimizing the search time. SharePoint 2010 Search provides intranet searches, people searches, and a platform to build search-driven applications, all on a single, cost-effective infrastructure.
- Contentment for Content Management—Content Management organizes data so that it can be found and acted on faster. Computer memory doubles yearly so data collection becomes a nebulous task. This is where the content management system helps organize the data for a user-friendly experience.
- Composites for Business Processes—Composites represent the replacement of PCs with bidirectional communication systems. This creates a large number of value solutions. SharePoint provides a workflow analysis engine that pinpoints the inefficient parts of the organization. This includes Visio and visualizing the supply chain. Lean Six-Sigma is also an integral tool in the understanding and dynamics of the business process.
- Insight for Business Intelligence—In many companies the content can grow by 40% to 70% or more per year. Business Intelligence makes sense of the increased data flow and presents to the user what is needed. The Pareto approach attempts to find the 20% and then presents the data to the manager faster.

In the past, using enterprise computing for every problem required multiple applications. Business Intelligence required Cognos or Business Objects. Document management projects required Documentum, Vignette, or Stellent. Unfortunately, these advances were costly and confusing. Using the SharePoint solution eradicates the need for multiple applications and saves 8% to 10% in search capabilities with an 8% savings in workflow analysis.

The next few tables translate VMware and blade technology savings into energy savings. Lean Savings is represented in Table 5-3, which shows how to compute dollar cost from kWh. The Green Savings from the VMware and blade technology is explored in Table 5-4. The table can be used to calculate an average CO_2 emission from the different ways of generating electricity. The result is a mean CO_2 emission from 1 kWh for the country.

Table 5-2 Calculating Gasoline Usage to Emissions in Pounds of CO_2 Emitted into the Atmosphere: Carbon Content in Motor Vehicle Fuels: Calculating CO_2 Emissions[10]

The Intergovernmental Panel on Climate Change (IPCC) guidelines for calculating emissions inventories require that an oxidation factor be applied to the carbon content to account for a small portion of the fuel that is not oxidized into CO_2. For all oil and oil products, the oxidation factor used is 0.99 (99% of the carbon in the fuel is eventually oxidized, while 1% remains unoxidized).[10]

To calculate the CO_2 emissions from a gallon of fuel, the carbon emissions are multiplied by the ratio of the molecular weight of CO_2 (m.w. 44) to the molecular weight of carbon (m.w.12): 44 / 12. CO_2 emissions from a gallon of gasoline are 2,421 grams $\times$ 0.99 $\times$ (44 / 12) = 8,788 grams = 8.8 kg/gallon = 19.4 pounds/gallon. CO_2 emissions from a gallon of diesel are 2,778 grams $\times$ 0.99 $\times$ (44 / 12) = 10,084 grams = 10.1 kg/gallon = 22.2 pounds/gallon.

Note: The previous calculations and the supporting data have associated variation and uncertainty. EPA may use other values in certain circumstances, and in some cases it may be appropriate to use a range of values.

Table 5-3 Computing Total Cost of Electricity from the kWh

Watts $\times$ Time / 1,000 $\times$ Cost per kWh = Total Cost

The figures are from the company maintenance department. The normal cost of electricity is 10 to 12 cents per kWh in the nine centers. This is a low cost because the centers are located in low-utility areas of the country. The normal range would be 10 to 14 cents per hour for the United States. Using an average of 12 cents per kWh leads to this calculation:

100 watts $\times$ 8,760 hrs. = 876,000 / 1,000 (converts to kWh) = 876 kWh times 12 cents = $105.12.

Table 5-4 Using the Cost of Utilities to Calculate the Pounds of CO_2 Emitted in the Atmosphere per Year[11]

- Coal = 44.9 % of the electric generation
- Nuclear power = 20.0%[12]
- Natural gas = 23.4%
- Hydroelectric = 6.9%
- Renewable = 3.6%
- Solar = .1% estimated
- Wind power = 1.8%[13]
- Petroleum = 1.2%[14]

How much carbon dioxide does 1 kWh create?[13] This is the calculated average amount of CO_2 in pounds used in the United States:

- Green Savings is 25% × 24,354,468.68 pounds of CO_2 in the atmosphere per year = 6,088,617.17 pounds of carbon dioxide saved per year.

- These numbers are in grams per kWh. The following shows how many grams depending on the method of generating electricity:[15]

  - Coal = 800 to 1,050

  - Natural gas (combined cycle) = 430 (average)

  - Nuclear = 6

  - Hydroelectric = 4

  - Wood = 1,500 without planting other biomass

  - Photovoltaic solar = 60 to 150

  - Wind Power = 3 to 22

  - Petroleum: 1 pound = 453.6 grams, so 1.969 pounds of CO_2[16] is generated by petroleum per kWh. This equals 1.969 pounds × 453.6 grams, or 875 grams.[16] This is used in Table 5-5.

So, using the information in Table 5-4, an average gram per kWh for the United States can be calculated. This averages the electricity generation with the number of grams of CO_2 per kWh. Table 5-5 shows the average amount of grams of electricity generated in the United States for one kWh of power.

Table 5-5 The Average Amount of Grams of Electricity Generated in the U.S. for One kWh

Electricity Generated in the U.S.	Grams of CO_2 per kWh	Total
Coal = 44.9%	950	425.55
Nuclear = 20.3%	6	1.218
Natural Gas = 23.4%	430	100.62
Hydroelectric = 6.9%	4	.276
Renewable Wood = 3.6%	1,500	54
Solar = .1%	105	.105
Wind Power = 1.8%	12.5	.225
Petroleum = .9%	875	7.875
Total = 101.9%		

The grand total of the grams of CO_2 per kWh in the U.S. is 590.879.

The corrected or normalized average is 590.869 / 1.019 = 580. The normalization was required because the percent total came to 1.019. The weighted average is necessary because it represents the blueprint of the entire continental United States. Companies with interests all over the continental United States need an estimate from coast to coast. This average is 580grams/kWh.

Calculate the Enterprise Dollar Cost of the Electrical Utilities

The enterprise cost of utilities per year is $0.5715 × the number of square feet. The average square feet is 450,000 for each of nine warehouses. The corporate square footage is also 400,000. The total square footage is 4,450,000 square feet. The total cost of utilities is equal to 4,450,000 × $0.5715 = $2,543,175 per year.

Calculate the Number of Kilowatt-Hours Used

To calculate the number of kWh used, take the kWh × 12 cents, which equals the cost in dollars. So in seeking the number of kWh used: kWh = Cost / .12 and kWh = $2,543,175/.12 = 21,193,125 kWh.

Calculate How Many Grams of CO_2 Are Used

- One kWh produces 580 grams of CO_2.
  - Calculate the number of grams of CO_2 = 21,193,125 kWh × 580 = 12,292,012,500 grams of CO_2 per year.
  - 1 gram = 0.00220462262 pounds so the yield of CO_2 is 0.00220462262 pounds × 12,292,012,500 grams = 27,099,249 pounds of CO_2 in the atmosphere per year.
  - The entire company through the electrical grid network emits 27,099,249 pounds of CO_2 in the atmosphere per year.
  - 40% of the electrical consumption can come from the server network and all the desktop and laptop computers and monitors. The data center accounts for 23% of the electrical usage.
- Cutting the electrical consumption by 20% to 30%, with the given Blade servers and VMware, the average savings will be 25%.
- The Lean Savings of the VMware and Blade Technology:
  - 25% of $2,543,175 = $635,793.75.
- The Green Savings of the VMware and Blade Technology:
  - 25% of 27,099,249 pounds of CO_2 = a reduction in CO_2 emissions of 6,774,812 pounds reduction of CO_2 in the atmosphere.

References

[1] http://www.dirjournal.com/business-journal/some-major-us-companies-that-went-bankrupt.

[2] http://evanmills.lbl.gov/pubs/pdf/ht_businesscase.pdf.

[3] http://www.energystar.gov/ia/partners/prod_development/downloads/EPA_Datacenter_Report_Congress_Final1.pdf.

[4] http://www.ijcse.com/docs/IJCSE10-01-04-15.pdf.

[5] The Climate Group for the Global e-Sustainability Initiative, "Smart 2020: Enabling the low carbon economy in the information age," http://www.smart2020.org/_assets/files/03_Smart2020Report_lo_res.pdf. Retrieved 2008-05-11.

(6) U.S. Environmental Protection Agency ENERGY STAR Program, "Report to Congress on Server and Data Center Energy Efficiency," http://www.energystar.gov/ia/partners/prod_development/downloads/EPA_Datacenter_Report_Congress_Final1.pdf.

(7) Silicon Valley Leadership Group, "Data Center Energy Forecast," https://microsite.accenture.com/svlgreport/Documents/pdf/SVLG_Report.pdf.

(8) "Best Practices Guide for Energy-Efficient Data Center Design," http://www1.eere.energy.gov/femp/pdfs/eedatacenterbestpractices.pdf, February 2010.

(9) http://www1.eere.energy.gov/femp/pdfs/eedatacenterbestpractices.pdf.

(10) "Carbon Content in Motor Vehicle Fuels" and "Calculating CO_2 emissions," http://www.epa.gov/oms/climate/420f05001.htm.

(11) http://natpa.org/publications/nuke4.pdf.

(12) http://www.eia.gov/kids/energy.cfm?page=nuclear_home-basics.

(13) http://www.eia.gov/cneaf/electricity/epa/epa_sum.html.

(14) http://www.eia.doe.gov/cneaf/electricity/epm/epm_sum.html.

(15) http://www.eia.gov/tools/faqs/faq.cfm?id=73&t=11.

(16) http://www.eia.doe.gov/cneaf/electricity/page/co2_report/co2report.html.

6

The Introduction of Enterprise Resource Programs (ERP)

ERP, an enterprise-wide system that integrates the business functions and processes of an organization, typically includes manufacturing, logistics, distribution, inventory, shipping, invoicing, and accounting. ERP requires companies to have the same definitions and the same computer screens across multiple departments. This eliminates the problem of one department presenting from one source and the other department answering from another source of information.

In most companies, ERP is the information backbone or pipeline needed to manage the daily transactions. Many of the internal functions of corporations are supported and shared by ERP systems. The advantage of ERP is that the software combines the data of formerly separate applications. This helps keep information in synchronization across multiple disparate systems. Because it standardizes the process, it will reduce the number of software specialists previously required.

Companies implementing ERP strive to derive the benefit of greater efficiency through integration. Companies can now operate in real time and run data as needed, rather than batch processes performed at the end of the day. To be best-of-breed, it is necessary to operate on event-driven processes that allow the computer to help in the decision process through decision support systems.

When ERP systems operate in real time, they can advise on alternate risk management paths for the enterprise. This will free up the managers' time in deciding because all departments have the same real-time data. In many best-of-breed companies, the system will make decisions for the projects and show results to the managers.

Integration and collaboration across multiple platforms frees up the managers to work on any anomalies.

Material management shares inventory and procurement order information. This allows for production and lead-time changes to be accounted for, increasing profitability for the supplier and the customer. The manufacturer can use material management data to make customer orders specific to CAD drawings, eliminating error.

Production is coordinated, which means less expediting of merchandise from and to the production floor because of an evened-out flow of demand. When customer and supplier collaborate, the demand process begins to match the supply requirements. One reason for this matching of the supply with the demand is the bullwhip effect. This was originally named with the PG and Wal-Mart collaborative efforts.

When suppliers and customers work in silos with little communication between them, the demand volatility for each step in the supply chain increases. This means that the demand volatility increases from the distributor to the customer. The manufacturer has a higher volatility than the retailer. Finally, the raw-material supplier has even higher volatility in the demand stream. This is called the bullwhip effect.

The solution is the use of collaborative technology between all parties in the supply chain. After there is collaboration in the supply chain, each successive partner in the supply chain can visualize the demand from the succeeding partner. There is no guessing or getting caught off guard. Expediting is minimized through information sharing, allowing each company in the supply chain to understand and anticipate changes made at any point in the supply chain. Data housing in the ERP systems can decrease safety stock by 20%. Sometimes this concept is called ERP II, because it involves reaching beyond the original company to the partners.

The collaborative fulfillment process can intelligently commit to delivery dates and increase accuracy. This is called available to promise (ATP) systems that can locate inventory, assets, personnel, and machines in real time. MySAP uses ERP to create collaborative hubs such as these:

- Collaborative Planning, Forecasting, and Replenishment (CPFR) allows the manufacturers to collaborate with their customers. This comes as an added module in some ERP packages. It allows companies to run on exception-based management systems where the entire supply chain sees abnormalities and works on them jointly. This allows both parties to raise revenues, improve service levels, and lower inventory levels while utilizing fewer people in the decision-making and logistics process.

- Vendor-managed inventory (VMI) comes as an added module in some ERP packages. This makes it easier to start the ERP process because a complete user's guide and instructions of EDI are generally available. The other advantage is that the process is fully integrated into the solution. Some of the development costs of the VMI package can now be defrayed. Another advantage is the community of people using the VMI package. They can be accessed at yearly conferences or through personal contacts to confer about new ideas or productivity tools.

- Enterprise portals increase utility to workflow management. Many of the documents and services can be automated through the Internet. Forms previously filled out by the distributor or retailer can now be filled out by the supplier. This can minimize the use of paper products and greatly enhance the performance of personnel. All new information can be relayed to the customer for promotions, revisions, and acceptance. The web-based tools also offer integration of third-party systems such as 3PLs and Software as a Service (SAAS) vendors. An example of SAAS or on-demand vendors is the CRM vendor SalesForce. com. This type of concept is in growing use in logistics and distribution. It even integrates into the customer's Facebook or Twitter accounts. The company can farm out the logistic services and distribution (3PLs) or coordinate the entire logistics function with the use of 4PLs. The ERP program can do the same productivity improvement process as SharePoint. It is equipped to facilitate the communication flow, enhancing collaboration.

- Within the Mobile Supply Chain, new paradigms of integration allow people to plan and execute decisions at alternate mobile points. There is no downtime for trying to contact and send information because it is sent in real time. Management can monitor all activities collectively and get the best consensus decisions. This moves into the world of "on-device" and "on-demand" computing. On-demand runs as SAAS architecture. Management executes and pays for only what is used. The software is generally hosted as an icon on the desktop that loads and executes with a click, which is how it came to be known as cloud computing.

- On-device computing allows for instant contact with employees through the information backbone ERP. Management can communicate immediately with employees using PDAs, iPads, Blackberries, and any other mobile device. Hard copies are not necessary, which cuts down on the amount of printing necessary. In manufacturing, any problems in production are corrected immediately from the assembly line by contacting the correct person via mobile device. Any conversation to select parties can be immediately sent to the manager, alerting the sales force of any designing changes that can be notified and approved immediately.

Business Processes and Analytics Features That Can Add to the ERP Software Solution

- Business Intelligence (BI)
- Artificial Intelligence (AI)
- Business Process Management (BPM)
- Data Warehouse (DW)
- Document Management (DM)
- Enterprise Document Management (EDM)
- Enterprise Asset Management (EAM)
- Field-Service Management
- Knowledge Management (KM)
- Supply Chain Management (SCM)
- Partner Relations Management (PRM)
- Portfolio Management
- Product Development
- Product Lifecycle Management (PLM)

- Project Management
- Risk Management
- SRM Supplier Relations Management
- Workflow Management

CRM Features

- Marketing Management
- Sales Management
- Order Management
- Product Configuration
- Order Fulfillment
- Customer Management
- Contact Management
- Customer Self-Service
- Account Management
- E-mail Tools
- E-Marketing Tools
- E-Selling Tools
- E-Fulfillment Tools
- E-Service Tools
- Mobile Sales
- Case Management
- Web Storefront Tool
- Marketing-Campaign Management
- Marketing Resource Management
- Mobile Access
- Opportunity Management
- Pricing
- Rental Management
- SFA (Sales Force Automation)
- Sales Management

- Sales Literature Creation
- Sales-Process Management
- Searchable Knowledge Base
- Marketing Intelligence (Analytics)
- Service Intelligence (Analytics)
- Service Management
- Sales-Order Management
- Target Marketing
- Targeted Offers

Financials Features

- Accounts Payable
- Accounts Receivable
- Activity-Based Costing
- Advanced Allocations
- Asset Management
- Balanced Scorecard
- Bank Reconciliation
- Budgeting
- Cash Management
- Cost Management
- Expense Management
- Financial Intelligence (Analytics)
- Fixed-Asset Management
- General Ledger
- Invoicing/Billing
- Properly Management
- Risk Management
- Tax Management
- Treasury Management

Human Resource Management Features

- Benefits Administration
- Employee Benefits and Compensation
- Employee Event Management
- Employee Self-Service
- HR Management
- Manager Self-Service
- Payroll
- Performance Management
- Personnel Administration
- Recruitment
- Talent Management
- Tax Administration
- Time and Labor/Attendance
- Time Management
- Training
- Work-Force Planning

Manufacturing Features

- Capacity Requirements Planning (CRP)
- Engineering Change Management (ECM)
- Forecasting and Planning
- Job Costing and Analysis
- Job Shop Floor Control
- Manufacturing and Production Cost Analysis
- Master Production Scheduling (MPS)
- Material Requirements Planning (MRP)
- Product Data Management (PDM)
- Quality Management (QM) and Quality Assurance

Supply Chain Management (SCM) Features

- APS (Advanced Planning and Scheduling)
- ATP (Available to Promise)
- Bin Management
- Capacity Requirement Planning CRP
- Collaborative Supply Chain CR, JIT, VMI, CPFR
- CTP (Capable to Promise) Inventory
- Demand Planning
- Distribution Management
- E-Design
- E-Procurement
- E-Supplier Portals
- Event Management
- Inventory Management
- Lead-Time Management
- Lean Manufacturing
- Logistics Management
- Manufacturing
- Manufacturing Intelligence (Analytics)
- Material Requirement Planning (MRP)
- Network Management
- Network Simulation (Analytics)
- Online Auction
- Private Exchange
- Purchasing
- Procurement
- Production Scheduling
- Promotions Management
- Purchase-Order Processing
- Quality Management
- Replenishment

- Requisition Management
- RMAs (Return Materials Authorizations)
- Sales-Order Management
- Serial and Lot Tracking
- Shop Floor Management
- Supply Chain Planning (SCP)
- Supplier Certification Program Vendor Performance Tracking
- Supplier Certification Program Carrier Performance Tracking
- TMS Transportation Management Systems
- WMS Warehouse Management Systems

The Quantifiable Benefits of an ERP System

The following sections describe the quantifiable benefits companies can reap from an ERP system.

Inventory Reduction

Improved planning and scheduling practices typically lead to inventory reductions of 20% or better.[1] In manufacturing, deliveries can be coordinated to actual need dates, and the bill of material is mated with inventory more readily over disparate sites. In distribution, a good supply chain solution and integration with suppliers can lead to a 1% to 2% inventory savings above and beyond the TMS savings for the inbound freight.

The additional productivity that ERP offers beyond Certification, VMI, WMS, and TMS programs adds 1% to inventory savings. Improved procurement practices lead to better vendor negotiations for prices, typically resulting in cost reductions of 5% or better. Valid schedules permit purchasing departments to focus on vendor negotiations and quality improvement rather than expediting shortages and getting material at premium prices.

Labor Cost Reductions

Improved manufacturing practices lead to fewer shortages and interruptions and to less rework and overtime. Typically labor savings is a 10% reduction in direct and indirect labor cost.[1] This savings is generated mostly in the office workforce and not so much in the distribution centers. At Do it Best Corp., the entire number of employees is 1,400, with around 800 in distribution. The 10% productivity pertains to roughly half this number because the other half is the professional staff and managers. The average wage is roughly $16 per hour. With an additional 25% for the perks and insurance, the wage increases to $20 per hour. The Lean Savings in dollars of labor time saved is 10% × $16 × 300 × 40 × 52 = $1,248,000.

Improved Customer Service

Improved coordination of sales and production leads to better customer service and increased sales. Improvements in managing customer contacts, making and meeting delivery promises, and shorter order-to-ship lead times will lead to higher customer satisfaction and repeat orders. Combining these improvements in customer services can lead to fewer lost sales and actually increase sales by 10% or more.

Improved Accounting Controls

Improved collection procedures can reduce the number of days of outstanding receivables, thereby providing additional available cash. The improvements include fast, accurate invoice creation directly from shipment transactions; timelier customer statements; faster credits to customer accounts for returns; faster return adjustments into inventory; faster credits from the supplier; faster follow-through on delinquent accounts; and being able to spot delinquency faster in an effort to avoid customer nonpayment. Credit checking during order entry and improved handling of customer inquiries further reduces the number of problem accounts. Improved credit management and receivables practices typically reduce outstanding receivables by 18% or better. This is when to use the applications in the ERP system to minimize the days in receivables. We used the e-commerce alternative with shareware.

The Lean Savings for the inbound freight of ERP:

- Inventory reduction is 1% × $195.7 million inventory = $1,960,000 reduction in inventory.
- Carrying cost reduction is $521,360.
- Freed-up cost of capital is .02 × $1,960,000 = $39,200.
- New inventory is at $194,040,000.
- The new turns are $931,000,000 / $194,040,000 = 4.80 turns.
- The Lean Savings in dollars of labor time saved is 10% × $16 × 300 × 40 × 52 = $1,248,000.
- Total Lean is $1,808,560.

The Green Savings:

- Damaged inventory cost represents .75% of $1,960,000 inventory = $14,700.
- Obsolete inventory cost reduction is 9% of inventory reduction = $176,400.
- Total Green is $191,100.

Total savings for the ERP Lean and Green from ERP is $1,999,660.

In summary, ERP efficiencies make a company lean. The Lean component will make a company green because it is using fewer resources and more efficient processes. Fewer people and less material and space will be needed to run the business with fewer wastes.

ERP's Sustainable Drive to Green

It is becoming an increasing responsibility for ERP systems to measure the sustainable metrics of the new green initiative. The systems need to save the details for the carbon labeling and carbon footprint metrics, which can be shared among the trading partners.

Make no mistake; ERP providers are making great strides in building their sustainability offerings. SAP has received countless awards and recognitions for its sustainability efforts. Its annual Sustainability Report highlights these achievements, and the company's recent acquisition of Clear Standards continues to support this trend.

SAP is not alone in these environmentally friendly endeavors. Oracle has teamed with ESS and Zogix, both of which specialize in carbon management and sustainability software, to enhance its offerings in the areas of sustainability reporting, planning, and management.

Although SAP and Oracle are the market leaders in ERP solutions, other options are available to meet the sustainability needs of businesses. Web-based tools such as Netsuite, Acumatica, and Nolapro and add-on solutions like Microsoft's Environmental Sustainability Dashboard are also available, being marketed primarily to medium-sized companies or divisions of larger corporations.

With Microsoft's Dynamics software they discuss the three elements of sustainability that constitute a corporate evaluation model measured by the so-called "triple bottom line," covering a company's impact on people, planet, and profit, respectively.

The reporting frameworks from the Global Reporting Initiative's (GRI's) G3 Guidelines provide an indication of what the core performance indicators are for economic, environmental, financial, and social sustainability. The GRI created a table that shows the key performance indicators for each of the four core performance indicators. The indicators are Economic, Environmental, Financial, and Social Sustainability.

Large or small, these solutions face similar challenges, including the rather tedious task of gathering data. Sustainability initiatives typically run the full length of a company's supply chain. So to really track and report success of corporate sustainability initiatives, these systems require complex streams of data. These streams include collecting product and SKU-level waste data from manufacturing sites, securing consignment-level emissions figures from transport providers, obtaining "real-time" energy consumption information from relevant utilities, and so on.[1]

One of the challenges in collecting this data is agreeing on scope and data standards. Interestingly enough, although the importance of common standards is universally recognized, there is no single standards-setting body or process with certified vendors in place today. Partners along the supply chain can agree to use a common dashboard of carbon pollutants and environmentally friendly processes. These standards can also be brought up in the common industry standards writing committees such as the American Hardware Manufacturer Association (AHMA).

Although the International Organization for Standardization is involved, it will be a long time before ISO standards proliferate; in the meantime, there is a need to drive consensus across nongovernmental groups to gain critical mass. Accenture is currently working with the World Economic Forum to address this need with organizations such as the World Business Council for Sustainable Development, the Carbon Trust and Business for Social Responsibility.[1]

Collecting and processing the green data across the supply chain is where the ERP platforms will make sustainable planning possible. The data can be shared with collaborative partners in real time to augment the collective responsibility of each partner to the reduction of emissions across the entire supply chain. The database for green sustainability indexes would not be possible without ERP systems. With these systems comes the creation of systems like ABC accounting, in which each unit or process is connected to the energy-generation process.

"SAP's customers," according to SAP, "produce one-sixth of the world's carbon emissions." Anything SAP can do to support sustainability, efficiency, and other green concepts could have a profound effect on its customers, and therefore a significant quantity of the world's emissions. And, because one of the main goals of SAP's sustainability initiative is to build software solutions that can lower these emissions while supporting more efficient and responsible use of other scarce resources like water, enterprise software companies like SAP can indeed become leaders in these efforts. For the moment, sustainability in the context of SAP is a maturing movement. In March of 2009, SAP announced plans to reduce its greenhouse gas emissions down to its year-2000 levels by the year 2020.

The Collaborative Sustainability Scorecard or KPI

Through the collaboration of many, there now exists a scorecard that can measure the success of a company's ERP system. It is a rough sketch of some of the key performance indicators or metrics that can be used by any company. These metrics can also be shared with suppliers and customers so that each member of the supply chain is on the same page.

The Recycle, Disposal, and Hazardous Metrics of Green

- Ratio of recycled waste to discarded waste
- Dollar amount of vendor return of faulty products
- Percent by vendor for vendor return of faulty products
- Dollar amount of refurbishing of damaged products
- Percent by vendor for refurbishing of damaged products
- Dollar amount of disposal in dump bins of damaged products
- Percent by vendor for disposal in dump bins of damaged products
- Hazardous waste disposal
- Nonhazardous waste disposal

Transportation Metrics of Green

- Miles per ton weight traveled
- Cost per route traveled to deliver goods
- Vendor fuel cost
- Vendor comparison by percentage of the cost of fuel
- Vendor comparison of revenue and fuel cost
- Cost of truck fuel

Utilities Metrics of Green

- Electric energy usage
- Fuel energy usage
- Water usage

See the Procter & Gamble KPIs Excel Spreadsheet[2]

- Improve environmental KPI
- Measure the environmental footprint
- Supplier Environmental Sustainability Scorecard
- Energy use
- Water use waste disposal
- Greenhouse gas emissions

References

[1] *Maximizing Your ERP System: A Practical Guide for Managers*, by Scott Hamilton.

[2] To access the spreadsheet, go to www.pgsuplidor.com and create an account.

7

Third-Party Provider

This is a case study of outsourcing logistics software to a company that can perform transportation scheduling and carrier selection more effectively and at a lower cost. Many companies choose third-party logistics (3PL) because they have more expertise and do more business with the carriers. This allows the 3PL to give a better freight rate. The 3PL also has longer standing relationships with the carriers, and this is important when a company needs to expedite merchandise or change existing routing.

So what are the advantages and technologies that a 3PL can offer that will improve the Transportation Management System (TMS)? There are incremental savings because of the 3PL's economy of scale. For a firm to successfully utilize the benefits of a 3PL, exposure to a TMS package is necessary. The TMS program, combined with the 3PLs, offers a visual of the supply chain so that everyone is aware of the location of all the carriers in real time and knows when each will ship. The 3PL concept can be used for inbound transportation because the 3PL can plan the carrier's deliveries with existing carriers and pool resources by combining existing shipments while lowering transportation cost.

A 3PL is the strategic formation of a partnership for risk reduction by focusing on core competencies, brand, customers, and new product introduction. Through the partnership some or all of the "nonstrategic activities," such as delivery, transport, and storage, can be outsourced. A 3PL solution empowers customers to focus resources on exceptions and provide management with the tools needed to minimize transportation spending by providing the tools covered in the following sections.

Multimodal

Using an array of rail and over-the-road multimodal carrier relationships, a 3PL can apply the right modes for the carrier to meet the service objective and cost constraints. The 3PL company can evaluate all the options, finding the quality, cost, performance, and reliability measures for each mode of transportation.

These Green statistics for intermodal and rail shipments cannot be ignored. According to the U.S. Department of Transportation, between 1980 and 2006, vehicle miles traveled increased by about 100%, while highway lane miles increased only about 5% during the same period. An intermodal train removes more than 280 freight trucks from the highway—the equivalent of 1,100 automobiles.[1] Every container shipped by rail equals one less long-haul truck on the highway, easing congestion, reducing pollution, and saving energy. Railroads are the most fuel-efficient mode of surface transportation. Steel wheels moving on steel rails, combined with the lower aerodynamic drag of a single train pulling hundreds of loads of freight, provides inherent advantages for rail. In fact, rail is more than three times as fuel-efficient as long-haul trucks. Wherever possible, without sacrificing service to the customer, intermodal shipments should be used.[2]

The 3PL offers many options to enhance company productivity. The following services are some of the more important options to consider in increasing productivity.

Onsite Supplier

An onsite supplier (OSS) is a 3PL representative who can place staff on location to manage a business. The onsite provider has all the tools and technology at his disposal to manage a transportation facility. The 3PL has extensive customer contacts and can provide shared coverage of the overhead cost to make it cost-effective.

The OSS can facilitate decision-making tasks between two companies, bridging the gap between any cultural, demographic, or logistical differences. The more tech-savvy the OSS, the greater the opportunity for in-house education opportunities. In the event of future issues, the employee who experienced the most direction from the OSS can be called on to problem-solve without having to seek additional onsite support.

Network Optimization

Network optimization can be used to simulate movement in the network and test for the optimum solution. All kinds of modifications can be performed to test the various scenarios:

- The warehouse location can be changed. The number of locations can also be visited. What are the results of this analysis on service, time of delivery, cost, and number of people needing to operate the system?

- A type of hub and spoke arrangement can be tested. Simulation of DRP arrangements can be run in this evaluation. (DRP is discussed later.)

- The mode of transportation can be analyzed for mode efficiency: Is it more efficient to ship by train, air, water, or a combination of those? Is it better to have LTL (less than truckload) or FTL (full truckload)?

- The freight can be merged with the other carrier's clients. This is called *consolidation*. It is one of the great advantages of the 3PL. You can analyze when and where it is best to merge two, three, four, or more clients' inventories to gain a competitive cost for the client. If it is possible to consolidate three clients, per-client shipping costs are cut by a third.

- The final assembly of a product can be postponed if necessary. The decision can be analyzed in a series of what-if scenarios. This offers a significant advantage in the number of end items to be stocked. It is now possible to build to the customer's specifications depending on the assembly parts available. Stocking only what is necessary significantly cuts inventory costs and allows the company to meet each customer's needs efficiently.

- The warehouse can receive merchandise and can fill the pending order from the receipts when there is an out-of-stock condition. This concept is called *cross-docking*. It can be used to add efficiency in the distribution center. In this system, the freight line notifies the receiver of the items to be received. This requires a series of combinations of EDI documents. An ASN tells the receiver of the item and quantity to be received, and an EDI 214 notifies the receiver of delivery time. Combining the receiver's Usage and Demand file with the EDI documents allows employees to see all incoming shipments and available warehouse inventory and space. Cross-docking then gives notification of the low-inventory incoming receipts to the receiving department to schedule movement to shipping. This avoids the problem of trying to stock an item before it's filled. This improves the level of service and cuts operation costs due to decreased double handling. In some cases the cost savings can be as much as 18% to 24%.

- Shipments can be merged to create full truckloads. This is called *merge-in shipment*, which can be performed on a series of LTL shipments to create an FTL full-truckload scenario. Management can merge other customers in the scenario to make the overall shipment less for each customer.

- The receipts can be simulated by the 3PL so that it is already on the truck and moving to the destination prior to the order trigger. This is called *continuous move* because the receipts are already moving to their destinations. It helps cut down the lead time to the customer because the product does not have to be picked and packed at the supplier's site.

- The retailers can control their own routing. This is called *dynamic routing*. It is a new form of routing that has a lot of merit. The routing technique can be utilized when the retailer has a series of pickups scheduled before the final long haul. For instance, it could come into play if the retailer needs to pick up at three locations and the shipments have been cubed by the 3PL. The 3PL knows that at the last pickup point it will have achieved a maximum cube to create a full load shipment to the final destination. This again utilizes an additional EDI document, 753. The retailer sends a vendor the 753 request for routing information to cross-check the weight, cube, and quantity. If everything can be shipped, the EDI document 754 is issued with the routing instructions given to the retailer's private fleet.

The vendor picks up the first shipment at point A. The total cube of the shipment is 35%. The next shipment is picked up at point B and now the total cube is 80%. The last shipment is picked up at point C and now the trailer has achieved 98% cube. It is ready to go the distance to the retailer.

- The network dynamics can be checked in real time. What if there is a road closing or a natural disaster? What does this do to the route analysis? What if a supplier is holding a shipment to load the merchandise? What does this do to the overall delivery time? Will customers be closed at the end of the daily run? In an event-driven evaluation like the one given previously, it may be necessary to bring in more carriers to help eliminate some of the obstacles and deliver on time.

- The company's fleet of incoming and outgoing carriers can be viewed on a computer. This is called *supply chain visibility*. This makes the system more dynamic because management knows where each carrier is in real time. The ship-to-arrival times also help the customer tell the buyer when the goods will be in stock. This is a great aid to CRM programs. The one customer service person at the desk can answer these kinds of questions accurately.

- The warehouse can use the 3PL's Carrier-Approved Shippers List to find the best carrier for their needs. This is a list of all the carriers the 3PL has partnered with. The 3PL may have a certified arrangement with some of the carriers such that they can deliver at a faster pace and at the least cost of delivery. In a certification agreement, the number of times the delivery meets the criteria is measured and agreed on. Consolidation helps the selected vendor expand their business, which improves service and lowers costs. In seeking a competitive edge, companies should consider consolidating wherever possible so that each helps the other grow.

- The freight payments can be automated by using the 3PL. With the use of the EDI transaction set 210, it is possible to automate a common execution platform across multiple facilities and various back-end systems. The Transaction Set 210 is the Motor Carrier Freight Invoice. This is probably one of the biggest advantages of a 3PL. The OSS has the time and incentive to create payment programs that would be far superior to the programs currently in use by the organization. Freight payment is arduous because each item requires rating by weight, class, hazard category, and distance. The regulations and classes may change or have new modifications. It takes a very well-trained individual to track this for the final freight payment. This is where the 3PL can really offer an advantage.

- The 3PL system can be used as a Web-based or cloud-based solution. The advantage of this is that the programs can be run at any location. They can be run from mobile devices and any phone can have apps to run a 3PL query.

- The 3PL system can show the firms' benchmarks and Key Performance Indicators (KPI). To justify the cost of any new technology, its success must be measured. The KPI is the major communication tool to be used with the management team to communicate successes. The KPI could measure the percentage of on-time deliveries. The metric is what management is trying to attain: for instance, greater than 80% on-time deliveries. Benchmarks in the system are a series of steps to the final metric. To achieve greater than 80% on-time shipments is impossible so it's necessary to set a benchmark at 70%. The benchmark measures success to the final metric. As long as the staff produces above the benchmark, management is pleased. They can measure the heartbeat of the organization in a real-time environment and know immediately when the system is not running correctly or is surpassing expectations.

Benefits of a 3PL

The first benefit of a 3PL is a reduction in staff. The industry norm is a 25% to 50% decrease in transportation staff. Typically, there is a smaller staff assigned to the transportation area. If there are five people in transportation, only three employees are now needed to do the same job. The average salary for this position is $60,000 per year. With approximately 25% benefit cost, the company saves $75,000 per employee annually. This is a Lean Savings of $150,000 per year for the company. Table 4-8 gives the Green Savings. This Green Savings is 2 × $490 = $980 saved in electricity usage from the reduction of two computers for the transportation group.

The fleet should experience a 9% decrease in the mileage for the inbound freight. The saving will be incurred by the consolidation, network optimization, merge-in transit, and multimodal technology.

Normally, a 3PL can show a substantial savings in fuel costs, and even reduce fuel costs by 40%.[2]

For the case of inbound transportation, the mileage of all the carriers into the warehouse is much greater. The best option in some cases is to use a TMS system to control the outbound transportation. This requires a lot of rescheduling and adjustments in routing, which can change frequently, to meet the customer needs. A 3PL is not recommended because it's imperative to keep close communication with the customers. It is unwise to outsource this area because customer service should remain the responsibility of the distributor. A 3PL was used for the inbound traffic from the suppliers to the distribution centers. The 3PL's job is to minimize the freight cost and mileage. This should be reflected in a lower cost of goods sold and fewer inventories needing to be stored if the lead time is decreased.

Lean Savings

Network optimization saves the company 2% in distance traveled by the fleet through the reconfiguration of the distribution centers and managing the transportation modes. The Lean cost is 2% × 6,800,000 gallons per year used × the cost of diesel, which is $3.12 per gallon = 2% × 6,800,000 × $3.12 = $424,320 per year.

The merge-in-traffic reduces the miles traveled per year by 1%. This is a lower figure than normal because of the frequent increase in lead times. The fleet runs at 6,800,000 gallons per year and at 6 miles per gallon. The fleet runs 40.8 million miles per year. The Lean Cost Savings is the cost of diesel, which is 6,800,000 gallons per year, × $3.12 per gallon used × 1.0% savings = $212,160 saved in gasoline.

The consolidation reduces the miles traveled per year by 6%. The fleet runs at 6,800,000 gallons per year, and at 6 miles per gallon the fleet travels 20.4 million miles per year. The Lean Cost Savings is the cost of diesel, which is 6,800,000 gallons per year, × $3.12 per gallon used × 6% savings = $1,387,200 saved in gasoline.

Reduced fuel rate cost would be 3% because of the better rates with the partnered carriers. The old fuel cost of 6,800,000 gallons per year × $3.12 per gallon = $10,608,000, making Lean Savings 3% × $10,608,000 = $318,240.

Lead times for transportation were reduced by four hours on average. This is due to the combination of better route optimization and network optimization programs. For every day the lead times were reduced, the inventory was reduced by 2.2%. The half-day reduction equates to a 1.1% reduction in inventory. The old inventory balance after the ERP contribution is $194,040,000. The new inventory is at 1.1% savings: $191,905,560. This is a $2,134,000 reduction in inventory. The carrying cost reduction is 26.6% × $2,134,000 = $567,761 reduction in carrying cost. The freed-up cost of capital is 2% × $2,134,000 = $42,688 increase in capital. The new inventory is at $191,905,560. Finally the new turns are $931,000,000 / $191,905,560 = 4.85.

Summary of Lean Savings of the 3PL:

- Network optimization = $424,320 per year.
- The merge-in traffic = $212,160 saved in gasoline.
- The consolidation routine = $1,387,200 saved in gasoline.
- The reduced fuel rate cost = $318,240 saved in gasoline.
- The lead times reduction:
  - Reduced lead times reduce the inventory by a 1.1% savings from the old inventory of $193,740,860 to a new inventory of $2,134,440.
  - Carrying cost reduction = $567,761.
  - Freed-up cost of capital = $42,688.
  - The new turns are $931,000,000 / $191,608,860 = 4.86 turns.

Total Lean Savings is $2,952,369.

Green Savings

- Damaged inventory cost represents .75% of $2,132,000 inventory reduction = $15,990.
- Obsolete inventory cost reduction is 9% of inventory reduction = $191,880.

- This represents $207,870 that would have been thrown away or put into a landfill.
- The savings in gasoline and CO_2 emissions. One of the primary determinants of carbon dioxide (CO_2) emission from mobile sources is the amount of carbon in the fuel. Carbon content varies, but typically average carbon content values are used to estimate CO_2 emissions.
- Table 4-10 is used to calculate the carbon footprint:
  - CO_2 emissions from a gallon of diesel are 2,778 grams × 0.99 × (44 / 12) = 10,084 grams = 10.1 kg/gallon = 22.2 pounds/gallon
  - This shows a carbon footprint of 22.2 pounds/gallon × 6,800,000 gallons used per year = 75,480 tons of CO_2 extracted into the air for the entire fleet per year.
  - The 3PL techniques save 75,480 tons of CO_2 × .09 = 6,793 tons of CO_2 from being released into the atmosphere. In this case, the savings is 9%.
- The Green Savings of 3PL:
  - Damaged inventory cost represents .75% of $2,132,000 inventory = $15,990.
  - Obsolete inventory cost reduction is 9% of inventory reduction = $191,880.
  - The route optimization techniques save 6,793 tons of CO_2 from being released into the atmosphere.
  - The Green Savings is 19 trucks × 9,600 cars × 5 days × 51 weeks = 107,712,000 fewer cars on the road per year.
- Total Green Savings is $208,090 per year for the 3PL.

Total savings for the 3PL Lean and Green program is $3,160,459.

References

[1] http://www.bnsf.com/communities/bnsf-and-the-environment.

[2] http://www.penskelogistics.com/newsroom/2010_4_22_logistics_sustainability.html.

8

Inventory Control

Pareto ABCDE Classification of Inventory

Forecasting systems are one of the most important parts of the supply chain. This can determine the nervousness or volatility of the supply chain system. This is also an area in which companies can cut waste in the logistics network. It is all about lowering the logistics and supply chain costs.

Inventory management is the process of controlling inventory with the fewest people and the least amount of inventory. Maintaining an optimum inventory is the most important aspect of inventory management. Implementing the techniques necessary to maintain an optimum inventory can equal massive company-wide savings.

ABC analysis is a technique used to prioritize inventory by its relative importance. The priority can be a number of factors. The following are generally the most commonly used priorities. The issue with these is that they are usually conflicting goals. For example, the highest selling strategy may sacrifice profit, and the maximum-revenue strategy makes it impossible to maintain a minimum inventory. The goals outlined are as follows:

- Maximize the revenue
- Maximize the profit
- Maximize the units sold
- Minimize inventory
- Maximize turns

These priorities cannot be collectively attained as one goal. Companies can choose to prioritize inventory on dollar sales, profit of the item, or number of items sold to maintain a minimum inventory and maximize turns. Each one of these has a definite impact on internal and customer goals.

Companies must maximize sales of the highest revenue items because sales fulfill the revenue goals set by upper management. In this case, the highest revenue and profit items should be coded as A items. This would tell the computer to stock more of the A item and so lessen the chance of out-of-stocks. The items that sell the highest quantity should also be categorized as A items because they will be the first to be noticed by the customer as the fill rate falls.

Fill rate is calculated as:

$$\% \ Line \ Fill = \frac{Quantity \ Filled \ in \ an \ Order}{Total \ Quantity \ of \ the \ Order}$$

A good example of fast-moving items is batteries. If a customer orders batteries and they are out of stock, the customer is dissatisfied with his shopping experience. Customers believe that commodity items should always be available. To avoid this problem, prioritize the inventory into five categories focusing on high revenue, high profit, and high quantity:

- Class A is the top 20% with 5% of the inventory.
- Class B is the next 20%, which generally is 10% of inventory.
- Class C is the next 20%, which is generally 18% of inventory.
- Class D items represent the next 20%, which accounts for 27% of the inventory.
- Class E items represent the next 20%, which accounts for the remaining 40% of the inventory.

At this point, it becomes necessary to run the distribution by line value (DBLV) report for the revenue items, the profit items, and the high line or quantity items in each department. The DBLV for profits will list the items in each department for each warehouse in sequence from high to low for the most profitable items. The DBLV report for fast-moving items will list the items in sequence from high to low for the fastest moving items inventory by department and by warehouse.

Now combine the first percentages for all three, add them together, and divide by 3 to get a global categorization. This allows for a blended approach of taking the best out of all three goals.

For example, item AA sorted by revenue may have a 3%, which means it is the top 3% of revenue growth in the department. Items sorted by profit may have a 12% figure, meaning they are ranked in the top 12% of profit for the department. The sort by SKU may rank item AA at the 30% rank. Now add all ranks together and divide by 3 to get the total global ranking by department for item AA = $\dfrac{3 + 12 + 30}{3}$ = 15% rank. This is still high enough to categorize item AA because it's the top 20%. This will be conducted for each item in the inventory by department and by warehouse.

Each category can be weighed differently. Weighted averages can be used to measure the priority within the company. Let's say the quantity ordered is the highest priority in the company because this is what the customer actually measures the company by. The customer in this case measures by line fill rate. So the quantity ordered has a weight of 45%. The next is the profitability, which receives a weight of 35%, followed by the revenue or highest price times demand, which is weighted at 20%. The new consolidated ranking by department for item AA is:

$$\frac{.20 \times 3 + .35 \times 12 + .45 \times 30}{1} = 18.3$$

which is still in the A category of top 20%. The operational savings is as shown next.

Lean Savings for the ABCDE Inventory Program

- Inventory before the ABC Classification program = $191,905,560.
- Sales before the ABC Classification program = $931,000,000.
- Turns before the ABC Classification program = $931,000,000 / $191,905,560 = 4.85 turns.

- Inventory reduction from the ABC Classification program is 1.2%.
- The Inventory Reduction results in a 1.2% × $191,905,560 = $2,299,306 reduction in inventory.
- The new inventory is $189,602,693.28.
- Carrying cost reduction = .266 × $2,299,306 = $611,615.
- Freed-up cost of capital = .02 × $2,299,306 = $45,986.
- There's a service-level improvement of 2%. This will increase sales. If there is 1% out of stock, three-fourths of the customers will wait until it is in stock. One-fourth will buy it direct from the manufacturer or buy it from a competing distributor. If the retailer is out of stock, only one-third of the customers come back to buy the product. This is a 66.67% reduction in sales because of out-of-stock. A 2% service-level increase represents a 2% × 25% = .5% increase in sales.
- The new increase in revenue is .5% × $931,000,000 = $4,655,000.
- The additional profit generated from the increase in sales is 18% × $4,655,000 = $837,900.
- This represents a new sales figure of 1.005 × $931,000,000 = $935,655,000.
- The new turns are $935,655,000 / $189,602,693 = 4.94 turns.

Total Lean Savings is $2,956,907.

Green Savings for the ABCDE Inventory Program

- Damage and Obsolescence is 9.75% × $2,299,306 = $224,182 per year in landfill savings.

Total Lean and Green Savings is $1,719,683.

The Substitution Program

A technique used to minimize out-of-stocks is called the substitution program. If a retailer or distributor is out of stock on an item, it sends a similar item in its place. The substitute item must have the same or very similar functionality. It must pass the following metrics:

- It must be within 7% of the original price. There may be other price rules that apply, depending on the unique nature of the product.
- It must have the same or better functionality.
- It must look the same as far as retail appeal.
- The item must be readily available.
- The item must have the same consumer acceptance as the primary item.
- The item must be shippable by UPS or small parcel shipping.

The substitute program allows for a decrease in the out-of-stocks by .50%, with a small inventory decline of .25%, which amounts to a $473,273.88 reduction on an $189,309,553 inventory.

Lean Savings for the Substitution Program

- Inventory before substitution program = $189,602,693.
- The Sales = $935,655,000.
- Turns before the substitution program = 4.94 turns.
- Sales before the substitution program = $935,655,000.
- Reduced out-of-stocks by .50%. This would increase sales as mentioned in the ABC classification section by $(1 + .5\% \times .25)$ = .125%. The sales increase is $1,169,568.
- Added profit from the sales increase = 18% × $1,169,568 = $210,522.
- Sales after the substitution program = 1.00125 × $935,655,000 = $936,824,568.
- Inventory reduction from the substitution program is .25%.
- The actual amount of Inventory Reduction is .25% × $189,602,693 = $474,007.
- The new inventory is $189,602,693 – $474,007 = $189,128,687.
- Carrying cost reduction = .266 × – $474,007 = $126,086.

- Freed-up cost of capital = .02 × $474,007 = $9,480.
  - Old turns = 4.95.
  - The new turns are $936,824,568 / $188,836,279 = 4.95.

Total Lean Savings is $346,088.

Green Savings for the Substitution Program

Damage and Obsolescence is 9.75% × $474,007 = $46,216 per year in landfill savings.

Total Lean and Green Savings is $392,304.

Central Stocking

The process of central stocking allows for fewer inventories to fill the needs of existing customers. If an item does not move well in one location, it can be moved into a different location in the hopes it will sell more quickly. When a retailer orders an item that was centrally stocked and the item is no longer stocked in that distribution center, it will be sent by UPS to their store from the closest center. The product will arrive generally a day later than is normal. The reasoning for central stocking is to allow for less variation in the demand level of a product.

It is a statistical fact that the more demand there is in a period, the less volatility is experienced on the item. This leads to a lower safety stock level and fewer out-of-stocks with a lower overall inventory. The question posed is why all the items in every warehouse are necessary when some of the items barely sell in other distribution centers. One reason for this is the lucrative client who demands to have a product to stock in a specific warehouse.

The item is stocked in the specified warehouse as well as the other seven warehouses, which barely have any movement. This low movement translates into a phenomenon known as lump demand. This pattern of demand is almost impossible to forecast. There may be months of very low demand or zero demand and then, unexpectedly, large demand patterns begin and are interspersed through the year. An example of this is SKU item BB's monthly demand from January to December:

January = 500, February = 0, March = 20, April = 0,
May = 0, June = 300, July = 40, August = 500, September = 0,
October = 0, November = 0, December = 500

If there is no clear pattern or seasonal explanation, it is considered lumpy demand. In some cases, the safety stock could be equal to three times the average usage. This is a waste of merchant and cash flow tied up in inventory.

The algorithm used in central stock items is to test the VI, or Volatility Index, of the item. If the Volatility Index is defined as:

$$\frac{MAD}{Average\ Demand}$$

and if the VI is < .20, then the item is not considered a central stock candidate. In forecasting terminally, MAD stands for Mean Absolute Deviation. The formula for MAD is:

$$\sum_{1}^{12} \frac{|xi - F|}{12}$$

where F is the forecast for the items throughout the year for each period. The xi is the monthly value of demand for the current year. Performance won't be improved much by central stocking the items if the VI is less than or equal to .20. The following represents the algorithm used for central stocking an item.

- If the VI is greater than .20 but less than .50, use Pareto analysis to central stock the items. The Pareto analysis is based on total dollar revenue per item. The top 20% of this value will be considered central stock only if
  - The inventory can be shipped by FedEx or UPS.
  - The percent cost for freight does not exceed 20% of the gross margin dollar.
- If the VI is greater than .50 and less than 1, try to central stock the next highest 10% of the stock from the Pareto analysis, which is the top 30%. The next set of inventory will be considered central stock only if
  - The inventory can be shipped by FedEx or UPS.
  - The percent cost for freight does not exceed 20% of the gross margin dollar.

- When the VI gets larger than 1, try to central stock all the items without using Pareto analysis. The key factor is that
  - The inventory must be shipped by FedEx or UPS.
  - The percent cost for freight does not exceed 20% of the gross margin dollar.

One last operation will be performed by the software:

- The central warehouse will be the warehouse with the largest outbound volume no matter what the VI value is.
- The item will be assigned to the warehouse that has the lowest UPS cost. This will override an earlier judgment if the software chose another warehouse. This costing function is performed by comparing the ZIP Code of the shipping warehouse to the ZIP Code of the customer. This is performed by the software that is provided by UPS and that is integrated into the shipping program.

The warehouse that has a VI less than or equal to .20 will not be central stocked. The warehouse with the same SKU with a VI greater than .20 will be up for consideration to move its stock to another warehouse using the preceding rules. The following rules apply to the dissemination of the warehouse inventory. Table 8-1 shows an example of an item in each warehouse by month. Notice that if the same item is stocked in one central warehouse, the demand volatility will be much less. This is represented in the last column.

The SKU is a class B item, so it will have a 94% service level assigned to it. This gives a k value of 1.94. The k is defined in the forecast section but it is similar to the Z factor in statistics. The k values are found in Table 21-1 in Chapter 21, "The New Sustainable EOQ Formula." It gives the relationship of k to the Z transform. For instance, a Z of 1 represents one standard deviation, which represents 69.27% of the sample. In this case, the k value of 1.94 states a desire for a level of safety stock that gives the customer a 94% service level or 6% out-of-stocks. The Order Quantity if the item minimum is 1 is equal to Q = (Avg. Demand/Month) * (LT + RT) + k * MAD * (LT + RT)$^{.7}$. This is also further explained in Chapter 19, "Forecasting Methodology and Gamma Smoothing: A Solution to Better Accuracy to Maintain Lean and Green." The lead time is 1.5 months and the review time is half a month = .5.

Table 8-1 Demand for Eight Warehouses

	Demand in DC1	Demand in DC2	Demand in DC3	Demand in DC4	Demand in DC5	Demand in DC6	Demand in DC7	Demand in DC8	Demand in All Central Stock
Jan.	500	0	1000	0	0	50	0	100	1650
Feb.	0	200	500	200	0	40	0	0	940
March	0	0	0	300	30	100	0	100	530
April	1000	50	300	50	0	0	0	200	1600
May	0	0	400	0	0	100	30	0	530
June	0	400	100	0	0	0	0	200	700
July	0	0	0	400	40	50	0	0	490
Aug.	0	40	0	200	0	40	0	100	380
Sept.	1000	300	500	0	0	0	50	200	2050
Oct.	0	0	400	200	0	0	20	0	620
Nov.	500	0	0	100	50	100	0	0	750
Dec.	0	100	300	0	0	50	0	100	550

The lower the coefvficient of variation (CV), the less safety stock is in the system and the lower the volatility is in the demand pattern. The formula for the CV is:

$$\frac{MAD}{Average\ Demand}$$

The following example shows the calculation of the OQ (Order Quantity) for each of the nine distribution centers:

DC1 OQ = (250) * (2) + k * 333 * (2)$^{.7}$ = 1,038 and CV = 1.333333333

DC2 OQ = (91) * (2) + k * 106 * (2)$^{.7}$ = 353 and CV = 1.168195719

DC3 OQ = (217) * (2) + k * 183 * (2)$^{.7}$ = 729 and CV = 0.846153846

DC4 OQ = (121) * (2) + k * 116 * (2)$^{.7}$ = 429 and CV = 0.959770115

DC5 OQ = (10) * (2) + k * 15 * (2)$^{.7}$ = 44 and CV = 1.5

DC6 OQ = (44) * (2) + k * 31 * (2)$^{.7}$ = 138 and CV = 0.698113208

DC7 OQ = (8) * (2) + k * 13 * (2)$^{.7}$ = 37 and CV = 1.5

DC8 OQ = (83) * (2) + k * 83 * (2)$^{.7}$ = 279 and CV = 0.833333333

CON OQ = (824) * (2) + k * 352 * (2)$^{.7}$ = 2,218 and CV = 0.428210313

Total Order Quantity for all warehouses (OQ) = 3,047, which stands for the total of all the order quantities for all the warehouses. The CON stands for the consolidated warehouse. For the central stocked warehouses the average demand per month is 824. This represents the average of the demand for all nine warehouses combined. There is less variation in the demand from month to month, so the MAD is lower as a percentage to the overall average. This is proven because the coefficient of variation is .428210314. This figure is lower than any one of the individual distribution center's CVs. This is the biggest reason that the overall inventory of the central warehouse is less than that of the individual warehouses combined. Note that Central Stock OQ = (824) * (2) + k * 352 * (2)$^{.7}$ = 2,218.

By definition, average inventory = 1/2 OQ. The analysis shows that for the warehouse that does not centrally stock its products, the average inventory would be 1/2 × 3,047 = 1,523. The warehouse that uses the central stock process has an average inventory of 1/2 × 2,218 = 1,109. This results in a 27.2% reduction in inventory with a higher service level because the product is being ordered more often. Interestingly, the central stock items are class C, D, and E items, which are not the fastest moving items. This is actually the area of inventory that needs minimized because it represents 60% of sales with 85% of inventory. The A and B items represent 40% of sales with 15% of inventory. If the inventory was $189,309,553 and the company central stocks 15% of this inventory, then the new inventory is 15% × 27.2% = 4.1%.

Lean Savings for the Central Stock Program

- Inventory before the Central Stock program = $188,836,279.
- The Sales = $936,824,568.
- Turns before the Central Stock program = 4.96 turns.
- Inventory reduction from the Central Stock program is 4.1%.
- The actual Inventory Reduction is 4.1% × $188,836,279 = $7,742,287.
- The new inventory is $188,836,279 – $7,742,287 = $181,093,991.
- Carrying cost reduction is .266 × $7,742,287 = $2,059,448.
- Freed-up cost of capital is .02 × $7,742,287 = $154,845.75.
- The new turns are $936,824,568 / $181,093,991 = 5.17 turns.

Total Lean Savings is $2,214,293.

Green Savings for the Central Stock Program

Damage and Obsolescence is 9.75% × $7,742,287 = $754,873 per year in landfill savings.

Total Lean and Green Savings is $2,970,335.

9

Promotional Forecast System

Promotional forecasting is the Achilles' heel of any system. Promoting an item may require selling in one month the amount normally sold in one year. In the case of Do it Best Corp., one-third of the revenue of the stock sales was produced by promotions. Sale merchandise generally has the poorest service levels and tends to have higher levels of stock left after a promotion. This process is in need of improvement.

To solve the problem, it is necessary to implement a promotional forecast system that uses exogenous variables, or variables outside the system. An excellent statistical package such as SAS is necessary for this process. The forecast is made with multiple regressions to add value to the understanding of the dynamics of the promotion. The system begins with a number of variables that need to be described.

Promotional lift is also called price elasticity to demand. It sets the level of sales depending on the price of the promotion. For instance, dropping the price by 10% may increase sales by 40%. This is a lift of 4. The correlation of price-to-demand has a number of factors that need to be analyzed. The forecast is different by warehouse and by vendor. The reason for this is that the centers are in different areas of the United States and demographics tend to play out in this scenario. The concept of buying power index (BPI) does influence the buying in many areas. This figure can be gained by Polk or Clarita's.

The promotional lift by item should be stored on a promotional database. The database will have a summary of all promotions and their associated lift, their margin, and the month promoted. It is very important to keep the promotions and regular demand in two different files. Do not add the promotional data to the regular usage sales file, or the demand data will be corrupted.

For example, if the same sale is not run next year and the promotional sales data is added into the regular demand data, purchasing will buy according to old information. The sales usage file shows inflated sales that will no longer be in effect because the promotion is outdated. When the data is stored properly, the purchasing manager can use the information to plan future promotions based on which items sold the best and at what price.

The dynamics of the optimal price for maximum profit can also be evaluated. The concept of cannibalization of gross margins must also be evaluated. This involves the idea that people will pay the regular price regardless of the promotion that has lowered the profit margin. Another consideration is the cross-correlation to other items. The concept of market basket analysis occurs when certain items are promoted, affecting the sales of other items.

Cross-correlation of promotion to stock sales addresses the fact that not all the customers take the promotional sale circulars. They tend to buy at the everyday low price or the stock price. The promotion increases the visibility of the product, and even the merchant not selling the item on promotion experiences an increase in sales. This amount of increase of regular sale items must be quantified. If the merchant thinks ahead, he could buy the merchandise on the promotional price and sell it at the regular price. This factor is known as PSD, or Promotion to Stock Demand.

It is necessary to have an indication of what the promotional sales are compared to regular stock sales. This is known as Promotion to Regular Usage (PRU). Not being aware of this information can be very dangerous. For example, running a promotion when the promotional forecast system says it is necessary to bring in a year's worth of merchandise can result in a significant amount of overstock.

One key to knowing how well an item will do on a sale is to have a database tracking past sales on the item. How well did it do and what was the overhang of merchandise after the sale? This should also be on the promotional item record. Here again it is imperative that all regular stock demand is shown only on the regular item usage file. All promotional demand for promotions is kept on the promotional item file. This is the only way to make the distinction of what sells best in each category.

The promotional usage file tracks by item, sale, and warehouse. This tracks the best timing and analysis by sale and by month. An item may be on sale for six months or so, placing the item on six circulars with each circular running for a month. Each sale is coded by the month in which it is run. This outlines the monthly analysis of how the sale worked. If the PRU is high, the promotion may result in overstocks. This is an opportunity to negotiate with the vendor to have the item shipped at different times so that the performance of the promotion can be evaluated.

Demographic information can also be used to selectively change some of the items on the sale circulars. A list of which items sell best in each region can enhance sales demographically. It also helps in actually increasing the sales of merchandise and effectively lessening the chance for poor sales and overstocks. Increasing sales results in lower after-promotion merchandise in the inventory, which decreases overhead.

After the regression analysis is completed, the supplier can be provided with the forecast in an electronic document called an EDI 830 transaction. With the added predictability of the regression analysis, it is possible to predict the overall monthly usage of promotional demand with 80% accuracy. Offering this information to suppliers in advance allows them to run their Material Requirement Programs. This is definitely a way to minimize the volatility of the downstream supply chain.

- It can minimize the expediting of merchandise throughout the promotion.
- Suppliers can ship on the correct date because of the added information. They have a clear plan for the Master Production Schedule.
- The supplier was able to run a more effective MRP program because unpredictable demand was eliminated. The demand is more predictable because of the regression forecasts.
- Running weekly simulations on the program can alert the supplier to any changes.
- The savings is in the out-of-stocks on promotional merchandise with a reduction from 20%-plus to around 10%-plus. The inventory has been reduced by 25% throughout the sales. The

key reason for this is that the long lead times on promotional items are longer than those on the normal stocking items. The lead times are longer because the amount of product being purchased is greater for a one-time event over a four- to six-week period.

- The schedule is dependable and the supplier can plan ahead. The orders are shipped on schedule, and if changes need to be made, they are usually small and the supplier can react to them. With this process, the order is not covering the entire sale period but is placed by the week throughout the sale period, lowering inventory amounts.

- The average inventory is considered as 1/2 the Order Quantity (AI = 1/2 OQ) of a forecast system. The order quantity is dictated as OQ = D × (LT + RT) + k × MAD × (LT + RT).

    - LT is the lead time in weeks.

    - RT is the review time in weeks.

- If inventory is reviewed every other week, the average LT = 18.5 working days for stock orders and LT = 25 days for promotional orders or 5 weeks. Lead times are now reduced for promotional orders from 25 days to 7 days, or 1.4 weeks of lead time. The reduction of Order Quantity should be $\dfrac{1.4 + 2}{5 + 2} = 3$ / 7 days or 48.57% decrease. If the order quantity is reduced by 48.57%, the average inventory is reduced by 48.57%.

Figure 9-1 shows graphically that the Average Inventory = 1/2 OQ Order Quantity. The following bullets describe the values on the graph.

- P1, P2, P3, and P4 are the order periods.

- P1 and P2 Order Quantity is 1,400 and it gives an average inventory of 700.

- P3 and P4 Order Quantity is 700 and it gives an average inventory of 350.

- The Y axis is the Order Quantity.

- The X axis is the time in periods 1 to 4.

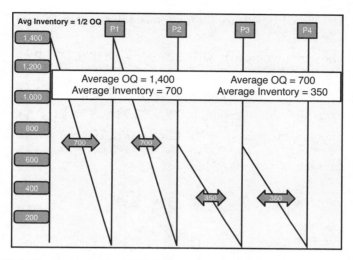

Figure 9-1 The computation of average inventory per period

This program allows for a cut in corporate inventory by 4.6%, which is an inventory savings of $16,000,000.

- The OQ is reduced by 48.57%.
- The Sales Promotions account for approximately 1/4 the sales of the company.
- The average prices of the promotional items average 40% of the average regular stocking items as a sample. By buying the merchandise on promotions, you can save 20% to 50% on the price, compared to nonpromotional periods.
- The reduction of overall inventory is calculated as .4857 × .25 × .40 = 4.6%.

Lean Savings for Promotional Forecast Program

- Inventory before the Promotional Forecast program = $181,093,991.
- The Sales are $936,824,568.
- Turns before the Promotional Forecast program = 5.17 turns.
- Inventory reduction from the Promotional Forecast program is 4.6%.

- The actual Inventory Reduction is 4.6% × $181,093,991 = $8,330,323.
- The new inventory is $181,093,991 − $8,330,323.59 = $172,763,667.
- Carrying cost reduction is 26.6% × $7,742,287 = $2,215,866.
- Freed-up cost of capital is 2% × $7,742,287 = $166,606.
- The new turns are $936,824,568 / $172,763,667 = 5.42 turns.

Total Lean Savings is $2,386,162.

10

An Introduction to Distribution Resource Management

Container Delivery Management

Distribution Resource Management (DRM) is the technology used for global scouring. This is the buying and storing of imported goods for sales. Purchasing items from overseas causes long lead times, which can destroy a company's order fill position. It may take two to three months to have the goods delivered and stocked in the warehouse. Replenishing out-of-stock items can take months! Customers won't tolerate the wait, even if the items are priced 50% to 60% cheaper than the domestic brands.

Another issue is the requirement that companies purchase in container loads for each warehouse, potentially causing an overstock situation. To avoid this problem, accumulate the sales of each item into one master file for all the monthly promotions for the entire warehouse combined. When it's time to purchase, do so for the entire company rather than each individual warehouse. This helps in making container loads for overseas shipments because of the combined demand for all warehouses. If it becomes necessary to increase or decrease the size of the container load, the whole company will see the effects.

After the order is received, it is stored in a central warehouse and dispersed as needed to each distribution center. This is known as distribution requirements planning (DRP). Combining warehouse volume minimizes the volatility in the demand. This allows for promotions to be run with less safety stock because of decreased volatility. In Six Sigma, variation is the enemy so it's necessary to do as much as possible to avoid it.

The center can act as a hub-and-spoke process. The nine warehouses will draw orders from the central warehouse based on their demand each month. The central warehouse is the hub and the nine warehouses are the spokes. The delivery cycle can be once a month from the central warehouse or hub rather than once every four to six months from overseas. To properly facilitate this operation, it is necessary to contact the freight forwarder or consolidator.

Using a freight forwarder provides Container Delivery Management by providing importers with information on a container's status. This information is known as *visibility*: It gives you the ability to visualize the status of your freight. It is also possible to interface electronically with the customer's forwarder to provide complete container cycle time. Lack of visibility of this information on a container's status can lead to any of the following:

- Storage fees assessed by the carrier due to late pickup of the container
- Charges assessed by the carrier due to late return of the container
- Production disruptions or distribution shortages caused by lack of information on incoming containers, effectively creating a bottleneck in the supply chain

Track and Trace allows for 24/7 Internet connectivity on the container location. Express bookings allow for electronic booking, receipt notifications, pickup arrangements, shipment tracking, and online documentation generation.

When a company is buying foreign goods, it may become necessary to bring in a container load of goods that could be equal to a year or more of inventory. This destroys inventory turns and takes up warehouse space. After the merchandise is stored in the hub warehouse, notice can be sent to have a month's worth of inventory shipped to each warehouse. The lead time is 7 to 10 days at the most, which is much better than the 30 to 60 days it would have taken to source from overseas. As an example, let's say the freight forwarder charges

10% and the profit margin on overseas goods is 40% to 50%. This still leaves a 30% to 40% profit on purchases.

Bringing merchandise into the warehouse and stocking it as a container load would require the housing of six months to a year's worth of inventory in each warehouse. The carrying cost would be too high and it may be necessary to pay outside storage fees. Let's say that 17% of the product is from overseas and the carrying cost is 26.6%. In the first scenario, consider buying overseas without the use of a freight forwarder. In the second, use the forwarder to perform the DRP functionality.

Buying from overseas without the forwarder, the total sales are $936,824,568. This would represent $936,824,568 × .17% = $159,260,176 for a year's worth of imported inventory. Purchasing six months of merchandise at each center, the average inventory would be $159,260,176 / 2 = $79,630,088. As discussed earlier, because the purchase is for a container load for each of the warehouses separately, this may represent six months of inventory. The $79,630,088 represents the total overall order quantity for each of the warehouses. The average inventory would be represented as 1/2 Order Quantity, which is $79,630,088 / 2 = $39,815,044. This is the average six months' inventory stored at each DC without using the DRP concept.

The norm for the industry's charge for storage can change for the type of product and the forwarder doing the scouring. This example uses a charge of 10% of the average yearly value of inventory for delivering and storing product at a central warehouse. It is necessary to provide the initial six months' PO and the product is brought in as three different shipments every other month from overseas. It is possible to cancel orders if they have not been shipped. The DRP system orders merchandise six times a year. It can be booked with other shipments to make the total cost less. The total charge comes out to be 10% to 30% of the average inventory. In this example, 25% × (their charge) × $39,815,044 / 3 (two months' average inventory) = .25 × $13,271,681 = $3,317,920 (two months' average inventory). This average will also be the average inventory for the year. The yearly charge to the freight forwarder is $1,327,168.

Bringing a month's worth of inventory from the hub into each of the DCs would represent $39,815,044 / 6 = $6,635,840 extra average inventory stored in other warehouses for nondomestic merchandise each month. If it was necessary to bring all this merchandise into the warehouse, the cost without the DRP system would be $39,815,044 – $6,635,840 = $33,179,203. Again, the $6,635,840 represents the one month's extra inventory that is in each DC from the DRP program. The $33,179,203 is the average inventory for all the warehouses when not using the DRP program for the nondomestic products for the year. Let's take a look at the Lean and Green effect of the DRP.

Lean Savings of DRP

The average inventory savings is $33,179,203 for the year for eight warehouses. To figure carrying cost, subtract two months of inventory from the six months required to carry. That is, the hub carries two months of inventory rather than the six months in each DC. Carrying cost savings represents 26.6% × the savings of four months of inventory. This figures out to be 26.6% × ($39,815,044 – 2 × $6,635,840) = $7,060,534 savings in inventory carrying cost dollars per year for the four months' inventory not carried.

This is not the only savings available with the forwarder. There is also the warehouse utilization cost savings. Warehouse space is expensive. It would be necessary to reposition the merchandise into overstock, and this involves double handling. If the warehouse is close to maximum utilization, an extension to the warehouse would have to be built or other facilities rented. To bring in the entire amount of inventory to the warehouse, more storage space would be needed. The nondomestic merchandise represents $159,260,176 for a year's worth of imported inventory. Six months of this is $66,358,406, which represents the initial shipment to all nine warehouses. On average, each warehouse would receive $66,358,406 / 9 = $7,373,156 as extra imported merchandise. The amount of increase is $66,358,406 / $173,031,187 = 38.4% in warehouse space required to house the additional inventory.

Typical warehouses employ 80 to 120 people. Using the average of 100 people in a warehouse, personnel savings is 38.4% × 100 = 38 people. The decrease in demand will not affect all employees, only the stocking and receiving personnel. This is a 38% increase in labor productivity in the distribution center. To compute the number of extra employees, multiply 100 per warehouse × 38% to see how many employees would be saved by the entire enterprise. This is equal to 342 employees not having to be hired to run in a non-DRP environment. At $18 per hour and with additional benefits of 25%, at 40 hours per week and 52 weeks per year, the direct labor savings is $46,800 per year per worker. Not needing to pay the 342 additional workers saves 342 × $46,800 per year = $16,005,600.

Green Savings

A new warehouse costs $14 million in inventory and $10 million in building costs, with an additional $3.517 million in additional infrastructure cost. An additional $3 to $6.5 million in furnishing, equipment, and racking and automation equipment would be needed. The total additional warehouse cost would be $14 million in inventory dollars + $3.517 million in additional infrastructure cost + $4.75 million in furnishing and equipment = $22,260,000 racking and automation equipment cost per building.

The total building cost savings would be 38% savings of warehouse space required × $22,260,000 = $8,458,800 × 9 = $76,129,200.

New warehousing construction cost of material and inventory is Cost Saved = $76,129,200. The savings introduced so far is totally from the company's perspective. It does not include the added cost if the hub warehouse has to expend to store and deliver merchandise. This does not include the added warehousing space needed. It would only be fair to temper some of these savings by sharing some of the expense with the hub warehouse. The premise is that the hub warehouse will have higher productivity. If, for example, the hub warehouse is 30% more efficient at the warehousing operation, then the $76,129,200 savings would be reduced by 70%. The new Green Savings is $22,838,760. This merely says that the warehouses are cubed 30% smaller because of more efficient economies to scale in lieu of their core business. This is a real possibility.

Added Utility Cost

- The added cost of utilities would be computed as $0.5717 per square foot annually. This is dependent on the amount of automated equipment in the warehouse. For a 450,000-square-foot warehouse, the average is 450,000 × $0.57170 = $256,500 spent annually on electricity. Utility cost savings is 38% × $256,500 × 9 = $877,230 in additional utilities.

- Table 4-8 in Chapter 4, "Transportation Management System (TMS)," shows that 3,060 kWh × $0.16 = $490 dollars were saved in less electricity usage by a reduction of one computer usage for the distribution center. There are 38 fewer people so the total reduction is $18,620.

Landfill Savings

- The savings to Damaged and Obsolescence is 9.75% of inventory. Table 4-9 shows the saving obtained through the freight forwarder program. Calculations show that 9.75% of $66,358,406 is $6,884,999.97 per year in Damaged and Obsolescence costs. In total, $6,469,944 per year was saved from being thrown away or put in landfills. This is not including the ROI calculation because the merchandise is still owned, even though it is not stocked in the warehouse.

Service-Level Savings

- Service level also has taken a great savings. Because we do not have to have two to three months in lead times, we have cut our out-of-stocks by more than 50%. This represents an increase in revenue of $936,824,568 × .17% (the percent bought from nondomestic sources) = $159,260,176. We have a normal out-of-stock of 26% on imported sale merchandise that is reduced to 13%, which is still too high. We figure that one-third of the out-of-stocks never gets filled because of members canceling orders or merchandise arriving after the sale is over. The lost sales then would be calculated as 13% / 3 = 4.33% of sales. This represents an increase in sales of $159,260,176 × 4.33% due to better service levels = $6,895,965. The profit margin that would have been lost is 30% × $6,895,965 = $2,068,789. The margin is higher than normal because we are buying from nondomestic sources where the price is much less.

Green Savings

- Savings in additional utilities is $877,230.
- Computer usage and purchase of computer equipment savings is $18,620.
- Landfill Savings of 9.75% of $70,833,333 is $6,884,999 per year.
- Total Green Savings is $22,838,760 + $877,230 + $18,620 + $6,884,999 = $30,619,609.

Lean Savings

The inventory savings is $66,358,406. One month is $6,635,840 and six months' inventory is $39,815,044. So 26.6% × ($39,815,044 – 2 × $6,635,840) = $7,060,534. The freed-up cost of capital is 2% × $66,358,406, and inventory savings is $1,327,168.

The following is a summary of the costs and profits:

- Service-level savings in increased sales is $6,895,965.
- Increase in profit from increased sales is 30% × $6,895,965 = $2,068,789.
- The cost of the forwarder is 25% × $13,271,681 = $3,317,920.
- Total Lean Savings Gain or (Loss) is $7,060,534 + $1,327,168 + $16,005,600 + $2,068,789 – $3,317,920 = $23,144,172.
- Turns prior the DRP = 5.41.
- Inventory prior to the DRP program = $173,031,187.
- Inventory after DRP = $165,703,133 with an inventory savings of $7,060,534.
- Sales prior to DRP = $936,824,568.
- Added sales from DRP = $6,895,965.
- Sales after DRP are ($6,895,965 + $936,824,568) = $943,720,533.
- New inventory turns are $943,720,533 / $165,703,133 = 5.69 turns.
- Total Lean Savings is $26,462,092 – (the cost of the forwarder, which is $3,317,920) = $23,144,172.

The timetable is now monthly rather than every six months. The extra trips from the hub to each warehouse do not need to be addressed when the backhaul system of routing is being used. A backhaul program uses the fleet to deliver the customer merchandise and pick up the imported supplies, returning them to their respective warehouses.

Four of the warehouses do not have this capability, so they have to expense the extra transportation to and from the hub to the four warehouses. The number of trailers is calculated as $66,358,406 / $40,000 per truck = 1,659 trailers every six months. Now to compute the number of trailers delivered per warehouse from the hub, divide the 1,659 by 9 = 173 trailers per warehouse. The four warehouses that are not backhauled have roughly half the volume of the other centers.

The nonbackhauled centers then receive 1/2 × 173 = 87 trailers every six months. They are receiving these trailers every month. This does not compute to 87 / 6 = 15 trailers per month. The trailers will be picking up exceptions and new danger-level items which could increase the monthly shipment by 25%. The total cost in this process is 15 × 4 × .25 × 400 miles round-trip × 6.1 miles per gallon × $3.12 per gallon = $3,069 in added expense in fuel costs.

Total Savings for the Freight Forwarder Program

Lean Savings is $26,462,092 – (the cost of the forwarder, which is $3,317,920) = $23,144,172.

Green Savings is $30,281,071.

Total Lean and Green Savings is $53,425,243 for the forwarder program.

11

Joint Order Allocation

Joint Order Allocation is used to create an order when the order is too small for the vendor minimum. In a case like this, test the system to see whether it is necessary to create a large order. Start by adding an extra period or fraction of the period to the order to make weight. The first thing to check is whether an order is needed in the warehouse. Do this by checking to see what the service would be when waiting for the next buying interval to place an order.

Remember, as with the ABCDE inventory classification system, the inventory is broken into five distinct groupings of importance. The importance level is denoted by the P_k or personalized service level, which dictates that this is the minimum service level accepted by this item because of its ranking on the ABCDE analysis. For example, if an item is an A category, it will have a $P_k = 98\%$ and this is the minimum accepted service level for this item. This means that an A item requires a higher level of safety stock than a D item.

- A items should have a service level of $P_k = 98\%$
- B items should have a service level of $P_k = 95\%$
- C items should have a service level of $P_k = 92\%$
- D items should have a service level of $P_k = 89\%$
- E items should have a service level of $P_k = 85\%$

Know the importance of all the items in the vendor in order to evaluate the criteria for placing or postponing the next order. The criteria used were to rank the vendor by service-level importance to the company. The process is to create a ranking scale for each vendor per warehouse. The vendor's item minimum service level is multiplied by its usage and then summed. When all items are summed and then divided, this is the sum of all the vendors usages. This creates a

173

minimum vendor service level called P, or vendor personalized service level. This is a weighted average of the vendors' overall service levels. Mathematically, this works out with the following formulas.

Vendor minimum is:

$$P = \sum_{k=1}^{k} (Pk \times Usagek)/Usagek$$

This is a weighted average by usage of all the P_k or personalized service level values assigned by the ABCDE system for all the items per warehouse. The P stands for the personalized service level for the vendor by warehouse. The P will range from 85% to 98%. Another name for P is the vendor minimum, which is called SSO, which stands for the Specified Service Overall by vendor by distribution center.

Let's say that the forecast system runs a simulation to determine the service level SSO that results by waiting a review period. Add the extra review period time into the forecast and see whether stock numbers greater than the (1 − SSO) deplete. The SSO is the service level needed to be maintained and the minimum out-of-stock would be formulated as (1 − SSO). As an example, if SSO is 98%, the minimum out-of-stock level is (1 − SSO) or (1 − .98) = 2%.

Now build the model. Let's say the lead time is four weeks and the review time is three weeks. An order would not be placed for an additional three weeks when waiting to order on the next review cycle. The total lead time to wait for the next order is 3 + 4 = 7 weeks. The nine weeks is equal to three usage buckets of demand. Each usage bucket represents three weeks of demand. Look ahead using the formula of OH − Forecast for three usage periods.

If it is a horizontal item, use the formula ESO (Expected Stock Outs) = OH − (f_{t+1} + f_{t+2} + f_{t+3}), where the f_{t+1} represents the forecast for the next period. The f_{t+2} represents the forecast for the demand two periods ahead. The f_{t+3} represents the forecast of demand three periods in advance. The ESO calculates the lost sales per item. If ESO is negative, this represents lost sales and the quantity is called ELS for Expected Lost Sales. An ELS shows the absolute value of the negative number if ESO is negative. For example, if ESO shows a value of -525, this represents an ELS expected out-of-stock of 525 units. Note that ELS is 0 when ESO is positive, which means there are no expected out-of-stocks. If the ESO value is equal to 47, the ELS value is 0. The ESOs are summed and weighted by vendor and by warehouse. This model assumes a nine-week lead time because it uses three forecast buckets that represent the forecast for the next three periods or $f_{t+1} + f_{t+2} + f_{t+3}$.

$$ESO = \sum [OH_k - (f_{kt+1} + f_{kt+2} + f_{kt+3})]$$

represents the ESO as a vendor value by warehouse. A note of caution: The ESO must be warehouse dependent for all vendors. With nine warehouses there will be nine values of ESOs per vendor. This independence is obviously based on the fact that there are separate warehouses. Each warehouse must have its own item and usage file. The total ESO by vendor is calculated by summing up all the items' values for the vendor by warehouse for its individual item ESOs. The following steps show the procedure:

- Each item ESO is defined by $ESO_k = OH_k - (f_{kt+1} + f_{kt+2} + f_{kt+3})$. The ESO by vendor is defined as

$$ESO = \sum [OH_k - (f_{kt+1} + f_{kt+2} + f_{kt+3})]$$

  for all the items in the vendor by warehouse.

- Every time ESO is negative, the absolute value of ESO is added to the ELS bucket for all the vendors' items by warehouse.

- If ESO is positive, it denotes the amount of extra or excess stock in the warehouse.

- The ELS is defined as the expected service level by vendor and by warehouse.

- Vendor $ESL = \sum [(f_{t+1} + f_{t+2} + f_{t+3}) - ELS] / (f_{t+1} + f_{t+2} + f_{t+3})$ This gives the expected service level by vendor and by warehouse.

- If ESO is less than SSO, buy before the next period.

- If ESO is equal to or greater than ESO, wait until the next period to order.

The beauty of this system is that it is personalized to the relative importance of the vendor to the overall average based on the importance of its items. Each vendor will have a different ranking based on its individual SSO.

When there is a trend item, use the FIT_t model for f_t, and for a seasonal model use the seasonal forecast mode FS_t, which would be weighted by the base index values explained earlier.

If ESO was greater than SSO, calculate each forecast by adding the extra review period to its forecast. This would now represent OQ = D * (LT + RT + k * RT) + k * MAD * (LT + RT + k * RT), where RT = the review period time. The k values are in Table 21-1 in Chapter 21, "The New Sustainable EOQ Formula," and give the relationship of k to the Z transform.

The k values on the preceding equations are for the amount of review time to put in. Begin with k = .5, which is a half review period. Calculate all the items in the vendor with this extra half review period and see whether the vendor made the weight for vendor minimum. If yes, use a k of .25 and simulate again. If the vendor still made weight, generate the forecast with an additional one-quarter extra review period. If it did not make weight, this means that the minimum shippable weight defined by the vendor was not met. Order a larger amount to make the vendor minimum weight. This means making the k value greater. In this case, try out the values of k = .25, .50, .75, 1.0. Use the lowest value of k that makes the vendor minimum weight. The scenario is if the system did not make weight with k = .50, then try k = .75 and finally k = 1.0. If the vendor minimum was made at .75, place the order. If k = 1 was used to make weight, place the order with k = 1.

If unable to make the vendor minimum weight with k = 1, use the regular forecast system without any additional review time put in, and place the order. The problem with this is that the freight may not be prepaid or discounted because less than the vendor minimum was purchased. The system would have to be notified whether the supplier would accept orders less than minimum. The rationalization for this is the need to satisfy customer demands with the smallest incremental change to inventory. The Green Savings to this is that the vendor minimum may be a full truckload and this will save the environment on wear and tear and the carbon footprint.

Let's take a look at the Lean and Green effect. Lean Savings of Joint Order Allocation is the first effect to be introduced. Reduced lead times reduce the inventory by using the minimum k value, which reduces the average inventory by an average of one week.

Lean Savings

- Twenty-five percent of the vendors need to make joint order calculations. One-third of this number cannot make the vendor minimum weight at all. This also means that 66.66% of the vendors can make weight.

- If the normal lead time is 18.5 working days and the joint vendor has an average of 7 days added to the lead time, this would give it a lead time of 25.5 days. The normal review time is 15 days. The total lead time is now (LT + RT + 7) = 40.5 days.

- Eight days are saved by not ordering the full review time. This is a savings of 8 / 40.5 lead time days, or 19.8%.

- The inventory reduction becomes 19.8% × .25% vendors need joint × 66.6% that actually make Joint Order Allocation = 3.33% reduction of inventory.

- Inventory values of the joint vendors are about one-fourth the value of vendors that don't need joint ordering. This brings new inventory reduction to 3.33% × .25 = .82% in inventory dollars.

- The inventory reduction in dollars is now .82% × $165,970,653 = $1,360,959.

- Carrying cost reduction is 26.6% × $1,360,959 = $362,015.

- Freed-up cost of capital is 2% × $1,360,959 = $27,219.

- The new inventory is at $165,703,133 – $1,358,765 = $164,609,694.

- The new turns are $943,720,533 / $164,344,368 = 5.73.

- Total Lean Savings is $362,015 + $27,219 = $1,388,178.

Green Savings

- Damaged inventory cost represents .75% of $1,360,959 inventory = $10,207.

- Obsolete inventory cost reduction is 9% of inventory reduction = $122,486.

- The Total Green Savings is $132,693.

Total savings for the Joint Order Allocation vendor program is $1,388,178 + $132,693 = $1,520,871.

12

Variable or Fixed Reorder Periods

There are many ways to review vendors for ordering. The models considered are the Fixed Period Model (FP), the Fixed Quantity Model (FQ), and the Variable Period and Quantity Model (VPQ). The Fixed Quantity Model and Fixed Order Model mean the same thing in this book and are used interchangeably. The fixed quantity refers to the fixed order quantity. The Fixed Period Model allows for ordering for a fixed period of time. It may be every week, every four weeks, or once a month. The key is that no orders are permitted between intervals. The Fixed Quantity Model can set up minimum inventory levels or reorder quantities per item. When the stock falls below this quantity, place another order in a fixed quantity every time. This quantity may be an economic order quantity, a container load, a box, a pallet, or some other vendor minimum. The Variable Period and Quantity with Look-Ahead option Model of ordering checks the out-of-stock conditions of waiting an additional day or period. If the system detects an out-of-stock situation by waiting, an order is cut that day. In this example the period and quantity can vary. Let's take a look at each model.

Fixed Period Model (FP)

The FP Model does not perpetually monitor the system for inventory levels that will cause some increases in out-of-stocks. The danger for stock outs occurring during the lead time is that the items will not be reviewed even if they are out of stock until the review period. The amount of safety stock in this system is greater than the FQ Model depending on the usage of the items. If an item has a very low demand with a high minimum order, the Fixed Period and the Fixed Order systems will be about the same.

An advantage to the Fixed Period Model is the option to review a vendor out of schedule. It is possible to plan a schedule that won't change as far as what and when vendors are reviewed. The reviewing process can be once a day or once a week but always on the same time or day of the week. The schedule can also be on a monthly basis such that the vendor is always reviewed on a particular day within a month. Nothing changes in the schedule. This is a saving of personnel time for the company because there are no unplanned orders. This minimizes the size of the purchasing staff.

The overall lead time (LT) is reprinted as (LT + RT), where RT is the length of the fixed period. The review period is defined as the time between reviews of the vendor for placing orders. When orders are reviewed every three weeks and the usage buckets are in weekly intervals, RT will equal three. The FP Model can be used to even out the workload of the purchasing people. The same number of items is reviewed each day with the same number of stock statuses or ordering forms.

The stock status, whether it is electronic or on paper, represents all the pertinent information about what is needed to place the vendor order. It will show the demand for a year, broken down into monthly time buckets. All the appropriate description, pricing, on-order, and on-hand information will be on the stock status. If the item is a faster moving item, it will be out of stock more often because of the volatility of demand. The Fixed Period Model will result in lower service levels and higher safety stocks. This will increase the size of the overall inventory. Overall lead times are the result of the supplier's lead time plus the review time. The supplier's lead time consists of the Manufacturer Lead Time plus Transit Time and also receiving and stocking time.

The Fixed Period Model can also be used to even out the receiving schedule on a daily basis throughout the month. If the vendor ships with a fairly regular lead time, the supplier can be told when to ship. This is accomplished with the ship date field of the purchase order. Some companies have actually simulated the optimum receiving schedule and back-dated the lead times to reflect the fixed review times for these vendors.

The ordering strategy is to order the amount that will equal the Predetermined Maximum Available inventory stock level, which equals PMA = OH + OO + SS – BO. The OH is the amount on hand at the order period. The SS stands for safety stock, which is equal to the extra stock needed to preserve the service level. The OO is the order quantity that needs to be ordered to reach the PMA level. If there are any backorders (BO), this amount will be subtracted from the PMA equation. This will increase the OO so the equation will equal the PMA.

Figure 12-1 shows the functionality of the Fixed Period Model in the perfect world where demand is constant from period to period. The terms used in Figure 12-1 are explained here:

- Safety stock, SS, is the predetermined amount of minimum stock needed to guarantee no stock outs. In this case, the safety stock is set to SS = $400 units.

- The OQ is the amount ordered to hit the Predetermined Maximum Available Inventory stock level, called PMA. The OQ is calculated as OQ = PMA – OH – BO. The assumption here is that the OH will not be negative. The minimum value for OH is $0.

- On-order, OO, is the amount on order.

- PMA is the predetermined maximum available stock level, which is equal to on-hand plus on-order, or OH + OO. The PMA value was determined to be $1,400 in this example.

- The average stock level is defined as 1/2 OQ in this example. OQ is constant so it's equal to $900. This is also calculated as 1/2 (beginning inventory level + ending inventory level) = 1/2 × ($1,400 + $400) = $900.

- In this case PMA is defined as $1,400. So PMA = OH + SS + OQ.

- Since demand is constant, the order quantity at the beginning of each period is $1,000.

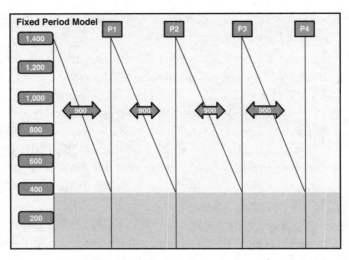

Figure 12-1 The Fixed Period Model average inventory

The final results for the Fixed Period Model are as shown here:

- PMA is $1,400.
- The average inventory is $900.
- Total sales is $4,000, which is composed of four periods of demand.
- Service Level is calculated as total sales / total demand.
- Total demand is calculated as total sales plus lost sales.
- There are no lost sales so the service level is 100%.
- The turns are calculated as total sales / average inventory = $4,000 / $900 = 4.44.
- The system should have turns equal to or greater than 4. However, demand in reality is not constant so the turns may change.
- The graph shows an order of $900 placed (the upper point or left point of each declining diagonal line). The order is received at the lower point of the diagonal line, and the P1, P2, P3, and P4 show the inventory levels when the product is received and stocked. At this time of receipt, the P values that represent the PMA values are equal to OO plus safety stock.

In the real world the FP Model does not have constant demand. It will vary over time. The best the FP Model can do in this example is the 4.44 turns with 100% service levels and $400 for safety stock when demand is constant and known. As demand starts to vary, the FP Model system begins to deteriorate. This process of deterioration is explained in the following analysis.

Figure 12-2 shows the FP Model for variable demand. The rectangles on top of the graph in Figure 12-2 show the total order quantity and the long dashed lines show when the order is placed. The short dashed lines show when an order is received, and the rectangles near the bottom show the available inventory.

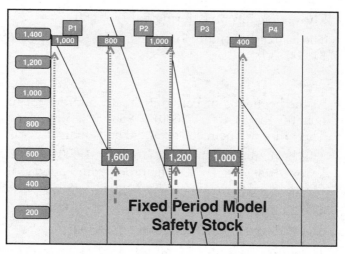

Figure 12-2 Fixed Period Model safety stock for variable demand

The system uses the Fixed Period Model with variable demand. At the beginning of each period, order the OQ. Remember that in a Fixed Period Model, an order is generated only once a period. In this case an order is generated at the beginning of each period as long as the available inventory at that time is less than $1,400. The PMA value is defined as = $1,400. At the beginning of each period, order when the available is less than 1,400. The available is defined as the sum of the on-hand and the on-order (OH + OO). Order the quantity that brings the available back to the PMA or $1,400. The OQ = 1,400 – OH – OO. The OQ will be placed as long as the value for OQ is positive. The graph shows the ordering procedure for the following demands:

- The Demand for Period 1 = $800.
- The Demand for Period 2 = $1,200.
- The Demand for Period 3 = $1,400.
- The Demand for Period 4 = $600.

- P1
  - Start the period with an OQ order quantity of $1,000. This order will be received at the beginning of Period 2.
  - The total sales or revenue for Period 1 = $800.
  - The beginning inventory in Period 1 (P1) is equal to = $1,400.
  - The ending inventory for Period 1 = $600.
  - The average inventory for the period is ($1,400 + $600) / 2 = $1,000.

- P2
  - At the beginning of Period 2, create an order for the order quantity of ($1,400 − $600) = $800 (the upper rectangle). This order will be received at the beginning of Period 3.
  - The beginning inventory = ($600 + $1,000) = $1,600 (the lower rectangle). That is, the order from Period 1 of $1,000 was received at the point where the inventory is $600.
  - The total sales or revenue for Period 2 = $1,200.
  - The ending inventory for Period 2 = $400.
  - The order quantity, at the safety stock level of less than $1,400, is created in Period 2 = ($1,400 − $400) = $1,000. This order will be received in the end of Period 3.
  - The ending inventory = $400. The receipt created in P2 will be received in Period 3.
  - The average inventory for the period is ($1,600 + $400) / 2 = $1,000.
  - Total sales or revenue = $1,200.

- P3
  - The receipt created from order quantity OQ from Period 2 is $800.
  - The beginning inventory is ($400 + $800) = $1,200 (the lower rectangle in Period 3).
  - Total demand is $1,400.

- Lost sales is $200 with a service level of 95%.
- Total sales is $1,400 – $200 = $1,200.
- The ending inventory is $0.
- The average inventory for the period is ($1,200 + $0) / 2 = $600.

- P4

  - The order quantity is $1,400 – $1,000 = $400 to be received in the beginning of Period 5.
  - The beginning inventory is $1,000 from the receipt of the $1,000 order created in Period 3.
  - Total Sales = $600.
  - The ending inventory = $400.
  - The average inventory for the period is ($1,000 + $400) / 2 = $700.

The final figures for the Fixed Period Model are as shown here:

- Total demand by period is $800 + $1,200 + $1,400 + $600 = $4,000.
- The lost sales are $200.
- Total sales are total demand – lost sales = $4,000 – $200 = $3,800.
- Average inventory is ($1,000 + $1,000 + $600 + $700) = $9,500 / 4 = $950.
- Turns are 4.61.
- The Fixed Period Model with variable demand has better turns of 4.61 compared to the Fixed Period Model with constant demand with turns of 4.44. The higher turns come with the expense of the lower service level of 95%.

Fixed Order Model (FQ)

The FQ Model perpetually monitors the system for inventory levels that will fall below the reorder point threshold. This reorder threshold is defined as the safety stock level. In this case it is defined as $400. The danger for stock outs occurs during the lead time when an item may be out of stock while still on order. The amount of safety stock in this system is less than the Fixed Period Model, depending on the usage of the items. This is because the inventory level should be less because the total overall lead time is less. (Recall that the total overall lead time is LT + RT.)

If an item has a very low demand and a high minimum order, the Fixed Period and the Fixed Order system will be about the same. The advantage to the Fixed Order Model is that the vendor does not require review every three or four weeks as in the Fixed Period Model. The vendor is reviewed only when the order falls below the minimum order. It may take several months before the vendor will be seen for review.

This saves time for the company because a stock status is not shown for this vendor until needed. The stock status is the form, either electronic or paper, which represents all the pertinent information about the vendor. It will show the demand for a year, which is broken down into monthly time buckets. All the appropriate descriptions, pricing on-order, and on-hand information will be present. If the item is a faster moving item, it will be triggered more often because of the volatility of demand. This results in a lower overall review time for the item.

Overall lead times are the result of the supplier's lead time plus the review time. If the item is reviewed more often, this makes the RT component smaller, which makes the overall lead smaller. The overall lead time is reprinted as (LT + RT). The Fixed Quantity can also be set to a minimum order which represents a discount quantity, a fixed run size to level an MRP run, or an economic order quantity. An example of the FQ, which refers to the Fixed Order Model, is as follows and also is illustrated in Figure 12-3:

- The lead time is one period in this example.
- The same Predetermined Maximum Available Inventory as in the above examples of FP Models is used.
- The only difference is the requirement for a triggering mechanism in the FQ Model to send the reorder notice. Ordering occurs when the item is less than the PMA. This allows for ordering at varying time intervals.
- The safety stock for the FQ Model is at SS = the PMA = $1,400.
- The fixed quantity is set to $1,200.

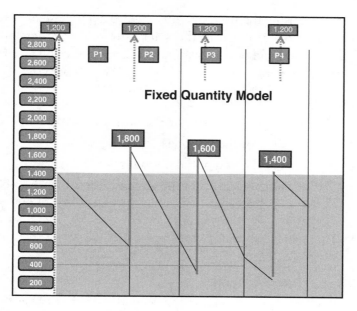

Figure 12-3 Fixed Order Model

- In the beginning of P1, the available inventory is at the safety stock level of $1,400, so Fixed Quantity Order is placed at $1,200.

- The dashed lines represent the fixed order quantity of $1,200, created at the start of Period 1.

- This order will be the receipt for the beginning of Period 2.

- The available inventory (AI) for Period 1 is OH + OO = $1,400 + $1,200 = $2,600.

- The new algorithm is what the safety stock is measured against. If AI falls below the SS level of $1,400, the system will place a fixed order quantity of $1,200.

- The middle rectangles represent the receipt of the last fixed order quantity of $1,200.

- This rectangle shows the new inventory level after the fixed order quantity of $1,200 is received.

- The dashed line shows when an order has been placed, and the middle box shows the fixed order quantity of $1,200.

- The top horizontal lines show the beginning and ending of each period.

- The square box represents the period number.

The system using the fixed quantity creates a purchase order only when the inventory is equal to the safety stock. This order level is where the on-hand and on-order is equal to P. The P value is defined as = $1,400. The graph in the figure explains the following:

- The FQ First Period:
  - The beginning inventory for Period 1 is $1,400.
  - The demand for the period is $800.
  - Inventory at the end of the period is $600.
  - The available inventory at the end of Period 1 is AI = $600 + $1,200 = $1,800. The safety stock level is above $1,400 so no new orders are placed yet.
  - The average inventory for Period 1 is ($1,400 +$600) / 2 = $1,000.

- The FQ Second Period:
  - Beginning inventory for the second period is equal to the ending inventory of the first period plus the receipt of the OQ from the first period, which is $600 + $1,200 = $1,800.
  - Total sales or revenue for Period 2 = $1,200.
  - If $400 of the $1,800 available inventories are sold, the stock level will be at the $1,400 safety stock level and another order for the third period will need to be placed. This will happen $400/$1,200 or 1/3 of the way into the second period. The new fixed order quantity will be received 1/3 of the way through the third period.
  - Ending inventory is ($600 + $1,200 – $1,200) = $600.
  - Average inventory is ($1,800 + $600) / 2 = $1,200.
  - The SS level is reached when the inventory drops another $400. This is equivalent to $400/$1,200 or 1/3 the way through the second period. At this time, create an order for $1,200. This order will be received 1/3 of the way into the third period.

- The FQ Third Period:
  - The third period begins with an inventory of $600.
  - Sales are $1,400.
  - There is an outstanding order for $1,200 to be received 1/3 of the way into the third period.

- Total available = $600 + $1,200 = $1,800, which is still above the safety stock level so do not order yet.
- Create another order when the inventory drops by $400 because the total available OH + OO is ($600 + $1,200) at the beginning of Period 4. This will be created at $400/$1400 or 29% or about 1/3 into the third period.
- At this time, the new available is $1,400 + $1,200 = $2,600.
- This order will be received 1/4 of the way in for Period 4.
- The ending inventory is $600 + $1,200 − $1,400 = $400.
- The average inventory for Period 3 is ($600 + $400) / 2 = $500.

- The FQ Fourth Period:
  - Starting inventory is $400.
  - Demand for the time is $600.
  - The order placed in Period 3 is received when the inventory drops to $400 − .29 × $600 = $226.
  - The availability is $226 + $1,200 = $1,426 and another order for $1,200 is placed when the inventory falls by $26. This order will be received in Period 5.
  - Ending inventory is $600 + $1,200 − $600 = $1,200.
  - Average inventory is ($400 + $1,200) / 2 = $800.

- The final figures for the Fixed Period Model are as given here:
  - Total demand by period is $800 + $1,200 + $1,400 + $600 = $4,000.
  - The average inventory for each period is the beginning inventory + ending inventory divided by 2.
  - Period 1 average = $1,400 + $600 = $2,000 / 2 = $1,000.
  - Period 2 average = $1,800 + $600 = $2,400 / 2 = $1,200.
  - Period 3 average = $600 + $400 = $1,000 / 2 = $500.
  - Period 4 average = $400 + $1,200 = $1,600 / 2 = $800.

- Average inventory is $1,000 + $1,200 + $500 + $800 = $3,500 / 4 = $875.
- The lost sales are $0.
- The service level is computed as total sales / total demand = 100%.

- The inventory turns are total sales / average inventory = $4,000 / $875 = 4.57 turns.

In this example, comparing the Fixed Period with the Fixed Quantity Models with 100% service levels shows very little difference. The turns for the FP Model with constant demand are 4.44. The turns with the FP Model with the variable demand is 4.61 but with a 95% service level. The turns for the FQ Models are 4.57. In comparing the FP Model with variable demand to the FQ, the turns are very close, 4.61 to 4.57. There is a 100% service level with the FQ Model; therefore, the FQ Model is better.

Variable Period and Quantity Model (VPQ) with Look-Ahead

The next comparison is with the Variable Period and Quantity Model (VPQ) with the Look-Ahead feature. This model looks ahead for each vendor and simulates whether it can wait until the next period to order. This is similar to the Joint Order Allocation Model in that the vendor minimum weight is not met, so an extra period or fraction of a period is added to make the required weight.

The VPQ Model looks ahead using the forecast system and does not have a fixed order period or fixed quantity to order. The order quantity or the review period can change. The new safety stock or PMA is the OQ = FCST – OH – OO. When the OQ is positive, an order can be placed. The FCST is the forecast for the purchasing periods being forecasted.

To begin, check to see whether an order is needed in the warehouse. Do this by checking to see what the projected demand against the on-hand and on-order is. Start the needs evaluation by checking the ABCDE inventory evaluation. Recall that the ABCDE inventory classification system breaks down the inventory into five distinct groupings of importance. Items must be classified in the ABCDE classification like this:

- A items have a service level of 98%.
- B items have a service level of 95%.

- C items have a service level of 92%.
- D items have a service level of 89%.
- E items have a service level of 85%.

It is necessary to know the importance of all the vendor items in order to evaluate the criteria for measuring the size of the safety stock and the need to order now. The criteria used was to weight the vendor items by service levels and see whether by waiting, the vendor would fall below the minimum threshold. Mathematically, this works out with the following formulas:

Vendor minimum service level is:

$$P = \sum_{k=1}^{k} \left(\frac{Pk \times USAGE}{USAGEk} \right)$$

This is a weighted average by usage of all the personalized service level values assigned by the ABCDE system for all the items per warehouse. The P stands for the Personalized Service Level for the system, which ranges from 85% to 98%. The vendor minimum is called P = SSO, which stands for the Specified Service Overall by vendor by distribution center. Another name for P is SSO.

Let's say a forecast system simulation is run to determine the service level at present if the order is placed at the next review time. Any vendors that are not experiencing immediate service-level problems, but cannot wait until the review period, are classified as danger-level vendors. Let's say the lead time is four weeks and the review time is three weeks. If the choice is made to wait until the next review period, the lead time calculations will be increased by an additional three weeks. The total lead time to wait for the next order is 3 + 4 = 7 weeks.

The system uses usage buckets that represent three weeks of usage. There are 7 weeks in total lead time, which was rounded up to 9 weeks in this example. To simulate this effect in the forecast system, use the following formulas. The nine weeks is equal to 3 usage buckets of demand. Each usage bucket represents three weeks of demand. So there are 17 usage buckets each year. When there are four-week usage buckets, there are 13 usage buckets per year. It does not matter how you break up the yearly time buckets, so in the example the three week usage was used. The next part is to develop the Look-Ahead feature for the system. This is performed by netting the forecast extended over the lead time against the current on-hand. If the system nets a negative value, the item needs to be ordered. The formula for the Look-Ahead feature is OH – Forecast × 3 usage periods.

The next few paragraphs are very similar to the process talked about in the joint order allocation discussion, but it is prudent to discuss this again due to the new methodology using the logic. This methodology is the Variable Period and Quantity Model (VPQ) with the Look-Ahead feature.

If it is a horizontal item, use the formula Expected Stock Outs (ESO) = OH – (f_{t+1} + f_{t+2} + f_{t+3}), where the f_{t+1} represents the forecast for the next period. The f_{t+2} represents the forecast for the demand two periods ahead, and the f_{t+3} represents the forecast of demand three periods in advance. The ESO calculates the lost sales per item. If ESO is negative, this represents lost sales and the quantity is called ELS for Expected Lost Sales. ELS shows the absolute value of the negative number if ESO is negative.

For example, if ESO shows a value of –525, this represents an ELS of 525 units that will be out of stock. Note that ELS is 0 when ESO is positive, which states that there are no out-of-stocks. This becomes a binomial decision. If ESO is negative, there is an out-of-stock condition. If ESO is positive, it is set to 0, which indicates no out-of-stocks. If the ESO value is 47, the ELS value is 0. The ESOs are summed and weighted by vendor and by warehouse. This model assumes a nine-week lead time because it uses three forecast buckets that represent the forecast for the next three periods, or f_{t+1} + f_{t+2} + f_{t+3}.

$$ESO = \sum \left[OH_k - \left(f_{kt+1} + f_{kt+2} + f_{kt+3} \right) \right]$$

represents the issue that the ESO is a vendor value by warehouse. A note of caution is that the ESO must be warehouse dependent. In the case of one vendor servicing nine warehouses, there are nine values of ESOs. This is calculated by summing up all the items' values for the vendor by warehouse for the individual item ESOs. The following list explains:

- Each item ESO is defined by $ESO_k = OH_k - (f_{kt+1} + f_{kt+2} + f_{kt+3})$. The ESO by vendor is defined as:

$$\sum [OH_k - (f_{kt+1} + f_{kt+2} + f_{kt+3})]$$

for all the items in the vendor by warehouse.

- Every time ESO is negative, the absolute value of ESO is added to the ELS bucket for all the vendor items by warehouse.

- If ESO is positive, it denotes the amount of extra or excess stock in the warehouse.

- The ESL is defined as the expected service level by vendor and by warehouse.

- Vendor $ESL = \sum [(f_{t+1} + f_{t+2} + f_{t+3}) - ELS]/(f_{t+1} + f_{t+2} + f_{t+3})$
  This indicates the expected service level by vendor and by warehouse.

- If ESO is less than SSO, buy before the next period.

- If ESO is equal to or greater than ESO, wait until the next period to order.

The beauty of this system is that it personalizes the relative importance of the vendor to the overall average. Each vendor will have a different ranking based on its individual SSO.

When using a trend item, use the FIT_t model for f_t, and for a seasonal model use the seasonal forecast model FS_t, which would be weighted by the base index values explained in Chapter 18, "A Technical Explanation of Forecasting Systems."

If ESO was greater than SSO, calculate each forecast. This is now represented as the variable order quantity of $OQ = D * (LT + RT) + k * MAD * (LT + RT)$. The order quantity (OQ) can vary also, and this is how it gets its name Variable Period and Quantity Model.

An example of the VPQ Model is as follows and also illustrated in Figure 12-4. A comparison to the other FQ or FP Models mentioned previously is included:

- The safety stock varies in this model. It looks at the next month's anticipated demand f_{t+1} and uses it to calculate the safety stock. Going into a period of increasing demand requires ordering the month before at a higher level. The order quantity is $OQ = f_{t+1}$

+ $200. As a policy decision, the $200 was added to ensure additional safety stock.

- The dashed lines represent the order quantity, $1,400 and $1,600.
- This VPQ created only two orders as opposed to the other models:
  - FP Model created three orders.
  - FQ Model created four orders.
- The line inside the period breaks represents the receipt of the last order quantity plus the existing on-hand.
- The rectangle in Periods 2 and 3 shows the new inventory level after the order quantity receipt.
- The long vertical lines show the beginning and ending of each period.
- The top box represents the period number.

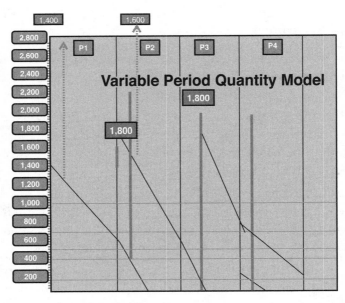

Figure 12-4 Variable Period Quantity Model

The system differs from the other models in that it tries to anticipate the future needs by using the forecast to predict the future.

- The First Period:
  - Beginning Inventory = $1,400.
  - Sales = $800.
  - Ending Inventory = $600.
  - The safety stock level at the beginning of Period 1 is set to $f_{t+1} = 1,200$. This is the Look-Ahead feature.
  - The order quantity is $f_{t+1} + \$200 = \$1,400$. This is also a Look-Ahead feature.
    - The example was simplified with only four periods and an estimate of the safety stock. There is no fixed safety stock level in this case. It can vary throughout the time series. In a real-time series analysis, use the following formula: OQ = OH + OO - D * (LT) + k * MAD * (LT)).
    - Note that the RT component is not included in the model OQ = OH + OO – D * (LT + RT) + k * MAD * (LT + RT)).
    - OH stands for on-hand inventory and OO stands for on-order or any inventory not yet received that has been ordered for delivery.
    - If the product is needed, there is no reason to wait to order it. Hence, there is no reason to include the RT component in the equation.
    - If the OQ becomes negative, an order determination must be made because the forecast is greater than the on-hand and on-order, so another order should be created to keep from running out of stock.
  - The OQ is created at the start of the period of $1,000. It will be received at the start of the second period.
  - The average inventory for the period is ($1,400 + $600) / 2 = $1,000.
- The Second Period:
  - Beginning inventory is $600.
  - Create an order when the available drops by $200 and this is $200 / $1,200 = 17% of the way into the second period. The inventory at the time of the receipt of the order is $400. The available = $1,800.
  - When the inventory drops by $400, create another order.

- The new safety stock is f_{t+1} = $1,400.
- The order quantity is f_{t+1} + $200 = $1,600.
- Total sales or revenue for Period 2 = $1,200.
- Ending inventory is ($600 + $1,400 − $1,200) = $800.

- The Third Period:
  - Beginning inventory is $800.
  - Two weeks into the third period an order is received for $1,600.
  - Sales are $1,400.
  - Ending inventory is ($800 + $1,600 − $1,400) = $1,000.

- The Fourth Period:
  - Starting inventory is $100.
  - Demand for the time is $600.
  - The ending inventory is $400.

- The final figures for the VQP Model are as shown here:
  - Total demand by period is $800 + $1,200 + $1,400 + $600 = $4,000.
  - The average inventory for each period is the beginning inventory + ending inventory divided by 2.
  - Period 1 average = $1,400 + $600 = $2,000 / 2 = $1,000.
  - Period 2 average = $600 + $800 = $1,400 / 2 = $700.
  - Period 3 average = $800 + $100 = $900 / 2 = $450.
  - Period 4 average = ($1,000 + $400) / 2 = $700.

- Average inventory is $1,000 + $700 + $450 + $700 = $2,850 / 4 = $712.50.
- The lost sales are $0.
- The service level is computed as total sales / total demand = 100%.
- The inventory turns are total sales / average inventory = $4,000 / $712.50 = 5.61 turns.
- This is well above the other two ways of forecasting FP and FQ.

In comparing the Fixed Period with the Fixed Quantity Models with 100% service levels, there is very little difference. The turns for the Fixed Period Model are 4.61. The turns for the Fixed Quantity Models are 4.57. The VQP Model indicates turns of 5.61, and this represents an increase in turns over the best model.

Let's take a look at the Lean and Green effect: Note that the VMI vendors are already taken out of this analysis. They are some of the largest vendors, which can make up to 30% to 60% of total sales. In this case, the VMI vendors are around 40% of sales. Taking the VMI vendors out allows for the remaining 60% of sales to be considered according to the Variable Period and Quantity Models.

Lean Savings of Variable Period and Quantity with the Look-Ahead Option

Reduced Early Order Stock

This is the stock that is brought in too early. It is different from safety stock, which is a statistical calculation of the amount of overage needed to satisfy predetermined service-level requirements. This can range from 2% to 10%. For this calculation, 3% will be used, multiplied by dollar inventory. So inventory is reduced by 3% through reducing early order stock. This implies better planning and scheduling, which is the function of the VPQ Model with Look-Ahead. The system looks ahead and calculates when it needs to add extra inventory based on the last two or three years' pattern of demand.

Reduced Inventory Levels

The order point for the safety stock model can and will change as time goes on. This probability system calculates the time closest to the predetermined service-level requirements and orders under these guidelines. Timing for order placement is more accurate. This can range from 3% to 15% of your inventory, but in this calculation inventory savings is set at 4%.

Reduced Lead Times

The reduced lead time reduces the wait on a minimum order level or predetermined time to buy. The calculations are more event-driven.

If something happens, it is observed and acted on immediately. The savings from the reduced lead time was included in the preceding reduced inventory savings. Using the non-VMI inventory for this analysis requires removing the VMI component from the inventory.

Lean Savings

- The inventory prior to the introduction of the VPQ with Look-Ahead is $164,609,694.
- Sales are at $943,720,533.
- Inventory turns are at 5.73 before VPQ.
- The inventory reduction in dollars for non-VMI merchandise is 60% × $164,609,694 48 = $98,765,816.
  - Early order stock reduction is 3% × $98,765,816 = $3,420,573.
  - Reduced inventory levels from order point are 4% × $98,765,816 = $4,560,764.
  - Total inventory savings is $3,420,573 + $4,560,764 = $7,981,337.
- New inventory level after the VPQ Model with Look-Ahead is $164,609,694 − $7,981,337 = $156,628,357.
- The new turns are $943,720,533 / $156,363,031 = 6.03.

Green Savings

- Carrying cost reduction is 26.6% × ($7,981,337) = $2,123,036.
- Cost of capital savings is 2% × ($7,981,337) = $159,627.
- Total Lean Savings is $2,123,036 + $159,627 = $2,282,663.
- The Green Savings:
  - Damaged inventory cost represents .75% of $7,981,337 inventory = $59,860.
  - Obsolete inventory cost reduction is 9% of inventory reduction = $718,320.

The Total Green Savings is $778,180.

Total Lean and Green Savings for the Variable Period and Quantity Model is $2,282,663 + $778,180 = $3,060,843.

13

Furthering Collaboration with Suppliers (CPFR)

A further enhancement to the supply chain is the concept of Collaborative Planning, Forecasting, and Replenishment (CPFR). The American Production and Inventory Control Society (APICS) defines collaborative planning, forecasting, and replenishment as "a collaboration process whereby supply chain trading partners can jointly plan key supply chain activities from production and delivery of raw materials to production and delivery of final product to end customers." CPFR is more than a generic description of cooperation among supply chain partners.

Formalized in 1998 by the Voluntary Interindustry Commerce Solutions (VICS) Association, CPFR is an evolving set of best practices that help supply chain partners jointly plan some or all key activities from the production of raw materials to the sale of finished products. Originally designed with retail supply chains in mind, the CPFR standards have been broadened somewhat to encompass lessons learned in other areas, including technology and chemistry. As more firms in different industries implement CPFR, the specific guidelines will undoubtedly continue to evolve.

CPFR is a web-based business tool that combines the knowledge of many trading partners, similar but more advanced than VMI, and is used to coordinate demand forecasting, production and purchase planning, and inventory replenishment functions. The savings seen with CPFR include an improvement in service levels, a corporate goal of 97%-plus, better promotional and seasonally accurate forecasting, increased sales, increased turnover, reduced inventory levels, greater efficiency in receiving inventory, and a fill rate increase from 1% to 4%, and in one case a vendor moved from a 93% to 97% fill rate.

The original CPFR model, introduced in 2001, started with a nine-step process:

1. **Develop collaborative planning**—This is the front-end agreement with the supplier and retailer, conducted quarterly. This is the first part of a partnership agreement. It is the hardest to accomplish because each of the corporations comes with its own mind-set and culture. Having a mind-set of being better than the competition has no place in CPFR. This all-knowing attitude is easy to spot and difficult to work with. It takes a very special person from both organizations to tie the knot on the agreement. Each must be professional and technical, self-motivated, extroverted, and energetic. Most of all, each must believe in the concept.

2. **Create a joint business plan**—After the companies agree to enter the partnership, this is the end result of the collaborative arrangements. It is important that each partner understands his role and knows whom to contact within the collaborative arrangement. It is also very important that both retailer and manufacturer have the backing of upper management. It actually is helpful that the owners of the CPFR project give quarterly results to the board throughout the year. This keeps the relevancy and importance of the project in front of upper management.

3. **Create the sales forecast**—This is to be reviewed weekly or monthly. The forecast is a joint agreement between the retailer and the manufacturer. There are many ways to collaborate on the forecast. One way is to agree to use the same forecasting methodology. The other way is to agree to a list of software vendors that the retailer and the manufacturer can both use. It is also possible to have the programs linked in order to share all exceptions.

4. **Identify exceptions**—Exceptions can be identified and must be communicated to the partners. The exceptions can vary:
   - Item on allocation
   - Severe weather patterns
   - Price changes
   - Item no longer available and to be discontinued
   - Giving the discontinued date
   - Substitute items

- New item
- Plant closing for vacation
- Shutdown time

5. **Resolve exceptions**—The exceptions are finally resolved through the collaborative information. Some of the resolutions are informational. It is assumed that the partners will act on this information.

6. **Create the order forecast**—The buyer creates the order and electronically sends it to the supplier. By this time, the order should have the input from the supplier and the retailer so that the level of communicated intelligence in the order is better than the silo approach.

7. **Identify exceptions**—The exceptions were listed previously.

8. **Resolve exceptions**—At this level the resolutions to the exceptions have been input into the forecast program.

9. **Generate orders**—The forecast has been accepted by all the prior steps and the order is sent to the supplier.

The New CPFR Model

The new CPFR Model, introduced in 2004, takes into account eight tasks that incorporate some of the previous nine steps in a revised edition. The new model completes the same functions as the older model but it breaks down the responsibilities. The new system has four activities that are shared between the retailer and the supplier: strategic planning, demand and supply management, execution, and analysis.

Each of these activities is broken into three tasks:

- **The Retailers Task**—This is the area where the retailer is responsible for performing the tasks. These are the tasks that the retailer can do a better job of than the manufacturer.

- **The Collaborative Task**—This is the area where both the supplier and the retailer can share their respective knowledge base. The event management and collaborative notifications occur with this task.

- **The Manufacturer Task**—This is the area where the manufacturer has the responsibility of performing the tasks. Again, these are the tasks that the manufacturer usually can do a better job of, compared to the retailer. Each activity is broken down into two enterprise activities per task. The total number of enterprise activities in the model is 4 (Activities) × 2 (Enterprise Activities) × 3 (Tasks) = 24 Enterprise Activities.

Figure 13-1 shows the four activities and the three collaboration tasks.

Retailer Task	Collaboration Task	Manufacturer Task
	A. Strategic Planning	
Vendor Management	Collaboration Arrangement	Account Planning
Category Management	Joint Business Plan	Market Planning
	B. Demand and Supply Management	
POS Forecast	Sales Forecast	Market Data Analysis
Replenishment Planning	Order Planning / Forecast	Demand Planning
	C. Execution	
Buying / Rebuying	Order Generation	Production and Supply Planning
Logistics / Distribution	Order Fulfillment	Logistics / Distribution
	D. Analysis	
Store Execution	Exception Management	Execution Monitoring
Supplier Scorecard	Performance Measurement	Customer Scorecard

Figure 13-1 The New Collaboration Model shows the relationship between the manufacturer and the retailer.

In the figure, the collaboration tasks appear in the center column; the enterprise tasks appear in the left column (Retailer Task) and right column (Manufacturer Task). This procedure forces cooperation between the retailer and the manufacturer. They have visibility into each other's demand chain. The four activities are broken into three tasks: Retailer Task, Collaboration Task, and Manufacturer Task. This gives 12 categories of tasks or action.

Strategic Planning Activity

In the Strategic Planning activity, the plan identifies significant events such as vendor promotions, retail promotions, special events, natural disasters, store grand openings and closings, competitive analysis, and new item product introductions.

Under the Retailer Task there are two activities:

- Vendor Management—This part of the strategic planning uses a macro concept of working with all the vendors, managing all details and communications with the suppliers.
- Category Management—This is the determination of how the retailer will display the supplier's merchandise, what the racking is, and what product groupings will be shown.

The center category, Collaboration Task, is the collaborative joint business plan. This utilizes the vendor and retailer partnership agreements. There are two Collaboration Task activities:

- Collaboration arrangement—This is the agreement between the supplier and retailer explaining how they intend to share the collaborative responsibility.
- Joint business plan—This spells out the intended goals and how both parties intend to meet them.

The Manufacturer Task involves two activities:

- Account Planning—This is the macro concept of how to plan and collaborate with all the retailers.
- Market Planning—This is the responsibility of the manufacturer. The manufacturer has the global view of all promotions and sales. They are in an excellent position to collaborate with the retailer on the revenue potential of certain categories of products.

Demand and Supply Management Activity

In the Demand and Supply Management activity, the manufacturer receives the point-of-sale demand from the retailer's stores. This is a very difficult task because of the nuances in the different retailers' cash register systems. There are three available techniques for retailer demand. The first technique is the point-of-sale system. The second is called member purchase history. The retailer demand is taken from invoices of previous purchases (note: these are purchases and not sales; however, there are some analytical benefits obtained by comparing the use of both). The third technique involves giving the manufacturer the usage file and certain item file fields.

The promotional forecast in EDI 830 documentation can also be passed along. In the distributor model, the manufacturer ships to the warehouse and the distributor then reships products to the retailer. Usage and certain regular item fields from the item file can be shared through the EDI transaction set 852. In choosing to use the distributor model, it is imperative to watch out for out-of-stocks.

The Retailer Task is broken into two activities:

- POS Forecast—It is the retailer's responsibility to prepare point-of-sale data, demand history, or the EDI document 852 and 830 for the manufacturer. Providing this documentation allows the manufacturer to plan the Manufacturing Requirements Planning (MRP) more effectively. The MRP program plans when to start production and in what quantities in order to match the ship date for purchase orders. The retailer can also notify the manufacturer of any special promotions they are planning and at what price.

- Replenishment Planning—This involves the actual summation of the POS forecast where the retailer sets the schedule and quantities of all the items needing replenished and assigns the ship dates to the purchase orders.

The Collaborative Task is broken into two activities:

- Sales Forecast—This represents the actual sales forecast developed by the collaborative effort between retailer and manufacturer.

- Order Planning Forecast—This is the actual planning of how to deliver the forecast to the retailer. It denotes the time schedule as well as the delivery schedule.

The Manufacturer Task is broken into two activities:

- Market Data Analysis—The vendor is in a unique position to see the effects of price changing in different areas globally and so can project the promotional lift of the price to elasticity-to-demand ratio changes. For instance, a price drop of 10% may increase sales by 30% that week. The manufacturer sees this from their customers, which allows them to assist in the planning process by using Demand Data Analysis.

- Demand Planning—The manufacturer analyzes market data and applies the unique events to each retail opportunity. In this phase, the Market Data Analysis is transformed into actual quantitative numbers called Demand Planning. The manufacturer can also receive the data from the POS information from the retailer. The data is only one week old and can be used for forecasting the next week's sales. The manufacturer will use the data to see whether there are any changes in the region or sale cycles. The supplier can see information right down to the retailers' shelves and anticipate increasing or decreasing inventory based on sales results. They can also spot instances in which the retailer is buying too much inventory in anticipation of a coming event.

This acts as a warning signal to the supplier to slow their production system down because the inventory-to-sales ratio of the retailer is becoming excessively higher. This helps the supplier become more proactive to the needs of the customer. Without this information, the supplier would continue to stock extra inventory based on past buying habits.

In the normal demand-driven system, the distributor would order every three to four weeks. Only then would the manufacturer receive the order quantity. If the distributor's inventory was high, they would need to delay their ordering by an additional one to four weeks or more. The distributor would then place the order at a later time.

The supplier works under the feast-or-famine modus operandi. After an order is received by the distributor, the retailer may have lowered the price of selected items. This may cause a run on these products. At this time, the warehouse or distributor would be placing an order much higher than usual. This is known as pent-up demand from the manufacturer's side or the feast side of the feast-or-famine equation. Collaboration minimizes the potential for the bullwhip effect.

The bullwhip effect was coined by Wal-Mart and P&G when they were working on VMI programs. The distributor or supplier can measure the relationship between the retailers' on-hand and its relative demand. If the retailer's inventory begins to grow, the supplier and distributor can be alerted to slow down on potential purchase orders. This is one of the reasons for major overstocks for promotions, because the distributor or supplier will still build inventory in lieu of the promotion in anticipation of larger demand.

The inventory-to-demand ratio denotes whether and when an increase in sales is materializing. Another important collaborative demand planning function is that the manufacturer communicates all plant shutdowns and vacation shutdowns to the retailers. The supplier would automatically add stock to the retailer's order just prior to the supplier's vacation shutdown. This issue gets ignored by many retailers and they wonder why their out-of-stocks go up in the summer.

Discontinued items and their last dates of ordering should be communicated. This is another thorny issue that leaves retailers wondering why they have outs on certain items, and later they discover that the items have been discontinued. The supplier should give an automatic issue of any substitute items available.

There is some difference between the supplier and the retailer in purchasing responsibilities. The manufacturer conducts demand planning, whereas the retailer undertakes replenishment planning. In many cases the demand planning is conducted with various sophisticated forecast models including SAP, Oracle, IBM, JDA, I2 (now part of JDA), Demand Solutions, and American Software.

Execution Activity

The Execution activity is also known as the "order-to-cash cycle." It is the plan to deliver goods to the retailer at the right time, at the right place, with the right quantity, and at the least cost.

The Retailer Task is broken into two activities:

- Buying/Rebuying—This is the actual placing of orders based on the algorithms in the system. After the orders are placed, they are electronically sent to the vendor or supplier. The orders are placed after all the collaborative efforts have been finalized. This activity also covers making payment or order payment.
- Logistics and Distribution—This is the shipping from the supplier to the receiving dock of the retailer. This represents the true transportation lead time.

The Manufacturer Task is broken into two activities:

- Production and Supply Planning—This is why the previous information is so important. For the supplier to do an excellent job in the MRP system, it needs to have excellent system visibility. Production and supply planning involves the production plan that matches the ship date given by the retailer in the retailer's buying and rebuying phase to the actual shipment delivery dates.
- Logistics and Distribution—This is scheduling and delivering the merchandise to match the retailer's delivery schedule.

The Collaborative Task involves two activities:

- Order Generation—This is the execution part of the supply chain. This function involves getting the orders to the plant door.
- Order Fulfillment—This involves getting the products from the plant to the retailer. This involves the logistic departments for both the manufacturer and the retailer.

Analysis Activity

The Analysis activity for the supply chain partners monitors planning and execution activities to identify exceptions. This is the quintessential continuous improvement activity. Analyzing execution highlights how a company can improve each step in the supply chain process. The partners also compile the results and calculate key metrics and the KPIs. This information is used to share insights and adjust plans as part of continuous improvement.

The Retailer Task is broken into two activities:

- Store Execution—The retailer or distributor receives and stocks the merchandise.
- Supplier Scoreboard—This measures the supplier's performance to the KPIs developed jointly with the supplier. Often, the manufacturer with the highest metrics receives the outstanding manufacturer of the year award. This definitely adds an incentive for the manufacturer to work more closely with the retailer because it's all about the retailer's reputation.

The Collaborative Task is broken into two activities:

- Exception Management—This involves execution monitoring by the manufacturer and the retailer. The objective is to identify the outlines that did not perform to the business plan. After the exceptions are identified, both parties identify any improvements. It is almost considered a living system because it's constantly growing and changing to the continuous improvement initiative.

- Performance Assessment—Manufacturers and retailers keep scorecards to assess each other's performance. The common performance metrics (KPI) are gross margin percent, return on investment and sales growth, in-stock percent at point-of-sale, inventory turnover, inventory level, sales forecast accuracy, potential sales lost due to stock-out, manufacturing cycle time, order cycle time, shipping cycle time, problem resolution time, rate of emergency or canceled orders, percent shipped or delivered on time, and mean number of back orders and timing of back orders.

The Manufacturer Task involves two activities:

- Execution Monitoring—The execution monitoring is the analysis of how well the supplier and retailer performed in the partnership. What are the pressure points in the system and what is causing the company pain? Perform a value stream mapping to see how much value was added and compare this to the previous plan.

- Customer Scorecard—This is the manufacturer's scorecard of how well the retailer performed when measured against the other retailers the manufacturer is partnering with. Many times this can be published in trade magazines as the outstanding customer award of the year. This definitely adds an incentive for the retailer to work more closely with the manufacturer. It is all about reputation.

Here is a summary of the metrics that can be used in CPFR which are very important in measuring the retailer's performance and the execution performance of the manufacturer:

- Gross margin percentage = $\dfrac{Revenue - Cost\ of\ Goods\ Sold}{Revenue}$.

- Return on Investment =

$$\frac{Gain\ from\ the\ Technology - Cost\ of\ the\ Technology}{(Cost\ of\ the\ Technology)}$$

- Sales growth:
  - If sales growth is positive = $\dfrac{Sales\ This\ Year}{Sales\ Last\ Year} - 1$

  - If sales growth is negative = $1 - \dfrac{Sales\ This\ Year}{Sales\ Last\ Year}$

- In-stock percent at point-of-sale = $\dfrac{Number\ of\ Filled\ Orders}{Number\ of\ Orders}$

- Service level by line = $\dfrac{Number\ of\ Lines\ Filled}{Number\ of\ Lines\ Orders}$

- Service level by dollar = $\dfrac{(\Sigma\ Lines\ Filled) \times C}{\Sigma(Lines\ Ordered \times C)}$

and C can represent the cost or revenue dollar for each line sold.

- Inventory turnover = $\dfrac{Cost\ of\ Goods\ Sold}{Average\ Value\ of\ Inventory}$

- Days of supply = (average value of inventory) / ((cost of goods sold) / 365)).

- GMROI (Gross Margin Return on Investment) = net profit margin × inventory turns.

- Sales forecast accuracy in a percentage =

$$\Sigma \frac{|Actual\ Demand - Forecast|}{12}$$

This assumes forecasting once a month for the vendor, and the percent is calculated for one year.

- Manufacturing cycle time = the total amount of time the manufacturer takes to complete the PO. It is measured from the receipt of the purchase order until the product leaves the plant.

- Transportation time = the amount of time the product takes to be picked up at the plant until it is received by the retailer.

- Receipt to stock time = the time the product is received until it is put away to stock and registered in on-hand inventory.
- Total lead time = manufacturing cycle time + transportation time + receipt to stock time. This is the metric to minimize. Note that it is a metric which is composed of the manufacturers, shipper, and retailer. To minimize, the collaborative presence of all three is necessary.
- Percent shipped or complete = $\dfrac{Orders\ Shipped\ Complete}{Orders\ Shipped}$

- Percent delivered on time = $\dfrac{Orders\ Shipped\ on\ Time}{Total\ Orders\ Shipped}$

- Percent back orders = $\dfrac{Lines\ Backordered}{(Lines\ Ordered)}$

- Number of back orders by vendor per year.
- Percent of back orders per vendor per year.
- Average length of time to complete the back order per vendor per year.
- Suppliers chosen for cost and quality.
- Product design that strives for maximum performance and minimal cost.

Installing VMI and other collaborative technologies minimizes the effect of CPFR because the inefficiencies are removed from the system. There is definitely an added value to installing CPFR, which is seen in the Lean and Green Savings.

Lean Savings of CPFR

- The service levels increase due to better demand management planning in promotions and also in new item introduction. The higher service level allows for a .5% increase in sales from $943,720,533 × 1.005 to $948,439,136.
- This is an increase of $4,718,603 in sales. This increases the profit by 18% × $4,718,603 = $849,348.
- Inventory levels decreased by 3% in the 3PL program. This results in an inventory reduction of $156,628,357 × .03 = $4,698,851. The new inventory level is at $151,929,506.

- A 2% increase in sales occurs because of the added collaboration between manufacturer and distributor. This further increases the sales from $948,439,136 to $967,407,918.38. This is a sales increase of $18,968,78, which adds an additional $18,968,783 × 18% = $3,414,380 profit to the company.

- The new turns are $967,407,918 / $151,929,506 = 6.37.

- The lower cost of transportation is a result of the collaborative effort between supplier and buyer. The reduction is 1.5%, which allowed for a drop in transportation costs by 1.5% because of better rates. The norm is 6,766,667 gallons per year × $3.12 per gallon = $10,608,000. A savings of 1.5% = $159,120.

- The carrying cost savings is .266 × $4,698,851 = $1,221,701.

- Cost of capital freed up on the inventory is 2% × $4,698,851 = $93,977.

- The total Lean Savings is $5,738,526.

Green Savings of CPFR

- Damaged inventory cost represents .75% × = $4,698,851 inventory = $35,241.

- Obsolete inventory cost reduction is 9% × $4,698,851 inventory reduction = $422,896.59.

- The Green Savings of reduced gasoline usage is 1.5% × 6,766,667 gallons per year = 101,500-gallon-per-year reduction in gasoline usage. As in the TMS model, one gallon of gasoline produces 2,778 grams of carbon content in the atmosphere. This is equal to a savings of 101,500 gallons per year × 2,778 grams = 281,967,000 grams of carbon content reduction per year.

- As discovered in the TMS section, CO_2 emissions from a gallon of diesel are 2,778 grams × 0.99 × (44 / 12) = 10,084 grams = 10.1 kg/gallon = 22.2 pounds/gallon.

- This is a 101,500-gallon-per-year reduction in gasoline usage × 22.2 pounds/gallon = 2,253,300 pounds of CO_2 reduction into the air for the entire fleet per year.

- Reduced wear and tear of the existing highway system:
  - As in the TMS model, one five-axle tractor semitrailer has about the same effect on concrete pavement as 9,600 passenger cars.
  - Using a similar analogy in the TMS system, the Green Savings is 9 trucks × 9,600 cars × 5 days × 51 weeks = 22,032,000 reduced cars on the road per year.
- The total Green Savings is $458,137.97.

The total Lean and Green Savings is $6,196,663.

Collaborative Transportation Management

One last topic to cover is the use of collaborative technology on transportation. This follows the same VICS initiative. The technology is called Collaborative Transportation Management (CTM). The CTM is actually building the same relationships built with CPFR but now extending this all the way through the transportation area.

The CPFR ends on order confirmation. The order has been sent and confirmed. The CTM phase continues through the delivery and includes all freight payments. The next paragraph illustrates the performance initiatives.[1] These pilot projects have demonstrated that the benefits of CTM are very real and substantial. Shippers and receivers have documented gains such as these:[2]

- On-time service improvements of 35%
- Lead-time reductions of more than 75% (for example, average lead time for one customer was reduced from 7 days to 1.5 days)
- Inventory reductions of 50%
- Sales improvements of 23% through improved service to customers
- Premium freight cost reductions of greater than 20%
- Administrative cost reductions of 20%

Carriers have recorded equally dramatic benefits from CTM pilot projects, including these:

- Deadhead mile reductions of 15%
- Dwell time reductions of 15%
- Fleet utilization improvements of 33%
- Driver turnover reductions of 15%

References

[1]   http://www.VICS.org.

[2]   http://www.idii.com/wp/ctm.pdf or *White Paper Version 1.0,* developed by the CTM Sub-Committee of the VICS Logistics Committee, April 6, 2004.

14

Material Handling Technology, Voice Pick, and Pick to Light Technologies

Material handling is the movement, placing, and lifting of goods using tools or equipment to help the worker. The equipment ranges from hand-held UPC guns to forklifts, Automatic Guided Vehicles (AGV), and ultimately the Automatic Storage and Retrieval Equipment (AS/RS). Material handling is used to automate logistics in the receiving, picking, or packing process.

In the logistics automation process, subsidiary software fully automates the logistics process. The software ties in the hardware and software processing and allows for communication between the hardware and the computer. Broadly defined as Supply Chain Management and Enterprise Integration Software, the solutions encompass the following:

- Supply Chain Management (SCM) systems
- Warehouse Management Systems (WMS)
- Transportation Management Systems (TMS)
- RF systems for communications (RF)
- Enterprise Resource Planning (ERP) systems

The supply chain is composed of three flows. The first is the material flow, which represents the movement of the goods and services of the product. The second is the information flow between the trading partners, which creates a knowledge network within the company; here information is transformed into knowledge. This secret ingredient is what makes the company different from the competition. The third is the financial flow, which represents all the processing and efficiencies added in the system for all the documents from the initial PO to the invoice and the final settlement of payment.

To begin, simply follow the money. Similar to the Pareto process or 80/20 rule, following the money constitutes asking, "What is the process that is causing the most pain? What activity is taking the longest to perform? Where are the most people working?" These questions, when answered, highlight areas with the most potential for productivity and throughput improvement.

The process of data mining uncovers the most profound problems, which will reveal opportunities to get the biggest productivity improvement. In most operations, those problems are discovered in order picking. Comparatively speaking, order picking is the most expensive activity. Table 14-1 shows the range of cost of each operation in a typical warehouse.

Table 14-1 The Operations Cost of Each Area in a Typical Company

Shipping area	19% to 22%
Receiving section	8% to 12%
Order picking section	54% to 59%
Storage area	13% to 17%

A typical order picker can walk six miles a day. Order picking can be the most labor-intensive activity in the warehouse, with as much as 75% of the employee's time spent in activities other than picking, highlighted in Table 14-2. This is where a value stream map (VSM) for the warehouse process becomes necessary. The software algorithm discussed earlier highlights the best flow for warehouse workers to follow in order to minimize work time. After the workflow is defined, it is necessary to determine which activity is taking the pickers the longest to complete.

Table 14-2 Breakdown of Order Pickers' Time

Searching	8% to 11%	NVA = 9.5%
Picking	21% to 26%	VA = 23.5%
Walking	55% to 70%	NVA = 62.5%
Writing	4% to 5%	NVA = 4.5%
All Activity		Total Time = 100%

Batch Order Summary Sheets

Note in Table 14-2 that only 21% to 26% of the time is spent is picking, and this is the only value-added activity in the table. In terms of six sigma analysis, the value-added (VA) for the picking process is 24.5%, which leaves plenty of room for improvement. Farther down, the chart denotes yet another problem: walking. This is where change must happen because the non-value-added (NVA) time is 62.5%, which indicates wasted activity. To fix this problem, begin by adding information system support to the picking operations without fully mechanizing it.

The first technique to start with is to batch-pick using a shelf cart. Since as much as 62.5% of the order picker's time is walking, the more orders picked in the same walk sequence, the less time the picker will spend walking. This is one way to increase the VA component. When the largest NVA element is decreased, the VA part of the process automatically increases.

For example, cutting the walking time down by 50% increases the VA process from 24.5% to 24.5% / (1 − 62.5% / 2) = 35.64%. Therefore, picking more than one order at a time can dramatically reduce walking time and increase productivity.

In batch order picking, multiple orders are grouped into small batches. An order picker will pick all orders within the batch with one pass using a consolidated summary picking list. Usually the picker will use a multitiered picking cart, maintaining a separate tote or carton for each order or customer. Each tote is a different color, representing the different customers on the consolidated picking list. The more successful systems vary the batch sizes depending on the average picks per order or cubic size of the items per order. Batch order picking takes a group of orders and arranges the items on these orders in warehouse location sequence, allowing the order picker to make one pass using a Batch Order Summary Sheet. The system should sequence the order picking for the different passes through the aisles to minimize the distance the workers have to travel. Table 14-3 shows a typical batch order sheet used to pick items in a warehouse.

Table 14-3 Batch Order Summary Sheet

Pick Location	Quantity	Item	Cart Location
A101A	3	iPod Mini Pink	1- for Customer 1, 2- for Customer 4
B1028	4	iPod Cover	2- for Customer 2, 2- for Customer 3
B107B	4	FM Transmitter	1- for Customer 5, 3- for Customer 6

The summary sheet highlights customers and quantities for ease of use. The Green Code represents customer one, and the code (1- for Customer 1) tells the operator to fill a quantity of one and put it in the green tote. The Blue Code represents customer two, and the code (2- for Customer 2) tells the operator to fill a quantity of two and put it in the blue tote. The Purple Code represents customer six, and the code (3- for Customer 6) tells the operator to fill a quantity of three and put it in the blue tote. This visual aid is a lean management technique. It is harder for the forklift driver to make a mistake since he is simply matching colors and quantities to place in the correct tote.

The computer sequences the routes for the drivers so that the totes are as evenly balanced as possible. This allows for each order picker to have about the same amount of work. If there are multiple order pickers, the computer tries to match their skills to the warehouse location they work best in. This is a concept of cellular management, matching the skills of the laborer to the skills of the job. The computer also tries to minimize the time of picking by using the best utilization of the workers in the process. These improvements are found in the Warehouse Management System described earlier.

Mechanized Takeaways

The next step in the automation process is to mechanize the takeaway process. Here, employees place items on takeaway conveyors that move the load to the docking area rather than the forklift driver doing the task. This is a more expensive alternative but the employees will not have to travel as far and so are able to pick more lines per hour. An automatic sorting order by customer saves in labor time.

The increased picking rate translates to faster consumer response and fewer employees needed to pick the merchandise. Balance this against the added cost to find the new ROI for the process.

Advanced Order Fulfillment System Technologies

The next step in the process is to use advanced order fulfillment system technologies for the picking system. The technology falls into three areas: Logistics IT, Picking Technologies, and Material Flow Technologies.

The Logistics IT Order Fulfillment Systems will perform the tasks listed next. This list is generally considered a wish list composed of a comprehensive list of the components of the entire order fulfillment system.

- Auditing/Claims/Freight Payment—This involves keeping the records accurate for the retailer and the customer.
- CRM (Customer Relationship Management)—All the documentation is available for the customer to see either on the Internet or from the customer service department.
- DM (Demand Management)—The order fulfillment system needs to balance demand with supply. If this is not done, the system will have service-level issues.
- Distribution Resource Planning/Material Resource Planning (DRP/MRP)—To fulfill a customer's order, the proper inventory must be scheduled with manufacturing or distribution.
- E-Business Functionality—This functionality gives the system the anytime, anywhere capability. This can also be used to show alerts of pending problems in the supply chain.
- ERP—The enterprise needs accurate data to follow all the transactions of the order fulfillment system. Enterprise Resource Management will make this possible.
- Global Trade Management—This process is similar to the 4PL process in which several 3PLs are controlled by one 4PL for the process of global control.
- Inventory Management—Inventory management controls inventory item minimums, EOQs, and fixed-period or fixed-quantity buying.

- Load Planning—The process ensures that the procured item is brought into or out of the enterprise at the fastest schedule and minimum cost. This is possible only with leveled flow for receiving, shipping, and/or manufacturing.

- Modeling/Forecasting—Using the correct forecast model will make it possible to have the lowest inventory with the highest service level to ensure the delivery of the product.

- Optimization—This can make possible the development of the process to allow inventory or profit to run at the highest possible levels with the lowest overhead.

- Procurement—This is the act of buying and should be done with the best terms and dating. This enables the organization to be the lowest cost provider of goods in the competitive arena.

- Product Life Cycle Management—This process helps determine whether to continue to make or sell the product. Cost and profitability of the product is measured throughout the four growth stages: Introduction, Growth, Maturity, and Decline.

- Reverse Logistics—This is the process of returning the customer order because of a wrong shipment or a defect. Not controlling this cost bleeds the profitability of the value-adding processes of the company. Reverse logistics is a non-value-added function and should be minimized as much as possible.

- RFID—This technology minimizes labor and maximizes the speed of the system. In the fulfillment system, it would help in getting the product delivered expeditiously.

- Routing/Scheduling—The routing refers to the network optimization presented earlier. The largest cost is in the network of the delivery of the product. Lower cost and faster delivery will magnify the difference between competitors.

- Security—If the customer feels unsafe buying the product, he will go elsewhere and sales will take a hit.

- Supplier/Vendor Management—This focuses on the collaborative efforts of the distributor with the suppliers and customers. It is all about partnering with suppliers to maintain the best compatible set of processes for both the supplier and the distributor or retailer. This enables the procurement process.

- Supply Chain Management—This is the largest cost for most companies. It is the movement of goods from raw material to product creation, disposition, and finally disposal of the product. There are a lot of flows in supply chain. These include the following:

- Information flow—the information needed to properly forecast and deliver the product
- Product flow—the movement of the product
- Financial flow—the procurement process

- Sustainability—This process uses the least amount of resources possible while meeting goals. Creating a lean environment with green sustainability accomplishes this task.
- Transportation Management System—In the world of procurement, saving mileage means delivering merchandise at a lower cost more expeditiously.
- Warehouse Management System—The system smoothes the labor schedule throughout the warehouse so that the merchandise can be received and picked at a faster rate. This allows for employing fewer personnel.
- Wireless/Mobile Technology—This system allows for 24/7 connectivity with personnel, "anytime and anywhere." This definitely acts as a stimulant to the supply chain by keeping all processes monitored.
- Yard Management—This acts as a product identifier in the yard which facilitates location, storage, and retrieval for procurement processes.

Picking Technologies are used to enhance the procurement system and enable faster throughput with better quality. This process is enabled only through the use of technology. The more commonly used technologies are listed here:

- Voice Picking—The WMS that allows the computer voice to regulate the flow to control the movement of the employee in the warehouse.
- Pick to Light—The WMS that allows the lighting on the bin to regulate the flow to control the movement of the employee in the warehouse.
- RF Pick Cart—The concept of using the RF gun to verify each pick or receipt. This helps maintain the highest accuracy of the procurement picking process.

- A-Frames—The system in which gravity drops the product at the base, allowing employees to go through the aisle and pick the product needed. The process speeds up the picking procurement process.
- Order Picking Robots—Mechanization of the process without the aid of a human.
- Automated Storage Retrieval Systems (AS/RS)—A fully mechanized system with high upfront costs but that enhances the picking procurement system.

Material Flow Technologies are used to control the flow of the goods in the warehouse. In its truest sense, it is considered a lean technology because it minimizes the amount of travel through the warehouse. In every economy, the fastest growing cost component of warehousing and order fulfillment is labor cost. The transportation cost of warehouse and fulfillment is approximately 35% to 40% and the logistics systems cost is approximately 54% to 66%. This can be further broken down into three categories:

- The inventory cost is 21% to 26%.
- The administrative cost is 3% to 5%.
- The warehouse fulfillment costs are 30% to 35%.

The use of Lean Six Sigma can be used to analyze the process to add more value to the operation. Technology, graphs, and charts are excellent tools to use in determining which processes are causing the most problems. Further, considering RF, Pick to Light, and voice-picking systems can increase productivity and enhance VA activity levels.

Order Fulfillment System

Order fulfillment represents the flow of information in the procurement process. It begins with the beginning of the order and extends to the final payment for the product. Modifications and changes are expensive and cannot safely be undertaken without a thorough understanding of the entire system.

- Product Inquiry—This involves the initial inquiry about offerings, visit to the Web site, and catalog request. This option maintains information on past customer purchases so that it can show options that can be considered by the customer in the future. If an item is out of stock, the system shows that there are items similar to the out-of-stock items that can be shipped immediately. If the customer is not interested in similar items, it will notify the customer of the date the item will be available. The Web site also offers up-selling opportunities.

- Sales Quote—This includes the Request for Quote (RFQ), which allows for quote creation with promotional credits and volume discounts factored in. The quote is also based on budgetary and availability constraints. The budgetary constraints are based on the buyer's credit history.

- Order Configuration—This configures a product based on the customer specifications. This value-added process performs the postponement option in distribution. The product is configured as the customer order comes into the shipping horizon.

- Order Booking—This step covers the formal order placement or closing of the deal using the customer's purchase order. The purchase number shows total dollars ordered and amount of credit left. The system must be very user-friendly.

- Order Acknowledgment/Confirmation—This involves confirmation that the order is booked and/or received. This is normally an e-mail sent just after the booking. The confirmation shows all future delivery times and any out-of-stocks.

- Billing—Billing is the presentation of the commercial invoice/bill to the customer. The billing procedure should also give allowance to members who pay within 30 days. The norm is 1% within 30 days or 2% over 30 days. The billing should also show all the future bills due and the current account payable in dollars.

- Order Changes and Order Processing—After all orders are ready to be processed, they are sent to the warehouse for filling and delivery.

- Shipment—This includes the shipment and transportation of the goods. The shipment process should use an Advanced Ship Notice to notify the customer of what product is in the shipment and that the shipment has been shipped.

- Delivery—The delivery of the goods to the consignee/customer. The important part of this concept is the scheduling options for the customer. Delivery must comply with customer expectations and needs, as well as transportation options according to delivery time-of-day.

- Settlement—This is the payment of the goods received. It is performed with the terms agreed to with the vendor. It is usually prepaid or collect. There may also be extra terms on the merchandise such as extended dating.
- Returns—In case the goods are filled wrong or have quality issues, the merchandise will be returned to the vendor. Each vendor can determine the requirements for this reverse logistics function. These are the four options generally used:
  - The vendor will pay for the return of the merchandise.
  - The vendor will charge a service or return charge. This may also include the cost of freight and restocking.
  - The vendor will give options for salvaging the product.
  - The customer must take a picture of the product's damage and send this to the vendor.

Recall from Table 14-1 that the picking operation has the highest value-added of 21% to 26%. Picking results in the highest non-value-added activity, walking, which is 55% to 70% of the order-picking time. The use of technology can increase value-added and decrease non-value-added in the picking process.

Picking without automation requires the use of paper. Picking by paper decreases picking rates by 30 to 60 lines per hour, depending on the industry and complexity of the operation. It requires careful reading of each document in low-light conditions. In today's competitive environment, it is necessary to utilize the available technologies to decrease errors and increase speed.

The Installation of the RF System

To improve the process, install the RF system. RF technology is the least expensive way to introduce automation in the warehouse. The RF system begins with receiving and unloading merchandise. It is then staged on the receiving floor and a piece count is verified. Full pallets of merchandise are labeled with a bar-coded license plate for tracking. The employee scans the tote after all the items are scanned and places it on the pallet. This creates the shipment identification file. This file allows for the following:

- Tracking of shipments
- Monitoring of carrier performance
- Reduction in paper documentation
- Receipt of multiple POs at one time

The scanning of the pallet will also give the receiver the priority of the merchandise on the pallet. It will provide the status of the shipment by showing the following information:

- Out of Stock—restock immediately
- On Sale—restock immediately
- Central Stock—send to other centers
- Discontinued—do not stock, return to supplier
- Replenishment Inventory—Not imperative so there is no rush to stock

If the merchandise is a new item, the scanner will scan the bar code for the UPC number. The new number is looked up and entered into the scanner. This process updates the table for associating UPC numbers with internal numbers.

Material will be expedited to stocking locations based on the status code provided. The license plate is scanned per pallet, so the employees know what product is on what pallet and the location of each pallet. Each item, carton, or bag is labeled with the appropriate bin location number. The RF system will track all locations within the warehouse. The system will recognize all empty overstock locations.

The Receiving Process and the Stocking Process

When merchandise is received, the RF system will search the warehouse for an empty location based on the size and weight of the pallet. The scanner will display the exact location the operator is to use to put away the merchandise.

At the stocking location, the operator scans the item again before putting it away. The location tag is scanned on the rack to make sure that the item is being placed in the correct spot. If the employee is in the wrong location, the WMS system shows an invalid location code on the scanner. This is an excellent way to cut down on errors in the system. If the location is correct, the operator places the merchandise in the bin. The operator verifies the quantities and keys it in the scanner. The receipt file is updated and the operator returns to the dock for the next pallet. The scanner will determine the sequence of put-away to reduce travel time and distance.

Here are some other considerations for order filling:

The forklift operator is directed to the location from which over-stock is to be pulled via display screen on the scanner. The scanner sequences the locations to be pulled in order by priority and for the shortest distance. There will be opportunities to fill member orders from overstock locations. The RF system will search locations to

- Combine bin replenishment and order filling with one move
- Avoid returning partial pallets to overstock—Automatic Let Down
- Fill orders requiring a full pallet of merchandise
- Remove partial pallets from overstock, opening locations for the storage of full pallets
- Scan the sequences of the locations to be pulled in the order by priority and for the shortest distance and time
- Direct the driver to the correct shipping door by the use of the scanner.

RF Productivity

The RF productivity level is generally within 99.2 to 99.6 increase in accuracy of the picking system. The RF picking productivity also increases to around 50 to 100 lines per hour. In a batch environment, the savings in number of picks is phenomenal because the outdated system resulted in picking the same items over and over again.

RF Picking System Metrics

- The RF system is acceptable to employees because they receive higher pay for increased productivity.

- Order filling experiences the greatest increase in productivity because orders are continuously filled with little distraction from other tasks. The only limit is the speed the worker could scan, fill, and walk. The average time needed to fill an order decreases by 40%.

- Productivity should be around 50 to 100 lines per hour as an average, depending on the type of product and the warehouse environment. The manual productivity with the use of paper is normally 30 to 60 lines per hour. This is an average of 66.66% savings in productivity.

- This is the least expensive way to start with the RF automation. At later stages, automation and other software can be tested for increased productivity. At this stage, any new productivity tools brought in to advance automation will assume the use of RF technology.

- Typical costs for hand-helds and related components range from $1,100 to $4,000 each, depending on the size, complexity, and environmental needs.

- Typical base costs for an RF system range from $30,000 to $80,000 including site analysis, consulting, and training.

- The average accuracy rate increases from around 99.2% without an RF system to around 99.5% or more, depending on the system design and the quality of the bar codes.

- The main issue with the technology is to the need for wireless access and the elimination of all dead zones in the warehouse. Site walk-off and site analysis require testing of all areas of the warehouse to make sure that the RF is not getting interference from other equipment in the facility. During this site analysis, a spectrometer is used to see whether any other device is giving off a 900 MHz signal that would interfere with the reader's 900 MHz signal.

Pick to Light Technology

When an order is delivered to the stocking area, it is delivered as a label. The label is then attached to the tote or container. The picker places the label on the container. The label is now scanned and this launches the picking process. The tote is put on a conveyor and goes to the first picker. The WMS has now configured the appropriate route and sequence the picker will follow as he or she picks the order for the customer. The entire order for that customer will now be picked into the tote or container.

Each operator works in a zone. The zone can also be configured by the computer. In the zone, the picker will scan the tote and the appropriate lights will turn on in the picker's zone. The entire picking process in is now visible to the employee. The lights will show the quantity to pick for each bin. After the worker has filled the bin, the picker will hit the confirm button and go to the next bin and start picking, hitting the confirm button when done. This process will continue until all the items in the zone are picked.

In the zone context, the picking of the order is called pick and pass. The operator stays in close quarters while picking the order. When done, he puts the tote on a conveyor and it is passed to the next picker, hence "pick and pass." In the world of lean, this is one of the best technologies. One of the eight wastes—walking—is almost eliminated because the worker stays nearly stationary. From this perspective, it is one of the greatest tools used to maximize worker productivity. Another advantage to the system is that it is visible to the manager. The worker's productivity and time of completion can be monitored on a real-time performance.

Light-directed order fulfillment systems use light indicator modules mounted to shelving, flow racks, workbenches, pallet racks, or other storage locations. Whenever product is needed from a particular location, the light indicator turns on, drawing attention where action is required. The operator picks the product quantity displayed. The operator then confirms the pick by pressing the lighted button.

Pick to Light works best in a piece-pick or broken-case-pick environment where there are high-density order picking areas. The general rule is if 80% of a distributor's item-level picking volume comes from 20% of the SKU base, Pick to Light is an ideal solution to optimize productivity and accuracy. Pick to Light can easily be configured to add performance and efficiency to many popular order-picking methodologies, including Order, Wave, Zone, and Batch picking techniques. Variations on light-directed technologies such as Put to Light or Pack to Light are ideal for high-speed sorting processes, in which a batch of orders is sorted to individual customer orders or used to maximize throughput for retail-store order distribution.

Pick to Light is acknowledged to be the fastest operator-based picking strategy available to execute broken-case quantity-order fulfillment operations. This is because the worker usually stands in a zone and has very little movement because the products are in close proximity. Ideal for team-based approaches like zone picking, the Pick to Light (P2L) solution increases the pick-rate productivity, accuracy, and cost efficiency of this labor-intensive operation by reducing the walk time, eliminating the reading errors, and simplifying the task throughout the pick process. Arguably, it is more expensive than Voice Pick or RF. This is why it is used based on the 80/20 rule. Only the 20% of the items which account for 80% of the volume use the P2L solution. A much smaller area configuration is needed for the P2L solution, but the entire area must be wired for the lighting.

Pick to Light Mechanics

The operator scans the tote, carton, or order bar code, which initiates the lights in the zone, as mentioned previously. The lights indicate where the order is to be picked and what quantity to pick for the active order. The item is confirmed picked by a press of the light/ button at the display. The tote is then passed to the next active zone to be completed until the order picking is done. The reason for using zones for P2L technology is that the worker is usually very busy. The worker does not move too far up or down his zone because the tote is usually delivered by a conveyor.

The employee fills smaller items and many more items are being picked per hour. The worker does not have time to walk too far so zone picking is the typical application. The dynamic balancing of zones is the key to high productivity. This is the result of the WMS system. Cellular technology allows for work to be done in groups by having expected work and individual productivity used to define zone groups and their size. P2L technology is for merchandise that will fit in a more compact area where employees can work in a fixed zone.

Voice Pick

Voice Pick can be used for almost all the warehouse functions. It can be used for receiving, stocking, replenishment, and shipping. One of the great productivity benefits of a voice-based system is that it allows operators to do two things at once, whereas other systems used in warehouses, such as paper or radio frequency guns, require the use of one hand on the gun with only one hand free. Many times, it is necessary to stop and read something before proceeding.

Each operator is given a voice-enabled RF device. These devices need not have screens or keypads—operators communicate with the system via headset. Managers use the WMS or middleware to assign operators work—jobs such as picking, put-away, replenishment, and truck loading. How this assignment process takes place is largely a function of the specific job, the specific skill of the workers, or the end result of the optimization of the work schedule from the WMS. For example, operators might be assigned to pick specific orders or load specific trucks based on their past qualifications and specified times of completing the work. Jobs are assigned priority codes based on the time of completion. The standardized job times for each worker can be used to schedule the entire day or might simply be used to assign picking or to place employees on the highest priority job.

With voice picking, the voice system directs the operator to perform each pick, giving directions to the pick location. The following is an example of a picking dialog:

It all starts with the voice training, which can last for up to 20 to 30 minutes. The system has to learn the user's voice inflection, tone, and speed. A computer voice directs the workers to their destinations in the warehouse. This gives the workers an environment in which they can have a hands-free and eyes-free operation. Work is transmitted from the host to the voice server and subsequently to the belt worn by the workers.

- Operators are guided by voice to a location and respond with a location check via digit(s). This can be either a UPC scan on the label on the bin or the operator responding with a voice command of the bin location.

- Operators are given quantity and respond with a verbal acknowledgement.
- Item verification with UPC check digit(s) is optional.

Guides to enhance the accuracy:

- Be cautions of inaccuracy due to confirming checks by digits of location before arriving and picking afterward from the wrong location. This is why some voice-directed systems make the user scan the location upon arrival.
- Inaccuracy occurs due to operators memorizing their SKUs and relating check digits instead of visually reading the check digits. This is done to cut down on the time of the picking operation. Any workers identified doing this should face loss of incentive pay per error.

Added Voice Pick functionality:

- Low- and high-hit-density environments work well with voice picking. The entire warehouse can actually be picked by one worker. If there are multiple workers, they should be assigned to sections in the warehouse to minimize their distance traveled. Work balancing and parallel picking can affect productivity. This again is the function of the WMS system. Its goal is to lay out the path for the worker in which it will minimize the workers' distance and time.
- The voice-directed picking system can be used to perform multiple warehouse tasks and receive multiple benefits:
  - It can be used in receiving to minimize the time of receiving. This can also cut the receiving-to-stock time that is part of overall lead time. Remember that cutting the lead time by one day can reduce overall inventory by approximately $3 million.
  - Put-away-to-stock is the second leg of dock-to-stock. If this can be shortened, all inventory gets into stock at a quicker pace and consequently improves service levels and also decreases the need for higher inventories.
  - Better error rate and speed in loading the picked stock into the outbound carriers can increase customer satisfaction by giving faster deliveries and reducing the cost of reverse logistics.

- There are two kinds of cycle counting: periodic and perpetual. In either case, the voice-directed picking system can help speed up the process. In the perpetual system, there is a quarterly count to see whether the system is actually working correctly. Use the voice-directed system to highlight all out-of-stock items and check whether the stock is really out. Check the sale items periodically to see whether the count has changed from the computer count. These self-checking techniques can be done daily by a small percentage of the workers after their main jobs have been completed. This keeps the checking process up to date.

- The voice-directed picking system can be used in cross docking to make it easier to match the receipts to the item file of the receiving company. The faster this matching process is, the more likely the cross-docking operation will be successful. This assumes that the item is out of stock and there is a pending order for the product. In the system not using cross docking, stock the item before picking it for the customer. In this scenario, the customer order may have been zeroed out because the shipment was sent before the item was filled. Cross docking knows in advance that the item is being received, and it can be taken from receiving and put on the customer outbound orders. The process creates an agile system able to adapt to changing conditions. In many cases, agility adds to customer satisfaction.

- It also has been noticed that worker motivation has increased because of the technology. The worker works at a faster pace and is paid incentives to perform the operation. As a result, there is less employee turnover.

- Other soft benefits derived from the Voice Pick system are the following:

  - A hands-free environment makes it easy for the worker to react and pick the merchandise.

  - The system provides real-time feedback for proactive management of people and processes. As the schedule changes, the entire staff is notified in real time.

  - As soon as the stock is entered or pulled, the system is updated in real time.

- Worker safety is improved in the warehouse because employees are more attentive to the operation. There are fewer distractions because of the hands-free environment.

- Training time is reduced considerably.

- The biggest cost benefit is the increase in efficiency and the increased accuracy. These two metrics have been the biggest contributor to the return on investment for the company.

Voice Pick Productivity Metrics

The typical costs for the system, the headset, and the related components range from $4,000 to $6,000 each, depending on the size of the warehouse, the complexity of the operation, and the environmental needs. With 50 employees in each warehouse who use the Voice Pick system, the cost for the headsets is 50 × 9 = 630 × $6,000. This represents a cost of $2,700,000.

The typical costs range from $80,000 to $225,000 per system, which also includes the site survey. The site survey is important because it is performed by the vendee or supplier of the software. If there are any dead spots in the warehouse, they must be found and rectified. If the dead spots cannot be resolved, performance in the voice-picking area is impossible. The communications network, server, chargers, and training and project services are also included in the pricing.

The productivity is typically 100 to 300 lines per hour with Voice Pick, depending on application. These figures were compiled during technology meetings with users:

- Increased accuracy: 99.9%-plus
- Increased productivity: 15% to 20%-plus

The average cost of a picking error for most wholesalers is in the range of $6 to $60. This is an average of the extra handling and reverse logistics cost.

With an accuracy of 99.8% using a voice-directed system and a conversion from an RF system in which the standard average of accuracy is 99.5%, the hypothetical wholesaler can now pick 500,000 cases per week with an error rate of two per thousand. This amounts to .002 × 500,000 × 52 = 52,000 errors per year. The analysis of the potential savings of the system is as follows:

- The old system had an error rate of .005 × 500,000 × 52 = 130,000 errors per year.
- The comparison of the error rate between the two systems is 130,000 − 52,000 = 78,000 fewer errors per year.
- Using an average of ($6 + $60) / 2 = $33 per year. The saving is represented as $33 × 52,000 = $2,574,000 annual savings. This more than pays for the cost of the system.
- The system cost is computed as ($80,000 + $225,000) / 2 = $152,500. Now add the total headset costs of $2,700,000 to the system cost. The total becomes an upfront cost of $2,852,000.

The ROI is now $2,852,000 / $2,574,000 = 1.1 years to break even. These figures are industry averages, but they show the possibility of absolute cost savings from the technology. The other thing to keep in mind is that after the first year, most of the cost of the equipment will have been paid, and the savings is still generated each year.

The previous explanation is a great introduction to the automated picking processes and its benefits. The Lean and Green increases in productivity include these:

- Training time cut by 50%. This allows for better employee cross-training. On vacation shifts and medical leaves, the staff is more efficient. This helps in the reduction of training time for new employees. Some of the employees are trained in two days when it took several weeks to fully train them in the past.
- Shortages and claims are reduced by 25%. This is a much more efficient use of the worker's time and minimizes the workload of the claims department. An average for retailing is .5% to 3% shortages and claims. Each 1% reduction in claims is equivalent to approximately $125,000 in savings. Assuming a 1.5% shortage and claims rate, the cost advantage for the reduced claims is 1.5 × $125,000 × 25% = $46,875.
- The returns and allowances have been reduced by 4%. This enables the staff to be more productive in not chasing the returns. The Lean cost of returns and allowances is 10% of the supply chain expense. This can be approximated as 10%

× \$954,373,200 × Gross Margin (18%) = \$17,178,717. The \$954,373,200 is the new revenue after the CPFR process. Reverse logistics accounts for 3% to 4% of a company's logistics cost.[1] It is also assumed that the cost of reverse logistics is 10% of the profit margin. The savings is now computed as the reduction of returns and allowances of 4% × \$17,178,717 = \$687,149.

- Warehouse labor hours dropped by 10%. A warehouse with 450,000 square feet of space would need about 125 workers using an existing WMS and RF system. This is not an exact formula so to be conservative the savings in employees is rounded to 1,000 employees. The 10% savings in voice-directed pick and stock operations allows for a savings of 100 employees, but to be conservative and for the purpose of this example, there is a reduction of 50 employees. Using 50 people with a savings of \$18 per hour and benefits of 25%, the total cost is \$22.50 per hour. Total savings is 365 days per year × 8 hours × \$22.50 × 50 people = \$3,285,000 in labor savings per year.

- Service levels improve slightly. Voice Pick is used not only to pick merchandise but also to stock the product into the stocking locations. The error rate goes down with this technology by a factor of .25%. The savings is much higher when an RF system is not used prior to the Voice Pick system. This is because a lot of productivity has already been added to the process because of the RF technology. For every 1% increase in error rate, the service level is decreased by .1%. In this example, the service level will be increased by .1% × .25 = .025% of sales. Assume that 1/3 of out-of-stock is lost to no sales. The added profit saving would be \$954,373,200 × .18 (GM) × .00025 = \$42,947.

Green Savings:

- The savings of 50 people is a 5% decrease in number of employees for 1,000 workers.
- There is less computer usage. Table 4-8 in Chapter 4, "Transportation Management System (TMS)," shows that 3,060 kWh × \$0.16 = \$490 dollars was saved in electricity usage by the reduction of one computer usage for the distribution center. With 50 fewer people the total reduction is \$24,500.

Lean Savings:

- The savings of 50 people on the payroll expense = \$3,285,000 in labor savings per year.

- Shortages and claims savings = $46,875.
- Returns and allowances savings = $670,320.
- Service-level increase to added profit = $42,947.
- Total Lean is $4,045,142.

Total Green of the voice-picking system:

- Less computer usage = $24,500.

Total savings of the voice-picking system is $4,069,642.

Conclusion summarizing the differences in the picking systems:

- Low- and high-hit-density environments work well with voice picking.
- Work balancing, slotting, and system layout, such as pick and pass or parallel picking, affect productivity and work best with Voice Pick and Pick to Light.
- Slow movers with large SKU counts and large real estate may best be served by RF picking.
- Medium movers with large SKU counts and large real estate may best be served by voice picking or light picking on a smart cart.
- Fast movers with high density may best be served by Pick to Light.
- No technology with human picking will currently outperform Pick to Light in close quarters.
- Broader applications with RF and voice for receiving, stocking, and so on enhance the value for these technologies, making them easier to justify.
- RF has a low cost of implementation and allows for flexibility, but it is not as productive as Voice Pick and Pick to Light.
- Pick to Light has the largest cost and is less flexible because you are picking in small zones. Usually you use the 80-20 rule: 20% of the inventory which accounts for 80% of the value may be a candidate for Pick to Light. This system may give the greatest accuracy compared to the other two technologies, RF and Voice Pick.

- Voice Pick has a high cost, but it is much less than Pick to Light. It is flexible because an order picker can go anywhere in the warehouse and use the system. Voice Pick is also accurate, and many times your greatest savings come from the accuracy of the system.

The employee picks the order after he has received instructions on location and quantity. Note that both hands are free. The P2L system also offers this advantage. The worker in the RF system usually has only one hand free because the other hand is used to hold the RF gun.

References

[1] http://scm.ncsu.edu/scm-articles/article/the-increasing-necessity-for-reverse-logistics.

15

The Visual and Visible Supply Chain

The visual supply chain and the visible supply chain mean different things in the world of logistics. It is important to note that the difference between the visible and the visual supply chain is often overlooked or not understood. The visible supply chain shows the network and allows the user to see the movement of traffic and bottlenecks. This visible display of assets on the move is important to the business planners. There is no simulation in the visible supply chain. The simulation is performed in the visual supply chain methodology.

The Visual Supply Chain

The visual supply chain systems simulate and animate the supply chain scenarios and network. The network may consist of a number of types. The description that follows will explain the types of networks used in the supply chain environment and will show the advantages of using the specific form of network.

The hub-and-spoke arrangement is one in which the warehouse delivers to an outlying center that is not as large as the central warehouse. The spoke acts as a relief warehouse when the transportation distances are large. This is an excellent way to extend the reach of the product delivery. The hub and spoke can also be used as a temporary bridge until expansion with another central warehouse in the area is possible. The hub can also act as a consolidation point for deliveries before they are delivered to the customer. The consolidation point could also receive merchandise from peddle runs from other main centers.

The regular Tier1, Tier2, and Tier3 warehouse allows the merchandise to be picked up at several centers. This is the network arrangement from the supplier's standpoint. Tier1 would represent the supplier-only exports. Tier2 implies that the supplier ships to a wholesaler who then delivers the goods. Tier3 represents the supplier having a distribution center network and also supplying the retailer. The advantages of the systems are obvious and the complexity of the system increases at each upgrade in the tiers.

Another network arrangement is the dead run, in which the merchandise is just delivered straight from the supplier to the retailer. This implies that the truck will come back empty. This is mileage for the supplier.

In the back-haul, the merchandise is delivered by a common carrier or the supplier's truck. It helps resolve the delivery back to the supplier with empty miles as in the preceding text. The system is more complicated than the dead run and it will increase lead times. The lead-time increase can range from a half-day to two days. The reason the lead time increases is due to the extra stops on the way back and also the additional lead time in receiving. Many times, the receiving personnel are reluctant to put away this merchandise first as compared to a common carrier load, which will charge demurrage if it is not unloaded at a specific time. The decrease in cost has to be weighed against the increase in safety stocks.

A consolidation-points network is one in which merchandise is consolidated for full freight charges, as compared to LTL freight rates. The system definitely offers transportation savings. The downside is the extra lead time and extra personnel needed to consolidate each supplier's merchandise before delivery.

The next network is the peddle run. It is usually used when the retailer wants to pick up the merchandise on their own truck close to its distribution point. It will follow a designated path before coming back to its home distribution center. The saving can be gained only with access capacity and when freight rates are less than those of the suppliers or common carriers.

Finally, there is dynamic routing, in which the retailer usually controls the delivery and it is picked up at predestined times from each supplier in a route that saves transportation dollars. The list is not exhaustive but includes some of the common network configurations.

To make the network analysis possible, the analytics must be input into the system. The system uses electronic information received through the Internet from its trading partners and suppliers in the visual supply chain. The data can also be read in the form of a dashboard. The system uses real demand data from the demand management system. The demand management system could be giving information on the current supply chain equilibrium or information from a trading partner. The inputs to the demand solutions program are used to balance the supply with the demand. A list of the inputs is as follows:

- Forecast method and smoothing—This includes the forecast model in use. It can be a moving average, a trend, a regression, or an exponential smoothing model.

- Seasonality method and smoothing—This includes the use of base indexing with three or more years of demand.

- The review of the statistical models—This can represent the class of fixed- and variable-period models introduced earlier. It may also represent a change in the forecasting model used in the past.

- OQ Order Quantity calculations and safety stock—This will be used, as introduced in the service-level option, in the demand forecasting. The example is $OQ = D * LT + k * MAD * .76$. This model includes all the safety stock and lead-time calculations with the required service level. This model will show the result of different simulations on inventory levels with changes in lead times or safety stock.

- Review of expediting opportunities—This should determine whether it's time to expedite or prolong the shipment. In modeling the event, the forecast program should show what ramifications to the network will result in changes to the ship dates. The ramifications are measured in total overall cost (TOC). Each change is associated with a change in TOC. The system gives you a chance to see all the network scenarios that will minimize the TOC.

- Review of any network changes and schedule changes—The network changes will result in road closings or different route configurations. The schedule changes will result from priority changes in the need of the merchandise at the designated times.

The supply chain network is a visual modeler which allows users to drag and drop changes to their network design. These changes can be used to see what strains are caused on the inbound or outbound network as changes to the system are made. Will deliveries be held up by the changes? Will customers miss their deadlines? What effect on the overall service level will these changes make to the system? Finally, the system highlights the new inventory scenario of the changed network relationship. Extra stock may need to be added to the inventory because of the network changes, which adds extra lead times to the system.

An entire supply chain can be designed and mapped against the Google Map service. Visually, the movement of goods and services is viewed at the actual street level or on geographical maps. The supply chain can be created by importing the shipment file and demand files from the system. The following issues can be resolved using the visual system:

- Inventory—What would a change in inventory policy do to the network as far as frequency of deliveries? Will it require more or less personnel? Would the added benefit subsidize the increase in cost?

- Sourcing—Which vendors or suppliers are the best choice to use? What are their locations and how does this influence the transportation costs? Is it best to follow the proverbial Keiretsu network of keeping the supplier as close to the facility as possible?

- Transportation policies—This issue can be included when seeking solutions to the future locations of warehousing and/or new hub-and-spoke opportunities. The choices will affect the network to the distributors and to the customers in an exponential fashion. It is also possible to measure what the effect of dynamic routing would be on the transportation policy.

The Visible Supply Chain

The visible supply chain will allow the common carrier network to be visible along the supply chain. It is used more for proactive planning because the results of decisions are simulated with the inputs.

The visible supply chain is more event-driven on the day-to-day activities. What is the best way to schedule the incoming shipment already on the way? Are there more important shipments that need to be brought in first? Incoming and outgoing deliveries are viewable on an integrated dashboard with the visible supply chain.

The supply chain becomes event-driven in the visual supply chain model because it will be motivated by Business Intelligence. The system notifies the user when there are problems with late shipments or adverse demand. It will even recommend solutions, if needed, using the analytics from the business intelligence module. The interesting part of this concept is that the manager will need to work on only the exceptions, freeing a great amount of his time to work on creative projects. The output of the system will also include score carding and evaluation of supplier performance. The performance will be measured in metrics and key performance indicators, tracking performance from last month or last year, as well as by industry.

The difference between visual and visible is because the terms are used almost interactively. An example of this is the use of Sterling Commerce visible supply chain software. The software measures critical bottlenecks and supplier performance along the way. It makes it easy to monitor and measure inbound supply activities. The system will include a dashboard of the integrated supply and demand. At any moment, purchase orders, shipment, and inventory information is available upon request. As supply disruptions occur, the system is alerted; it notifies the user through integrated business intelligence and offers intelligent alternatives.

The use of the business intelligence actually makes the system visual in some respects. When purchase orders on shipments are sent to the customer, several decisions should be made. Is it best to expedite the shipment, transfer from another warehouse, use a substitute item, or increase the purchase system's ordering? The system also automates supplier performance for score carding and evaluation. Score carding is accomplished with predetermined KPIs. The suppliers can also share the information with their customers, as well as retailers with their suppliers.

The shared information can show on-time delivery, damaged goods, and order fulfillment measurements. This allows for complete integration, flexibility, and configurability, with lower inventories and higher customer satisfaction. The visible supply chain is what makes the rest of the technologies introduced in the book more meaningful and easier to use.

16

Master Data Alignment and Item Synchronization

Master data alignment is sharing data within the supply chain between the trading partners. A common feature used between partners is electronic catalogs. The supplier and distributor and/or retailer can share item information for their catalogs. This is also much more than just sending data for a catalog change. This allows companies to share data to minimize the discrepancies of separate silos.

Item data accuracy is paramount in today's era of increased collaboration. These are some applications that require accuracy:

- Product Life Cycle Management (PLM)—PLM is a strategic business approach that applies a consistent set of business solutions in support of the collaborative creation, management, dissemination, and use of product definition information across the extended enterprise from product concept to end of life. It integrates people, processes, business systems, and information to create an environment in which companies can improve the efficiency and effectiveness of their product development programs. Normally, 50% to 85% of the cost of the product is committed in the design phase. Make sure the information is accurate at this phase.

- Digital Manufacturing—Digital Manufacturing represents an integrated suite of PLM tools that supports manufacturing process design, tool design, plant layout, and visualization through powerful virtual simulation tools that allow the manufacturing engineer to validate and optimize the manufacturing.

- Just in Time (JIT)—Just in Time programs ensure that there is no interruption in the supply chain. All data must be accurate and available in real time. As in manufacturing, the merchandise is delivered at the point it is needed at the assembly line.

- Efficient Consumer Response (ECR)—Creates an environment and tools that enable the distributor and supplier trading partners to work collaboratively to deliver superior value on the products and services they offer consumers. The benefits that retailers realized from Quick Response include the use of bar coding, data warehousing, EDI, RF, and RFID. The grocery industry initiated ECR in the 1990s. The requirements of ECR are efficient assortment, efficient replenishment, efficient new product development, and efficient promotions.

The Global Data Synchronization (GDS) and Electronic Product Code (EPC) are used together. Global data synchronization is an industry-wide initiative to create standardized formats for product information that can be shared globally and electronically by manufacturers, distributors, and retailers. This information would be housed in one data source. The EPC is the electronic product code for each item to identify the product by its unique number.

The number for the EPC is broken into four distinct fields. The first is the header. The second is the manager, which is the vendor code. The third is the SKU code, which could be used as a UPC number. The fourth is the serial numbers, which give each product with the same UPC number a unique number, or DNA. Each product is now unique.

If 12 bottles have the same UPC number, they will each have unique serialized numbers. If an RFID gun scans a carton of the same 12 bottles, each will be considered unique. This option can't be beat for productivity in inventory counting. The EPC is used in the concept of RFID, discussed throughout the book. The point here is that data is exploding. After it is sent out globally, it can't be taken back, so it must be of the highest quality and entirely accurate.

The accuracy and consistent data sharing for product and production details is lacking today. In fact, Capgemini's research found that more than half of the items in company systems contain incorrect data (for example, wrong values and duplicate or obsolete entries). Master data alignment is about improving this situation by having the product data across the various business systems consistent, complete, accurate, and available in a timely manner.

To make all this possible on a global scale, UCCnet, which is a subsidiary of the Uniform Code Council, was created. This is a not-for-profit company whose function is to facilitate industry-wide sharing of data by trading partners. The manufacturers who subscribe to UCCnet download their catalog information to the UCCnet's Global Registry. This information is a comprehensive detail of catalog information, as shown in Table 16-1. This table is a summary of the item configuration that can be saved in the data pool.

The advantage of this scheme is that it makes the supply chain more efficient and accurate. Let's take the example of the manufacturer. They have to send out price changes, new items, or catalog changes to all the customers worldwide. This is a daunting task. Today, with the B2B commerce sites, some larger retailers have portals connecting to the suppliers to send item detail information back and forth. An advantage is that the data on the data pool is straight from the supplier. It should be error free. This eliminated the errors in cataloging and also in customer pricing discrepancies. One of the biggest problems in out-of-stocks occurred when a supplier discontinued an item. The supplier hardly ever gave notice on a global scale, leaving the customers unaware of the change. Now the cancellation date is published in advance and sent to the data pool.

The global view of item synchronization is that all manufacturer information is sent to the Global Registry (GS1). GS1 stands for Global Standard 1 and it is the registry for all information to be stored in the common data pool. It gives the permission for the source, usually the supplier, to store the data, and for the recipient, usually the retailer, to receive the data stored globally. This creates a network connecting trading partners all over the world. It is truly a one-stop opportunity. The information is saved in a large information base called a data pool. The data pools are interoperable electronic catalogs of standard master data. This data consists of the master data information shown in Table 16-1. This is only a partial list of the data that can be stored in the data pool.

Table 16-1 A Partial List of the Data Stored in a Data Pool

UPC Number	Target Market	Return Good Code
Negotiated Cost	Order Multiple	Less Case Multiple
Inner Pack	Full Case Multiple	Vendor Name
Vendor Number	New Item Date	Harmonized Product Code
Manufacturer (GLN)	Start Available Date	Parent Item
Child Item	POS Description	Case Width
Case Weight	Case Height	Case Length
Unit Length	Unit Width	Unit Height
Retail Pack	Shelf Life in Days	Tihi (Tier × Height)
Cases per Layers in a Pallet	Cases Per Pallet	

The synchronized data will be used to populate forms or automate processes with the corporations. These processes need accurate and timely information to make them world-class. The following list shows some of the processes that can be automated with data synchronization:

> New items can be added to the catalogs with greater accuracy and speed. This requires accurate pricing, cube, weight, bullet descriptions, return code authorization, vendor number, unit, our cost, retail, height, width, length, UPC number, less case, inner pack, full case, and so on.

> Claims are a very important area needing accurate data. Otherwise, the claim is never settled or is settled wrongly. This is an area of great frustration for the customer. Item synchronization will always show the prices and promotional prices at select periods of time.

> Price Changes can be automated and sent out to all retailers at the same time. All the price changes are from a common source, which eliminates the chance of error.

> Shipping Errors are easily rectified with the accurate information. Many times an item is set up as a subitem from the supplier. The retailer may wonder why they got the product. This notifies the customer of the exact timing of the change.

> File Maintenance can be done through downloading new information from the supplier. It can be item- or vendor-related

detail. The information can range from change in cost to change in bulletined descriptions for the retailer files or electronic catalog.

Pricing and Dating from everyday low price or promotional periods are downloaded from the supplier to the data pool and eventually to the subscriber or the retailer. The extended dating for each sale can be downloaded for each promotion throughout the year. It is critical to keep this information synchronized from the supplier to the retailer.

Return Authorization is given by the supplier and this can change in time. Certain items in the line may have different return authorization codes. Some returns are merely marked as destroy and the supplier will refund the retailer.

Non-Stock Order Form is the order form used when the dealer or customer buys merchandise from the supplier that the distributor does not stock. These are usually direct to store delivery when a distributor is involved.

Receiving Reports can perform the triple-check for accuracy. The invoice will be checked against what the receiving report shows as the price. Then the purchase order will be checked against the receiving reports price. This minimizes the error rate and all prices are sent electronically from the data pool.

Credit Memo can show the amount of credit from the supplier for certain conditions. There may be adjustments for sale or everyday low pricing.

Catalog Cut & Description is for the companies using the electronic catalog or for promotions to be sent out as fliers. The information is sent and downloaded each time there is a change. This definitely has a large effect on the productivity of the catalog department.

Market Specials Form is used when the retailer or distributor has an offsite event for promotions. The customers may meet in a convention center for the suppliers to demonstrate what is new in their line for the next year. These are special prices and terms. The forms will automatically be filled out at the distributor's site because the data has been downloaded automatically to the distributor's item files. All they have to do now is print the form off for the customer and it is prepopulated with the correct information. This is definitely a step in the right direction for the productivity and Green Savings.

The next part on this master data alignment scheme after global data registry is to have unique numbers for all the items listed in the EAN.UCC system. The EAN stands for European Article Number and it is the counterpart of the UCC. With the introduction of the EAN.UCC, there exists a global registry of items called GTIN numbers. GTIN stands for Global Trade Identification Numbers. It allows for items made or sold globally to be numbered. It also dictates the level of packaging the item is sold in. It is possible to have an item number, a number for the container, and, if needed, a separate number for the pallet. The GTIN number is a 14-digit number indicating the following:

- The first digit is the packaging indicator, which in the following example, and for simplicity, will be a 0.
- The second digit in this GTIN is a 0.
- The supplier in this example was issued a six-digit GS1 company prefix of 123456. This tells everyone that the item belongs to XYZ Manufacturer.
- The supplier has five digits to assign an item reference number for that product. This is either a SKU number or the UPC number.
- The last digit is a single-digit "check digit." This is used in case the number is wrong, and the machines scanning this can use the authentication scheme to double-check the authenticity of the number.

Here's the example of the four fields of the 14-digit GTIN number:

First Field				Company Prefix		Item Ref #		Check Digit		
0	+	0	+	123456	+	00001	+	3	=	14 digits

The GTIN is a 14-digit number composed of four data standards. These standards are for the United States and Europe.

Table 16-2 shows the four standards.

Table 16-2 The Four Standards Used in North America and Europe

The **UCC-12 (UPC-A)** is a 12-digit number used primarily in **North America.**

The **EAN/UCC-8 (EAN-8)** is an 8-digit number used predominately **outside of North America.**

The **EAN/UCC-13 (EAN-13)** is 13-digit number also used predominately **outside of North America**

The **EAN/UCC-14 (EAN/UCC-128 or ITF-14)** is a 14-digit number used **to identify trade items at different packaging levels.** Scan the case to discover how many items are inside. This saves from having to open the case and count the items.

As mentioned previously, the GTIN is composed of four fields:

- The packaging indicator, I, is the first digit.
- The company prefix is the next seven digits and is set to 0 + Company Prefix 0 + C. In this case each unique company indicator is five digits long and is represented as C.
- The next five digits make up the serial number, U.
- The last digit is the check digit, C.
- The layout is as follows: I0CCCCCCUUUUUC.

Table 16-3 shows the data structure for the UCC-12 using the GTIN configuration with the various packaging levels.

Table 16-3 The Two Ways of Representing the Packaging Levels for the UCC-12

Showing the item reference for higher levels of packaging can be done in two ways. The first example is when the package indicator is always 0; then the serial number must be different for each level of packaging, as below.

UCC-12	UPC or UCC-12	GTIN
Each	012345633317	00012345633317
Case	012345633324	00012345633324
Pallet	012345633331	00012345633331

The second example is when the package indicator is different for each level of packaging because the serial number is the same for each level of packaging, as below.

UCC-12	UPC or UCC-12	GTIN
Each	012345633317	00012345633317
Case	012345633314	20012345633314
Pallet	012345633311	40012345633311

Note that at each level of the packaging the GTIN is different. The difference is achieved by either a different packaging indicator or a different unrelated item reference. It is possible to make both the packaging indicator and the unrelated item reference different for each level of packaging. The one area of caution is that the packaging indicator is always 0 at the lowest level.

The check digit is very important for readers because they must be able to differentiate between various bar codes and their representations. The check digit guards against fraudulent or bad bar codes. The following example shows how you can calculate the check digit for the UPC-12 number 012345633317. The check digit is equal to 7 and is the last digit in the bar code.

- UPC = 1st + 3rd + 5th + 7th + 9th + 11th = 0 + 2 + 4 + 6 + 3 + 1 = 16.
- Multiply the answer by 3, which yields 3 × 16 = 48.
- UPC = 2nd + 4th + 6th + 8th + 10th = 1 + 3 + 5 + 3 + 3 = 15.
- Add the 48 and the 15 = 63.
- What number is used to round the 63 to a number divisible by 10? Answer is 7. So 63 + 7 = 70. The check digit is 7.

The calculation for the GTIN is the same as discussed except that there are 13 digits to calculate rather than the 11 in the UPC.

Figure 16-1 shows the bar codes used in each of the four data standards.

A major advantage for item synchronization is the drill-down procedure in this master data alignment scheme which groups the data into categories. Similar items are stored in many departments, causing double the inventory. This occurs as a result of multiple orders being placed by different department heads with little communication between them. Each has a preferred method for naming products. There are companies, such as Byte Manager, that specialize in categorizing items to avoid this issue.

The first level is the department, the second level is the category, the third level is the subcategory, and the last is the product. This is very important in data management for analysis and accuracy. For example, one department is labeled for tools. A category could be hammers, the subcategory could be all claw hammers, and the product would be the specific type of claw hammer carried by all the vendors.

Figure 16-1 The GTIN family of data structures[1]

This information is very important when using category management techniques to analyze the category movement in a company or store. It is also important to include in the advertising analysis of promotions. The content management is so important it is recommended that departments, such as the Electronic Publishing Department, be renamed to Content Management Department as it is responsible to act as librarians over all company content.

References

[1] GTIN info http://www.gtin.info. See also the following: http://www.gs1us.org/ http://www.gs1.org/barcodes/technical/idkeys/gln Σhttp://www.gs1.org/1/gtinrules/.

17

Internal Supply Chain

Environmental Facts

This is an excerpt from a Perspective Software white paper:[1] "Paper—it's used and wasted every day. Hundreds, thousands, millions of sheets are printed, written on, exchanged between hands and then discarded to help an organization operate. In the United States, an average office worker uses 10,000 sheets of copy paper each year, and a total of 4 million tons of copy paper are used annually across the country."[2]

The Environmental Paper Network points out, "Paper production causes a wide range of environmental impacts, so by using less of it you can press many environmental buttons at once: you can reduce your pressure on forests, cut energy use and climate change emissions, limit water, air and other pollution, and produce less waste."[3]

Printing paper also means an increased use of ink and toner that are toxic for the environment. More than 350 million ink and toner cartridges are thrown out annually in the United States. Toxic ink and toner aren't free. Companies spend a small fortune on printer ink and toner every year.[4]

Designing a Paperless Environment with Software

The current environment is a poor use of the supply chain system by allowing paper to travel the entire value chain. Today, people make copies of their paperwork and store it for later use. First of all, it takes time and motion to go to the copy machine and make the copies. Time is wasted when people stand at the copy machine and talk. Add into the consideration the time and expense involved in hand-delivering mail to each employee in the company. The combination of time, space, and wasted printing supplies adds up to a key area for improvement along the supply chain. Approximately 10% of office space could be saved by using digital data from the Enterprise Content System, and every choice made in the office affects other areas along the supply chain, such as the post office.

A proactive green policy is a sign of good governance. It gives a favorable brand association and a positive image for staff. It gives the management a chance to reduce waste and to electronically capture the paper-flow process. This is called workflow and it's used for creating a measurable environmental impact that cannot be overstated. The manager can see the entire set of workflow daily because it is sent to his computer electronically. He can see the overload areas and inefficient processes and see how long each person is taking to perform the task at hand.

For companies with an incentive plan, this really helps in maintaining lean goals. With quantifiable, documented evidence of how each person is doing in the company, employee reviews and progress tracking during training programs is simplified. The goal here is to create a paperless office and measure its performance with a series of metrics to create a world company with a world-class environment.

These waste issues can be resolved through the use of document management systems that provide storage, versioning, metadata, and security, and boast indexing and retrieval capabilities. Document Management (DM) is an electronic system or software that stores and tracks documents, images, and scanned paper documents. Enterprise Content Management (ECM) is the parent of Document Management. Document Management is a subset of Enterprise Document Management Systems. ECM covers document management, Web content, and collaboration with other companies' data, workflow management, and scanning. All of these systems are controlled through Digital Asset Management (DAM), which performs the following functions:

- Storage—This stores documents in places where they will be easily accessible. It will also mark when the item was saved. This speeds up file retrieval through date searches. Some of the ECM uses cloud computing to either store or back up the data.

- Retrieval—This allows for abbreviation of the filename that will represent what the file is. For instance, the monthly billing for April reads: "Monthly Billing April 2011." This makes it easier to find. Complicated queries with Boolean expressions of AND, NOT, and OR can be performed.

- Distribution—This allows for sending as an e-mail attachment, or a protected document, and allows for sending to all or a select few. There are many other options that can be used for the distribution for internal and external collaboration.

- Security—There is a secured firewall with all the password combinations and protection.

- Work Flow—This can help management detail how each worker is performing the tasks. They will be able to see the problems and queries in each of the work centers. In some of the software, a simulation teaches how to expand and maximize the workers' performance by setting up the parameters of a shorter work time and asking the system to simulate the scenario and see whether this is possible within the current work-flow environment. If the system comes up with a better solution, it will show the new network and new chain of responsibility.

- Collaboration—This will enable the ECM to communicate to trading partners on scheduled or timely bases. The option exists to allow outside partners to view files and data and vice versa.

- Versioning—This saves older versions and updates documents into newer version formats. This process can be automated or kept as an on-permission basis.

- Publishing—This version allows for the creation of a Web page using available data. It can be published by being sent as an HTML document.

- Content Virtualization—This is an important part of the productivity improvement initiative of the work-flow analysis. The system uses graphics to represent data to enhance the analysis.

- Searching—This is all about indexing the products so that it is easier and faster to retrieve the data. Are keywords an option? How many keywords are linked to the item? Herein lays the ultimate paradox: If an item has too many keywords linked to it, the search process is slowed. However, having the item indexed properly maintains specific records. There must be a happy medium. Searching uses a few key concepts in its quest to represent all types of queries:

- Normalization—This is the process used to expand the abbreviations and acronyms to full, uniform, and correct terminology. For instance, one supplier may list black ballpoint pens using the abbreviations "Black," BLK," "Pen Black." Another supplier may refer to the same pen as "Ballpoint, BK." Through normalization, both abbreviations are expanded to the uniform description "black ballpoint pen."

- Rationalization—This incorporates only the data that every supplier provides. The common standard is to expand to include all content categories.

- Categorization—Items are categorized so that the computer can sort all categories of the item depending on how specific the search is. For instance, in searching for drills, all power and cordless drills in the category from all vendors are listed. A more specific search of cordless 3.8" drill will result in a list of all the suppliers for this size of cordless drill. This is an excellent technique for using category management in a marketing scheme. An entire category can be sorted and its performance measured in comparison to others over a specified period. Available categories include the United Nations Standard Product and Service Classification (UNSPSC) agency, which attempts to classify all products or the National Hardware Retail Association (NHRA), which attempts to break up all the items into departments like Sporting Goods, Toys, Tools, Building Products, Electrical, Plumbing, and so on.

Mobius Software: A Division of ASG Software

Mobius software allows for a significant reduction in the number of copies used in the company and also forces proactive decision making. The system digitizes printed documents off the mainframe computer. To access a report, click the Mobius icon, which opens a screen separated by departments. Click the department of choice, and document retrieval by name or document number is permitted. The software allows for scanning and printing any section or all of each document.

The ability to become more proactive in the use of the software becomes more apparent as the software options are explored. In many companies, data is listed only in a printed document and not on file. This system performs data mining on the electronic documents. For instance, if a document lists all the sales of the entire country, it can be separated out by division and then by sales representative. The data can be filtered by most logical operators. For instance, to download all sales above $300,000 for the months of January through March in the Northeast region, the digital information is passed to an Excel spreadsheet, Access database, or SQL database. The analytics needed to show better presentations to a management group or employees is easily accessible. After the data is downloaded, it can be presented in a graph, it can be sorted, or all kinds of analytical analysis can be performed on the information to add to the knowledge base.

System Advantages

Saving in paper use becomes apparent. When six 50-pound boxes of green screen paper are used daily for miscellaneous reports, Mobius cuts the paperwork by 50%. This is a savings of six 50-pound boxes of landscape paper per day. This represents $6 \times 50 \times 360 = 108,000$ pounds of paper saved per year. The letterhead paper has a savings of two boxes per week. The savings here are $2 \times 50 \times 52 = 5,200$ pounds of paper saved per year. The total for all the forms is 113,200 pounds of paper saved per year.

Lean Savings

- The 113,200 pounds of paper saved at $0.50 per pound[5] is $56,600 saved per year.
- The programming change backlog time is a soft issue. With Mobius programming change options, six months of time can be saved by permanently changing how to view forms, group

documents, or sort data. The data can come from existing reports that may be the only depository of the data. Two of 25 programmers can be taken out of the program change stream. Each programmer typically makes $55,000 per year with salary and fringe benefits. This is an $110,000 savings per year on personnel costs. The purchasing and marketing group also becomes more productive, but it is hard to put a direct measurement on this.

Total Lean is $110,000 + $56,600 = $166,600.

Green Savings

- From Tables 4-3 and 4-6 in Chapter 4, "Transportation Management System (TMS)," a tree produces roughly 800 pounds of paper. Dividing 113,200 by the 800 equals a savings of 142 trees per year.
- As documented in Table 4-7 in Chapter 4, a healthy tree stores about 13 pounds of carbon annually.[6]
  - Savings in CO_2 is 13 pounds.
  - It may take up to 10 years before the tree can start producing at the ultimate level. So for every tree cut, it will take up to ten years to hit this maximum 13 pounds of CO_2 out of the atmosphere. With an average of five years to represent the loss of carbon dioxide absorption, there are five years of loss for each tree cut and replanted.
  - The amount of extra CO_2 taken out of the atmosphere is 13 × 5 × 142 = 9,230 pounds of CO_2 per year.

The Lean and Green summary of the Mobius system is $166,600 saved in paper and 142 fewer tress cut, enabling the environment to extract 9,230 extra pounds of CO_2 per year.

Oracle Content Management

Oracle Content Management adds further credence to the Lean and Green Savings of document management. The paper brings into perspective the internal savings which is considered internal supply chain savings. Now it is necessary to deal with the external supply chain events in a more expeditious fashion in order to lower the cost of operations.

By permission from Oracle, included here is the actual white paper that demonstrates the Lean and Green Savings that can be gained through the use of Content Management.

Go Green with Oracle Content Management[6]

An Oracle White Paper

November 2009

INTRODUCTION

Organizations are constantly looking for ways to cut costs, but don't realize that those cost cutting measures may also have positive environmental effects that can increase goodwill and shareholder value. Oracle Fusion Middleware solutions provide tremendous return on investment, but also make your organization more environmentally conscious or "green" by cutting the consumption of electricity, paper, fossil fuels, and the emission of greenhouse gases. Many organizations around the world are utilizing information technology solutions to realize their green initiatives. To quantify these efforts, Oracle has created the Oracle Document Management Green Calculator. This online tool, and the accompanying spreadsheet, will enable you to see how your organization can effect environmental change by moving printed information online. This document will help explain the tool and provide background information on how these figures were arrived at.

> *"While data center greening hasn't really become a play in this software sector yet, the reduction of information and content in various formats that are moved into digital storage shows what ECM can offer green initiatives."*
>
> John William Toigo, Information Week (2007)

There are many government-sponsored green initiatives currently underway already. For instance, in 2003, the United Nations Economic Commission for Europe enacted a strategy to form a "Roadmap for Paperless Trade.[1]" This sought to eliminate the paper bottlenecks created by customs during the trading process. The commission discovered that by moving from paper document processes to electronic technologies, they increased security and transparency in supply chains and provided both government and private sector with higher revenues and costs savings of billions of dollars a year.[1]

> *"Green IT: This is a path that more and more companies are taking as a socially responsible strategy."*
> Carl Claunch, Gartner Group (2008).

Several local governments within the European Union have also adopted similar green initiatives. In 2005, Styria, Austria, launched its green initiative for reducing paper in favor of managing content electronically. Styria reduced the time consuming and expensive generation and circulation of paper used during the parliamentarian process. Additionally, this enhanced the transparency of parliamentarian processes and public access to documentation. It was the first workflow program in Europe which allowed parliamentarian work without the use of any paper. Parliamentarians use this program from the first day of a new idea or legislative initiative until the final decision and voting of the parliament. This program saves up to € 200.000 per year and hastens the legislative process by reducing the average amount of time for producing new laws from two months to two weeks.

Another effective example of government green initiatives can be found in Germany, which has established an eGovernment-system for the handling of the "Ordinance on Records of Proper Waste Management," now mandated by German law. Using this green paperless system, a formerly very complex administrative procedure containing a number of forms and handwritten signatures was replaced by a more manageable electronic method. This method contains a qualified electronic signature methodology as well as the mandatory archiving of digital certificates, thereby improving workflow. The rationalization and simplification caused by the project benefits both the public and private sector. A nation-wide deployment could lead to savings of approximately 50 M.€ ($63.6 Million US) per year, 80% of this sum being saved in the private sector.

Oracle Content Management Solutions:

Universal Content Management
Imaging and Process Management
Universal Records Management
Information Rights Management
Document Capture
Distributed Document Capture

ORACLE CONTENT MANAGEMENT

Oracle Content Management enables organizations to control the creation, routing, approval, and publishing of documents. Many organizations use documents in paper format such as invoices, patient records, insurance forms, and corporate policies. These documents are typically copied and dispersed to wherever they are needed— often to too many disparate locations. By converting these paper based documents and processes to electronic procedures, a single copy can be accessed electronically from any location without it being printed, shipped and then later archived or discarded.

Calculating Return on Investment

With content management, return on investment is typically calculated based upon processing speed. By processing invoices faster, an organization requires fewer people to process those invoices, which makes up the largest savings. Often there are additional savings due to cash flow or discounts. An accounts receivable group will show how cash inflows or days sales outstanding have improved. An accounts payable group will demonstrate how invoices are paid faster, taking advantage of discounts for early payment. A large real estate company reduced invoice processing from $33 per invoice to $2.75 per invoice using Oracle Content Management. Most of this gain was due to processing invoices faster by having them electronically available in the transaction processing screens. By processing invoices faster, they were able to reduce their invoice processing team from 25 people to 5 people. Another company reduced A/P cycles by 20+ days, reduced their billing cycle by months, and is saving at least $100,000 annually, and has been able to provide substantial ROI within months.

Call centers will show how customer call times have dropped based upon faster answers to customer questions, and how leaner staffing can address the same call volume. A large telephone utility cut call center times by as much as 75% by implementing content management.

Beyond faster business processes, there are other ways to show return on investment as well—paper costs, shipping costs, and storage costs, while not necessarily the largest returns, can nonetheless contribute to the overall return on investment a company can realize from content management. These areas have direct correlation to an organization's green initiatives by reducing the usage of trees and oil, and reducing the emissions of carbon.

CUSTOMER PROFILES
Embry Riddle

Embry Riddle is an aeronautical university with 130 locations worldwide. Universities are highly information intensive—applications, financial aid forms, insurance documents, transcripts, housing information—admitting and tracking each student generates a tremendous amount of information. Embry Riddle typically kept a copy of each document at the campus where the student attended, and forwarded a copy to the central office. Often these documents would also have to be duplicated at other offices. By implementing Oracle Content Management, Embry Riddle was able to have a centralized server to store the information, where any location could access it. This made student, loan and payment processing faster, and also cut paper and shipping costs.

Paper Costs

Applicants, 2007		15,473
	Average Pages	
Application	30	
Transcripts	10	
Institutional Supporting Documents	20	
Other Supporting Documents	5	
Total	65 [× 15,473 =]	1,005,745 [pages]
Accepted Students, 2007	10,315	
	Average Pages	
Financial Aid Forms	5	
Transfer Credit Documents	5	
Academic Evaluations	5	
Military Approvals	5	
Total	20 [× 10,315 =]	206,300 [pages]
Existing Students, 2007		27,421
	Average Pages	
Intercampus Transfers	5	
Web Based/forms	5	
External Documents	5	
Total	15 [× 27,421 =]	411,315 [pages]
Duplicate Copies at HQ		
Student Folder		1,005,745
Total Pages	2,629,105	
Paper Rate	$6/Ream	$0.012 [per page]
Other Print Costs (ink, maintenance)	$3/Ream	$0.006 [per page]
Total Paper Cost	$47,324	

Embry Riddle also estimates a $100,000 annual savings in shipping costs.

Swedish Medical

Swedish Medical is a care provider collection of 4 hospital locations and 70 clinics located in Seattle, Washington. Content produced includes photocopies of insurance cards, consent forms, paper records, reports, patient health information and business information. At Swedish, paper documents were shipped and stored, faxed and couriered between clinics, hospitals, and offsite storage. With Oracle Content Management, electronic faxes are ingested into their content management system, resolving redundancy, image quality and access time issues.

While implementing Oracle Content Management, Swedish, along with their partner ImageSource, also integrated it with their Epic Electronic Medical Records System. Switching to Epic required a vast amount of retraining of their personnel.

Rather than printing, shipping, and storing training materials, they created a dynamic training system that enabled users to select the training they required.

Paper Costs		
Training		1,400,000
Documentation		93,000
Patient Information		373,000
Other Supporting Documents		134,000
Total		2,000,000
Total Pages		2,000,000
Paper Rate	$6/Ream	$0.012
Other Print Costs (ink, maintenance)	$3/Ream	$0.006
Total Paper Cost		$36,000

Swedish also estimates that they save about $200,000 in shipping costs annually.

Standard Forwarding

Standard Forwarding Company was started in 1934 and has grown from a dedicated contract carrier for John Deere to a diversified Midwest regional LTL (Less Than Tuckload) carrier. Their fleet of 300 tractors and 790 trailers operated by 430 drivers allows them to provide a variety of effective transportation services. Standard Forwarding's commitment to state-of-the-art information technology meant they wanted to provide a reliable and scalable content management solution to minimize the duplication of efforts in company processes and procedures. In order to meet these specific goals, Standard Forwarding, along with partner Midland Information Resources, integrated Oracle Universal Content Management with their Carrier Logistics software to automate invoice processing and enable secure e-mails. This saved the company more than $150,000 annually by automating the invoice process and eliminating associated manual processing and postage costs.

Paper Costs		
Invoice		290,152
Supporting Documentation		435,228
Envelopes		145,076
Total		870,456
Total Pages		870,456
Paper Rate	$6/Ream	$0.012
Other Print Costs (ink, maintenance)	$3/Ream	$0.006
Total Paper Cost		$15,668
Postage cost savings		$60,932

Emerson Process

Emerson Process is a diversified global technology company that provides products and services for a wide range of industries, commercial markets, and end-users, including consumers. Emerson wanted easy global search and retrieval capabilities for Engineering and Quality Documentation and hoped to eliminate millions of pages of documents that were being printed each year. Emerson's implementation was done with the help of their Oracle implementation partner. "Emerson started out with one implementation of Oracle Content Management," said John Klein, VP of Business Development for Redstone Content Solutions. "When they saw what it could do, it quickly expanded to many more projects."

Based on a Forrester study[2], just one application at Emerson will realize a total savings of $574,354 in printing costs and $158,074 in shipping costs including gas, tires, and vehicle maintenance in one year. Today, Emerson has over 200 applications using Oracle Content Management.

Missouri Division of Professional Registration

Missouri division of Processional Registration handles professional licensing for industries such as cosmetologists, barbers, and dieticians. They handle over 400,000 constituents in 240 professional trades, and 39 boards. This results in twelve million new documents every year. The Division, along with their implementation partner Tallgrass Technologies, had a goal of improving the processing of licenses. They reduced license issuing time from 3 weeks to 2 days, resulting in a tremendous return on investment. They reduced filing costs by 76%, and reduced copier costs by 62%. But they also reduced paper consumption by 50%, and eliminated 90% of mailing, shipping, and other delivery costs.

GREEN CALCULATOR

Paper Savings

The savings realized by these companies can be translated into positive effects on the environment. The Oracle Document Management Green Calculator works on commonly accepted figures:

- 1 tree makes 16.67 reams of copy paper or 8,333.3 sheets
- 1 ream (500 sheets) uses 6% of a tree

http://www.conservatree.com/learn/EnviroIssues/TreeStats.shtml

Calculating Swedish's paper savings	
Total Pages	2,000,000
Reams of Paper (500 sheets/ream)	4,000
Number of Trees Saved (17 reams/tree)	235

Oil and Carbon Savings

The industry standard percentage for fuel as the cost of hauling is 43.5%.

http://www.mlive.com/businessreview/western/index.ssf/2008/06/shipping_costs_manufacturers.html

After removing 6% of Emerson's shipping cost for profit, we take 43.5% of the remainder for our calculation (40.89% of the original number). We are not calculating the cost of oil and tires to run the trucks, but that is an additional area that could be calculated.

Calculating Emerson's oil savings:	
Cost of shipping	$158,074.00
Total gas cost (40.89%)	$64,636.46
Total gallons of gas (gallon of diesel, $5.15)	12,550
Total barrels of oil (9 gallons/barrel)	1,395

After accounting for how many barrels of oil have been used in shipping, you can calculate how many pounds of carbon were released into the atmosphere. There are 9 gallons of diesel fuel in each barrel of oil, and each gallon of fuel burned releases 22.2 pounds of carbon.

Calculating Embry Riddle's carbon savings:	
Cost of shipping	$100,000.00
Total gas cost (40.89%)	$40,890.00
Total gallons of gas (gallon of diesel, $5.15)	7,940 [gal]
Total pounds of carbon (22.2 per gallon) [× 7,940]	176,264 [lbs]

Overall Results

When we add the results for all of these customers, we see savings of thousands of trees and barrels of oil, and tons of carbon emissions avoided.

	Emerson	Embry-Riddle	Swedish Medical	Standard Forwarding	Missouri Division of Professional Registration	Total
Dollars Saved in Printing Costs	$574,354	$47,324	$36,000	$15,668	$264,000	$937,346
Dollars Saved in Shipping Costs	$158,074	$100,000	$200,000	$60,932	$2,565,391	$3,084,397
Trees Saved	3,754	309	235	102	1,726	6,126
Barrels of Oil Saved	1,395	882	1,764	538	22,632	27,211
Pound of Carbon Emissions Avoided	278,627	176,264	352,527	107,401	4,521,853	5,436,672

OTHER BENEFITS

Real Estate

Not storing paper has two benefits regarding real estate—paper storage space and office space. Swedish is targeting 60% cut in storage costs—a $600K annual savings—by not having to store documents in paper form. This is space that would require energy consumption for heating, lighting, and humidity control, providing an additional green benefit by avoiding those energy costs. Beyond that there is also the impact on the environment of using the physical space as a warehouse as opposed to, say, a wetland reserve.

Another example of the real estate impact of storing physical documents is the fact that a paper document is only available at a single location. By storing documents electronically, they can be accessed in multiple locations, even simultaneously. PG&E (Pacific Gas and Electric) is implementing electronic documents because employees can access them from home as they perform their business processing, further saving on real estate by reducing necessary office space.

Lifestyle Benefits

As well as reducing real estate requirements, putting documents online reduces the number of employees who are commuting to an office. An employee commuting to work has environmental impact in terms of fuel consumption, tire consumption, and carbon emissions. By enabling employees to work from home, these effects on the environment are removed. While this has tremendous impact on the environment, it also has an impact on employee lifestyle.

Some organizations are beginning to assign lifestyle scores to corporate initiatives. While analyzing return on investment and other facets of a project, organizations can assess the impact on employee lifestyle. These organizations use the lifestyle benefit factors in recruiting to demonstrate that they are a more attractive employer.

Culture Change

Making these kinds of changes in your organization can require a huge culture change. As Nancy Richards of Swedish Medical Centers put it, "In the healthcare industry, it's not real if it's not on paper."

Many organizations have had similar concerns and even hesitation to change their current standard operating procedures in favor of green initiatives. Beyond the clear ROI of improving business processes with electronic documents, presenting the clear ROI of adopting green initiatives to the Chief Compliance Officer or other executives, or arming your CEO to publicize these efforts with shareholders in earnings reports can have a positive impact. The key is to find paper-based processes that can benefit from electronic documents. Broadening those use cases to other business processes that can benefit from going to electronic documents compounds the gains. Furthermore, constituents, possibly in other departments, such as facilities or operations who would also find clear advantage in benefits such as lowered real estate and/or storage costs can further increase the green benefits. Going green always means good press, so you should take up the subject with your organization's PR department to see how well such initiatives would resonate within your industry, potentially leading to a competitive advantage.

CONCLUSION

From various examples we have seen how companies can report to their shareholders, employees, and customers the impact they have had on the environment using Oracle Fusion Middleware solutions. Organizations which use Oracle Fusion middleware solutions are also well-positioned to meet their business challenges as they now have a scalable and manageable technology platform which is hot-pluggable—meaning it can be integrated with other standards-based applications and tools.

More and more, we are seeing materials written for executives of all ranks, industrial designers, and laypeople eager to learn more about eco-friendly products and business practices and the benefits gained from their implementation. Oracle Corporation proudly stands among organizations committed to bettering our environment through green initiatives—both as a provider of leading technology solutions to meet green initiatives at all levels around the globe, as well as an implementer of such initiatives throughout our own organization.

Sources:

[1] "A Roadmap towards Paperless Trade," United Nations Development Account; 2003.

[2] Further Topics: "Total Economic Impact of Oracle Universal Content Management," Forrester Research, Dec 2007.

Oracle

Go Green with Oracle Content Management

November 2009

Authors: Brian Dirking

Oracle Corporation

World Headquarters

500 Oracle Parkway

Redwood Shores, CA 94065

U.S.A.

Worldwide Inquiries:

Phone: +1.650.506.7000

Fax: +1.650.506.7200

oracle.com

References

(1) "Going Green? Choose ECM," Perspective Software, http://www.aiimhost.com/whitepapers/Perceptive_GoingGreen_ChooseECM.pdf.

(2) Environmental Protection Agency, Paper Recycling Frequent Questions, http://www.epa.gov/osw/conserve/materials/paper/faqs.htm.

(3) Environmental Paper Network January 2008, "Increasing Paper Efficiency" Fact Sheet, http://www.borealbirds.org/resources/factsheet-epn-paperefficiency.pdf.

(4) Environmental Protection Agency, www.epa.gov.

(5) http://eetd.lbl.gov/paper/ideas/html/copyfactsA.htm.

(6) "Go Green with Oracle Content Management: An Oracle White Paper," November 2009, http://www.oracle.com/us/products/middleware/content-management/059500.pdf.

18

A Technical Explanation
of Forecasting Systems

This section represents the forecast systems used in the corporate environment to add greater productivity to the corporation. Forecasting is very important in the new collaborative era. As companies are becoming increasingly interconnected, it is more important to fine-tune the forecast. The more accurate the system is, the less variance there is in creating in the entire supply chain. Because of connectivity and real-time information, decreased accuracy in-house decreases the accuracy of the collaborative partners as well. This creates a cascading effect all the way down the supply chain. This is why there is a lot of time spent on the forecasting methodologies. For example, in Six Sigma and Lean the enemy of the process is variation.

The chapter is technical in nature. The forecasting algorithms have been improved to allow the corporation to achieve an even better level of service and increased turns for the customer. The list of forecasting techniques is varied because the system is not used only to predict demand. Algorithms predict promotions, the effects of advertising, site selection, target marketing, and economic growth in different regions. The final classification of the general models used is as follows, and the forecast systems can be grouped into the following categories:

- The Algebraic Model, which includes the Multivariate Regression Model
- Trigonometric Models
- The Logistics Model
- The Logarithmic Models

- Exponential Smoothing Models, which include the Horizontal, Trend, Seasonal, and Trend Seasonal Models

The rest of the chapter explains the analysis of the variance in the forecast system. This is found in the "Dispersion of Demand" section. The chapter ends with an example of each type of exponential smoothing in the "Finding the Correct Forecast Model" section.

- The Algebraic Models and the Multivariate Regression Models are basically the same as far as the R^2 and multivariate coefficients. The only difference was that they were developed for different purposes. The Algebraic Models were developed from the SAS software for predicting the promotional forecast of sale circulars. Promotions are the Achilles heel of the supply chain system, and this gives outstanding accuracy in predicting the promotional quantity needed per item for each sale. The Multivariate Regression Models were developed from the use of Minitab software. This system was used in predicting target marketing and categorical management.

- The next models presented are the Trigonometric Models used in some software packages as an alternative to seasonal forecasting.

- The Logistics Model is used to associate the advertising effect on sales revenue.

- The Logarithmic Model is used to predict new item introduction, new category introduction, or the effect of fads.

- The next series of models, which are the Exponential Smoothing Models, are used for the forecasting systems in a time series environment.

The Algebraic Model

The Algebraic Model allows the expression of forecast as a function of an independent variable multiplied by a coefficient. This forecast can be represented as a sum of the independent variables with different exponents. An example of this is $Q_0 = X_1 * d_1 + X_2 * d_2 + X_3 * d_3 + X_4 * d_4 + X_5 * d_5$. The values can be determined by a good statistical package—in this case, SAS.

The number of variables will be determined by the R^2 in the model. Do not add too many variables into the system because it increases the nervousness of the forecast system when too many extraneous variables are added. Using backward regression, measure the R^2 of each independent variable added in. The R^2 determines how much of the variation the equation explains. If the R^2 measures a 43 for an independent variable, this means that the variable explains 43% of the variation when added to the equation.

To limit the number of extraneous variables, make a management policy that no one adds a variable to the forecast if it cannot explain 5% or more of the variance. This minimum percentage for R^2 can change from the type of forecast needed and the management philosophy. Typically, a backward regression system will list the R^2 values with the independent variable. The R^2 value in a backward regression lists the variables with the highest R^2 to the lowest. Always start to add the largest values of the R^2 into the forecast first. For example, the system has listed the following set of values:

- $R^2 = 40\%$ for X_1
- $R^2 = 30\%$ for X_2
- $R^2 = 12\%$ for X_3
- $R^2 = 8\%$ for X_4
- $R^2 = 5\%$ for X_5
- $R^2 = 2\%$ for X_6

In the preceding case, select only the top five variables because the sixth variable has an R^2 under 5%. The forecast system is represented as $Q_0 = X_1 * d_1 + X_2 * d_2 + X_3 * d_3 + X_4 * d_4 + X_5 * d_5$. The values represent a new forecast for the next month. The d_1 is the demand for the current month. The d_2 is the demand for the last month, and the d_3 is the demand for the month two periods in the past. The total explanation of the variation is 95%, which is the sum of the R_2s. The forecast model typically represents the data in monthly terms to make it easier to understand. The forecast for January, run in December, is $Q_{jan} = X_1 * d_{dec} + X_2 * d_{nov} + X_3 * d_{oct} + X_4 * d_{sep} + X_5 * d_{aug}$ with an R^2 of 95%. *Note:* The d and X values do not need to just be demand values. They can denote other events that show correlations to the dependent variable. The other conditions can help by predicting the price elasticity to demand when running a promotion. How much will sell at this price? How will the effect of increased advertising in an area increase sales? Which items should be selected in a target market?

Multivariate Regression Models

Regression Models using regression analysis can be used to infer causal relationships between the independent and dependent variables. The forecast uses external data as the independent data to represent its forecast. This approach is used to help increase the accuracy of the forecast by including external variables such as these:

- Housing starts
- Interest rates
- GDP growth
- Spendable income
- Price elasticity to demand
- Ethnic variables
- Type of home in an area
- Age in the community

The illustrated Regression Model shows three forms of forecast models. The model that predicts the demand with the greatest amount of accuracy has the least MAD or highest R^2. The Regression Model uses the Minitab software. The three forms are the linear, the quadratic, and the cubic forecast models. The graphs were also drawn from the Minitab software. The regression can be linear like $Y = \beta_0 X + C$ where β_0 is the coefficient and C is the constant. This can represent a Horizontal or Trend Model in a cyclical demand pattern graphed in Figure 18-1. Note that the R^2 shows a 0%, which indicates that the model does not predict the demand at all.

It can be parabolic or to the power of two like $Y = \beta_0 X_1 + \beta_0 X_2^2 + C$. Note that the R^2 shows as 8.2%, which explains that the parabolic model accounts for only 8.2% of the variation. This is illustrated in Figure 18-2, which shows the improvement over the previous model by introducing the quadratic model. This is not the appropriate model for the demand pattern. A quadratic model is used when the demand shows a maximum or minimum and turns the other direction after hitting the maximum or minimum.

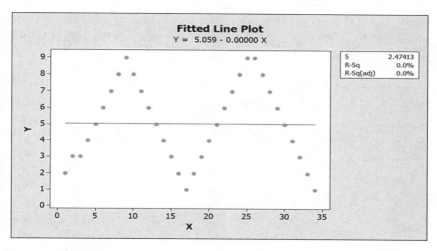

Figure 18-1 Using a Horizontal or Trend Model in a seasonal or cyclical demand pattern

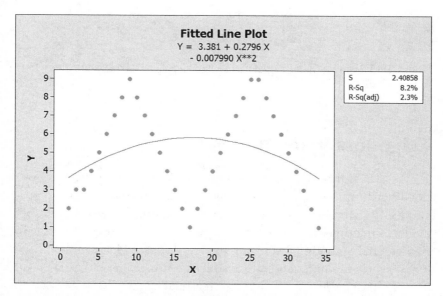

Figure 18-2 Using a Quadratic Model in a seasonal or cyclical demand pattern

Finally, it can be to the power of three known as a cubic model like $Y = \beta_0 X_1 + \beta_1 X_2^2 + \beta_2 X_3^3 + C$. Note that the R^2 shows as 9.6%, which explains that the parabolic model only accounts for 9.6% of the variation. This is illustrated in Figure 18-3, which shows the improvement over the previous model by introducing the cubic model. This is also not the appropriate model for the demand pattern. The appropriate model would be a seasonal forecast model, as explained in the following chapter on exponential smoothing.

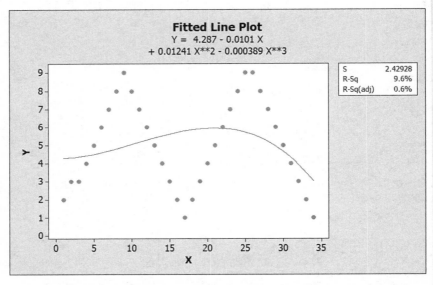

Figure 18-3 Using a Cubic Model in a seasonal or cyclical demand pattern

Trigonometric Models

As a classification, the Trigonometric Model would be the Fourier Transform. The transform could be available in the software program as an alternative to the exponential smoothed seasonal indexing model. Sometimes people use this concept versus seasonal indexing in Exponential Smoothing Models, which is discussed later in this chapter. Because the independent variable is a time value, it can be used in predicting cycles, oscillations, or seasonal cycles. Both are used to forecast seasonal or cyclical data patterns. Compare both models to see which one gives the more accurate solution. This is determined by seeing which system gives the lowest mean absolute deviation (MAD). The concept of MAD is discussed later.

The Logistics Model

The Logistics Model can be used to approximate sales and advertising. This approach measures advertising spending to actual sales increases. The advertising dollars are the independent variable and sales are the dependent variable. An example of the logistics formula would be $y = a / (1 + b\ e^{-kx})$, $k > 0$. As an example using the preceding formula, the system calculates the following results:

- a = $100,000, which is the maximum reachable revenue. This means that the maximum revenue, no matter how many dollars are spent, is $100,000.
- b = 200,
- k = 1,
- e = 2.718282,
- The X axis is the increase in adverting dollars as a percentage:
  - X = 1.0: No increase.
  - X = 1.1: Increase advertising 10%.
  - X = 1.2: Increase advertising 20%.
  - X = 10.9: Increase the advertising by 10.9 times the original value.
- The graph in Figure 18-4 illustrates the effect of the Logistics Model. The top line represents sales. The bottom line represents change in advertising. This shows the relationship of advertising dollars to sales.

The maximum increase in sales is when adverting is increased by 45, denoted by the flattening out of the change line. At this point, the slope of the line is zero, which means you have achieved a maximum. The bottom line represents change in sales for each percentage of increase in advertising dollars. After this point, the change becomes negative. This represents a 350% increase in adverting budget. Beyond this point, returns diminish.

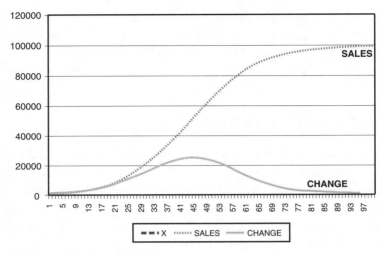

Figure 18-4 Graph showing the relationship of advertising dollars to sales

The Logarithmic Models

These models are used to forecast a new item introduction when it is expected to act as a fad-changer. This predicts the growth curve of the product. The Logarithmic Model has a period of rapid increase of sales, followed by a period when the growth slows. The interest is in the beginning growth portion of the graph because it is the hardest to forecast. The main difference between the models is that the Exponential Model begins slowly and then increases rapidly as time increases, whereas the Logarithmic Model begins fast and then decreases rapidly as time increases. Figure 18-5 shows the rate of increase of sales for a new item over time.

This is the formula for the Logarithmic Model: $y = a + b * \ln x$.

- $a = 1$. This is the point where the graph starts to depart from the Y axis and begins its logarithmic slope.

- b = the coefficient or percentage contribution of the ln function, and it is set to 40 in this case. As a good rule of thumb, take the b value and multiply it by 5 and the curve will cross the Y axis value at approximately the 145 period. This is significant because now there is a template in which to overlay the sales pattern. For example, if the forecast reads that the sales will be $200,000 in approximately 5 months, then use a b value of $200,000 / 5 = 40,000. The result is the higher the b coefficient, the greater the Y axis values or anticipated sales. Another rule of thumb is that as you increase b you multiply the initial growth by 6.9315. The initial growth when b is equal to 40 is 277 units sold the first month. If you set b to equal 80, then you forecast sales of 80 * 6.9315 = 555 units sold the first month. This is just another tool in using the model. If you estimate the first month's sales, the rest of the graph can be estimates. After your first month's sales are available, you can adjust b to match the actual first month's sales. The adjusted graph may give a better prediction of the future months' sales.

- x = the number of months after introduction.
  - x = 1 means 1 month after introduction.
  - x = 2 means 2 months after introduction.
  - x= 100 means 100 months after introduction.

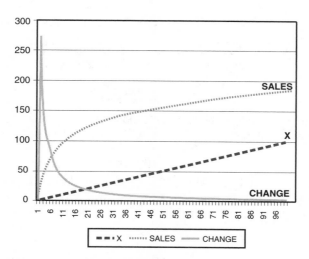

Figure 18-5 Using Logarithmic Models to model the growth curve of a new item with a = 1 and b = 40

- The X axis shows the month after the introduction of the new item.
- The descending line shows the decline in the amount of positive change in sales over time.
- The top line is the anticipated sales over time. With a value of a = 1 the sales go above the 150 in Period 42.

- The point of diminishing returns would be around 10 to 13 months.

The effect of a on the graph is the point where the graph forms the logarithmic curve. The a value is set to 10 in Figure 18-6 and note the curve leaves the Y axis at the point of 10. In other words, it starts its sales growth at a higher level. With a value of a = 10, the sales go above the 150 in Period 34 as opposed to Period 42 in Figure 18-5.

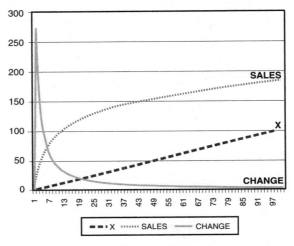

Figure 18-6 Using Logarithmic Models to model the growth curve of a new item with a = 10 and b = 40

Figure 18-7 shows when a = 100, the curve leaves the Y axis at 100. This means that the sales will begin at a higher value as opposed to using the a value of 1 or 10. With a value of a = 100 the sales go above 150 in Period 4.

Exponential Smoothing

Gamma smoothing is a unique contrast to exponential smoothing. Exponential smoothing is the use of a constant like α = .1 to change the forecast. Alpha α = .1 means to take 10% of the most recent data in figuring the new forecast. The formula is New Forecast = Last Forecast + .1 * (Current Demand – Last Forecast). This actually weights the importance of the most recent demand to the demand in the past. Table 18-1 shows the percentage contribution to the current demand and the past demand.

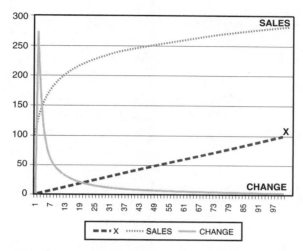

Figure 18-7 Using Logarithmic Models to model the growth curve of a new item with a = 100 and b = 40

Table 18-1 Percentage Contribution

Forecast Month	Current Month	Percent Contribution	Cumulative Contribution	$(1 - Alpha)^n$	Month $= n$
January	Dec	0.1	0.1	0.9	1
	Nov	0.09	0.19	0.81	2
	Oct	0.081	0.271	0.729	3
	Sep	0.0729	0.3439	0.6561	4
	Aug	0.06561	0.40951	0.59049	5
	Jul	0.059049	0.468559	0.531441	6
	Jun	0.0531441	0.5217031	0.4782969	7
	May	0.04782969	0.56953279	0.43046721	8
	Apr	0.043046721	0.612579511	0.387420489	9
	Mar	0.038742049	0.65132156	0.34867844	10
	Feb	0.034867844	0.686189404	0.313810596	11
	Jan	0.03138106	0.717570464	0.282429536	12
	Dec	0.028242954	0.745813417	0.254186583	13
	Nov	0.025418658	0.771232075	0.228767925	14

Forecast Month	Current Month	Percent Contribution	Cumulative Contribution	$(1 - Alpha)^n$	Month = n
	Oct	0.022876792	0.794108868	0.205891132	15
	Sep	0.020589113	0.814697981	0.185302019	16
	Aug	0.018530202	0.833228183	0.166771817	17
	Jul	0.016677182	0.849905365	0.150094635	18
	Jun	0.015009464	0.864914828	0.135085172	19
	May	0.013508517	0.878423345	0.121576655	20
	Apr	0.012157665	0.890581011	0.109418989	21
	Mar	0.010941899	0.90152291	0.09847709	22
	Feb	0.009847709	0.911370619	0.088629381	23
	Jan	0.008862938	0.920233557	0.079766443	24
	Dec	0.007976644	0.928210201	0.071789799	25
	Nov	0.00717898	0.935389181	0.064610819	26
	Oct	0.006461082	0.941850263	0.058149737	27
	Sep	0.005814974	0.947665237	0.052334763	28
	Aug	0.005233476	0.952898713	0.047101287	29
	Jul	0.004710129	0.957608842	0.042391158	30
	Jun	0.004239116	0.961847958	0.038152042	31
	May	0.003815204	0.965663162	0.034336838	32
	Apr	0.003433684	0.969096846	0.030903154	33
	Mar	0.003090315	0.972187161	0.027812839	34
	Feb	0.002781284	0.974968445	0.025031555	35
	Jan	0.002503156	0.9774716	0.0225284	36
	Dec	0.00225284	0.97972444	0.02027556	37

The table shows the relative importance of each month in the past to the forecast. The last month influences the forecast by 10%. The month prior shows a 9% contribution to the forecast with a total cumulative contribution for the two months of 19%. The third month shows an 8.1% contribution to the forecast with a total contribution for the three months of 27.1%. Now consider yearly numbers. With an exponential smoothing constant of .1, the last 12 months have a 71.76% influence on the forecast. The last two years will influence the forecast by 92.02%.

Changing the exponential smoothing constant can have a large effect on the amount of planning horizon of the forecast. For instance, changing the alpha from .1 to .2 results in subsequent changes. The last month influences the forecast by 20%. The month prior shows a 16% contribution to the forecast with a total cumulative contribution for the two months of 36%. The third month shows a 12.8% contribution to the forecast with a total contribution for the three months of 48.8%.

Consider yearly numbers again. With an exponential smoothing constant of .2, the last 12 months have a 93.13% influence on the forecast. The last two years will influence the forecast by 99.5%. By using an exponential smoothing constant of .2, any disturbances in the first year will have a 93.13% effect on the forecast.

Changing the A constant seeks the quantity that minimizes MAD. In the last models of regression, R^2 was used as a measure of fit. MAD could also have been used as a measure of fit.

Exponential Smoothing for a Horizontal Model

The Horizontal Model is the forecast of demand for a time series that does not experience trends, cyclicality, or seasonality. This is also known as single exponential smoothing.

The formula for exponential smoothing is $F_t = F_{t-1} + \alpha(A_{t-1} - F_{t-1})$.

- F_t = new forecast for the next month.
- F_{t-1} = forecast for current month.
- α = the exponential smoothing constancy and is generally .1 to .15.
- A_{t-1} = actual demand from the current month.

The next example illustrates how it works. It starts with a current demand of 50. The example fills the numbers in to show how the exponential smoothing works in an applied fashion.

- F_{t-1} = forecast for the current month = 580.
- α = .10.
- A_{t-1} = actual demand for the current month = 700.
- $F_t = F_{t-1} + \alpha(A_{t-1} - F_{t-1}) = 580 + .10(700 - 580) = 580 + 12 = 592$. The F_t is the forecast for the next month, which equals 592.

Figure 18-8 shows the relationship of the forecast to demand. A represents actual demand and F_t is the forecast generated from the horizontal forecast model. Note that the MAD is 94.65. Whichever model is selected should have the smallest MAD.

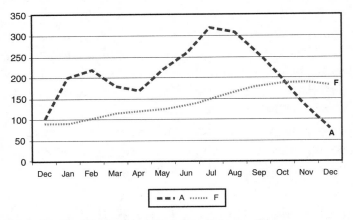

Figure 18-8 Graph of the horizontal exponential smoothing

Exponential Smoothing for a Trend Model

This is the time series model which incorporates the Trend Model. It is sometimes referred to as double exponential smoothing because it has two steps to the process and uses two smoothing constants, α and β. It is calculated as follows:

- $F_t = \alpha(A_{t-1}) + (1 - \alpha) * (F_{t-1} + T_{t-1})$.
- β = usually 2 * α or greater depending on choice.
- $T_t = \beta(F_t - F_{t-1}) + (1 - \beta) * T_{t-1}$
- Step 1 is to compute F_t.
- Step 2 is to compute T_t.
- Step 3 is to calculate the forecast $FIT_t = F_t + T_t$, which represents forecast with trend.

Begin with the actual demand noted as Actual in Table 18-2. There must exist an initial forecast called F, and the initial trend to start the model has to be estimated. The trend can be estimated by inspection of the graph or simply calculated as the average amount of growth between several points. This can be represented as T. The α is the exponential constant and the β is the smoothing constant for the trend element T. It is usually twice the alpha constant. If α = .10 then β will equal .20. In this case, the β = .40. The first line with the given demand of 100 followed by the estimate of the forecast and trend begins the process. This allows you to have the initial data to begin the trend forecast.

Table 18-2 Calculating Forecast Including Trend

Actual	FIT	F	T	α	β
100		90	6	.1	.4
110	102.56	96.4	6.16	.1	.4
120	109.7616	103.304	6.4576	.1	.4
130	117.6526	110.7854	6.867136	.1	.4
140	126.2484	118.8873	7.361033	.1	.4
150	135.5346	127.6235	7.911099	.1	.4
160	145.4709	136.9812	8.489714	.1	.4
170	155.9947	146.9238	9.07088	.1	.4
180	167.0263	157.3952	9.631093	.1	.4
190	178.4737	168.3237	10.15004	.1	.4
200	190.2374	179.6263	10.61109	.1	.4
210	202.2153	191.2137	11.0016	.1	.4

The graph in Figure 18-9 shows the forecast versus actual demand. The MAD is calculated as 86.39. This is lower than the Exponential Smoothing Model of 94.65. In this case, use the Trend Model. Graphically, the Trend Model shows that the forecast is closer to the actual demand compared to the Horizontal Model.

Exponential Smoothing for a Seasonal Model

The seasonal model uses base indexes (BI) to calculate the forecast for future months. The indexes also give a very good idea of the seasonal profile. How is it that some months consistently sell more than or less than the other months throughout the year? At this point, average out the last three years, denoted as Avg. Now calculate the average per month for the three years. For example, take the last

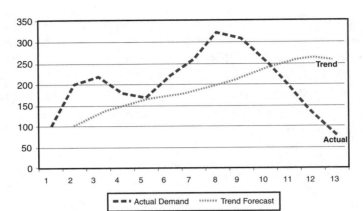

Figure 18-9 Graph of the trend exponential smoothing

three January sales for each of the last three years and find the average. Do the same for February all the way to December. This is called the monthly average M_t. The reason for using the last three years' consumption is that it averages out late or early seasonal patterns.

- M_t is the average of the monthly demand per month for three years.
- The BI = M_t/Avg.
- The Avg is the three years average of all 36 months.
- The M_t is calculated in the following table and again is all three months' sales for each year added together and divided by three. After this is calculated, the BI base index is determined by dividing each month's M value by the overall three-year average called Avg. Table 18-3 shows you how the base index (BI) is calculated.

Table 18-3 Calculation of the Base Index

Month	A for 2008	A for 2009	A for 2010	Avg 3 months M_t	Over Avg	BI
Jan	200	210	230	213	198	213/198 = 1.08
Feb	190	200	220	203	198	1.03
Mar	150	160	180	163	198	.82

Month	A for 2008	A for 2009	A for 2010	Avg 3 months M_t	Over Avg	BI
Apr	140	150	170	153	198	.77
May	190	200	220	203	198	1.03
Jun	230	240	260	143	198	1.23
Jul	290	300	320	303	198	1.54
Aug	280	290	310	193	198	1.48
Sept	230	240	260	243	198	1.23
Oct	170	180	200	193	198	.92
Nov	100	110	130	113	198	.57
Dec	50	60	80	63	198	.32
			Total =	2,380		
			Average =	198		

The next step is to determine how to forecast seasonality using exponential smoothing. As an example, in November 2010 the deseasonalized F_t was equal to 220. The deseasonalized value is the average for the month with seasonality taken out. Begin the forecast with a deseasonalized value. This is the average value for all 12 months. Find the deseasonalized value for each month. This starts by creating the base index for each month. With the base index values configured, divide the month's actual sales by the base index to see what the demand would be for the months without any seasonal influence.

To more easily follow the development of the forecast in the following step-by-step process, a few terms need to be defined. *FS* stands for the seasonalized forecast created from the deseasonalized demand multiplied by the base index. *FD* stands for the forecast for the month deseasonalized, which is synonymous with the average demand for the year. *BI* is the monthly base index, synonymous with the ratio of the month's expected demand above or below the mean. The next step is to create the new seasonal forecast, which is a two-step process:

- To create the new forecast for January, use the deseasonalized demand for December. The calculation is as follows:

$$FD_{DEC} = (FS_{DEC} + \alpha * (A_{DEC} - FS_{DEC})) / BI_{DEC}$$

- The new seasonalized forecast for January is $FS_{JAN} = BI_{t\text{-}11} * FD_{DEC}$.
- The index t-11 used on the BI stands for the 11th month back from the current month when the current month is December. The 11th month back is January 2010. $BI_{t\text{-}11}$ is the base index for January 2010 and is used to calculate the forecast for January 2011.

  - FD_{DEC} stands for December's deseasonalized average.

  - $BI_{t\text{-}11}$ stands for the base index for January 2010 and is used to calculate the forecast for January 2011.

  - FS_{JAN} stands for January 2011's seasonalized forecast average.

- Now that January's demand is calculated, February's forecast can be completed:

  - Calculate the deseasonalized demand for January:

$$FD_{JAN} = (FS_{JAN} + \alpha * (A_{JAN} - FS_{JAN})) / BI_{JAN}$$

  - A_{JAN} is the actual demand for January 2011. So the equation smoothes the difference of how far the forecast missed the actual demand. At this point, take a percentage of the miss, which is α, and add it onto the new smoothed January deseasonalized demand.

  - This deseasonalized demand for January is used to compute the seasonalized demand for February. All seasonal forecasts begin with the deseasonalized demand and use the two-step approach.

  - The new deseasonalized demand for February is used to calculate the March seasonalized demand forecast through the same two-step approach:

$$FD_{FEB} = (FS_{FEB} + \alpha * (A_{FEB} - FS_{FEB})) / BI_{FEB}$$
$$FS_{MAR} = BI_{T\text{-}11} * FD_{FEB}$$

- Table 18-4 shows the rest of the months filled in.

Table 18-4 Calculating the Seasonalized Demand from the Deseasonalized Demand

Month	A	BI	FS	FD
Jan	250	1.08	226	212
Feb	240	1.03	218	214
Mar	200	.82	177	217
Apr	190	.77	168	220
May	240	1.03	226	222
Jun	280	1.23	272	222
Jul	340	1.53	340	222
Aug	330	1.48	329	222
Sep	280	1.23	273	223
Oct	220	.92	206	224
Nov	150	.57	128	228
Dec	100	.32	73	237

The chart in Figure 18-10 shows the tracking of the exponential smoothing constant and the tracking of the seasons within the time series.

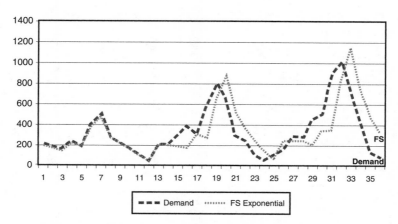

Figure 18-10 The comparison of the demand pattern with the seasonal forecast.

Note the closeness in the forecast FS and the actual demand. The next operation to complete is to smooth the BI values for each month because these values can change over time.

Exponential Smoothing for a Trend Seasonal Model

Figure 18-11 highlights the trend in the forecast that we must address.

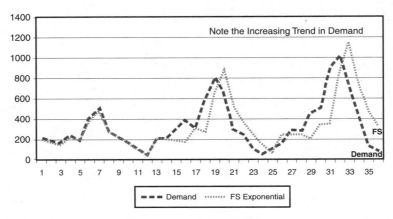

Figure 18-11 Emphasizing the trend component of the seasonal forecast

The formula for exponential smoothing, including trend, is $FD_{T+1} = \alpha(A_t) + (1 - \alpha) * (FD_t + T_t)$.

β is usually $2 * \alpha$ or greater depending on choice. In the last example, the choice was $4 * \alpha$.

This follows a four-step process:

1. Compute FD_{t+1}, where $FD_{T+1} = \alpha(A_t) + (1 - \alpha) * (FD_t + T_t)$.
2. Compute T_{t+1}, where $T_{t+1} = \beta(FD_{t+1} - FD_t) + (1 - \beta) * T_t$.
3. Calculate the forecast $FITD_{t+1} = FD_{t+1} + T_{t+1}$, which represents Forecast with trend for the next period.
4. Calculate the seasonal forecast $FITS_{T+1} = FITD_{t+1} * BI_{T-11}$.

An example of this forecast is as follows:

Trend Seasonal

MAD

The initial MAD is calculated as the absolute value of the demand minus the average for one year, $MAD_0 =$

$$\sum_{1}^{12} \frac{|xi - Average|}{12}$$

This stands for the initialized value of MAD. After this is calculated, the MAD is updated by using the following formula over time:

$$MAD = \sum_{1}^{12} \frac{|xi - forecast|}{12}$$

How much is the forecast missing the actual demand? In the beginning, the first smoothed value uses the initial estimate MAD_0 to smooth against the deviation between the forecast and the actual demand or the MAD value. This value is smoothed over time as each month is tracked. Reinitialization is the time the initial values for the forecast system were calculated and then double-checked to determine whether any forecast model changes needed to be made. The MAD_0 is calculating from the last 12 months. This first value gives a base to start with. After the initial MAD is calculated, the rest of the calculations for the future values are determined through exponential smoothing.

The formula for the new MAD is as follows:

$$MAD_1 = MAD_0 + \alpha / 4 * (A_0 - F_0)$$

- MAD_1 = the MAD for the next month based on the current absolute deviations.

- $\alpha / 4$ = the current exponential rate used in the Horizontal Model divided by four. The alpha is divided by four to minimize the variation in the MAD calculation. If it is not divided by four, volatility is introduced into the forecast model.

- The rest of the calculations are represented by the following formula. CSFE stands for the Cumulative Sum of the Forecast Errors:

$$MAD_i = \sum_{1}^{12} \frac{|xi - F|}{12}$$

Table 18-5 shows the initialized value of the

$$MAD_0 = \sum_{1}^{12} \frac{|xi - AVG|}{12}$$

With the beginning MAD in place, calculate the MAD by $MAD_i = \sum\limits_{1}^{12} \dfrac{|xi - F|}{12}$

Remember that a beginning forecast is not necessary but an average is.

Table 18-5 The Creation of MAD Mean Absolute Deviation

	A	F	alpha	A – F	RSE	CSFE	A – AVG	MAD
Jan	100	90	0.1	0	0		–103.846	103.846
Dec	200	91	0.1	109	109	109	–3.846	3.846
Nov	220	101.9	0.1	118	118.1	227	16.154	16.154
Oct	180	113.71	0.1	66	66.29	293	–23.846	23.846
Sep	170	120.339	0.1	50	49.661	343	–33.846	33.846
Aug	220	125.3051	0.1	95	94.6949	438	16.154	16.154
Jul	260	134.7746	0.1	125	125.2254	563	56.154	56.154
Jun	320	147.2971	0.1	173	172.7029	736	116.154	116.154
May	310	164.5674	0.1	145	145.4326	881	106.154	106.154
Apr	260	179.1107	0.1	81	80.88932	962	56.154	56.154
Mar	200	187.1996	0.1	13	12.80039	975	–3.846	3.846
Feb	130	188.4796	0.1	–58	58.47965	917	–73.846	73.846
Jan	80	182.6317	0.1	–103	102.6317	814	–123.846	123.846
	203.8462							56.450

$$MAD = \frac{3186.57}{13} = 56.450$$

Now that the average mean from initialization is calculated, the new MAD for future months can be determined. Consider that the MAD in the preceding chart was calculated in December. Use this value to calculate the forecast for January. At the end of January, measure the demand for that month, assumed for this example to be 150. From the initial calculation, smooth the MAD for the subsequent months. The February MAD is

$A_J = 150.$
$\alpha = .10.$

F_J = 182.6317 forecast for January 2011 calculated in the chart. MAD_J = 56.450, which was calculated from the initialization phase.
$MAD_F = MAD_J + \alpha / 4 * (A_J + F_J)$ = 56.450 + (.10 / 4) * (150 – 182.6317) = 56.3684.

The MAD for March would be calculated the same way, or $MAD_M = MAD_F + \alpha / 4 * (A_F + F_F)$. This process will calculate the MAD for each month in the time series.

Order Quantity

The order quantity calculation can vary by type of forecast model.

- Horizontal Model: $OQ_H = F_t * (LT + RT) + k * MAD * (LT+RT)$.[7]
- Trend Model: $OQ_T = FIT_t * (LT + RT) + k * MAD * (LT+RT)$.[7]
- Seasonal Model OQ_S is explained as follows:
  - $OQ = \Sigma(BI_{t-8} + BI_{t-9} + BI_{t-10} + BI_{t-11}) * FD_{t-1} * (LT + RT) k * MAD * (LT+RT)$[7] where $\Sigma(BI_{t-j})$ represents the number of periods or partial periods in $(LT + RT)$.
  - In forecasting the OQ in December for next year and $(LT + RT)$ = 4, then the equation would be represented this way:
    $OQ = \Sigma(BI_{APR} + BI_{MAR} + BI_{FEB} + BI_{JAN}) * FD_{DEC} * (LT + RT) k * MAD * (LT+RT)$[7]
- The k values are found in Table 21-1 and give the relationship of k to the Z transform. The system uses the k values for MAD, and using the standard deviation requires the use of the Z value. This is only showing the comparison for illustration.

Dispersion of Demand

With the concept of adoptive forecasting, the alpha constant can be changed when the forecast error begins to increase. This is accomplished with the use of tracking signal trips (TS) and the Running Sum of Errors (RSE). $TS = \dfrac{RSE}{MAD}$. The RSE is the accumulative difference between the demand and the forecast for the same period. The tracking signal is tripped when it reaches a value of > 3 or < 3. The tracking signal also determines whether there is too much forecasting being done or whether the forecast is on the high or low side.

The Demand Filter (DF) indicates whether the target is consistently missed on the high or low side. $DF = \dfrac{(Demand - F)}{MAD}$. When DF > 6, it will trip the Demand Filter. The Demand Filter can also calculate whether the demand is changing dramatically or the demand is an outliner. The term "outliner" is used because it is a computer program that organizes text into discreet groups. "Outliner" represents the outliers in terms of discreet numbers. An outliner is defined as a very high or low demand that does not represent the demand pattern. It is usually excluded or taken out of the calculation. In this case, ignore smoothing the variables because the demand is probably an error. The Tracking Signal with the Demand Filter will signify that closer attention must be paid to the forecast and one of the following corrective measures is necessary:

- Reinitialize the forecast or reevaluate the forecast model. Should it be Horizontal, Trend, Seasonal, or Trend Seasonal? If the model changes, run the reinitialization on the item to see what new model fits the demand better. During reinitialization, set the default MAD into the file. Remember, the default MAD is calculated as

$$MAD_0 = \sum_{1}^{12} \frac{|xi - AVG|}{12}$$

  After the software has selected a new model, the TS indicator should be reset to zero. It isn't necessary to change the alpha for the Exponential Smoothing Model yet. If it still continues to trip the tracking signal limits after the forecast model has changed, begin reevaluating a change in the alpha value in the model.

- If the model stays the same, change alpha. The TS indicator will be reset to 0.

Table 18-6 shows the forecast F, FE, RSE, AFE, CAFE, TS, and DF and is used to calculate the TS tracking signal and DF Demand Filter.

Table 18-6 Forecast Through the Tracking Signal and MAD

Month	Demand	F	FE	RSE	AFE	CAFE	DF	TS	MAD
Jan	670	604	66	66	66	65.625	1.00	1.00	66
Feb	750	613	137	203	137	203	1.35	2.00	101
Mar	610	613	-3	200	3	205	−0.04	2.92	68
Apr	680	616	64	264	64	269	0.95	3.92	67
May	620	617	4	267	4	273	0.06	**4.90**	55
Jun	690	620	70	337	70	343	1.23	**5.90**	57
Jul	500	620	−120	217	120	463	−1.82	3.27	66
Aug	400	633	−233	-16	233	696	−2.67	−0.18	87
Sep	630	612	18	2	18	714	0.23	0.03	79
Oct	690	615	75	77	75	789	0.95	0.98	79
Nov	640	625	15	92	15	803	0.20	1.25	73
Dec	800	636	164	256	164	967	2.04	3.17	81

The columns for Table 18-6 are defined here:

- **F** = The Forecast for the Period
- **FE** = Forecast Error
- **RSE** = Running Sum of Errors
- **AFE** = Absolute Forecast Error
- **CAFE** = Cumulative Absolute Forecast Error
- **DF** = Demand Filter
- **TS** = Tracking Signal
- **MAD** = Mean Absolute Deviation = CAFE/N
- **N** = Number of Periods Measured in the CAFE

In the table, if the tracking signal gets larger than 3 or 4, consider either reinitializing to change the forecast model or changing the alpha constant. In this case, the tracking signal is 4. In May, the TS = 4.90. This is a problem because there is a strong positive bias to the forecast that must be addressed. In some cases, there may be a few false trips with the tracking signal but each one requires further investigation.

The demand filter is used to check individual forecast errors. The amount of deviation from the demand and the forecast is divided by MAD. If the DF > 6, look at the usage as a possible outliner or potential change in demand. DF = (Demand − Forecast) / MAD. In this case, the limit for the demand filter is set for values above 3.33.

$$MAD = \sum_{1}^{12} \frac{|xi - avg|}{12}$$

A Tracking Signal (TS) trip of 3 would signal the system to possibly change the alpha from .1 to .13. As the forecast is continually missed, the α alpha constant is changed. After the tracking signal has been tripped and the α alpha constant is changed, for example, from .1 to .13, then the TS is zeroed out and the calculation begins again. If demand starts to change, the correction will be a stepladder approach. Each time the TS is tripped it is zeroed out and then the TS must accumulate the biased errors either negative or positive before it is tripped again. One approach, if the forecast model has not been changed, is to successively increase the alpha content from .1 to .13, then .16, then .20. It is possible to extend the increase of alpha beyond this point but sometimes it brings in too much nervousness in the system.

Finding the Correct Forecast Model

Initialization is scanning the set of forecast models to find and use the correct one for each item in the warehouse. It should be noted that each item is warehouse-dependent, meaning that an item may have a different forecast model for different warehouses. Each item in the inventory will probably possess its own unique demand pattern. Some warehouses may be trend whereas others may be horizontal and a few could be seasonal.

The correct procedure to determine the model is to wait for a tracking signal trip. After the item has been tripped, it will go through the process of initialization. This process compares the MAD for each successive forecast model. The usages used in this calculation are the last year's usage based on the smallest MAD. This visual approach is used only for demonstration. In the normal process, the computer only looks at the MAD in its quest to find the correct forecast model.

The Horizontal Exponential Smoothing Model

The first comparison is for the Horizontal Model in Table 18-7. The **A** represents actual demand. The **F** is the forecast for the period. The alpha is the smoothing constant (A − F), which represents the difference between the actual and the forecast. The calculations for the MAD follow Table 18-7. The Horizontal Forecast Model is represented by the formula $F_t = F_{t-1} + \alpha(A_{t-1} - F_{t-1})$. The RSE represents the Running Sum of Errors. The Running Sum of Errors should net out close to 0. In this case it does not because the forecast is always below the demand. There is a trend component in the demand and the forecast is not using the horizontal model instead of the trend model. In a case like this, consider changing the forecast parameters or changing to a Trend Forecast Model. Figure 18-12 shows how the forecast does not keep up with demand because of the large gap between A (actual demand) and F (the forecast).

Table 18-7 Exponential Smoothing Including Horizontal and Trend

A	F	alpha	A − F	RSE
100	**90**	**0.1**	0	0
200	91	0.1	109	109
220	101.9	0.1	118	227.1
180	113.71	0.1	66	293.39
170	120.339	0.1	50	343.051
220	125.3051	0.1	95	437.746
260	134.7746	0.1	125	562.971
320	147.2971	0.1	173	735.674
310	164.5674	0.1	145	881.107
260	179.1107	0.1	81	961.996
200	187.1996	0.1	13	974.797
130	188.4796	0.1	−58	916.317
80	182.6317	0.1	−103	813.685

$$\text{MAD} = \sum_{1}^{12} \frac{|xi - avg|}{12} = 94.65898$$

The MAD from these values is 94.65898.

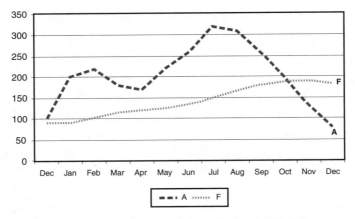

Figure 18-12 Demand versus forecast for the Horizontal Model

The Trend Exponential Smoothing Model

The next comparison is for the Trend Model. The A represents actual demand. The FIT is the forecast including trend for the period. The alpha is the smoothing constant. A – F is the difference between the actual and the forecast including trend. The MAD is calculated for the Trend Model in Table 18-8.

Table 18-8 The Calculation of MAD from a Trend Model

A	FIT	MAD
100		
200	102.56	97.44
220	122.3616	97.6384
180	146.0886	33.91142
170	164.7993	5.200689
220	180.847	39.153
260	201.856	58.14396
320	227.0899	92.91006
310	259.5168	50.48316
260	289.7204	29.72039
200	310.7148	110.7148
130	319.1811	189.1811
80	312.2336	232.2336
		0
	MAD	86.39421

The graph in Figure 18-13 represents the actual demand and forecast for the Trend Model. Note that the MAD for the Trend Model is 86.394, which is 8.2647 lower than the Horizontal Model's MAD of 94.65898. This is an improvement over the Horizontal Model. It's noted that the gap between the actual and the forecast is greater for the Horizontal Model. As the MAD becomes smaller, the gap between the actual demand and the forecast becomes smaller.

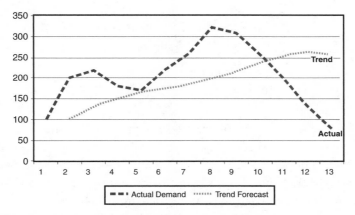

Figure 18-13 Demand versus FIT (forecast including trend) for the Trend Model

The Seasonal Exponential Smoothing Model

The final comparison is for the Seasonal Model. The A 2010 represents actual demand. The FS2 is the forecast seasonalized by the use of base-index values. The alpha is the smoothing constant. The MAD calculations for the seasonal model are performed shown in Table 18-9.

Table 18-9 The Calculation of MAD in a Seasonal Model

A 2010	FS2	MAD
	210	
200	215	15.29415
220	219	1.235262
180	177	2.565164
170	169	1.310159

A 2010	FS2	MAD
220	227	6.52331
260	273	12.69806
320	341	20.84892
310	330	19.53005
260	273	13.39914
200	206	6.482976
130	128	1.520381
80	73	6.999956
TOTAL =		108.408
Average =	212.5	9.03396
	MAD	9.03396

The graph shown in Figure 18-14 is the actual demand and forecast for the Trend Model. Note that the MAD for the Trend Model is 86.3942. The Seasonal Model is 77.3602, which is 9.034 lower than the Trend Model. This is a large improvement over the Trend Model. In comparing the two graphs, note that the FS tracks the peaks and values of the demand. This is why the MAD is much lower for the seasonal forecast.

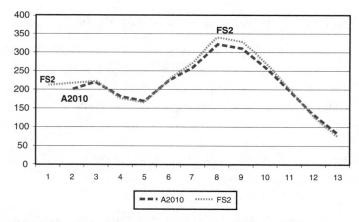

Figure 18-14 Demand versus forecast using the Exponential Smoothing Seasonal Model

19

Forecasting Methodology and Gamma Smoothing: A Solution to Better Accuracy to Maintain Lean and Green

Introduction of Gamma Smoothing

Gamma smoothing is the culmination of a detailed examination of past forecast programs and their failures. The primary focus of this concept is a holistic integration of the needs of fortune 500 companies worldwide. It has been in practice for 20 years and continues to prove its superiority with increased service levels, turns, and low inventory.

Description of the Theory and the Formulas

Gamma smoothing always includes an underlining trend indicator (TI) to minimize the chance of out-of-stocks. The TI is a parameter that tells the system to add more trend component to the forecast. This becomes an automatic trend-detection system. It is not a filter that has to wait for two or three periods to trip the system as some forecast systems require.

Gamma smoothing also avoids the stair-step process of evaluating the tracking signal (TS). The process is constantly evaluating the change in demand and is more responsive to the variation in demand when calculating safety stock. With gamma smoothing, the safety stock is calculated with the variability of the demand pattern in mind.

Start by calculating the Dispersion Measure of the demand pattern:

- A_{t-1} is the actual demand for the last period.
- F_{t-1} is the forecast for the last period's demand.
- γ Gamma = the smoothing constant for gamma smoothing = .10.
- δ Delta = the smoothing constant used for trend smoothing = .20.
- P or percent changed = $D_n / D_{(n-1)}$, which is the most recent demand divided by the last period demand.
- P_t is the initial smoothed value of P to be used in TI_{CUM} mentioned in the following text.
- TI = a running average of the trend component of demand pattern for the years.
- TI_{cum} = the cumulative trend over the time series.
- (DM) Dispersion Measure is defined as follows:
  - $DM_{t-1} = (A_{t-1} / F_{t-1} - 1)$ when $A_{t-1} / F_{t-1} > 1.00$. This formula is used when the actual demand is greater than the forecast.
  - $DM_{t-1} = (1 - A_{t-1} / F_{t-1})$ when $A_{t-1} / F_{t-1} < 1.00$. This formula is used when the actual demand is less than the forecast when measuring the magnitude of the actual demand as less than the forecast.
- F_t is the forecast for the Horizontal Gamma Soothing Model and it is calculated as follows:

  If $A_{t-1} / F_{t-1} < 1$ then:
  - $DM_{t-1} = (1 - A_{t-1} / F_{t-1})$
  - $F_t = (1 - DM_{t-1} * \gamma) * F_{t-1}$

  If $A_{t-1} / F_{t-1} > 1$ then:
  - $DM_{t-1} = (A_{t-1} / F_{t-1} - 1)$
  - $F_t = (DM_{t-1} * \gamma + 1) * F_{t-1}$
- The mathematics behind the trend pattern follows by using the trend indicator:
  - P or percent changed = $D_n / D_{(n-1)}$, which is the most recent demand divided by the last period demand.

If P < .80 it is set to P = .80. This is a default value to limit the variation or noise in the system for the lower bounds.

If P > 1.2 then it is set to P = 1.2. This is a default value to limit the variation or noise in the system for the upper bounds.

For values ≥ .80 and ≤ 1.2 use the P = $D_n / D_{(n-1)}$ value. This variation is within the tolerance of the system. Do not filter any of the forecasts P or Percent changed values.

- P_t = the Percent changed, which is the initial smoothed value for P. The smoothing constant for P is called Delta δ. Here use the value of Delta δ = .20.

  If P < 1 use $P_t = (1 - P) * δ$.

  If P ≥ 1 use $P_t = (P - 1) * δ$.

  - If the P value of the demand is $D_n / D_{(n-1)} = 1.10$ this means a 10% increase from this period compared to the last.

  - After the smoothed value, increase the cumulative trend by 2%. $P_t = (1.1 - 1) * .2 = .02$. This value is used as a multiplier of TI_{cum}, which in this case would be $TI_{cum} * (1.02)$.

- For example:

  - TI = trend indicator is the cumulative trend of P where P = D_t / D_{t-1}. This is the cumulative smoothed value of TI_{cum} for the time series. The TI_{cum} is smoothed and updated throughout the year.

  - TI_{cum} is calculated in two different ways:

    If P < 1 then $TI_{cum+1} = (1 - P_t) * TI_{cum}$.

    If P > 1 then $TI_{cum+1} = (1 + P_t) * TI_{cum}$.

    If P = 1 TI_{cum} is not changed.

  - Assume that the TI_{cum} value at this time is 1.04.

  - Given the P_t = .02.

  - Now calculate the new value for TI_{cum+1}, which is $(1 + P_t) * TI_{cum} = 1.02 * 1.04 = 1.06$.

  - The TI_{cum} is a multiplicative sum of the average trend in the time series throughout the series.

  - The Forecast Gamma (FG) will now have a trend component for the time series, which is represented as $F_{n+1} = F_n * TI_{cum+1}$. This stands for the forecast without safety stock.

- The forecast with safety stock and trend is equal to FS_{N+1} = F_{N+1} * TI_{cum+1} + k * MAD * β, where beta β is the coefficient determined by the Volatility Index (VI). The VI is based on the relative variation in the forecast values over time. If the system has decreased volatility, use a lower value of beta β. This FS_{N+1} is called OQ G because the focus is to compute safety stock and eventually a forecast using gamma smoothing.

- Including lead time in the preceding equation to calculate the OQ order quantity changes the formula to OQ G = F_{N+1} * (LT + RT) * TI_{cum} + k * MAD * (LT + RT) $^{.7}$ * β.

A Comparison Using Gamma Smoothing and Exponentials Smoothing

Figure 19-1 shows the forecasts for exponential smoothing as FE and gamma smoothing as FG. FE and FG are the initial forecast without safety stock. The graph also shows the order quantity using exponential (OQ E) and gamma smoothing (OQ G), which includes the safety stock calculation. As a matter of convention, reference to an order quantity always includes the safety stock calculation in the forecast.

The data in Tables 19-1 has a slight trend that is not enough to trip the TS. But the TI picks it up in gamma smoothing. Figure 19-1 shows both the gamma smoothing and the exponential smoothing with and without the safety stock portion. Table 19-2 is without the use of the TI and it compares this to the Exponential Smoothing Model. The gamma smoothing can accelerate the findings of small trends that can go undetected in some systems. The results were simulated in an Excel spreadsheet and over time indicated the average turns and service levels.

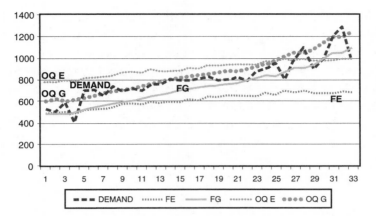

Figure 19-1 The comparison of exponential smoothing versus gamma smoothing without the TI

Table 19-1 The Exponential Smoothing Metrics for Figure 19-1

T. Revenue	25656			77,550	**LS =**	0
		Avg INV	2,350		**N =**	11
		Turns =	10.91745		**T =**	3.090909
	Service Level =		100.00%			

Table 19-2 The Gamma Smoothing Metrics Without TI and Beta at .50

T. Revenue	25656			65,044	**LS =**	0
		Avg INV	1,971		**N =**	12
		Turns =	13.01654		**T =**	2.833333
	Service Level =		100.00%			

Note that the differences in turns have accelerated between the exponential smoothing and gamma smoothing, from turns of 10.9 to 13.01. With the additional protection of the TI, the risk of out-of-stocks is reduced, making the forecast more accurate. This can be concluded by the lower MAD in the series as it was simulated over the past year. Reinitialization is necessary whenever a change is made to the forecast model to determine whether it is a better model. Because the MAD is lower, it's necessary to simulate the new value for beta. In this model, a lower value for beta is used because the forecast is improved by the addition of the TI also shown graphically in Figure 19-2. The inclusion of the TI causes less variance in the forecast, which results in a lower MAD. The gamma smoothing metrics with TI uses a beta of .38 instead of the .50 used without the TI, as shown in Table 19-3.

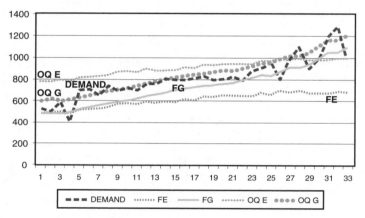

Figure 19-2 The gamma smoothing metrics with the use of the TI

Table 19-3 The Gamma Smoothing Metrics with TI and Beta at .38

T. Revenue	25656		56,740	LS =	0
		Avg INV	1,719	N =	12
		Turns =	14.92141	T =	2.833333
		Service Level =	100.00%		

Note that the gamma smoothing with the TI seems to get its turns from having a lower inventory in the beginning of the graph. As the trend begins to pick up, the OQ G picks up more sharply as compared to the previous graph without the trend indicator. To summarize, turns have improved from 13.01 to a value of 14.92 using the TI value. Note that the Order Quantity levels are higher at the end. This is because of the inclusion of the trend.

An Applied Example of the Gamma Smoothing Calculations over Time

If the demand in November was 500 and the forecast for November was 400 for an item carried by XYZ Retailer, then the actual demand in December was 600. What is the forecast for January when calculating in November? After December's forecast is calculated, January's can be done.

- A_{t-1} for November = 500.
- A_t for December = 600.
- F_{t-1} = 400.
- Gamma γ = .10. This is the gamma smoothing constant similar to α in exponential smoothing. In gamma smoothing, the γ is the smoothed average for the ratios of increase or decrease in the system between the actual demand and its forecast. In exponential smoothing, the α represents the smoothed average of the difference between the latest demand and the forecast for that period.
- Delta δ = .20 is used to smooth the trend component for TI.
- Calculate the forecast for December = F_t:
  - Now $A_{t-1} / F_{t-1} > 1$ so
    - $DM_{t-1} = (A_{t-1} / F_{t-1} - 1) = (500 / 400 - 1) = 1.25 - 1.00 = .25$
    - The forecast for December is $F_t = (DM_{t-1} * \gamma + 1) * F_{t-1} = (.25 * .10 + 1) * 400 = (1.05) * 400 = 410$.
- Calculate the forecast for January = F_{t+1}:
  - Now $A_{t-1} / F_{t-1} > 1$ so
    - $DM_t = (A_t / F_t - 1) = (600 / 410 - 1) = 1.46 - 1.00 - .46$
    - The forecast for January is $F_{t+1} = (DM_t * \gamma + 1) * F_t = (.46 * .10 + 1) * 410 = (1.046) * 410 = 429$.
- Introduce the TI for any possibility for trend to use as the TI_{cum} for January.
  - Assume that the TI_{cum} = 1.06 for November.
  - December demand = 600 and November demand = 500.

- The analysis is as follows:
    - $P = D_t / D_{t-1} = 600 / 500 = 1.2$
    - If $P < 1$ then
        - $P_t = (1 - P) * \delta$
        - $TI_{cum+1} = (1 - P_t) * TI_{cum}$
    - If $P > 1$ then
        - $P_t = (P - 1) * \delta = (1.2 - 1) * .2 = .04$
        - $TI_{cum+1} = (1 + P_t) * TI_{cum}$
        - $TI_{cum+1} = (1 + P_t) * TI_{cum} = (1 + .04) * 1.06 = 1.10$
- The forecast for January is $F_{n+1} * TI_{cum+1} = 429 * 1.10 = 471.5$.

The Trend Section of Gamma Smoothing Using TI

Gamma smoothing automates the trend model rather than forcing the user to wait for reinitialization notification. Gamma smoothing highlights the change in forecast models and reacts to it before a problem exists. This is especially true when using the trend indicator. If the actual demand gets larger or smaller than expected through time, the TI calculates the trend forecast system.

The system also measures various amounts of volatility in the demand pattern. This measurement is calibrated by the Volatility Index (VI), which equals MAD / AVG. The VI measures the volatility of the demand; the larger the value, the more volatility exists in the demand pattern. As the VI increases, so does the need to add extra safety stock.

VI will be valued at .069 and the gamma versus exponential smoothing results are graphed in Figure 19-3 to demonstrate this comparison.

The value FE is the forecast value for exponential smoothing without safety stock. The value of FG is the forecast value for gamma smoothing without safety stock. Note that gamma smoothing corrects faster to the change in demand from demand periods 7 to 25. At the finish, both systems end up at approximately the same point. Both systems ride on the bottom edge of the demand pattern. This is the reason for safety stocks. The concept of ABCDE analysis discussed earlier can also be applied to improve the weighting values for safety stocks. The concept and calculation of safety stock will be covered in the dispersion section. The comparison begins with a very low-volatility demand pattern measured by the VI which equals .06845, as shown in Figure 19-4. As the chapter proceeds, the effects of safety stocks are measured with the different VIs compared in the next scenario of comparisons. The VI of .069 is very low, which indicates that the MAD does not deviate from the overall average very much.

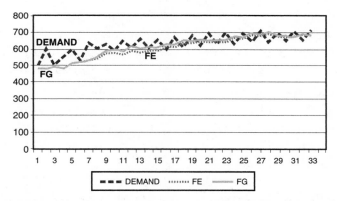

Figure 19-3 Graph using a VI = .069 and showing the gamma versus exponential smoothing

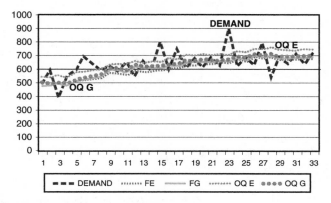

Figure 19-4 The graph of VI = 0.06845

Dispersion Measurement

This section discusses the concept of telling the computer what safety stock level is needed for the appropriate service level. Figure 19-4 shows a VI of 0.06845, which is a very low value indicating that the MAD variation compared to the average is 6.85% of the mean demand for the year. If confidence bands surrounded the mean, there would be a plus or minus 6.85% deviation around the mean. This is small so it's considered a very stable demand that needs very little safety stock.

Add safety stock only selectively when it's called for. Fast-moving items need only a small amount of safety stock because their pattern is so regular and this results in a low VI value. In most classic cases, more safety stock is added to the fast-moving items. This is not always necessary. It all depends on the volatility of the demand pattern. When demand is predictable, it makes sense to lower the safety stock level.

Figure 19-4 shows a demand pattern that moves from low to high. It also has a low VI which indicates that if the demand drops it will pick up in the near future. A low VI, in other words, says that the demand is predictable. This is called the wave pattern. When this pattern exists, the stock must be at a level that is a little higher than the wave patterns in the demand column. In this case, multiply the safety stock by the beta coefficient β. This is what makes gamma smoothing unique. There is a different beta coefficient for each VI. In this case, the VI is 0.06845. The beta used is .50. Beta is multiplied by the MAD to yield a reduced MAD. The new MAD = MAD * β, which = MAD * .5.

The next coefficient used is the k factor. This is used because of the importance of the item to overall service level, item demand, or profit margin. This was determined in the ABCDE hierarchy of inventory. The k values are in Chapter 21, "The New Sustainable EOQ Formula," in Table 21-1, which gives the relationship of k to the Z transform. It's necessary to balance the risk of the item with its priority or importance. The concept for determining safety stock is a two-step approach:

- Multiply MAD by β to get the correct risk factor for the demand pattern.

- Multiply MAD by k to get the correct service level for the ABCDE classification. How important is the item if sales are lost? What is its priority? This step converts the MAD into safety stock.

The safety stock is now prioritized by risk and priority.

For example, the calculation for safety stock is SS = k * MAD * β.

The demand pattern in Figure 19-5 follows a fairly predictable wave pattern. A larger value of VI is used for this example to illustrate the differences between the two systems. Exponential smoothing usually follows at the top of the wave pattern. It is marked as OQ E. The OQ G usually rides in the middle of the demand pattern. This is because it looks at the Volatility Index to check for a predictable wave pattern. It keeps the order quantity at midwave level, where half the demand will fall above and half will fall below. This assumes a stable wave pattern as measured by the VI indicator. If the demand drops, there is a reasonable probability it will increase in the next period or two. The converse is also accepted. If the demand increases, there is a reasonable probability that it will decrease in the next period or two.

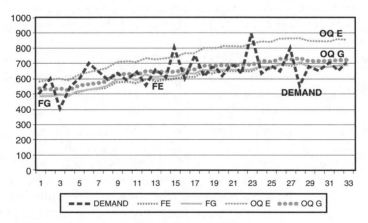

Figure 19-5 The graph of larger than VI = 0.06845

The β beta values are calculated from the VI as presented in the following bullet points. The list is only an example and each system requires its own analysis. To calculate, simulate the demand pattern history and use the beta values for a specific company. Those values may be different than the ones listed here:

- VI ≤ .10 yields β of .5 to .70 depending in the spikes in the demand. This means that the variation is less than 10% of the mean value for the time period.

- VI > .10 and ≤ .20 yields β of .50 to .80 depending in the spikes in the demand. This means that the variation is greater than 10% but less than or equal to 20% of the mean value for the time period.

- VI > .20 and ≤ .30 yields β of .50 to .80 depending in the spikes in the demand. This means that the variation is greater than 20% but less than or equal to 30% of the mean value for the time period.

- VI > .30 and ≤ .40 yields β of .50 to .80 depending in the spikes in the demand. This means that the variation is greater than 30% but less than or equal to 40% of the mean value for the time period.

- VI > .40 and ≤ .50 yields β of .50 to .80 depending in the spikes in the demand. This means that the variation is greater than 40% but less than or equal to 50% of the mean value for the time period.

- VI > .50 and ≤ 1.0 yields β of .50 to 1.0 depending in the spikes in the demand. This means that the variation is greater than 50% but less than or equal to 100% of the mean value for the time period.

- VI > 1.0 and ≤ 1.1 yields a β of .50 to 1.0 depending in the spikes in the demand. This means that the variation is greater than 100% but less than or equal to 110% of the mean value for the time period.

- VI > 1.1 indicates a need to check the TI, the TS tracking signal, the DF demand filter, and the OI for the outliner index. All of these are covered in the "Error Measurement" section later in this chapter. This means that the variation is greater than 110% of the mean value for the time period. This definitely needs more safety stock in the system to minimize the out-of-stock conditions.

Observing the Effects of Increasing the Volatility Index

This section graphs the various combinations of the Variability Index (VI). The section starts with VI ≤ .10 yields β of .50. This represents a point that is slightly above the average of the peaks and troughs of the demand pattern. The original VI from Figure 19-5 is 0.06845. Figure 19-6 shows an instance of VI = .0819, which is getting closer to .10, the first break point.

The following list explains the values used in the forecast:

- Demand = the usage per the period.
- FE = the exponential smoothed forecast without safety stock.
- FG = the gamma smoothed forecast without safety stock.
- OQ E = the order quantity using exponential smoothing and including safety stocks.
- OQ G = the order quantity using gamma smoothing and including safety stocks.

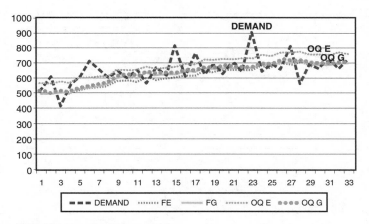

Figure 19-6 The graph of VI = .0819

Note that the OQ G is in the middle of the wave pattern and it is fairly consistent.

Figure 19-7 represents a VI of .10, and safety stock needs to be added because the volatility has increased from the VI of .0819. Note that as the VI indicator increases, the OQ E gap widens from the OQ G.

Notice as the VI increases to VI = .15 (Figure 19-8), the amplitude of the waves gets larger. Gamma smoothing is still at midlevel. The OQ G is still in the midrange of the demand patterns because the waves are still fairly predictable.

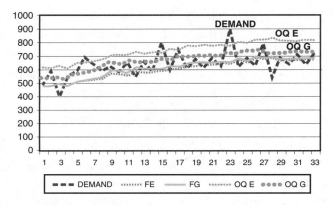

Figure 19-7 The graph of VI = .10

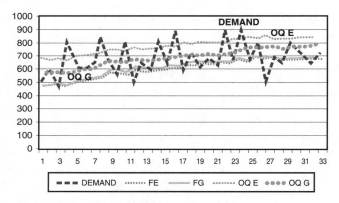

Figure 19-8 The graph of VI = .15

Amplitude increases as VI increases. A good service level exists because there are no real outliners and the waves are still predictable. This results in the OQ G being positioned in the middle of the demand patterns even with the large spikes in periods 10, 12, and 16 (Figure 19-9).

The next period requires additional safety stock analysis. Spikes should be analyzed to see whether they are occurring in a seasonal fashion. Are there any extraneous explanations to this sudden increase or decrease? Have inventory prices dropped or are there any promotions during this time? This is where inventory progress is made as long as there is no service-level sacrifice.

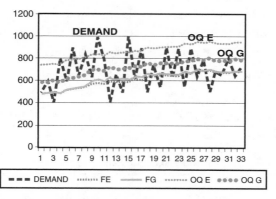

Figure 19-9 The graph of VI = .20

Inventory Control Metrics for Various VI Patterns

This section of the chapter compares the actual metrics in the various combinations of VI including the turns, number of times ordered, and service levels between the exponential smoothing systems and gamma smoothing systems using the various VI combinations. The section compares the Exponential Smoothing and Gamma Smoothing Models with the following combinations of VI at 0815, .20, .50, and finally at VI equal to 1.0. This section shows, in numerical terms, what happens to both systems as volatility goes up.

1. The following list compares the turns and service level for exponential smoothing and gamma smoothing.

2. Definitions:
    - Demand = monthly demand.
    - OQ E = order quantity for exponential smoothing, which is a one-period forecast.
    - OQ = the OQ E multiplied by 4. As a standard, the company wants four periods of stock to be carried to cover lead time or any unexpected changes in demand. This is a normal procedure for most firms. The number of periods held in stock may change from one company to the next.
    - OH = on hand.
    - PO = purchase order created.
    - Lost Sales = lost sales this period.

- n = 1 for any purchase orders created. This value is used in tracking the number of orders placed in the year.
- N = number of orders placed in the year.
- T = time between the orders.

Inventory at VI = .08187 with Exponential Smoothing and Gamma Smoothing

Inventory at VI = .08187 with Exponential Smoothing

Demand	OQ E	OQ	OH	PO	Lost Sales	n
500	630	2,520	2,020	0	0	0
600	638	1,913	1,420	0	0	0
400	645	1,934	1,020	1,934	0	1
550	638	1,913	470	1,913	0	1
600	675	2,024	1,804	0	0	0
700	692	2,077	3,017	0	0	0
640	705	2,116	2,377	0	0	0
600	719	2,158	1,777	0	0	0
630	753	2,260	1,147	2,260	0	1
590	760	2,279	557	2,279	0	1
650	755	2,266	2,166	0	0	0
550	777	2,331	3,895	0	0	0
660	771	2,313	3,235	0	0	0
600	779	2,337	2,635	0	0	0
660	791	2,372	1,975	0	0	0
600	812	2,435	1,375	2,435	0	1
750	817	2,451	625	2,451	0	1
610	846	2,537	2,450	0	0	0
680	845	2,534	4,221	0	0	0
620	855	2,565	3,601	0	0	0
690	854	2,562	2,911	0	0	0
630	857	2,572	2,281	0	0	0
700	868	2,605	1,581	2,605	0	1
630	892	2,677	951	2,677	0	1
690	889	2,667	2,866	0	0	0
640	910	2,731	4,903	0	0	0

Inventory at VI = .08187 with Exponential Smoothing

	Demand	OQ E	OQ	OH	PO	Lost Sales	n
	710	911	2,732	4,193	0	0	0
	550	915	2,745	3,643	0	0	0
	700	895	2,684	2,943	0	0	0
	650	894	2,683	2,293	0	0	0
	710	893	2,678	1,583	2,678	0	1
	650	904	2,711	933	2,711	0	1
	720	901	2,704	2,892	0	0	0
T. Revenue	$20,860			75,763	**LS =**	0	
			Avg INV	2,296		**N =**	10
			Turns =	9.085985		**T =**	3.4
		Service Level =		100.00%			

Inventory at VI = .08187 with Gamma Smoothing

	Demand	OQ G	OQ	OH	PO	Lost Sales	n
	500	535	2,141	1,641	0	0	0
	600	528	1,585	1,041	1,585	0	1
	400	534	1,602	641	1,602	0	1
	550	522	1,566	1,676	0	0	0
	600	552	1,656	2,678	0	0	0
	700	559	1,678	1,978	0	0	0
	640	570	1,710	1,338	0	0	0
	600	585	1,755	738	1,755	0	1
	630	627	1,882	108	1,882	0	1
	590	633	1,898	1,273	0	0	0
	650	622	1,867	2,506	0	0	0
	550	654	1,961	1,956	0	0	0
	660	642	1,925	1,296	0	0	0
	600	645	1,936	696	1,936	0	1
	660	644	1,932	36	1,932	0	1
	600	660	1,981	1,372	0	0	0
	750	657	1,972	2,554	0	0	0
	610	685	2,055	1,944	0	0	0
	680	680	2,040	1,264	2,040	0	1

Inventory at VI = .08187 with Gamma Smoothing

	Demand	OQ G	OQ	OH	PO	Lost Sales	n
	620	690	2,070	644	2,070	0	1
	690	686	2,057	1,994	0	0	0
	630	689	2,066	3,434	0	0	0
	700	686	2,057	2,734	0	0	0
	630	711	2,132	2,104	0	0	0
	690	705	2,116	1,414	0	0	0
	640	728	2,183	774	2,183	0	1
	710	722	2,167	64	2,167	0	1
	550	733	2,199	1,697	0	0	0
	700	712	2,137	3,164	0	0	0
	650	712	2,137	2,514	0	0	0
	710	709	2,126	1,804	0	0	0
	650	721	2,162	1,154	2,162	0	1
	720	716	2,147	434	2,147	0	1
T. Revenue	$20,860			50,665	**LS =**	0	
			Avg INV	1,535		**N =**	12
			Turns =	13.5868		**T =**	2.833333
		Service Level =		100.00%			

When comparing the two methods of forecasting, note that neither system experienced out-of-stocks or lost sales.

The Exponential Smoothing Model has the following benchmarks:

- Turns = 9.085.
- Lost Sales = 0.
- N = number of orders placed = 10.
- T = interval between orders = 3.4.

The Gamma Smoothing Model has the following benchmarks:

- Turns = 13.587.
- Lost Sales = 0.
- N = number of orders placed = 12.
- T = interval between orders = 2.8.

The difference becomes apparent. Gamma smoothing will increase the turns by 50%, from turns of 9.085 to turns of 13.587. There is also no sacrifice in lost sales. The number of orders placed throughout the year with gamma smoothing will also increase by 20%, from 10 to 12. This is because less stock is carried. If transportation is an issue, it will need to be addressed with higher stock levels.

Inventory at VI = .20 with Exponential Smoothing and Gamma Smoothing

Inventory at VI = .20 for Exponential Smoothing

Demand	OQ E	OQ	OH	PO	Lost Sales	n
500	800	3,200	2,700	0	0	0
600	808	2,423	2,100	0	0	0
400	815	2,444	1,700	0	0	0
800	821	2,462	900	2,462	0	1
600	858	2,573	300	2,573	0	1
900	885	2,656	1,862	0	0	0
640	899	2,696	3,795	0	0	0
840	925	2,775	2,955	0	0	0
630	959	2,877	2,325	0	0	0
1000	986	2,959	1,325	2,959	0	1
800	990	2,969	525	2,969	0	1
400	1,004	3,011	3,085	0	0	0
660	998	2,993	5,394	0	0	0
500	1,001	3,002	4,894	0	0	0
1000	1,022	3,067	3,894	0	0	0
600	1,043	3,130	3,294	0	0	0
900	1,057	3,170	2,394	0	0	0
500	1,080	3,239	1,894	3,239	0	1
750	1,082	3,247	1,144	3,247	0	1
550	1,089	3,266	3,833	0	0	0
900	1,099	3,296	6,180	0	0	0
630	1,102	3,307	5,550	0	0	0
900	1,113	3,339	4,650	0	0	0
550	1,133	3,399	4,100	0	0	0

Inventory at VI = .20 for Exponential Smoothing

	Demand	OQ E	OQ	OH	PO	Lost Sales	n
	900	1,140	3,421	3,200	0	0	0
	640	1,162	3,486	2,560	0	0	0
	800	1,162	3,486	1,760	3,486	0	1
	500	1,164	3,491	1,260	3,491	0	1
	690	1,143	3,430	4,056	0	0	0
	650	1,143	3,429	6,897	0	0	0
	800	1,146	3,439	6,097	0	0	0
	650	1,157	3,472	5,447	0	0	0
	720	1,155	3,465	4,727	0	0	0
T. Revenue	$22,900			106,800	**LS =**	0	
			Avg INV	3,236		**N =**	8
			Turns =	7.075828		**T =**	4.25
			Service Level =	100.00%			

Inventory at VI = .20 for Gamma Smoothing

	Demand	OQ G	OQ	OH	PO	Lost Sales	n
	500	612	2,447	1,947	0	0	0
	600	593	1,778	1,347	0	0	0
	400	590	1,769	947	1,769	0	1
	800	574	1,721	147	1,721	0	1
	600	602	1,806	1,317	0	0	0
	900	608	1,825	2,137	0	0	0
	640	618	1,855	1,497	0	0	0
	840	633	1,899	657	1,899	0	1
	630	675	2,024	27	2,024	0	1
	1000	682	2,046	926	2,046	0	1
	800	672	2,016	2,150	0	0	0
	400	703	2,110	3,796	0	0	0
	660	691	2,073	3,136	0	0	0
	500	696	2,088	2,636	0	0	0
	1000	695	2,084	1,636	0	0	0
	600	708	2,123	1,036	2,123	0	1
	900	706	2,117	136	2,117	0	1

Inventory at VI = .20 for Gamma Smoothing

	Demand	OQ G	OQ	OH	PO	Lost Sales	n
	500	734	2,202	1,759	0	0	0
	750	731	2,193	3,127	0	0	0
	550	742	2,225	2,577	0	0	0
	900	739	2,216	1,677	0	0	0
	630	741	2,223	1,047	2,223	0	1
	900	739	2,216	147	2,216	0	1
	550	764	2,293	1,819	0	0	0
	900	760	2,279	3,135	0	0	0
	640	783	2,348	2,495	0	0	0
	800	778	2,333	1,695	0	0	0
	500	789	2,366	1,195	2,366	0	1
	690	764	2,292	505	2,292	0	1
	650	763	2,290	2,222	0	0	0
	800	762	2,286	3,714	0	0	0
	650	774	2,321	3,064	0	0	0
	720	768	2,304	2,344	0	0	0
T. Revenue	$22,900			58,003	LS =	0	
			Avg INV	1,758		N =	11
			Turns =	13.02858		T =	3.090909
		Service Level =	100.00%				

When the two methods of forecasting are compared, the difference is clear. Neither system experienced out-of-stocks, notated as LS for lost sales. The exponential smoothing has the following benchmarks:

- Turns = 7.
- Lost Sales = 0.
- N = number of orders placed = 8.
- T = interval between orders = 4.25.

The gamma smoothing has the following benchmarks:

- Turns = 13.03.
- Lost Sales = 0.

- N = number of orders placed = 11.
- T = interval between orders = 3.09.

Gamma smoothing will increase the turns by 84.1%, from turns of 7.075 to turns of 13.028. There is also no sacrifice in lost sales. The number of orders placed throughout the year will also increase by 38%, from 8 to 11.

Inventory at VI = .50 with Exponential Smoothing and Gamma Smoothing

Inventory at VI = .50 with Exponential Smoothing

Demand	OQ E	OQ	OH	PO	Lost Sales	n
500	1,090	4,360	3,860	0	0	0
600	1,098	3,293	3,260	0	0	0
100	1,089	3,268	3,160	0	0	0
300	1,069	3,208	2,860	0	0	0
200	1,086	3,258	2,660	0	0	0
200	1,078	3,233	2,460	0	0	0
100	1,063	3,189	2,360	0	0	0
100	1,051	3,154	2,260	0	0	0
200	1,063	3,189	2,060	3,189	0	1
300	1,054	3,163	1,760	3,163	0	1
400	1,037	3,112	4,549	0	0	0
500	1,056	3,169	7,213	0	0	0
600	1,047	3,141	6,613	0	0	0
700	1,061	3,182	5,913	0	0	0
800	1,072	3,216	5,113	0	0	0
900	1,108	3,325	4,213	0	0	0
1000	1,127	3,381	3,213	0	0	0
1400	1,196	3,588	1,813	3,588	0	1
1200	1,222	3,665	613	3,665	0	1
900	1,246	3,739	3,301	0	0	0
700	1,246	3,738	6,266	0	0	0
600	1,248	3,744	5,666	0	0	0
500	1,238	3,715	5,166	0	0	0
550	1,258	3,775	4,616	0	0	0

Inventory at VI = .50 with Exponential Smoothing

	Demand	OQ E	OQ	OH	PO	Lost Sales	n
	400	1,240	3,719	4,216	0	0	0
	300	1,244	3,731	3,916	0	0	0
	300	1,218	3,655	3,616	0	0	0
	700	1,230	3,691	2,916	0	0	0
	900	1,221	3,662	2,016	3,662	0	1
	1500	1,264	3,793	516	3,793	0	1
	1200	1,288	3,864	2,979	0	0	0
	1300	1,332	3,997	5,471	0	0	0
	1000	1,345	4,034	4,471	0	0	0
T. Revenue	$20,950			121,091	**LS =**	0	
			Avg INV	3,669		**N =**	6
			Turns =	5.70935		**T =**	5.666667
		Service Level =		100.00%			

Inventory at VI = .50 with Gamma Smoothing

Demand	OQ G	OQ	OH	PO	Lost Sales	n
500	586	2,345	1,845	0	0	0
600	571	1,714	1,245	0	0	0
100	571	1,714	1,145	0	0	0
300	555	1,666	845	1,666	0	1
200	584	1,751	645	1,751	0	1
200	590	1,770	2,111	0	0	0
100	600	1,799	3,762	0	0	0
100	614	1,843	3,662	0	0	0
200	657	1,972	3,462	0	0	0
300	665	1,994	3,162	0	0	0
400	654	1,963	2,762	0	0	0
500	685	2,056	2,262	0	0	0
600	670	2,009	1,662	0	0	0
700	675	2,026	962	2,026	0	1
800	674	2,023	162	2,023	0	1
900	690	2,069	1,288	2,069	0	1
1000	687	2,062	2,311	0	0	0
1400	716	2,147	2,979	0	0	0

Inventory at VI = .50 with Gamma Smoothing

	Demand	OQ G	OQ	OH	PO	Lost Sales	n
	1200	712	2,137	1,779	0	0	0
	900	724	2,171	879	2,171	0	1
	700	720	2,161	179	2,161	0	1
	600	724	2,173	1,750	0	0	0
	500	722	2,166	3,411	0	0	0
	550	747	2,240	2,861	0	0	0
	400	742	2,226	2,461	0	0	0
	300	765	2,295	2,161	0	0	0
	300	760	2,279	1,861	0	0	0
	700	769	2,308	1,161	2,308	0	1
	900	749	2,248	261	2,248	0	1
	1500	751	2,252	1,069	2,252	0	1
	1200	748	2,243	2,117	0	0	0
	1300	760	2,280	3,069	0	0	0
	1000	756	2,268	2,069	0	0	0
T. Revenue	$20,950			63,366	**LS =**	0	
			Avg INV	1,920		**N =**	10
			Turns =	10.91042		**T =**	3.4
		Service Level =		100.00%			

When comparing the two methods of forecasting, notice that neither system experienced out-of-stocks. The exponential smoothing mode has the following benchmarks:

- Turns = 5.71.
- Lost Sales = 0.
- N = number of orders placed = 6.
- T = interval between orders = 5.66.

The gamma smoothing has the following benchmarks:

- Turns = 10.91.
- Lost Sales = 0.
- Service Level = 100%

- N = number of orders placed = 10.
- T = interval between orders = 3.4.

Gamma smoothing increases the turns by 53%, from turns of 5.71 to turns of 10.91. There is also no sacrifice in lost sales. Exponential smoothing and gamma smoothing had a 100% service level. The number of orders placed throughout the year will also increase by 66.67%, from 6 to 10.

Inventory at VI = 1.0 with Exponential Smoothing and Gamma Smoothing

Inventory at VI = 1.0 with Exponential Smoothing

Demand	OQ E	OQ	OH	PO	Lost Sales	n
500	3,756	15,025	14,525		0	0
200	3,758	11,274	14,325	0	0	0
100	3,769	11,308	14,225	0	0	0
300	3,760	11,279	13,925	0	0	0
800	3,791	11,373	13,125	0	0	0
600	3,799	11,397	12,525	0	0	0
900	3,806	11,419	11,625	0	0	0
7000	3,817	11,451	4,625	11,451	0	1
500	3,847	11,540	4,125	11,540	0	1
600	3,852	11,556	14,976	0	0	0
10000	3,844	11,532	16,516	0	0	0
800	3,867	11,601	15,716	0	0	0
900	3,857	11,572	14,816	0	0	0
1000	3,865	11,595	13,816	0	0	0
1100	3,866	11,597	12,716	0	0	0
1200	3,886	11,659	11,516	0	0	0
1300	3,885	11,655	10,216	0	0	0
10000	3,914	11,741	216	11,741	0	1
1500	3,911	11,732	−1,284	11,732	−1284.33	1
2000	3,922	11,765	8,457	0	0	0
700	3,919	11,756	19,488	0	0	0
600	3,923	11,769	18,888	0	0	0

Inventory at VI = 1.0 with Exponential Smoothing

Demand	OQ E	OQ	OH	PO	Lost Sales	n
500	3,921	11,763	18,388	0	0	0
550	3,946	11,839	17,838	0	0	0
400	3,942	11,825	17,438	0	0	0
300	3,965	11,895	17,138	0	0	0
300	3,960	11,879	16,838	0	0	0
700	3,971	11,913	16,138	0	0	0
900	3,951	11,853	15,238	0	0	0
2000	3,952	11,856	13,238	0	0	0
10000	3,949	11,847	3,238	11,847	0	1
1300	3,961	11,884	1,938	11,884	0	1
5000	3,958	11,873	8,786	0	0	0
$64,550			405,297	**LS =**	−1284.33	
		Avg INV	12,282	**N =**	6	
		Turns =	5.360349	**T =**	5.666667	
	Service Level =		98.01%			

Inventory at VI = 1.0 with Gamma Smoothing

	Demand	OQ G	OQ	OH	PO	Lost Sales	n
	500	2,734	10,936	10,436	0	0	0
	200	2,736	8,207	10,236	0	0	0
	100	2,747	8,241	10,136	0	0	0
	300	2,737	8,212	9,836	0	0	0
	800	2,769	8,306	9,036	0	0	0
	600	2,777	8,330	8,436	0	0	0
	900	2,788	8,363	7,536	0	0	0
	7000	2,803	8,409	536	8,409	0	1
	500	2,846	8,538	36	8,538	0	1
	600	2,853	8,560	7,845	0	0	0
	10000	2,843	8,529	6,384	0	0	0
	800	2,874	8,622	5,584	8,622	0	1
	900	2,862	8,585	4,684	8,585	0	1
	1000	2,866	8,599	12,306	0	0	0
	1100	2,865	8,594	19,791	0	0	0

Inventory at VI = 1.0 with Gamma Smoothing

	Demand	OQ G	OQ	OH	PO	Lost Sales	n
	1200	2,883	8,650	18,591	0	0	0
	1300	2,880	8,640	17,291	0	0	0
	10000	2,907	8,721	7,291	0	0	0
	1500	2,902	8,707	5,791	8,707	0	1
	2000	2,912	8,736	3,791	8,736	0	1
	700	2,908	8,724	11,798	0	0	0
	600	2,911	8,733	19,934	0	0	0
	500	2,908	8,724	19,434	0	0	0
	550	2,932	8,797	18,884	0	0	0
	400	2,927	8,781	18,484	0	0	0
	300	2,949	8,848	18,184	0	0	0
	300	2,943	8,830	17,884	0	0	0
	700	2,954	8,862	17,184	0	0	0
	900	2,934	8,801	16,284	0	0	0
	2000	2,934	8,803	14,284	0	0	0
	10000	2,931	8,793	4,284	8,793	0	1
	1300	2,943	8,828	2,984	8,828	0	1
	5000	2,938	8,815	6,777	0	0	0
T. Revenue	$64,550			361,972	**LS =**	0	
			Avg INV	10,969		**N =**	8
			Turns =	5.884847		**T =**	4.25
			Service Level =	100.00%			

When comparing the two methods of forecasting, notice that neither system experienced out-of-stocks. The exponential smoothing mode has the following benchmarks:

- Turns = 5.36.
- Lost Sales = $1,284.
- Service Level = 98.1%.
- N = number of orders placed = 6.
- T = interval between orders = 5.66.

The gamma smoothing has the following benchmarks:

- Turns = 5.89.
- Lost Sales = 0.
- Service Level = 100%.
- N = number of orders placed = 8.
- T = interval between orders = 4.25.

Gamma smoothing will increase the turns by 10%, from turns of 5.36 to turns of 5.89. In the Exponential Smoothing Model, there are lost sales of 1.99%. The dollar amount of lost sales is $1,284. The service level is still high in the Exponential Smoothing Model at 98.01%. There is no sacrifice in lost sales for the Gamma Smoothing Model. The service level for gamma smoothing is 100%. The number of orders placed throughout the year will also increase by 33%, from 6 to 8, with gamma smoothing.

Turns began to fall at each level of VI for the Exponential Smoothing Model. At VI = .5 and VI = 1.0 the turns seemed to plateau on the low side at five plus turns. The Gamma Smoothing Model also decreased in turns as the VI increased but not as fast as the Exponential Smoothing Model. The Gamma Smoothing Model received its worst turns when VI = 1.0. The Gamma and Exponential Smoothing Models were close in turns at VI = 1. Normally, as the Volatility Index increases, the spread between the turns of exponential smoothing versus gamma smoothing increases in favor of gamma smoothing. In the last case where VI = 1.0, the spread between exponential smoothing and gamma smoothing was close due to the spikes in demand. This is registered by the outliner index (OI).

In this case the OI registered at 4. The OI monitors the number of outliners in the forecast. An outliner indicates that the demand is beyond the forecast's capability to measure. Because the outliner cannot be measured, it represents an unpredictable spike or decrease in demand that cannot be forecasted in the model. To make things worse, the 4 out of 32 demand buckets indicates an incapability to measure demand on 12.5% of the demand series. Each increment of the OI will add significantly to the extra safety stock carried by the gamma smoothing. In this case, it's necessary to carry extra safety stock because there are four instances in which the demand can't be forecasted. This also explains the decrease in turns.

VI = 1.0

- The OI outliner index = 4 in the system. This means that there are four large spikes in demand. Figure 19-10 illustrates the four OI outliners on the demand line.
- FE = forecast using exponential smoothing without safety stocks.
- FG = forecast using gamma smoothing without safety stocks.
- OQ E = the order quantity for exponential smoothing, forecast plus safety stock.
- OQ G = the order quantity for gamma smoothing forecast plus safety stock.

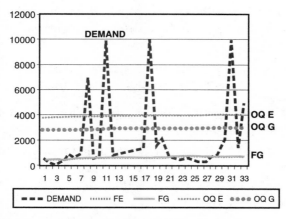

Figure 19-10 The graph showing the four outliners

Seasonal Exponential Smoothing and Seasonal Gamma Smoothing

The seasonal model uses base indexes for the monthly usage. It averages out the last three years' monthly usages to create 12 monthly averages. Then divide each monthly average by the three year over-age average to create 12 monthly base indexes. The reason for using the last three years' usage is that it averages out late or early seasonal patterns.

How is forecasting using exponential smoothing and using the F_t value done? F_t stands for the current forecast for the current month.

F_{t+1} stands for the next month's forecast. Table 19-4 is used for creating the appropriate forecast and base index values for the forecast.

Table 19-4 shows the usages for three years and will be used in the calculations.

The average demand for all three years is equal to 327.50. Looking at the example of December 2010, the FD_t for December is the overall average of 327.50, and the base index for December is equal to .1933. Both gamma smoothing and exponential smoothing use the concept of deseasonalized averages, termed FD to create the forecast.

All values calculating the demand for January, February, and March of 2011 will be smoothed in the future. Table 19-4 shows how to create the process. In forecasting terminology this is called initialization. Initialization is the creation of all the default values necessary to begin the forecasting and the eventual smoothing of all the values for future forecasts.

In this example are the forecasts for January, February, and March starting in December for exponential smoothing.

- FD_{Dec} stands for the new average for December and the average again is 327.50.
- FD_{Jan} stands for the new average for January after the month is complete.
- The alpha used in the smoothing of base index values and deseasonalized demand is .20.
- After January is completed, calculate the new deseasonalized demand for January = FD_{Jan}.
- A_{Dec} = the actual demand for December.
- FS_{Jan} = the seasonal forecast for January, which is FS_{T+1} = $FD_T * BI_{T-11}$. Note that the BI_{T-11} says to use the base index 11 months back from December, which would be January 2010. The BI is .15908. So the new forecast for January 2011 or FS_{Jan} = $FD_{Dec} * BI_{Jan\ 2010}$ = 327.50 * .15908 = 170.
- FS_{JAN} stands for January seasonalized forecast.
- After January's demand is set at 130, the two contents of exponential smoothing can be considered.

Table 19-4 Calculation of Initial Base Indexes (BI)

Month	Year	Demand	Month	Year	Demand	Month	Year	Demand	Average Monthly Demand	BI
Jan	2010	100	Jan	2009	210	Jan	2008	200	170.00	0.519084
Feb	2010	160	Feb	2009	200	Feb	2008	190	183.33	0.559796
Mar	2010	290	Mar	2009	280	Mar	2008	150	240.00	0.732824
Apr	2010	280	Apr	2009	390	Apr	2008	230	300.00	0.916031
May	2010	450	May	2009	300	May	2008	190	313.33	0.956743
Jun	2010	500	Jun	2009	600	Jun	2008	400	500.00	1.526718
Jul	2010	900	Jul	2009	800	Jul	2008	500	733.33	2.239186
Aug	2010	1,000	Aug	2009	670	Aug	2008	280	650.00	1.984733
Sep	2010	680	Sep	2009	300	Sep	2008	220	400.00	1.221374
Oct	2010	380	Oct	2009	240	Oct	2008	170	263.33	0.804071
Nov	2010	130	Nov	2009	110	Nov	2008	100	113.33	0.346056
Dec	2010	80	Dec	2009	60	Dec	2008	50	63.33	0.193384
Average per Year		412.5			346.6667			223.3333	327.50	

- Next, smooth the forecast for changes in demand. Update the FD and BI constants:
  - $BI_{Jan\ 2011} = A_{Jan\ 2011} / FD_{Dec\ 2010} = 130 / 327.50 = 0.397$.
  - Smoothed $BI_{Jan\ 2010} = 0.519084 + .20 * (0.397 - 0.519) = 0.495$. This is the new smoothed base index for January 2011. This is the BI for the year when forecasting for January 2012.
  - $FD_{Jan\ 2011} = (FD_{Dec} + .2 * (A_{Jan\ 2010} / (BI_{Jan\ 2010}) - FD_{Dec\ 2010}) = 327.50 + .20 * (130 / 0.519084 - 327.50) = 351.588$.
- After January is complete, it is time to calculate the forecast for February.
- The new forecast for February is $FS_{Feb\ 2011} = BI_{Feb2010} * FD_{Jan\ 2011} = 0.559796 * 351.588 = 196.818$.
- FS_{Feb} stands for February seasonalized forecast.
- Smooth the forecast for changes in demand. Update the FD and BI constants:
  - $BI_{Feb\ 2011} = A_{Feb\ 2011} / FD_{Jan\ 2011} = 200 / 351.588 = 0.569$.
  - Smoothed $BI_{Feb\ 2011} = 0.560 + .20 * (0.569 - 0.560) = 0.5616368$. This is the new BI for February 2011. This is the BI used next year when forecasting for February 2012.
  - $FD_{Feb\ 2011} = (FD_{Jan\ 2011} + .2 * (A_{Feb\ 2010} / (BI_{Feb\ 2010}) - FD_{Jan\ 2011}) = (351.588 - .20 * (200 / 0.559796 - 351.588) = 352.725$.
- After February's demand is calculated, March's forecast can be determined.
- The new forecast for March is $FS_{Mar\ 2011} = BI_{Mar\ 2010} * FD_{Feb\ 2011} = 0.732824 * 352.725 = 258.4853454$.
- $FS_{Mar\ 2011}$ stands for March seasonalized forecast.
- Next, smooth the forecast for changes in demand. Update the FD and BI constants:

  - $BI_{Mar\ 2011} = A_{Mar\ 2011} / FD_{Feb\ 2011} = 380 / 352.725 = 1.077$.
  - Smoothed $BI_{Mar\ 2011} = 0.733 + .20 * (1.077 - 0.733) = 0.801$. This is the BI used next year when forecasting for March 2012.
  - $FD_{Mar\ 2011} = (FD_{Feb\ 2011} + .2 * (A_{Mar\ 2010} / (BI_{Mar\ 2010}) - FD_{Feb\ 2011}) = (352.725 - .20 * (380 / 0.732824 - (352.725) = 385.888$.

Another calculation that can be utilized is the demand for the next three months, January through March. If starting in December, the equation is $FS_{(J \text{ to } M)} = FD_{Dec} * (BI_{t-11} + BI_{t-10} + BI_{t-9})$. This calculates the seasonalized demand for January through March.

Figures 19-11 and 19-12 show the difference between exponential smoothing and gamma smoothing. In gamma smoothing, the calculated BI for the month required taking the actual demand for the month and dividing it by the 12-month average demand. This is performed each month. The monthly average is the new FD. To calculate the new forecast for the next month, use the following formula:

$$FS_{n+1} = FD_n \times BI_{n-11}. \text{ Where } BI_n = A_n / (\sum_1^{12} D)/12$$

This is done instead of smoothing the BI from period to period as was done previously. The big difference in the two algorithms is that the gamma smoothing system measures the Volatility Index and prorates the safety stock based on the degree of predictability in the demand patterns. Again, the formula for VI = MAD / (Average Demand). The Average Demand is for 12 months. The VI is 1.304 and this indicates a use of 40% of the safety stock values because the pattern is still predictable. As the VI gets larger, greater amounts of safety stock are necessary. For a good comparison, Figure 19-11 graphs the exponential smoothing seasonal forecast, and Figure 19-12 graphs the gamma smoothing seasonal forecast.

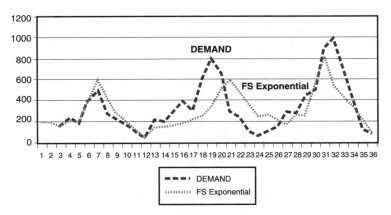

Figure 19-11 The exponential smoothing seasonal forecast

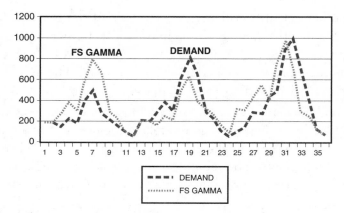

Figure 19-12 The gamma smoothing seasonal forecast

Figure 19-13 is a comparison of both exponential and gamma smoothing on the same graph versus demand. Note that in both models, the gamma smoothing does not lag as does the exponential smoothing. The Gamma Smoothing Model does initially include a lower amount of stock, which is based on the Volatility Index.

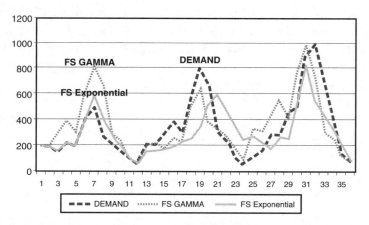

Figure 19-13 The graph compares exponential smoothing and gamma smoothing.

Graph of Exponential Smoothing Order Quantity

The order quantity is the forecast with safety stock added in for the Exponential Smoothing Model. The equation is OQS Exp = FS Exponential + k * MAD. The FS Exponential is the forecast seasonalized as described previously for the exponential model, where $FS_{N+1} = FD_N * BI(N - 11)$. The OQ Exponential $= FS_{N+1} = FDN * BI_{(N-11)} + k * MAD$.

The formula for the forecast for gamma smoothing is $FS_{N+1} = FD_N * BI_{(N-12)}$. The order quantity is the forecast with safety stock for the Exponential Smoothing Model. The OQ Gamma $= FS_{N+1} = FD_N * BI_{(N-12)} + k * MAD * \beta$, where beta β is the coefficient determined by the VI.

The Gamma Smoothing Model gives a closer fit to the demand pattern. This is because it measures the volatility of the demand pattern with the Volatility Index. This measures its predictability and reduces the need for unnecessary safety stock with the beta β coefficient.

Tables 19-5 and 19-6 show the effect on turns, number of times ordered, and inventory level using the two approaches. The order quantity (OQ) is the order quantity seasonalized and bought for three periods. This is a policy decision that can change from company to company. The three periods' quantity is established to match the lead times and any large demand pattern.

Table 19-5 Seasonal Exponential Smoothing

Demand	OQS EXP	OQ	OH	PO	Lost Sales	n
200	1,056	3,167	2,967	0	0	0
190	1,048	3,143	2,777	0	0	0
150	1,011	3,034	2,627	0	0	0
230	1,070	3,210	2,397	0	0	0
190	1,055	3,164	2,207	0	0	0
400	1,245	3,734	1,807	3,734	0	1
500	1,453	4,358	1,307	4,358	0	1
280	1,267	3,802	4,761	0	0	0
220	1,140	3,421	8,899	0	0	0
170	1,052	3,156	8,729	0	0	0
100	964	2,893	8,629	0	0	0
50	906	2,718	8,579	0	0	0
210	1,009	3,028	8,369	0	0	0
200	1,011	3,033	8,169	0	0	0

Demand	OQS EXP	OQ	OH	PO	Lost Sales	n
280	1,023	3,069	7,889	0	0	0
390	1,046	3,138	7,499	0	0	0
300	1,080	3,239	7,199	0	0	0
600	1,108	3,325	6,599	0	0	0
800	1,200	3,599	5,799	0	0	0
670	1,370	4,111	5,129	0	0	0
300	1,452	4,355	4,829	0	0	0
240	1,324	3,972	4,589	0	0	0
110	1,213	3,640	4,479	0	0	0
60	1,102	3,307	4,419	0	0	0
100	1,121	3,362	4,319	0	0	0
160	1,081	3,244	4,159	0	0	0
290	1,027	3,081	3,869	0	0	0
280	1,121	3,362	3,589	0	0	0
450	1,109	3,326	3,139	0	0	0
500	1,410	4,231	2,639	4,231	0	1
900	1,676	5,028	1,739	5,028	0	1
1,000	1,411	4,233	4,971	0	0	0
680	1,289	3,867	9,319	0	0	0
380	1,198	3,595	8,939	0	0	0
130	1,059	3,176	8,809	0	0	0
80	948	2,845	8,729	0	0	0
11790			194,874	**LS =**	0	
		Avg INV	5,413		**N =**	4
		Turns =	2.178028		**T =**	8.5
	Service Level =		100.00%			

Table 19-6 Seasonal Gamma Smoothing

Demand	OQ G	OQ	OH	PO	Lost Sales	n
200	454	1,363	1,163	0	0	0
190	435	1,306	973	0	0	0
150	399	1,196	823	0	0	0
230	472	1,415	593	1,415	0	1
190	435	1,306	403	1,306	0	1

Demand	OQ G	OQ	OH	PO	Lost Sales	n
400	627	1,881	1,418	0	0	0
500	718	2,154	2,224	0	0	0
280	517	1,552	1,944	0	0	0
220	463	1,388	1,724	0	0	0
170	417	1,251	1,554	0	0	0
100	353	1,059	1,454	0	0	0
50	307	922	1,404	0	0	0
210	462	1,386	1,194	0	0	0
200	441	1,323	994	0	0	0
280	404	1,213	714	1,213	0	1
390	485	1,455	324	1,455	0	1
300	450	1,349	1,237	0	0	0
600	688	2,063	2,092	0	0	0
800	775	2,325	1,292	2,325	0	1
670	560	1,680	622	1,680	0	1
300	540	1,619	2,647	0	0	0
240	506	1,517	4,087	0	0	0
110	410	1,230	3,977	0	0	0
60	339	1,016	3,917	0	0	0
100	583	1,749	3,817	0	0	0
160	556	1,667	3,657	0	0	0
290	661	1,983	3,367	0	0	0
280	776	2,328	3,087	0	0	0
450	626	1,878	2,637	0	0	0
500	961	2,882	2,137	0	0	0
900	1,101	3,302	1,237	3,302	0	1
1,000	850	2,550	237	2,550	0	1
680	517	1,550	2,859	0	0	0
380	503	1,509	5,029	0	0	0
130	382	1,147	4,899	0	0	0
80	331	994	4,819	0	0	0
11,790			76,547	**LS =**	0	
		Avg INV	2,126		**N =**	8
		Turns =	5.544827		**T =**	4.25
	Service Level =		100.00%			

When comparing the two methods of forecasting, note that neither system experienced out-of-stocks, notated as LS for lost sales. The Exponential Smoothing Model has the following benchmarks:

- Turns = 2.18.
- Lost Sales = 0.
- Service Level = 100%.
- N = number of orders placed = 4.
- T = interval between orders = 8.5.

The gamma smoothing has the following benchmarks:

- Turns = 5.55.
- Lost Sales = 0.
- Service Level = 100%.
- N = number of orders placed = 8.
- T = interval between orders = 4.25.

Gamma smoothing increases the turns by 155%, from turns of 2.18 to turns of 5.55. There is no sacrifice in lost sales. The number of orders placed throughout the year increases by 100%, from four to eight.

Error Measurement

In this case, the VI is 0.06845. This results in beta β of .50. This figure is multiplied by the MAD to yield a reduced Mean Absolute Deviation. The new MAD = MAD * β, or MAD * .5. This measure is used with the k factor as well so that the user can selectively create the ABCDE hierarchy of inventory based on the importance of the item to overall sales. The theory requires a multiple-step approach:

- The Volatility Index measures the variation and degree of unpredictability:
  - Multiply safety stock to get the correct risk profile for the demand pattern. This is determined by the VI and VI = MAD /AVG.
  - VI is a measurement of instability in the demand pattern, and it dictates the need to add or subtract more safety stock from the system.

- Add safety stock only selectively when necessary. Many fast-moving items need only a small amount of safety stock because their pattern is so regular. In most classical cases, the experts say to add more safety stock to the fast-moving items. This is not necessarily true. It all depends on the volatility of the demand pattern.
- The VI indicates what beta β value to use to approximate the risk in volatility in the demand pattern.

- Priority is measured using the k factor:
  - Next, multiply safety stock by k to get the correct service level for the ABCDE classification.
  - The safety stock is now prioritized by risk and order of importance. When balancing both priorities, the new calculation for safety stock is SS = k * MAD * β.
  - When including lead time (LT) and review time (RT) values of the Order Quantity, the formula becomes OQ = FS * (LT + RT) + k * MAD$^{.7}$ * β.
  - Taking the MAD components to the .7 power was determined to give the best multiplicative coefficient for the lead-time variability on MAD. To simulate this, multiply MAD for both the exponential smoothing and the gamma smoothing by a constant equal to .764.

- Outliner Indicator (OI):
  - This system checks for outliners or spikes in the demand pattern that cannot be anticipated.
  - OI = D_t / AVG_t
  - D_t = the current demand.
  - AVG_t = the average demand for the last month.
  - If OI > 3 then this is an exception and the OI is set from 0 to 1.
  - This system counts how many times in a rolling year there is an exception.
  - It increases the safety stock level for the system as follows:
  - Safety stock = k * MAD * (β + .1 * OI). This could change by system. If it changes, use a different coefficient other than the .1, for example .15 or .20 value.

- If the Volatility Index states a beta of .5 with three exceptions, or OI = 3 throughout the year, the new beta will be equal to .80, or .5 + .3.= .8
- Updated safety stock is k * MAD * .8 = k * MAD * .7.
- Tracking signal indicator (TS):
- The tracking signal traces the running sum of errors (RSE) in the system. Over a period of time as these errors accumulate, they will show either upward or downward bias in the forecast system.
- The formula for the tracking signal is TS =

$$\sum \frac{Actual\ Demand - Forecast}{MAD}$$

- Any value greater than a 3 is a concern.

- Downward or upward bias can be tracked using the demand filter.

- Demand Filter (DF):

  - DF = cumulative forecast error divided by the MAD. The formula notation is DF = $\dfrac{(Demand - F)}{MAD}$.
  - A value of DF > 6 will trip the Demand Filter device.
  - This option checks how many MADs are over or under in the forecast.
  - Any value above a 6 or below a –6 is a concern. The filters of plus or minus 6 are not cast in concrete. A 4 or 5 may also be used, depending on the importance of demand change.

- Error measurement is the process of closing the loop in the system. It will notify the user when one of the following conditions arises:
  - Forecast is erroneous.
  - There exists spurious demand.
  - The demand pattern is changing.
  - The beginning of a fad is present.
  - Similar items are on promotion.
  - A competitor advertised the items.

20

The Characteristics Needed
in a Forecast Program

This chapter is designed to list the sundry differences of many systems and their applicability. The information was created in collaboration with customers and suppliers. It was also accumulated as a wish list for future program changes in the system. When designing or buying a system, the following list can be used as a guide to what each system requires.

1. Many purchasing managers base their service level on different criteria. Some want to stock three or four weeks' worth of stock as an average. This does not offer a quantitative view of how to reach the company goal. When trying to maintain a 97% service level with three weeks' worth of stock on hand, this does not correlate. This is why the service-level metrics are important in a forecast system.

   a. Service level by item. This enables the user to show and measure the service levels by item to include a hit list for the items which are at the worst service level. The information should be analyzed and developed further in collaborative department meetings. The only way to create solutions to existing problems is to know which items are causing them. Raising the service-level requirements on these items may solve the issue.

   b. Service level by vendor. This is a good assessment technique for evaluating vendor performance. This can be used on a vendor scorecard when it is time to measure the vendor execution.

   c. Service level by warehouse. If there is a large difference in the service levels among the various warehouses, there may be a logistics or personnel problem. This comparison should be readily available on a billing report. Many times this is also a metric used for training the trainer. Key people in the warehouses with the highest service levels and turns can train the personnel for new warehouses. The same personnel can share their ideas in semiannual management meetings.

   d. Service level by department. The department service level is used as a barometer for future improvements. It is recognized that each department may vary from the next because of the uniqueness of the products carried. Comparing each department's service level for improvement may not be the issue. Some departmental categories will historically carry a lower service level. It may be helpful to collaborate with the vendors involved to see whether they have better ideas for improvement. Internal improvement teams should meet with suppliers regularly.

   e. Service level using the ABC. The final concept using the classification approach needs to be measured and input into the system. As discussed earlier, it is the weighted average of the volume, revenue, and profit models in calculating the k factor for the safety stock.

2. Scheduling inbound freight should be performed with the information from the forecast master file. The issues in this category revolve around logistics visibility. It is imperative to use an Advance Ship Notice (ASN) and software programs to match the delivery of a truck to a destination and time. The EDI 214 is also useful for freight scheduling from the carriers.

3. Seasonal profile forecasting is the concept that allows the computer to aggregate the seasonal patterns. When category management is used, lift by season for all the categories is outlined. This helps select the correct items for each season and lumps all like classes together. It is a good idea to lump products by their master codes. For instance, the National Hardware Retailer Association (NHRA) has categorized products by their type and use. These item categories can be further broken down to the end item. In the tools and drills department, comparisons by demand for a 12-volt variable-speed cordless drill versus cord model are optional. All vendors who make this type of drill will have the same NHRA code. When changing or adding vendor lines, all the suppliers are listed. The reference codes come in handy when looking for new items or seasonal patterns. This is a fast way to increase forecast accuracy. If the buyer can offer a rough estimate of the average sales for the item, it can be overlaid as a deseasonalized demand with the seasonality profile, which offers a better idea of how and when to buy the product.

4. Automatic reinitialization occurs when the computer automatically changes the smoothing rate and/or forecast models to minimize forecast errors. The system constantly checks for accuracy and determines whether the correct forecast model is being used. This is done by using demand filter and tracking signal limits. When the system sees problems, it will go back in and evaluate the current model for improvements. If the model needs corrected, it automatically performs the corrections. For example, around Father's Day, certain items sell at higher rates over the weekend. The computer automatically notices the seasonality change and selects the correct model: horizontal, trend, seasonal, trend seasonal, or lumpy.

5. Adaptive forecasting is a system used for short-range and long-range forecasts. This is a term that denotes the capability to change the forecast constant as demand varies. In this case, the exponential constant is changed from something like .1 to .15 or .2, depending on the system suggestion. The beta constant for the safety stock also changes as the Volatility Index varies.

6. Modified EOQ occurs when software packages deviate from the conventional EOQ concept. This is accomplished through changes in the following areas:

    a. Allowing quantity discounts to be entered into the calculations.

    b. Making lead-time adjustments and considering how they will change the EOQ.

    c. Making adjustments to allow EOQ to vary with seasonality.

    d. Varying the EOQ to coincide with capacity.

    e. Varying the EOQ to coincide with the minimum order multiple.

7. The use of regression analysis studies external changes and what their effect will be on the forecast. This is a useful technique in the evolution of demographic studies or categorizing items by region. This model is also used in the optimum pricing strategy and in promotional lift evaluations.

8. The management of correlation and data graphics services uses correlation analysis to tell how much of the variation in a forecast is explained by the independent variables. The data graph-

ics services are used when management needs to see the activity of the item. In this case, the results are displayed graphically. This may be used for the following reasons:

a. Discovering exceptions in demand—What causes the demand to change?

b. Reviewing an early order strategy—What will happen if the merchandise is brought in early?

c. Reviewing critical items—Will the system will show the critical items and their performance?

d. Reviewing seasonal items—Is the best seasonal inventory maintained? What unique categories are influencing the demand?

e. Finding cross correlations—Is there a category of items that influence the movement of other items such as Market Basket Analysis?

9. Fixed or variable intervals are used for the review periods to evaluate a vendor on a fixed or variable interval. This usually depends on the purchasing policy or the relative importance of the vendor. A variable interval reviewing system is best used to minimize the inventory, and the number of orders and unpredictability of the vendor reviews is not as important. The fixed review system is in place when it is very important that a schedule of vendor reviews is kept in place.

10. Look-ahead options cover forecast systems that use advance planning to look ahead and anticipate the next move. This feature is used in the following areas:

a. Scheduling of production—What happens if production is delayed?

b. Scheduling of receiving—What happens upon waiting until the next review period?

c. Scheduling of demand planning—How does the receiving schedule change if the demands of subsidiary warehouses change?

11. Demand patterns will be able to track five ways: horizontal, trend, seasonal, trend seasonal, and lumpy.

12. Shelf life is used in the food and drug industry but is not limited to only these two industries. Some companies have used the concept of shelf life on very expensive inventory items.

13. The open-to-buy system is established with a commitment from the retailer to buy a fixed amount over time from the supplier. This amount can be changed as long as enough lead time is given before any significant changes are made in the consumption planning. This is called an open-to-buy orientation. It is used or modified for the following:

    a. Minimum inventory allocation. This implies a long-term contract for purchasing a minimum amount of inventory over time to ensure service to customers. The minimum amount stands at the average inventory level. Any additional inventory or safety stock can be added later.

    b. Item service level. In the open-to-buy system, it is best to use a service level per item rather than an overall service level by vendor. It's necessary to get down to the micro level because purchasing out for six months is required. Any item overages on item inventories will be magnified. In any case, the item-service-level plans inventory using the ABCDE inventory analysis.

    c. Grouped vendor allocation. It may be advisable to buy for all warehouses as one long-range purchase agreement to the supplier. This purchase can be drawn from over time, with the items sent to the appropriate warehouses. This option reduces demand volatility in the forecast.

14. Expediting systems recognize the need to expedite and request a faster delivery date. This would alert the system of a pending shortage if the vendor stays on its normal manufacturing lead-time consideration. The system will decrease the lead time and ask for a quicker delivery. An order would be generated if needed with a shorter lead time. The system can be modified to review the vendor only if absolutely necessary.

15. Capture lead times in a forecast system can increase accuracy in the forecast system. The more relevant the information, the likelier the system will increase its accuracy. The lead times should be exponentially smoothed over time to keep an average lead time per vendor, per distribution center by vendor, per item, or per item by distribution center.

16. Fixed order quantities can be used for discount buying, freight savings, or receiving and stocking optimization.

17. Min/Max strategy stands for Minimum/Maximum Strategy; it yields a bounded solution to purchasing when necessary. It is

used when certain constraints in either buying or warehouse capacity are present.

18. Seasonal profiles can be used in the following areas:

    a. Grouping like seasonal products. Using a profiler highlights areas where purchasing can be grouped together to buy in larger, consolidated shipments where volume discounts apply.

    b. Determining the maximum period of sales. This can be used in grouping like products for freight savings. Knowing when and where the maximum shipment will occur offers additional leverage with the carriers for added discounts for volume shipments over time.

    c. Profiling new items. A new item does not have any seasonal characteristics added to its forecast profile. A new item may actually be seasonal and the buyer will complete two important steps to ensure that all new items have the correct profile if needed.

        i. The buyer will give an overall average for new items. This can be entered manually or approximated by a similar item with the same item classification code. The item classification code indicates that the item is the same as or similar to an existing item in inventory. It would make sense to use a similar demand average for similar items.

        ii. There will be an overlay of the new item with the same seasonal profile or template as the similar item described previously. This helps in maintaining a better forecast seasonality on new demand.

19. Seasonal indexing is a relatively new concept for the evaluation of seasonal merchandise. It will aid in the following areas:

    a. Predetermining a slight pre-buy. It uses seasonal base indexes that measure the amount of increase or decrease by period for demand. Any period with a base index above one will be considered as selling above the average.

    b. Increasing or decreasing of safety stock. After seasonality is determined, increases or decreases in safety stocks based on the index values are implemented. Entering a low-demand season requires lowering the safety stocks in advance.

    c. Increasing or decreasing the forecast. If you increase your forecast because of the base index, mentioned in step b, you would also increase your safety stock. If you lowered your forecast because of the base index, mentioned in step b, you would lower your safety stock.

20. The joint order system process allows for adding to an order to make the minimum shipment. The system looks ahead and analyzes whether the order results in a dip below the minimum service level. The order may not be accepted because it does not meet the vendor minimum weight requirements. If that occurs, the system will increase the order size to match the vendor minimum. In this case, the system determines the service-level threshold and looks at future demand.

21. Management information systems or queries can be incorporated into the following:

    a. Vendor modeling—This is used in modeling for different inventory scenarios for optimum inventory and service-level strategies.

    b. Vendor sundry reports—This involves offering many different reports that can be made by the user.

    c. Lead-time simulation—This involves testing the lead-time changes of several vendors to see what effect they will have on the inventory.

21

The New Sustainable EOQ Formula

The Economic Order Quantity (EOQ) is the amount needed to be ordered to minimize the variable cost. The EOQ formula looks only at the activity on the plant floor or in the distribution area. This chapter takes this formula to a new dimension. It expands the horizon of the EOQ formula to the entire supply chain and into the sustainable age of Green. The EOQ is the amount of inventory purchased that will balance the ordering and holding costs. Inventory is composed of the following parts:

- Raw materials and purchased parts from outside suppliers.
- Components and subassemblies that are awaiting final assembly.
- Work in process, which is all materials or components on the production floor in various stages of production.
- Finished goods, which are the final products waiting for purchase or to be sent to customers.
- Supplies, which are all items that are needed but that are not part of the finished product, such as paper clips, duplicating machine toner, and tools. This also includes the Maintenance Repair and Operations items.

Inventory Management is the process of ensuring that the firm has adequate inventories of all parts and supplies needed within the constraint of minimizing total inventory costs. The total inventory costs are composed of ordering (setup) costs, acquisition costs, holding (carrying) costs, and stock-out costs.

To be Lean and Green, the transportation component must be minimized. The existing EOQ formula is concerned only with the effect of holding and receiving costs. As the order quantity (OQ) increases, a Total Cost (TC) curve hits a minimum where the slope equals zero. After that, the TC slope turns positive and the total costs will start increasing.

Including the freight component along with the holding and receiving costs represents the transportation phase of the supply chain. When decreasing the EOQ to lower inventory cost, the transportation cost must be added to the EOQ equation. As the EOQ increases, the transportation costs decrease due to less-frequent shipping. Holding costs increase but the number of deliveries decreases.

The Old Economic Order Formula

There is a trade-off between lot size and inventory level in the former economic order formula. Frequent orders, sometimes called JIT or just in time orders (small lot size), have higher ordering costs and lower holding costs. Fewer orders (large lot size) have lower ordering costs and higher holding costs. The ABC Inventory Management tends to decrease the inventory levels because the extra safety stock is used for only the most important items.

- Inventory is divided into three dollar-volume categories—A, B, and C—with the A parts being the most active (largest dollar volume). The idea is to focus most on the high-annual-dollar volume A inventory items, then to a lesser extent on the B items, and even less on the C items.

- Inventory A items have the highest safety stock to guard against costly stock-outs. This can be performed in a number of ways. These are the variables:

  - Q = number of pieces per year.
  - EOQ = optimum number of pieces per year.
  - D = annual demand in units of inventory items per year.
  - S = setup cost or ordering cost for each order in $.
  - H = holding or carrying cost per unit, per year, in $.
  - d = demand during a demand period.
  - F = freight rate.
  - P = purchase price or cost of inventory.
  - N = number of orders per year which yields $\dfrac{D}{Q}$.

- LT = the lead time for the vendor.
- RT = the time between reviews of the supplier, called review time.
- Annual setup costs (SC) = $\dfrac{D}{Q} \times S$. The ordering cost can also be used for this analysis depending on what is minimized.
- The average inventory is defined as $\dfrac{Q}{2}$.
- Annual holding costs (HC) = $\dfrac{Q}{2} \times H$.
- Optimum inventory is found when the annual setup costs = annual holding costs.
- Where $\dfrac{D}{Q} \times S = \dfrac{Q}{2} \times H$.
- So $Q^2 = \dfrac{2DS}{H}$.
- $Q = \sqrt{\dfrac{2DS}{H}}$.
- So the total cost (TC) = $\dfrac{D}{Q} \times S + \dfrac{Q}{2} \times H$ of inventory is minimized when holding costs equal setup costs.

Let's use the preceding concept to create a graph of the EOQ formula (Figure 21-1), using the following values:

- D = $1,200 annual demand.
- S = the ordering costs are $5.00 per order.
- H = the holding cost of inventory, which is an annualized figure of 25%.

Figure 21-1 shows the simulation of the EOQ formula run for 52 periods. The graph in Figure 21-1 shows the minimum point in the EOQ formula where ordering cost and holding costs cross each other.

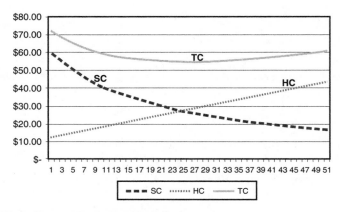

Figure 21-1 The graph of the EOQ formula

Note that the point where the holding costs equal the ordering costs is where the EOQ = 219. The calculation is

$$\sqrt{\frac{2 \times \$5.00 \times \$1,200}{25\%}}$$

On the graph, the period at 26 places the EOQ at 220. This is where the HC graph crosses the SC graph, resulting in the lowest total cost.

At this point, it is necessary to introduce the safety stock because the entire order quantity is made up of the forecast plus safety stock minus on-hand and on-order. The order quantity is now ordered in multiples of the EOQ.

In forecasting, the value k measures the amount of safety stock to use. The k is the equivalent of Z in a probability transform. The k value is used with the mean average deviation (MAD), whereas the Z value is used for standard deviation. The k measures the amount of safety stock needed according to the required item service level.

When the system reads a higher k value, it orders more safety stock. With k set for a 98% fill rate for A items and a 90% fill rate for B items and 85% fill rate for C items, this is called forecasting using the service level to determine the ABC analysis. The formula is OQ = d * (LT + RT) + k * (LT + RT)$^{.7}$.

- d = the demand for the period.
- OQ = the order quantity.

- LT = the lead time including manufacturing lead time plus transit time and receiving to stock time.
- RT = the review time, which is the time between reviews. This assumes a fixed-period forecasting schedule.
- k = the forecast standard deviation used for determining service level when using MAD.
- The $(LT + RT)^{.7}$ to the .7 power is used to get the most accurate lead-time variability for MAD.

It is possible to alternatively add extra lead time for A items and decrease the extra lead time for C items, but this does not result in a quantified answer to the service-level goal. It simply allows for adding to improve the service level. There is no guide available to indicate what the improvement will be. Using the k values results in enough measurable performance criteria on which to base the reason for increasing or decreasing safety stock.

Now ordering occurs only when the items are needed or according to company policy, which could increase transportation costs. The new formula for OQ takes into account the OH (on-hand) and the OO (on-order). The term AVAIL (available) is used to reference OH + OO. The calculation of OQ is now $OQ = AVAIL - (d * (LT + RT) + k * (LT + RT)^{.7})$. If the order quantity is negative, no order is placed. If the order quantity is positive, an order can be created.

The new formula results in lower average inventory because the lead time does not include review time. This methodology will dramatically increase the transportation component. The safety factor k averages 1.25 × the normal Z transform. This is an accepted approximation of k when not using Table 21-1. The increase accounts for the MAD.

Table 21-1 The Relationship of k to the Z Transform

Service Level	K	Z	=NORMSINV(B1)
55	0.16	1.25 ° Z ° 1.02	0.125
60	0.31	1.25 ° Z	0.2533
65	0.48	1.25 ° Z	.3853
70	0.65	1.25 ° Z	.5244
75	0.84	1.25 ° Z	.6744

Service Level	K	Z	=NORMSINV(B1)
80	1.05	1.25 ° Z	.8416
85	1.3	1.25 ° Z	1.036
90	1.6	1.25 ° Z	1.282
91	1.68	1.25 ° Z	1.3407
92	1.76	1.25 ° Z	1.4051
93	1.85	1.25 ° Z	1.4758
94	1.95	1.25 ° Z	1.5548
95	2.06	1.25 ° Z ° .99	1.6649
96	2.23	1.25 ° Z ° .1.02	1.7505
97	2.37	1.25 ° Z ° 1.01	1.8807
98	2.56	1.25 ° Z	2.0538
99	2.91	1.25 ° Z	2.3264
99.5	3.2	1.25 ° Z	2.5758
99.9	4	1.25 ° Z ° 1.105	3.0902

The way to solve the increase in transportation is to group the forecast by vendor. Tally the vendors' total overall service level of expected or forecasted out-of-stocks against the vendor predetermined specified service-level objective. After it is determined that total vendor out-of-stocks will fall below the predetermined minimum service level, the vendor will order in quantity. The new formula is Q = d * (LT) + k_v * $(LT)^{.7}$. The k_v Service factor is for the vendor and indicates a weighted average of all the k values in the vendor line. It weights the k value by demand and gives an overall service factor for the vendor on all items.

The service-level factor is figured by the sum of the item service-level factors multiplied by demand and divides this by total vendor demand. This gives a prorated vendor service level created by the relative importance of its items. The formula for this is:

$$K_v = \left(\sum di \times ki \right) / \left(\sum di \right)$$

If the system forecast of the sum of out-of-stocks for the vendor shows a value lower than the k_v value, it's time to order. This minimizes the number of shipments because orders are placed only when needed. It is also based on quantifiable measures of vendor service level. To compute the order quantity for each item in the line, match each order quantity against the vendor minimum or EOQ. The process is as follows:

- Average inventory (AI) is computed as 1/2 * OQ.
- The size of each item order is rounded out by the EOQ formula as directed by the next example, where $Q_{EOQ} = |Q/EOQ + .5|$ * EOQ. The vertical bars indicate an integer value of OQ value rounded by .5.
- The Q_{EOQ} is the item rounded for the new EOQ.
- Now the average inventory = 1/2 * Q_{EOQ}.

The EOQ formula is based on a simple formula used to determine the most economical quantity to order so that the total of inventory and setup costs is minimized. The following assumptions are in place:

- Constant per-unit holding and ordering costs
- Constant withdrawals from inventory
- No discounts for large quantity orders
- Constant lead time for receipt of orders

The EOQ is determined as the lowest point on the total cost from Figure 21-1.

There is a relationship between total inventories to the service-level criteria. As the need for higher service level increases, the safety stock begins to increase exponentially. It really takes a turn when it goes above 95% service levels. The values from Table 21-1 give the relationship of k to the Z transform. The k value is plotted against the service level.

Here the EOQ formula transforms from the old version to the new version, which includes the supply chain. The calculations are as follows for the older version:

- $SC = \dfrac{D}{Q} \times S$

- $HC = \dfrac{Q}{2} \times H$

- $TC = \dfrac{D \times S}{Q} + \dfrac{Q \times H}{2}$

- The lowest total cost is where the slope is equal to zero. This requires the first derivative of the total cost curve or

$$\frac{dTC}{dQ} + \frac{d}{dQ}\left(\frac{DS}{Q} + \frac{HQ}{2}\right) = 0$$

- After the differentiation the equation becomes $-DS / Q^2 + H / 2 = 0$.
- Now to solve for Q, the formula becomes $Q^2 = 2DS / H$.
- The EOQ is the Q calculated as $\sqrt{\dfrac{2DS}{H}}$.

For example:

- Suppose annual requirement (AR) = 10,000 units.
- Cost per order (CO) = $2.
- Cost per unit (CU) = $8.
- Carrying cost percentage (percentage of CU) = 0.02.
- Carrying or holding cost per unit = $0.16.
- The freight cost as an average per item = 4%.

- The EOQ $= \sqrt{\dfrac{2DS}{H}} = \sqrt{\dfrac{2 \times 10,000 \times \$2}{\$8 \times 0.02}}$.

- Economic order quantity = 500 units.

Now consider the increase in EOQ and the increased cost of holding the inventory versus the decreased cost of transportation:

- The holding cost is a yearly cost of 16%.
- Freight cost is 4%.
- In this case, do not include the freight in the EOQ calculation. The number of times ordered per year is calculated this way:
  N = number of orders per year = D / EOQ = 10,000 / 500 = 20.

As the transportation price increases, the number of inbound shipments will decrease, which begins to make sense using the new EOQ formula.

The New Economic Order Formula

The new total cost formula is total cost = total cost of goods sold (PD) + ordering cost (DS / Q) + holding cost (HQ / 2) + freight cost (DFP / Q). The equation is TC = PD + DS / Q + HQ / 2 + DFP / Q. Take the first derivative and find the point where the slope is equal to zero.

$$\frac{dTC}{dQ} + \frac{d}{dQ}\left(\frac{DS}{Q} + \frac{HQ}{2} + \frac{DFP}{Q}\right) = 0$$

After the differentiation, this is the formula: $-DS / Q^2 + H / 2 - DFP / Q^2 = 0$. Now it's time to solve for Q to get the new EOQ formula which takes into account the logistics, or, more specifically, the cost of freight:

$Q^2 = (2 * D * (S + F * P)) / (H)$

$$Q = \sqrt{2 \times D \times \frac{S + F \times P}{H}}$$

$EOQ_1 = 538.5$

$EOQ = 500$

There is a shortcut method that can be applied to the old style of calculated EOQ. If the system calculates this EOQ, simply multiply it by a constant coefficient of:

$$\sqrt{\frac{(S + F \times P)}{S}}$$

The new EOQ, known as EOQ_1, is calculated as:

$$EOQ_1 = \sqrt{\frac{(S + F \times P)}{S}} \times EOQ$$

where EOQ represents the old style of calculating the economic order quantity.

The following analysis also suggests that as the freight costs increase relative to the cost per order, the importance of transportation becomes more apparent. For instance, if F (freight cost) was 15% instead of 4%, the new EOQ would be 632.

$$Q = \sqrt{\frac{2 \times D \times S}{H}} = \sqrt{\frac{2 \times 10,000 \times 2.00}{.15}} = 516.39$$

Note that at period 19 on Figure 21-2, the minimum cost for the old EOQ is 77.46154.

Figure 21-2 shows the lowest point on the Total Cost Curve to be around period 19.

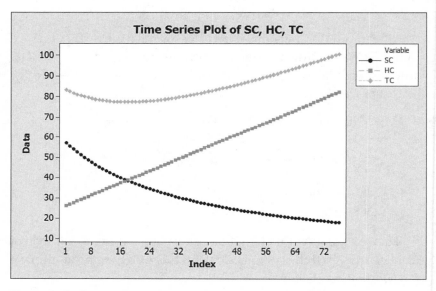

Figure 21-2 Plot of the holding and set up cost for the EOQ formula

Figure 21-3, which is an Excel spreadsheet, shows the minimum total cost at period 19 with an EOQ of around 520, which matches the calculation of 516.39. It is the lowest point on the spreadsheet. Close to period 19 the cost gets lower, and after that point the cost begins to rise. The Q on the spreadsheet represents the EOQ.

F33 | f_x | 660

	D	H	S	Q	SC	HC	TC	P		TCS
	D	H	S	Q	SC	HC	TC	P		TCS
12	10000	0.15	2	450	44.44444	33.75	78.19444	0.16	8	106.6389
13	10000	0.15	2	460	43.47826	34.5	77.97826	0.16	8	105.8043
14	10000	0.15	2	470	42.55319	35.25	77.80319	0.16	8	105.0372
15	10000	0.15	2	480	41.66667	36	77.66667	0.16	8	104.3333
16	10000	0.15	2	490	40.81633	36.75	77.56633	0.16	8	103.6888
17	10000	0.15	2	500	40	37.5	77.5	0.16	8	103.1
18	10000	0.15	2	510	39.21569	38.25	77.46569	0.16	8	102.5637
19	10000	0.15	2	**520**	38.46154	39	**77.46154**	0.16	8	102.0769
20	10000	0.15	2	530	37.73585	39.75	77.48585	0.16	8	101.6368
21	10000	0.15	2	540	37.03704	40.5	77.53704	0.16	8	101.2407
22	10000	0.15	2	550	36.36364	41.25	77.61364	0.16	8	100.8864
23	10000	0.15	2	560	35.71429	42	77.71429	0.16	8	100.5714
24	10000	0.15	2	570	35.08772	42.75	77.83772	0.16	8	100.2939
25	10000	0.15	2	580	34.48276	43.5	77.98276	0.16	8	100.0517
26	10000	0.15	2	590	33.89831	44.25	78.14831	0.16	8	99.84322
27	10000	0.15	2	600	33.33333	45	78.33333	0.16	8	99.66667
28	10000	0.15	2	610	32.78689	45.75	78.53689	0.16	8	99.52049

Figure 21-3 The Excel spreadsheet showing the minimum cost for the EOQ formula

Now consider the new EOQ calculation of including the transportation cost. Assume the following values:

D = 10,000 and S = $2.00 and H = $0.15 and F = .16 and P = 8

$$Q = \sqrt{2 \times D \times \frac{S + F \times P}{H}} = \sqrt{2 \times 10,000 \times \frac{2.00}{H}} = 661.31$$

Figure 21-4 indicates that the EOQ has shifted from period 19 to around period 33. The top line shows a Minitab line graph showing the minimum at approximately period 33.

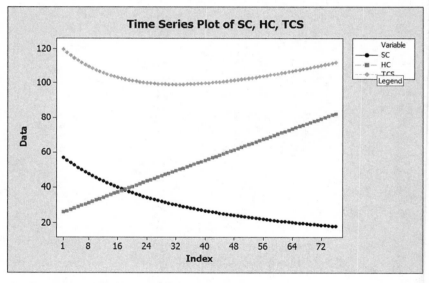

Figure 21-4 Shift on minimum to period 33

The Excel spreadsheet in Figure 21-5 shows the new Total Cost at period 33 with the EOQ_1 at around 660, which matches the results on the Excel spreadsheet of 661.31. The Q on the spreadsheet represents the EOQ_1.

F33 ▾ | fx | 660

	D	H	S	Q	F	SC	HC	TC	F	P	TCS
19	10000	0.15		2	**520**	38.46154	39	**77.46154**	0.16	8	102.0769
20	10000	0.15		2	530	37.73585	39.75	77.48585	0.16	8	101.6368
21	10000	0.15		2	540	37.03704	40.5	77.53704	0.16	8	101.2407
22	10000	0.15		2	550	36.36364	41.25	77.61364	0.16	8	100.8864
23	10000	0.15		2	560	35.71429	42	77.71429	0.16	8	100.5714
24	10000	0.15		2	570	35.08772	42.75	77.83772	0.16	8	100.2939
25	10000	0.15		2	580	34.48276	43.5	77.98276	0.16	8	100.0517
26	10000	0.15		2	590	33.89831	44.25	78.14831	0.16	8	99.84322
27	10000	0.15		2	600	33.33333	45	78.33333	0.16	8	99.66667
28	10000	0.15		2	610	32.78689	45.75	78.53689	0.16	8	99.52049
29	10000	0.15		2	620	32.25806	46.5	78.75806	0.16	8	99.40323
30	10000	0.15		2	630	31.74603	47.25	78.99603	0.16	8	99.31349
31	10000	0.15		2	640	31.25	48	79.25	0.16	8	99.25
32	10000	0.15		2	650	30.76923	48.75	79.51923	0.16	8	99.21154
33	10000	0.15		2	660	30.30303	49.5	79.80303	0.16	8	**99.19697**
34	10000	0.15		2	670	29.85075	50.25	80.10075	0.16	8	99.20522
35	10000	0.15		2	680	29.41176	51	80.41176	0.16	8	99.23529

Figure 21-5 An Excel spreadsheet showing the minimum at 33

The Green Effect of the New EOQ Formula

It's time to determine what the Green effect of the new EOQ_1 is with a freight rate of 16%. The number of deliveries per year with the old EOQ is calculated as N = number of orders per year = D / EOQ = 10,000 / 500 = 20. The new EOQ is 661.31, and this translates into D / EOQ_1 = 10,000 / 661.31 = 15.125 deliveries per year. For the sake of argument, there are now 16 deliveries per year. This represents the following:

- A 20% decrease in deliveries to and from the supplier to the customer.
- A 20% decrease in the amount of mileage needed to deliver the product from supplier to customer.
- A 20% decrease in the amount of gasoline used from the supplier to the customer.
- A 20% decrease in the amount of CO_2 put into the atmosphere from the decreased usage of gasoline because of the decreased number of deliveries.

Figure 21-6 shows how the freight rate and the number of deliveries are correlated to the freight rate "F." The chart indicates the number of deliveries that should be made to minimize the total cost of the supply chain. It begins with a freight rate of 1% and then increases by adding 3% to each successive value until it gets to 85%. The freight rate is the Y axis. The graph is calibrated in percentages divided by 10 to make the graph more proportional. A bottom line is F and the top line is N. The F line of 5 is interpreted as a freight rate of 50%. The X axis indicates the number of deliveries per year. Deliveries can be scheduled according to the rate of freight rate increases. For instance, if the freight rate increases from 3.4% to 6.4%, the number of deliveries per year should fall from 16 to 14. This represents an 85% increase in the freight rate, which will cause a 12.5% decrease in the number of deliveries made per year. The data is shown in Table 21-2.

Table 21-2 The Excel Spreadsheet Showing the Effect of Freight Rate "F" on the Number of Deliveries "N"

F	N
3.1	16.35175
3.4	**16.09557**
3.7	15.85107
4	15.61738
4.3	15.39373
4.6	15.17942
4.9	14.97382
5.2	14.77635
5.5	14.5865
5.8	14.40378
6.1	14.22776
6.4	**14.05804**
6.7	13.89425
7	13.73606

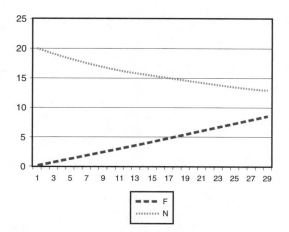

Figure 21-6 The effect of freight rate "F" on number of deliveries "N"

22

Consequences of the Industrial Revolution

Before the Industrial Revolution, the amount of carbon dioxide (CO_2) and other greenhouse gases released into the atmosphere was in a rough balance with what could be stored on Earth. Natural emissions of heat-trapping gases matched what could be absorbed in natural sinks. For example, plants take in CO_2 when they grow in spring and summer, and release it back to the atmosphere when they decay and die in fall and winter.

Industry took off in the mid-1700s, and large amounts of greenhouse gases were being emitted.

Fossil fuels were burned more and more to run cars, trucks, factories, planes, and power plants, adding to the natural supply of greenhouse gases. The gases—which can stay in the atmosphere for at least 50 years and up to centuries—are building up beyond the Earth's capacity to remove them and, in effect, are creating an extrathick heat blanket around the Earth. The result is that the globe has heated up by about one degree Fahrenheit over the past century—and it has heated up more intensely over the past two decades.

According to the National Oceanic and Atmospheric Administration's Earth System Research Laboratory, carbon dioxide concentrations in the atmosphere increased from approximately 280 parts per million (ppm) in preindustrial times to 382 ppm in 2006, a 36% increase. Almost all the increase is due to human activity. The current rate of increase in CO_2 concentrations is about 1.9 ppmv (parts per million by volume). Currently, the CO_2 concentrations are higher than at any time in at least the past 650,000 years. See Figure 22-1 and Figure 22-2 for a record of CO_2 concentrations from about 420,000 years ago to present.[1]

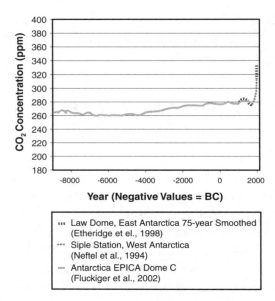

Figure 22-1 CO_2 concentrations from 8947 BC to 1975 AD[1]

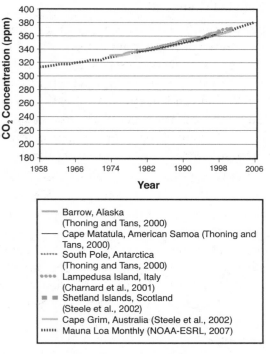

Figure 22-2 CO_2 concentrations from 1959 AD to 2006 AD[1]

Scientists expect that, in the absence of effective policies to reduce greenhouse gas pollution, the global average temperature will increase another 2.0 degrees Fahrenheit by 2100.[2] Even if the temperature change is at the small end of the predictions, the alterations to the climate are expected to be serious: more intense storms, more pronounced droughts, and coastal areas more severely eroded by rising seas. At the high end of the predictions, the world could face abrupt, catastrophic, and irreversible consequences.[2]

The last four complete years of the Mauna Loa CO_2 record plus the current year are outlined in Figure 22-3. Data are reported as a dry air mole fraction defined as the number of molecules of carbon dioxide divided by the number of all molecules in the air, including CO_2 itself, after water vapor has been removed. The mole fraction is expressed as parts per million (ppm). Example: 0.000400 is expressed as 400 ppm.

In Figure 22-3, the dashed line with the most volatility represents the monthly mean values, centered on the middle of each month. The smoothed line with the square symbols represents the same, after correction for the average seasonal cycle. The latter is determined as a moving average of seven adjacent seasonal cycles centered on the month to be corrected, except for the first and last three-and-a-half years of the record, where the seasonal cycle has been averaged over the first and last seven years, respectively.

The last year of data is still preliminary, pending recalibrations of reference gases and other quality-control checks. The Mauna Loa data are being obtained at an altitude of 3,400 meters in the northern subtropics, and may not be the same as the globally averaged CO_2 concentration at the surface.

It is important to study the data from the Mauna Loa Observatory from 1960 to 2010. The carbon dioxide data measured as the mole fraction in dry air on Mauna Loa constitutes the longest record of direct measurements of CO_2 in the atmosphere and is the volatile data on the graph. This work was started by C. David Keeling of the Scripps Institution of Oceanography in March of 1958 at a facility of the National Oceanic and Atmospheric Administration.[3] NOAA started its own CO_2 measurements in May of 1974, and they have run in parallel with those made by Scripps since then.[3] The stable line in the center represents the seasonally corrected data.

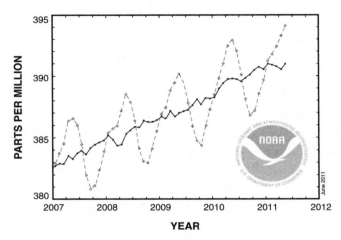

Figure 22-3 Represents the recent monthly mean of CO_2 at Mauna Loa[4]

Data are reported as a dry mole fraction defined as the number of molecules of carbon dioxide divided by the number of molecules of dry air multiplied by one million (ppm). Figure 22-4 shows the rise in parts per million.

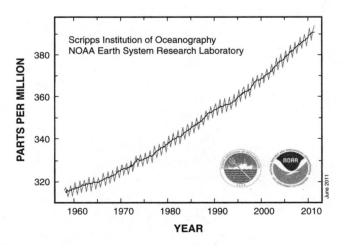

Figure 22-4 Atmospheric CO_2 at Mauna Loa Observatory from 1960 to 2010, Hawaii[4]

Now review the current increase in global temperatures. The data presented documents the increase in global temperature over the time span of 1890 to the current date (see Figure 22-5). Furthermore, 2009 was tied for the second-warmest year in modern record, according to a new NASA analysis of global surface temperature. The analysis, conducted by the Goddard Institute for Space Studies (GISS) in New York City, also shows that in the Southern Hemisphere, 2009 was the warmest year since modern records began in 1880.[5]

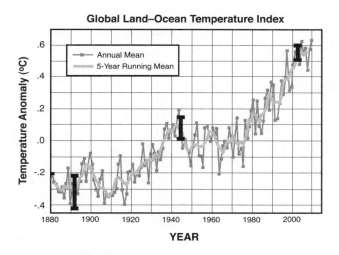

Figure 22-5 Global Land–Ocean Temperature Index[5]

Although 2008 was the coolest year of the decade—due to strong cooling of the tropical Pacific Ocean—2009 saw a return to near-record global temperatures. The past year was only a fraction of a degree cooler than 2005, the warmest year on record, and tied with a cluster of other years—1998, 2002, 2003, 2006, and 2007—as the second-warmest year since record keeping began.[5]

January 2000 to December 2009 was the warmest decade on record. Throughout the last three decades, the GISS surface temperature record shows an upward trenvd of about 0.2°C (0.36°F) per decade. Since 1880, the year that modern scientific instrumentation became available to monitor temperatures precisely, a clear warming trend is present. In total, average global temperatures have increased by about 0.8°C to 1°C (1.44°F to 1.8°F) since 1880 (see Figure 22-6).

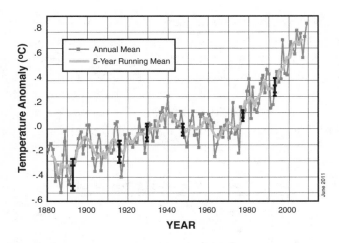

Figure 22-6 Global temperature[6]

References

[1] http://www.epa.gov/climatechange/science/recentac.html.

[2] EDF Environmental Defense Fund. http://www.edf.org/climate/basics-global-warming.

[3] http://www.esrl.noaa.gov/gmd/ccgg/trends, referencing C.D. Keeling, R.B. Bacastow, A.E. Bainbridge, C.A. Ekdahl, P.R. Guenther, and L.S. Waterman, "Atmospheric carbon dioxide variations at Mauna Loa Observatory, Hawaii," *Tellus*, 28 (1976): 538–551 and K.W. Thoning, P.P. Tans, and W.D. Komhyr, "Atmospheric carbon dioxide at Mauna Loa Observatory 2. Analysis of the NOAA GMCC data, 1974-1985," *Journal of Geophysical Research-Atmospheres*, 94 (1989): 8549–8565.

[4] http://www.esrl.noaa.gov/gmd/ccgg/trends.

[5] http://www.nasa.gov/topics/earth/features/temp-analysis-2009.html.

[6] http://data.giss.nasa.gov/gistemp/graphs.

23

Different Organizations' Green Supply Chain Management and LEED

In recent years, public attitude and opinion have changed remarkably regarding the way in which the environment is viewed. Over the past decade, many studies have been conducted regarding how the earth's environment is being destroyed due to the way in which people consume many of the earth's natural resources without replacing them, along with the harmful pollution that is continually pumped into the environment.

This change in attitude has primarily been brought about due to increased awareness of the harm caused by everyday lifestyle choices. The resulting attitude shift has sparked campaigns focused on educating people on how to make a difference. This shift increases pressure on organizations to improve their operations to reduce the amount of harm they cause on the environment. Consumer awareness has resulted in different buying choices being made based on which companies are cognizant of environmental protection strategies. This has forced many organizations to change the way they operate and learn new ways to operate a sustainable organization.

Various initiatives have been put in place to build a healthier and more sustainable environment for the years to come. Many organizations are continuously developing new technologies that will make the world a more environmentally friendly place. One such initiative in place is Leadership in Energy and Environmental Design (LEED), which was created by the United States Green Building Council (USGBC). It provides a general set of standards in the development of green buildings and green renovations and leads the effort toward developing Green supply chain management.

Green supply chain management is certain to be around for years to come and will inevitably be the cornerstone of sustainable organizations concerned with manufacturing and production. Green supply chain management will be vital to customer relationship management's success in providing consumers with proof of an organization's Green manufacturing and supply chain management processes. Organizations today need to look into their own carbon footprint and try to reduce it as much as possible.

There are thousands of programs and initiatives worldwide that have been designed and implemented to not only help make the environment sustainable for the future but also ensure business sustainability. The first example of this is the LEED requirements. Another initiative discussed is the study conducted by the Supply Chain World Conference titled *Best Practices in implementing Green Supply Chains.*[1] This considers the field of construction and its many facets, such as building codes and what new materials have been produced to cause less of an impact on the environment than traditional materials.

The majority of large companies today have taken steps to reduce their organizational impact on the environment. This transformation has proven the link between improving environmental performances and financial gain. Supply chain management is a key area for implementing green improvements that result in increased financial strength. Organizations that have improved their supply chain and environmental performance have found that the organization incurs lower waste disposal and employee training costs, as well as a decrease in cost of materials. Combining these cost-saving activities with lower environmental permitting fees, organizations can experience enormous savings.

So what exactly is Green supply chain management? According to LMI Government Consulting, "Green Supply Chain Management recognizes the disproportionate environmental impact of supply chain processes in an organization."[1] In an article published by the *Harvard Business Review,* Carter and Narasimhan state that Green supply chain management has the following advantages:

- Improves agility—Green supply chain management helps mitigate risks and speed innovations.

- Increases adaptability—Green supply chain analyses often lead
  to innovative processes and continuous improvements.

- Promotes alignment—Green supply chain management
  involves negotiating policies with suppliers and customers,
  which results in better alignment of business processes and
  principles.[2]

Traditionally, Green supply chain management programs were
associated with assuring compliance, minimizing risk, maintaining
health, and protecting the environment. However, organizations are
starting to notice an emerging value creation that is being brought
about through implementation, such as enhanced supplier and customer relations, rise in organizational productivity, increase in innovation, and growth. Organizations that successfully implement Green
supply chain management strategies give themselves a much greater
chance for long-term sustainability, regardless of external forces such
as competition or economic health. The inability of an organization to
change will result in the organization's being susceptible to failure.[2]

In *Strategic Management* by Dess, Lumpkin, and Eisner (2006),
it is written: "Environmental sustainability is now a value embraced
by the most competitive and successful multinational companies. For
many successful firms, environmental values are now becoming a central part of their cultures and management process...environmental
impacts are being audited and accounted for as the third bottom line."

According to one 2004 corporate report, "If we aren't good corporate citizens as reflected in a Triple Bottom Line that takes into
account social and environmental responsibilities along with financial
ones—eventually our stock price, our profits, and our entire business could suffer." *Strategic Management* also describes a report
conducted by KPMG studying 350 firms: "More big multinational
firms are seeing the benefits of improving their environmental performance.... Firms are saving money and boosting share performance by
taking a close look at how their operations impact the environment....
Companies see that they can make money as well."

Shaw Industries, a subsidiary of the Berkshire Hathaway Company, has managed to reinvent itself through taking drastic action and
developing an environmentally stable business plan. Shaw Industries
produces industrial carpet for offices. Traditionally, the company

used a PVC plastic to produce their product, which was potentially toxic and harmful. Old, used carpet was dumped in landfills, with over 95% of the carpet being nonreusable. The carpet industry was also susceptible to increases in raw material prices because petroleum is one of the primary products used to produce carpet. These factors prompted Shaw Industries to rethink their business strategy and create a new way of producing carpet.

The company developed a brand-new way of manufacturing carpet that is not only nontoxic, but extremely eco-friendly. Shaw Industries was awarded by the Environmental Protection Agency (EPA) with the Presidential Green Chemistry Challenge Award for their ingenuity. As of 2008, Shaw Industries had 500 million square feet of their new carpet, EcoWorx, laid in offices throughout the world. This example shows how good strategic planning that takes into account the changing external environment helps organizations achieve sustainable growth.

In recent years, LEED has looked at tackling how to reinvent previously harmful products so that they are eco-friendly. The goal is to set guidelines for the construction industry with the intent of improving performance in energy conservation, water efficiency, carbon dioxide emissions reductions, indoor environmental quality, and stewardship of resources and sensitivity to their impact. LEED was developed by the United States Green Building Council in 1998 and is continually becoming ever more present in the design of new buildings and communities and the redevelopment of existing structures. According to the United States Green Building Council, LEED is flexible enough to be applied to both commercial and residential structures. The USGBC states: "It works throughout the building lifecycle—design and construction, operations and maintenance, and significant retrofit. And LEED for Neighborhood Development extends the benefits of LEED beyond the building footprint into the neighborhood it serves."

In a report titled *Foundations of LEED*, published by the USGBC, the mission of LEED is as stated: "LEED encourages and accelerates global adoption of sustainable and green building and neighborhood development practices through the creation and implementation of a universally understood and accepted benchmark encompassing existing and new standards, tools, and performance criteria." The first LEED Pilot Project Program was launched in 1998 and is known as LEED Version 1.0. With the green building industry guidelines and initiatives constantly changing, new guidelines and initiatives are being introduced daily. Project teams must be aware of changes made in order to comply with the latest version of the LEED rating system so that all construction qualifies for LEED approved and certification. Currently, LEED Version 3 has been in use since its launch in April 2009.

LEED is focused on continuous improvement and is updated through regular development cycles. *The Foundations of LEED* report identifies three basic types of LEED development:

1. **Implementation and Maintenance of Current Version** includes the improvement of LEED through the correction and clarification of credit language. Credits refer to gaining credits for green rights. For example, a permit is required to allow the holder to emit one ton of carbon dioxide. Credits are awarded to countries or groups that have reduced their greenhouse gases below their emission quota. Carbon credits can be traded in the international market at their current market price. The carbon credit system was ratified by the Kyoto Protocol. Its goal is to stop the increase of carbon dioxide emissions. If an enterprise or a group plants enough trees to reduce emissions by one ton, the corporation will be awarded one credit. If emissions are produced above quota, a credit must be purchased from the environmental group.

2. **Adaptations** to the existing version include the ability for both specific space types and international projects to be addressed through the creation of credit adaptations. This allows new paths to be introduced in existing credits to meet the needs of projects that would otherwise be unable to utilize the requirements in LEED.

3. **Next Version** is the comprehensive improvement phase of LEED development through a periodic evaluation and revision process. This phase includes multiple avenues for stakeholder input and final approval by USGBC membership. The ideas generated during the development of next version LEED credits are often pilot tested by LEED project teams prior to ballot.

The LEED Green Building Rating System is voluntary and no developer is confined to follow the set guidelines. The rating system is also consensus-based and market-driven. The rating system is structured around existing and proven technologies, and evaluates the environmental performance of a whole building over the building's or neighborhood's life cycle, providing a benchmark standard for what is deemed a green building in not only design but also construction and operation.

The rating system is designed so that new or existing commercial, institutional, and residential buildings, along with new neighborhood developments, can be rated on the same standards. Accepted energy standards, along with environmental practices, serve as the base of the rating system, and it aims to strike a balance between known, established practices and emerging, innovative concepts. The USGBC sets Minimum Program Requirements (MPRs). All projects must follow these minimum requirements to be eligible for LEED certification. These MPRs are in place to clarify the types of buildings that the LEED Green Building Rating System was designed to measure, and taken together these serve three goals:

1. To give clear guidance to customers.
2. To protect the integrity of the LEED program.
3. To reduce complications that occur during the LEED Certification process.[3]

Developers must be aware that the LEED Certification can be revoked at any time if the project fails to uphold the MPRs. The reason the MPRs are in place is to ensure the understanding of the fundamentals of green building. The rating system designed by the USGBC covers the following various topics:

- Sustainable Sites
- Water Efficiency
- Energy and Atmosphere
- Materials and Resources
- Indoor Environmental Quality

- Awareness and Education (Homes)
- Smart Location and Linkages (ND*)
- Neighborhood Pattern and Design (ND*)
- Green Infrastructure and Building (ND*)
- Innovation in Design/Operations
- Regional Priority

* ND stands for neighborhood development. In the future, HUD may begin giving grants based on the LEED ND scores. The ratings are divided into five areas.

- Smart Location and Linkage   Points 27
- Neighborhood Pattern and Design   Points 44
- Green Infrastructure and Buildings   Points 29
- Innovation and Design Process   Points 6
- Regional Priority Credit   Points 4
- Possible Total   Points 110

The rating system is designed around a 100-point scale, with an additional 10 bonus points granted for innovative design and exceptional performance. Additional credit is granted for achieving regional importance regarding a project's location. The weighting of points is split between human benefit and environmental benefit, such as global warming, greenhouse gas emissions, fossil fuel use, toxins and carcinogens, air and water pollutants, and indoor quality. The USGBC awards different project certifications in accordance with the following scale, which is determined on the amount of points obtained:

40–49 Points	Certified
50–59 Points	Silver
60–79 Points	Gold
80+ Points	Platinum

References

(1) http://postconflict.unep.ch/humanitarianaction/documents/02_08-04_05-25.pdf.

(2) "The Triple-A Supply Chain," Lee, *Harvard Business Review*, October 2004 and "Environmental Supply Chain Management," Carter and Narasimhan, CAPS Research, 1998.

(3) U.S. Green Building Council Board of Directors, June 15, 2010.

24

Case Study: Sweetwater Sound

The green building should take advantage of a number of elements:[1]

Building site—The site must be well suited to take advantage of the mass transportation system so that mileage to and from can be minimized.

Energy efficiency—This includes passive design strategies such as orientation of the building, natural lighting, and passive solar and building design.

Material efficiency—This involves selecting sustainable building products. These products should be as reusable and recyclable as possible.

Water efficiency—Plans need to be in place to use recycled water or limit the usage of water by creative options such as these:

- Ultra-low-flush toilets
- Low-flow shower heads and other water-conserving fixtures
- Recirculation systems for centralized hot water distribution
- Point-of-use hot water heating systems for distant locations

Occupant and health and safety—The proper vitalization and clean-air quality will cut down on allergy reactions and respiratory disease.

Sweetwater Case Study[2]

On June 26, 2011, Sweetwater's Leadership in Energy and Environmental Design (LEED) Platinum Certification was recognized at a special ceremony where the award and certificate were presented to Sweetwater Founder and President, Chuck Surack, by Fort Wayne, Indiana, Mayor Tom Henry and Liz Ellis, representative of the Indiana Chapter of the U.S. Green Building Council. This was the first award given in the State of Indiana for a commercial building. Present at the ceremony were representatives for the USGBC, representatives from Senator Richard Lugar's local office, several city council members, and representatives from Corporate Construction and MSKTD, the construction company and architectural firm responsible for Sweetwater's LEED Platinum Certification success.

Sweetwater's headquarters building is the first commercial structure in northeast Indiana to receive LEED Platinum Certification by the U.S. Green Building Council. The LEED award recognizes Sweetwater's commitment to preserving natural resources and providing a safer, healthier workplace. To accomplish these goals, Sweetwater employed a combination of state-of-the-art technology, rapid-renewal materials, and recycling during construction and in their day-to-day operation. These practices benefit the entire community. The two key partners for the project were MSKTD Associates in Fort Wayne, Indiana, an Architect and Design firm; and Corporate Construction out of Auburn, Indiana.

The remainder of this chapter presents some of the features of the new campus.

Rapidly Renewable Materials

Every effort was made to use rapidly renewable materials—products derived from plants that are harvested within a 10-year or shorter cycle, including cork, bamboo, pine, and okan wood. For example, the sales manager offices were constructed of bamboo.

Glass

Insulated, heat-treated glass is used on the east, south, and west building faces to reduce solar heat gain and limit the cooling load placed on the building's mechanical systems. The heat-fused coating on the glass also reduces glare to improve the comfort of building occupants.

Texturing on the glass reduces glare and improves the comfort for the building occupants.

Light Sensors

Sensors throughout the building respond to natural light levels and occupancy, automatically adjusting the amount of light as necessary. In some instances, occupancy sensors detect the presence of people and turn on the lights as they pass through the halls or enter rooms.

Roof Membrane

The buildings feature a highly reflective white roof membrane that reduces solar heat gain.

Insulation

Insulation was added to the roof to increase energy efficiency.

Daylight and Views

Windows and skylights throughout the building help to reduce or eliminate the need for electric lighting, creating a stimulating and productive environment. Eighty percent of the building has access to sunlight. Sensors are integrated to increase or decrease the amount of light in the building as it changes throughout the day.

Recycling

Recycling reduces waste that would otherwise end up in landfills. Shredded paper and cardboard boxes are reused in the warehouse for packing and shipping orders.

Construction-Waste Management

Throughout the construction process, materials were sorted to identify items that could be reused or sent back to the manufacturers.

Recycled Content of Materials

At the onset of construction, an older building stood on-site. When parts of the building were demolished, 98% of the total waste materials, such as concrete, plastic, wood, and glass, was recycled. Construction materials were carefully selected to ensure that recycled content would be used wherever possible. Carpet, fabric, and steel throughout the facility contribute to the total recycled percentage of 31.4%.

Regional Materials

More than 44% of the building's materials, such as steel, stone, stone cladding, drywall, insulation, and doors, was extracted, harvested, recovered, or manufactured within 500 miles of the project site. All the warehouse's structural steel and panels were manufactured just north of Fort Wayne; the stone that clad the new recording studio and auditorium spaces was quarried in Glenmont, Ohio.

Water Use Reduction

Sweetwater's restrooms employ water conservation strategies, resulting in a 40% efficiency increase and reducing the burden on municipal water supply and wastewater systems. Waterless urinals, low-flow/automatic faucets, and dual-flush toilets all contribute to water savings.

Water-use reduction techniques result in a 54% annual water savings.

Certified Wood

At least 50% of the wood-based products used in the facility are certified in accordance with the Forest Stewardship Council's

Principles and Criteria. These components include structural framing, flooring, subflooring, wood doors, and finishes.

Low-Emitting Materials

Low-emitting materials are those that emit zero or minimum pollutant into the environment. Wherever possible, these materials were used to eliminate odorless indoor air contaminants that are irritating or harmful to the occupants. All adhesives and sealants used on the interior of the building comply with standards for air quality control. Low Volatile Organic Compound materials including carpet, paints, coatings, glues, sealants, and wood products free of urea-formaldehyde resin were specified to ensure compliance with air-quality measures.

Building Flushing

Prior to occupancy, the building air was flushed to reduce/eliminate harmful vapors and toxins that may have been left behind after the construction was completed.

Ice Storage

During off-peak overnight hours, ice storage tanks on the campus produce ice for the mechanical system's cooling needs, reducing overall power consumption and the load on the utility grid. The cost of this system will be offset in annual energy savings within five years.

Commissioning of Mechanical Systems

The mechanical systems were commissioned and carefully analyzed by specialists throughout the design process. Energy modeling, through testing and balancing of different components, was calculated to improve efficiency.

Outdoor Air Delivery Monitoring

Air monitoring systems, designed to help sustain occupant health and comfort, are integrated into the building. This system regulates indoor air quality, introducing fresh outdoor air as necessary, to flush out contaminants that may be present.

Tobacco Smoke Control

The entire campus inside and out is smoke free to minimize exposure of building occupants, indoor surfaces, and ventilation systems to tobacco smoke.

References

[1] http://www.calrecycle.ca.gov/GREENBUILDING/Basics.htm#What.

[2] Video: http://www.youtube.com/watch?v=CIcexWH0kck.

Other videos:

The Sustainable Building Center, http://www.youtube.com/watch?v=Q7XZAc2CD6s&feature=related

25

Case Study: Behavioral Health

This chapter highlights the Lean and Green philosophy by showing the results of the use of a researched methodology, Lean Six Sigma, in the hospital process. The goal is to maximize the value-added process, which inherently adds less waste to the system. The rest of the case study follows the steps of the Lean Six Sigma philosophy to emphasize the profitability and sustainability possible in any company.

Lean Six Sigma is the marriage of two disciplines, Lean and Six Sigma. Lean is the philosophy of the focus on nonvalue activities. This is where the concept of value stream mapping (VSM) comes from. Identify the number of activities that have value and divide by the total process. The total process is composed of activities that have values and activities that do not add directly to the value of the product. These activities are called non-value-added. Create a map of the current processes, identifying the nonvalue activities, and eliminate as many as possible. Then map the activities of the improved model with future processes in mind. The comparison of the value stream mapping of the process and the ratio of value-added should be greater than the VSM of the current process.

Six Sigma is the business management strategy developed by Motorola. It is a philosophy and set of methods companies use to eliminate defects in their products and processes. It seeks to reduce variation in the processes that lead to producing higher inventories or inefficient processes. The introduction of process improvement Six Sigma is now about helping the organization make more money by improving customer value and efficiency. Six Sigma breaks the process improvement effort into five phases, called the DMAIC process: Define, Measure, Analyze, Improve, and Control.

In the Define phase, the problem is identified. This can be very difficult for some companies because problems vary by department. Defining the customer-related issues is a good company-wide starting point. Using value stream mapping will help in determining process goals and delineating a clear problem statement.

In the Measure phase, problems or inaccuracies in the system are measured, defects are defined, and opportunities for improvement are evaluated. During this phase, a process map is developed and data collection procedures begin. Using Pareto charts, histograms, bar charts, and control charts will simplify the introduction of causal relationship strategies.

Analyze is the phase used to quantify what was found in the Measure phase. In this step, define performance objectives, identify value and nonvalue process steps, and determine the root cause of the inefficient process. The Pareto analysis, statistics, ANOVA, and brainstorming techniques can be utilized in this phase.

In the Improve phase, use the preceding steps to determine where to improve the process. Brainstorming, 5S, line balancing or work flow, poka-yoke, and hypothesis testing are excellent methods for completing this analysis.

Control is the last, and perhaps hardest, phase. After the entire plan is developed and implemented, a plan is needed for keeping the process improvement effort in line in the future. If the new environment is too relaxed, it becomes easy to lose focus. Techniques available for maintaining the new status quo include control charts, mistake proofing, process control plans, and training plans.

Case Study of the Six Sigma DMAIC Approach in Health Care

The following case study follows all five phases. This case study in the application of Lean Six Sigma in a hospital measures the efficacy and potential savings of adding Lean Six Sigma into the corporate philosophy. For privacy reasons, the name of the hospital is withheld.

Behavioral Health

In-Patient Admission

EXECUTIVE SUMMARY

The team was asked to integrate the basic principles of Lean Six Sigma into the in-patient admission process. The team examined the patient admission process from the time of arrival to the time of discharge.

Purpose

The objective of the project was to identify probable variables that are a direct result of slow-speed admissions and customer dissatisfaction. The total average time for patient admission was three hours.

Analysis

Due to the large scale of the projected, limited data collection, and allotted time, the group decided to focus on the process flow. The team discovered that patients were being asked the same questions at one or more points in the communication chain. After examining the process flow, it was concluded that different mediums of communication created a constraint in the flow of information.

Goals

- To achieve a 50% decrease in the amount of time spent on nurse assessment by June 2009
- To increase revenue by increasing the number of patients from 10 to 12 per day
- To decrease patient assessment by 33%

Define Phase

The Behavioral Health hospital is a 24-hour comprehensive mental health program located in Fort Wayne, Indiana, offering specialized inpatient and outpatient services to children, adolescents, adults, and older adults suffering from emotional, behavioral, and chemical dependency problems. The facility opened in August 2000 and currently employs over 200 full- and part-time employees, providing a total of 107 beds, making it the second-largest unit in the hospital family.

The purpose of this project is to provide Behavioral Health Hospital an educational insight concurrent to the methodologies found in the Lean Six Sigma philosophy and to apply that knowledge to Behavioral Health in-/outpatient process flow. The Behavioral Health staff is interested in reducing the cycle time it takes a patient to complete the admission process from entry to exit.

The team's mission is to look into this data and determine the key input variables that are the root of slow admission processes and determine how to correct or improve on these situations. The mapped process includes five main processes that require the patient to be interviewed and examined by a licensed nurse/physician. These processes include a brief clinical, nurse assessment, social history examination, psychiatric evaluation, genealogy, family history, and physical examination.

Problem Statement

There are four different communication mediums utilized for each admission process: one written, three dictations, and one electronic. Using different mediums has created communication constraints within the process and uses valuable resources to create non-value-added to the process. Often, the same questions are repeated in the five processes, creating frustration for the staff and the patient. The duplication results in inconsistent documentation, wasteful staff resources, and patient dissatisfaction.

The brief clinical is currently processed in written form, whereas the nurse assessment is processed electronically through the hospital's central computer software. These steps utilize different methods of storing information, which results in data redundancy. The information gathered from the other areas is imaged into their database. Each of these systems offers a means of communication and collaboration but stores data on separate systems. This makes it difficult to access information from one system to the other. The duplication of questions and the inability to transfer answers to questions from one step to the next proves to be a major concern. All the mentioned variables combined result in slow admission speed and patient dissatisfaction.

The process map (see Figure 25-1) illustrates the various steps a patient follows throughout the admission process. In the brief clinical, there are 19 main questions, 12 of which are repeated in nurse assessment. A patient who is already suffering from a mental problem may become more frustrated with recurring questions throughout the process. The Behavioral Health Center is striving for 100% customer satisfaction; however, due to their current system structure, they are unable to meet this goal.

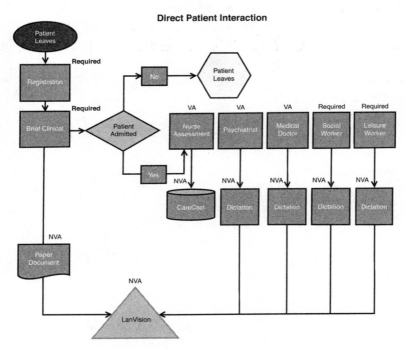

Figure 25-1 Current process flow map

Scope of Analysis

Upon data collection, the team examined each process from the time of patient arrival until the time of discharge. The group focused on the brief clinical questionnaire in comparison to all other processes to determine the number of questions that were repeated in each process. The scope of the project is to eliminate the 15 most time-consuming, duplicate questions from the admission process based on cycle time. A data set has been created to demonstrate how much time can be saved after eliminating the recurring questions.

Purpose

The objective is to examine each process and create alternative opportunities for improving the admission process. This includes identifying internal and external factors that are creating slow admission speed, exploring the channels of communication to improve the process, and eliminating data redundancy. The current time interval for the patients to complete the admission/discharge process is estimated to be three hours. Table 25-1 shows the total amount of time wasted per year, which results in a total cost of $171,250, including 60 minutes of wasted time per patient, resulting in $91,250 in wages for a $25-per-hour salary. The total dictation cost would include the $80,000 salary of $40,000 per year for two employees.

Table 25-1 Cost of Wastage Amount of Time

Current Process Time and Wastage of Time in Complete Process

Average Patient/Day	Wastage Time/ Patient (Min)	Total Wastage Time/Day (Min)	Total Wastage Time/Year (Min)
10	60	600	219,000

Total Extra Cost Per Year for Complete Process (Assumption That Average Salary per Employee is $25)

Average Hourly Salary of Employees	Wastage Time/ Day (Min)	Wastage Money/ Day in Salaries	Wastage Money/ Year
$25	600	$250	$91,250

Total Extra Cost from Dictation

Dictation Employees	Salary/Year	Total Cost of Dictation/Year	
2	$40,000	$80,000	
	Total Cost/Year	$171,250	

Goals

- To increase customer/staff satisfaction through elimination of repetitive questions and improvement to the process flow
- To achieve a 50% decrease in the amount of time spent on the nurse assessment by June 2009
- To increase revenue by increasing the number of patients from 10 to 12 per day

- To decrease the amount of time spent for the complete patient assessment process by 33%

Measure Phase

To understand the process, different data and variables collected during the first phase of the project was reviewed. The staff provided the team with their current process flow of inpatients (see Figure 25-1). Due to privacy and confidentiality, the team was unable to physically collect data throughout the five process phases. The staff was able to provide the team with templates for each stage. The total process consisted of six stages; however, the team narrowed the process down to five due to the insignificant value/time the last stage provided.

The team researched each process beginning with the brief clinical. In this portion of the process, an assessor or a nurse performs a written brief clinical to evaluate the patient. Questions focus on better understanding the patient's chief complaint, presenting problem, and performing a suicide assessment. The average time for a patient to complete a brief clinical was measured at 40 minutes (see Figure 25-2). If assessors believe that the patient is mentally unstable, the patient is moved into the nurse assessment stage.

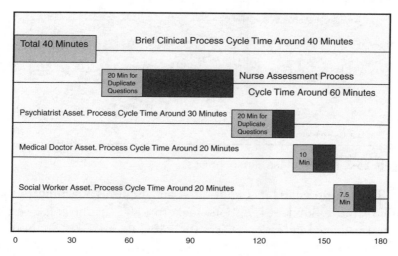

Figure 25-2 The Behavioral Health Center process flow

In this stage, questions about psychiatric, physical, and overall health of the patient are entered into the computer software Care-Cast. This process typically takes an average time of 60 minutes per patient. In the third stage, a psychiatrist performs a mental status evaluation of the patient averaging 30 minutes. In the fourth stage, a medical doctor completes a thorough physical evaluation of the patient, which takes an average of 20 minutes to complete. For the final process, a social worker will ask the patient personal information including family history and abuse history. This assessment takes an average of 20 minutes per patient.

During the measure phase, the team decided to focus on the brief clinical as a base foundation for the redundancy of the questions asked throughout all processes. Based on the data gathered, the Dotplot chart illustrates the number of repetitive questions asked throughout the process (X) and the time in seconds (Y) each question takes. The time for each question ranges from 0 to 600 seconds (see Figure 25-3).

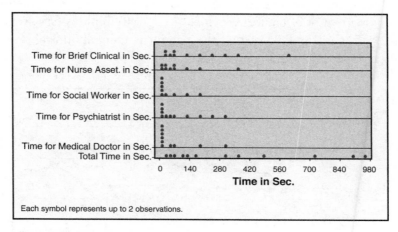

Figure 25-3 Dotplot of the current process

The Pareto charts in Figure 25-4 and Figure 25-5 indicate that 50% of the redundant questions make up 80% of the total wasted time. Further examination proves the initial findings. It is important to understand that the Pareto chart in terms of "time" is more important than the Pareto chart in terms of "redundancy" because, although a question may be asked several times throughout the process, the question may take only a few seconds to answer and will not be relevant to reducing time. This can also be viewed in Figure 25-3. Notice that the time, the X axis, is clustered with questions that are less than 200 seconds; however, they become stagnant as time increases.

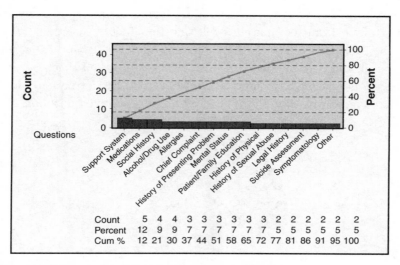

Figure 25-4 Pareto chart on redundancy-based process

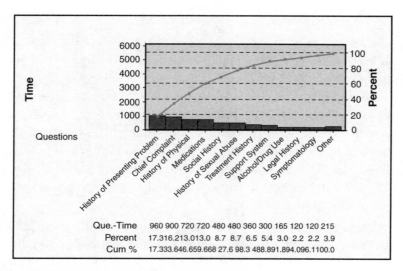

Figure 25-5 Pareto chart on time-based process

Analysis Phase

Given the measure and data provided, the team concluded that 54.08, or 29%, of the questions create wasted time (see Figure 25-6) due to redundancy of data and based on the amount of time each question takes. This was calculated by taking 15 questions from the brief clinical and comparing each question to the questions asked in the processes of social history, psychiatric evaluation, history and physical, and nurse assessment, and selecting questions that pertained to a frequency greater than one. Questions that had a frequency level less than one were considered relevant, nonrepetitive questions.

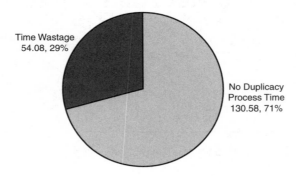

Figure 25-6 Complete process time

Although many of the frequencies were greater than one, the team examined each question and concluded that some of the questions measured took longer in patient assessment. There may be extreme variations depending on the patient; however, the mean concluded an approximate time for each question to complete. An analysis measured each process and determined the length of each repetitive question, measuring how long each question takes for each process. The findings concluded that recurring questions that took greater than 100 seconds to answer made up 80% of the total wasted time and should be looked at first.

Although the team focused on question redundancy, a closer look at the fish-bone diagram (see Figure 25-7) reveals several factors that may create cause and effect for slow admission speed and customer dissatisfaction. After sitting through several meetings with the staff, the team found lack of collaboration among the doctors and the hospital staff. This may be due, in part, to employee enforcement by management. Many of the doctors are reluctant to use the software provided, either because they don't think it is user-friendly or because they lack the patience to use the new technology tools available. The nurses feel that due to the nature of the patient's state of mind, it would be inappropriate to interview the patients while recording data on the computer. The staff argues that loss of eye contact through the use of computers during interviews detracts from their ability to build trust with the patient. Also, the hospital has certain state and government policies to follow that prohibit the staff from following a uniform process flow.

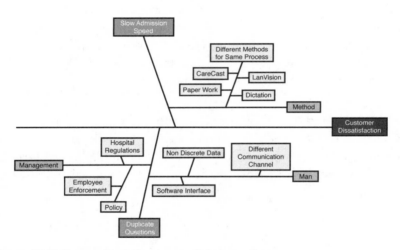

Figure 25-7 Cause-effect diagram, or fish-bone diagram

The major cause of slow admission could be pinpointed at the different methods used for the same process. With several different communication channels, the hospital is unable to flow the process from one stage to the other. It operates on central software but does not utilize this software to its maximum potential. Instead, information is manually written in the brief clinical as opposed to being entered into the system's software.

The brief clinical is electronically stored into the system database, which is software that stores all the patients' medical records as images throughout each stage of the admission process. In the second phase, the nurse interviews the patient and inputs the information into the software, which is imaged into the database. It is important to note that the software does not have the capacity of storing information for more than one month. The third and fourth phase involves a contracted psychiatrist and medical doctors who provide their own medical form and dictate the information from each patient. The information is later typed by staff and scanned into the database. This creates many non-value-added processes and redundancy between all processes and uses four means of communication throughout the patient admission process.

Another possible cause for slow admission is the software itself. The software is structured to have data flow from one task to the next; however, the software has some constraints of its own. Comments entered by doctors/staff are considered discrete data and do not allow flow to another task process. If the doctors/staff would like to see the comments made on the nurse assessment, they have to log in to that specific task process.

The selected area in Figure 25-8 should be an area of focus for Behavioral Health. The graph indicates an overall picture of the time in seconds each repetitive question takes to complete. The hospital has the potential to improve its performance by simply eliminating non-value-added data.

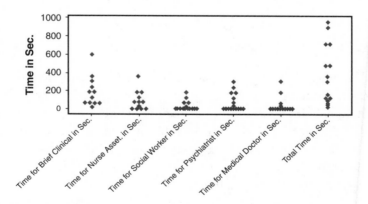

Figure 25-8 Individual value plot for current process phases

Improvement Phase

The analysis provided the team with insight on ways to improve the patient admission process, beginning with implementing an effective process to eliminate recurring questions. The total time to complete the admission process is estimated to take three hours. Figure 25-9 shows how the recurring questions could streamline the time, reducing it by 60 minutes or 33%.

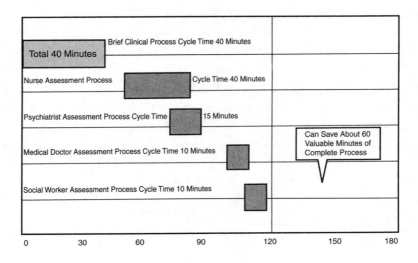

Figure 25-9 The Behavioral Health Center recommended process flow

Improvement is possible through the trials of hardware and software tools currently on the market. For example, Hosp-Cad is a tool used in hospitals that works much like the clipboards used by nurses to write down notes while interviewing patients. The clipboard is a digital device capable of scanning multiple forms while allowing the nurse or doctor to write notes as if it were paper. The Hosp-Cad alleviates the concern for maintaining eye contact with the patient and would be no different than writing on a piece of paper. The staff could then upload the information in digital format straight to the computer. This would eliminate the written brief clinical and the doctor's paper trail while storing the information in digital form. Hosp-Cad along with Script 1.1, software designed to convert handwriting to digital writing, would allow the information technology department to write software that would interact and input the data into the software.

The current practice for dictation is for the doctor to record his conversation with the patient. At a later time, a hospital staff member dictates the conversation to paper form. A possible solution would be to purchase software called Dragon, a voice-to-digital converter that will eliminate the tedious task of a staff member listening to a monologue and typing it into the system. The software allows the user to speak to the patient while wearing a headset. The headset is connected to a computer input and converts verbal information into digital format.

The cost to implement such tools would be insignificant in comparison to the benefits of implementing the hardware/software. Table 25-2 provides an approximation of the cost to implement the information technology tools. Another system available that performs similar functions is the Tablet PC; although the device is a high-cost product, the benefits would outweigh its short-term cost.

Table 25-2 Costing Table for Recommended Solutions

Hardware/Software	Cost/Unit	Total Requirement	Total Cost
Tablet PC	$2,000	10	$20,000
Hosp-Cad	$200	10	$2,000
Dragon software	$2,000	1	$2,000
Dragon headphone	$100	10	$1,000
Script 1.1	$60	1	$60
Total Cost			$25,060

Upon implementation of the improvements previously mentioned, the team was able to construct an improved process flow (see Figure 25-10) that eliminated the manual brief clinical form. Now a paperless process not only saves the company resources, including the use of and finance for paper, but also eliminates the process of physically having to image the file to the database. Through the elimination of redundant questions, each process was also improved by more than 50%.

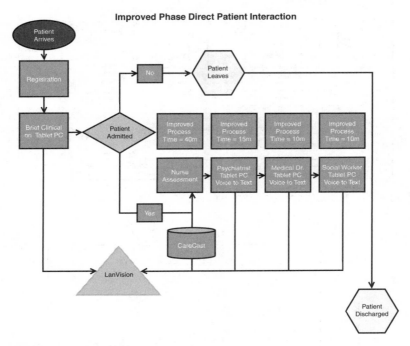

Figure 25-10 Improved process map

A confidence interval was created to determine the effect of the redundant questions in comparison to the amount of time that could be reduced. The team concluded with a certainty of 95% that questions greater than 370 seconds create 80% of the time wasted for all processes. The summary chart for total time (see Figure 25-11) clearly shows the 95% confident intervals for improvements.

Figure 25-12 visibly depicts the comparison of the current time for a patient to complete the process and the improvement of the time reduced by 30%. With the implementation of this improvement, Behavioral Health will eliminate non-value-added, which will result in an increase in the number of patients who are admitted daily and increase patient revenue by more than 20%.

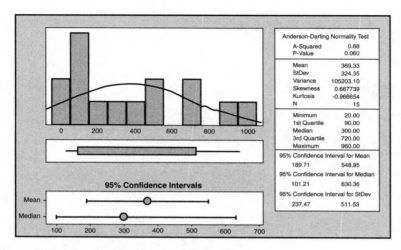

Figure 25-11 Summary chart for total time

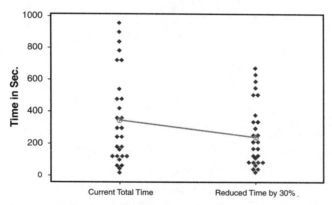

Figure 25-12 Individual value plot of comparison between current and improved time

Through the reduction process, the team expects to increase patient load by 2% per day, which would increase company revenue by $2,640,000 per year, as seen in Table 25-3.

Table 25-3 Revenue Table

Current Revenue Report			
Average Patients/Day	Patients/Year	Revenue/Patient	Total Revenue/Year
10	3,500	$3,000	$10,500,000
Predicated Revenue Report			
Average Patients/Day	Patients/Year	Revenue/Patient	Total Revenue/Year
12	4,380	$3,000	$13,140,000
Increased Revenue Per Year from Patient		$2,640,000	

Control Phase

The team concluded that the nurse assessment process was the most time-consuming process. The results were based on the length and breadth of the questions extending throughout the process, whether psychological, physical, family based, background check, or treatment based. After a conversation with one of hospital's nursing staff, it was discovered that most of the information is already in the system or on paper; however, the nurses don't have access to the information. This causes the nurse to ask identical questions to the patient throughout all stages.

One of the most critical areas needing correction is the head-to-toe physical examination. The nursing staff reported that almost one-third of their patients come from the Main Hospital Unit. The Main Hospital Unit collects patient information during their head-to-toe examination and stores the data in the center's database. When the patient arrives in the Behavioral Center, he is taken through the same head-to-toe examination. This particular process can take 10 to 20 minutes. Future research must center on the potential for eradicating this duplication through information-sharing technology between the two treatment units. Information sharing could save both facilities time, money, and resources, as well as increase customer satisfaction.

The Summary of the Lean and Green Technologies

Technology	Lean	Green	Total
VMI	21.22%	27.23%	23.01%
Certification	1.02%	0.82%	0.96%
WMS Program	3.64%	0.14%	2.60%
RF in the Warehouse	1.02%	0.91%	0.99%
TMS	10.49%	13.38%	11.32%
Vendor Portal	0.51%	0%	0.35%
New Item Portal	1.72%	0%	1.20%
Customer, Commodity, and New Product Portal	26.07%	0.05%	18.30%
ERP	1.29%	0.32%	1.00%
3PL	2.11%	0.35%	1.59%
ABCDE Classification	1.07%	0.38%	0.86%
Substitution Program	0.25%	0.08%	0.20%
Central Stock	1.58%	1.27%	1.49%
Promotional Forecast	1.71%	1.37%	1.61%
DRP	16.56%	51.45%	26.98%
Joint Order Allocation	0.99%	0.22%	0.76%
VPQ with Lookahead	1.63%	1.31%	1.54%
CPFR	4.10%	0.77%	3.11%
MH and Voice Pick	2.89%	0.04%	2.04%
Mobius	0.12%	0.00%	0.08%
Total	**100%**	**100%**	**100%**

Index

Symbols

3PL (third-party logistics), 137
  benefits of, 142-143
  Green Savings, 144-145
  Lean Savings, 143-144
  multimodal, 138
  network optimization, 139-142
  OSS (onsite supplier), 138-139

A

ABC analysis, 147-148
ABCDE classification of inventory, 147-149
  central stocking, 152-157
    Green Savings, 157
    Lean Savings, 157
  Green Savings, 150
  Lean Savings, 149-150
  substitution program, 150-151
    Green Savings, 152
    Lean Savings, 151-152
accounting controls, benefits of ERP (Enterprise Resource Programs), 130-131
adaptive forecasting, 347
Advance Ship Notice (ASN), 15, 19
  EDI savings, 20-22
  TMS (Transportation Management System), 90

advanced order fulfillment system technologies, batch order summary sheets, 219-222
advanced planning, forecast programs, 348
affinity analysis, staff training, 5
Algebraic Model, 276-278
American Production and Inventory Control Society (APICS), 199
Analysis activity, CPFR (Collaborative Planning, Forecasting, and Replenishment), 207-210
analytics features, ERP (Enterprise Resource Programs), 124-125
Analyze phase, Six Sigma, 390
  Behavioral Health Hospital, 398-400
animal industry, RFID (Radio Frequency Identity Tags), 54
APICS (American Production and Inventory Control Society), 199
apparel industry, RFID (Radio Frequency Identity Tags), 52-54
Apple, 4
  iMac, 4
ASN. *See* Advance Ship Notice (ASN)
AS/RS (Automatic Storage and Retrieval Equipment), 215
Asset Life Cycle Management, RFID (Radio Frequency Identity Tags), 57
ATP (available to promise), 122-124

auto industry, RFID (Radio Frequency Identity Tags), 55

automated forecast system, TMS (Transportation Management System), 83-90

automatic re-initialization, forecast programs, 347

automation, distribution portal, 107

automation savings, EDI (VMI), 19-20

Autonomic Supply Chain Management, 59

available to promise (ATP), 122-124

Average Inventory, 162-163

B

B2B (business-to-business), 97

customer portals, 101

  competition's sales choices, 102-103

  lift by category, 101-102

  lift by item, 102

  lift by month, 102

  Merchandising Optimizer, 103

  operational savings, 106-107

  price optimizer, 102

  productivity enhancements, 103-104

  savings, 104-105

  variable pricing, 102

distribution portal, 107

  automation, 107

  iPad used in distribution setting, 107-108

  IT green savings, 109

  savings of new items using new item portals, 108

green IT

  energy efficiency, 110-115

  energy usage, 109-110

  greenhouse gas emissions, 110

vendor portals

  automation of Show Market Bulletins, 98-99

  closeout and discontinued items, 100-101

  new items portal, 100

  new items portal, savings, 100

  special events, 101

  special prices, 101

back order time to completion, WMS (Warehouse Management System), 33

back-haul, visual supply chain, 240

batch order picking, 217

batch order summary sheets, 217-218

advanced order fulfillment system technologies, 219-222

mechanized takeaways, 218-219

order fulfillment systems, 222-224

BD&L (broken, damaged, and lost inventory), 64

Behavioral Health Hospital

Six Sigma, 390-391

  Analyze phase, 398-400

  Control phase, 405

  Define phase, 391-395

  Improve phase, 401-404

  Measure phase, 395-397

benefits of ERP (Enterprise Resource Programs)

improved accounting controls, 130-131

improved customer service, 130

inventory reduction, 129

labor cost reductions, 130

BI (Business Intelligence). *See* Business Intelligence

blade servers, 114

Borders, 109

broken, damaged, and lost inventory (BD&L), 64

building flushing, Sweetwater, 387

building site, 383

bullwhip effect, 12, 57

Business Intelligence,7

SharePoint, 115

business processes, ERP (Enterprise Resource Programs), 124-125

business-to-business. *See* B2B (business-to-business)

C

calculated vendor lead time, WMS (Warehouse Management System), 33

calculating

carbon dioxide emission, 116

enterprise dollar cost of electrical utilities, 118

grams of carbon dioxide used, 119

number of kilowatt-hours used, 118

pounds of carbon dioxide emitted per year, 116-117

cannibalization of gross margins, 160

carbon dioxide emission, 81, 90, 369-373

calculating, 116

calculating pounds emitted per year, 116-117

carbon dioxide emissions, calculating grams used, 119

central stocking, ABCDE classification of inventory, 152-157

Green Savings, 157

Lean Savings, 157

certification programs, 12, 24-26

savings, 26

certified wood, Sweetwater, 386-387

chain of custody, pharmaceutical industry, 56

Change Management, 6

characteristics of forecast programs, 345-351

check digits, 252

closeout items, vendor portals, 100-101

Collaborative Planning, Forecasting, and Replenishment. *See* CPFR (Collaborative Planning, Forecasting, and Replenishment)

Collaborative Transportation Management, CPFR (Collaborative Planning, Forecasting, and Replenishment), 212-213

commissioning of mechanical systems, Sweetwater, 387

Commodities Catalog Savings, customer portals, 105

communities for portals, SharePoint,115

competition's sales choices, customer portals, 102-103

components of RFID (Radio Frequency Identity Tags), 50

composites for business processes, SharePoint, 115

computing cost of electricity, 116

consigning, inventory, 11

consolidation-points network, visual supply chain, 240

construction-waste management, Sweetwater, 386

Container Delivery Management, 166

contentment for content management, SharePoint, 115

Control phase, Six Sigma, 390
Behavioral Health Hospital, 405
Corporate Construction, 384
correlation analysis, forecast programs, 348
cost of electricity, computing, 116
cost of implementing RFID (Radio Frequency Identity Tags), 49-50
cost of RFID implementation, distribution industry case study, 69-71
cost of utilities, calculating pounds of carbon dioxide emitted per year, 116-117
CPFR (Collaborative Planning, Forecasting, and Replenishment), 123, 199-202
Analysis activity, 207-210
CTM (Collaborative Transportation Management), 212-213
Demand and Supply Management activity, 203-206
Execution activity, 206-207
Green Savings, 211-212
Lean Savings, 210-211
Strategic Planning activity, 202-203
CRM features, ERP (Enterprise Resource Programs), 125-126
cross docking, WMS (Warehouse Management System), 30
CTM (Collaborative Transportation Management), CPFR (Collaborative Planning, Forecasting, and Replenishment), 212-213
customer portals, 101
Commodities Catalog Savings, 105
competition's sales choices, 102-103
lift by category, 101-102
lift by item, 102
lift by month, 102
Merchandising Optimizer, 103
New Product Merchandising Portal, 105
operational savings, 106-107
price optimizer, 102
productivity enhancements, 103-104
savings, 104-105
variable pricing, 102
customer service, benefits of ERP (Enterprise Resource Programs), 130

D

Daily Sales Product Activity Data 852, 17
DAM (Digital Asset Management), 256
Darwin, Charles, 4
data mining, 216
data pools, item synchronization, 247
data synchronization, item synchronization, 248-249
data warehouse, 98
daylight, Sweetwater, 385
DBLV (distribution by line value), 149
dead run, visual supply chain, 240
Define phase, Six Sigma, 390
Behavioral Health Hospital, 391-395
Demand and Supply Management activity, CPFR (Collaborative Planning, Forecasting, and Replenishment), 203-206
Demand Filter (DF), 298
demand patterns, 348
demographic information, 161
designing paperless environments with software, internal supply chains, 255-258

DF (Demand Filter), 298, 344

Digital Asset Management (DAM), 256

Digital Manufacturing, 245

directed putaway, RF (Radio Frequency), WMS (Warehouse Management System), 45

discontinued items, 206

  vendor portals, 100-101

dispersion measurement, gamma smoothing, TI, 314-316

dispersion of demand, 297-300

distribution industry case study, RFID (Radio Frequency Identity Tags), 63-70

  cost structure of RFID implementation, 69-71

  future recommendations, 74-75

  implementing RFID, 68-70

  ROI (return on investment), 70

  savings, 73-74

distribution portal, 107

  automation, 107

  iPad used in distribution setting, 107-108

  IT green savings, 109

  new items portal, 108

  savings of new items using new item portals, 108

distribution requirements planning. See DRP (distribution requirements planning)

Distribution Resource Management (DRM), 165-168

DM (Document Management), 256

Do it Best Corp, 12

  certification programs, 25

  savings, 22

  SharePoint, 97

Document Management (DM), 256

documents, VMI partner document, 12

dollar fill rate, WMS (Warehouse Management System), 32

DRM (Distribution Resource Management), 165-168

DRP (distribution requirements planning), 166, 168

  freight forwarder program, savings, 172

  Green Savings, 169, 171

    landfill savings, 170

    service-level savings, 170

    utility costs, 170

  Lean Savings, 168-169, 171-172

dynamic routing, visual supply chain, 240

E

EAN.UCC, 250

ECM (Enterprise Content Management), 256

economic order formula

  new, 361-364

  old, 354-360

Economic Order Quantity. *See* EOQ (Economic Order Quantity)

economical routing, TMS (Transportation Management System), 80

ECR (Efficient Consumer Response), 246

EDI (electronic data interchange)

  automation savings (VMI), 19-20

  savings, 14-17

    Advance Ship Notice, 20-22

    invoices, 20-22

    PO (purchase order), 20-22

transaction sets, 14-17

   summary, 18

Efficient Consumer Response (ECR), 246

efficient servers, 111

electricity, average amount of grams of electricity generated in U.S. for one kWh, 117

electronic data interchange. *See* EDI (electronic data interchange)

Electronic Product Code (EPC), 51

Ellis, Liz, 384

Embry Riddle, Oracle Content Management, 264-265

Emerson Process, Oracle Content Management, 267

employee retention, 5

employees, incentives, 6

energy efficiency, 383

   green IT, 110-115

energy usage, green IT, 109-110

Enterprise Content Management (ECM), 256

enterprise dollar, calculating cost of electrical utilities, 118

enterprise portals, 123

Enterprise Resource Programs. *See* ERP (Enterprise Resource Programs)

environmental facts, internal supply chains, 255

Environmental Paper Network, 255

EOQ (Economic Order Quantity), 1, 353-354

   determining economical quantity to order, 359

   forecast programs, 347

   formulas, 355-356

   Green effect, 366

   transportation costs, 360

EPC (Electronic Product Code), 51, 246

ERP (Enterprise Resource Programs), 121-122

   benefits of

      improved accounting controls, 130-131

      improved customer service, 130

      inventory reduction, 129

      labor cost reductions, 130

   business processes and analytics features that can be added, 124-125

   CRM features, 125-126

   financials features, 126

   human resource management features, 127

   manufacturing features, 127

   Procter & Gamble KPIs Excel spreadsheet, 135

   recycle, disposal, and hazardous metrics of green, 134

   SCM (Supply Chain Management) features, 128-129

   sustainable drive to green, 131-133

   transportation metrics of green, 134

   utilities metrics of green, 134

ERP environment, 7

ERP II (Enterprise Resource Management), 9

error measurements, 342-344

   VI (Volatility Index), 342-343

ESO (Expected Stock Outs), 174

event driven, 55

execution, 7

   technology, 7-8

Execution activity, CPFR (Collaborative Planning, Forecasting, and Replenishment), 206-207 expediting systems, 349

exponential smoothing, 284-287

    versus gamma smoothing, 308-310

    Horizontal Model, 287-288

    inventory control metrics, VI (Volatility Index) = .08187, 320-321

    MAD (mean absolute deviation), 294-297

    Seasonal Model, 289-293

    Trend Model, 288-290

    Trend Seasonal Model, 294

    VI (Volatility Index) = 1.0, 329-330

    VI (Volatility Index) = .20, inventory control metrics, 323-324

    VI (Volatility Index) = .50, 326-327

Exponential Smoothing Models, 280-281

    benchmarks, 322

exponential smoothing order quantity, graphs, 338-340

F

fans, variable-speed fans, 111-112

fill rate, 148

financials features, ERP (Enterprise Resource Programs), 126

finding forecast models, 300

fixed order quantities, 349

Fixed Period Model. *See* FP (Fixed Period Model)

Fixed Quantity Model, 179, 185-190

forecast models, finding, 300

Forecast Planning Schedule 830, 17

forecast programs

    adaptive forecasting, 347

    advanced planning, 348

    automatic reinitialization, 347

    characteristics of, 345-351

    correlation analysis, 348

    EOQ (Economic Order Quantity), 347

    intervals, 348

    joint order system process, 351

    management information systems, 351

    open-to-buy system, 349

    regression analysis, 347

    seasonal indexing, 350-351

    seasonal profiles, 350

    service-level metrics, 345-346

Forecasting and Ordering Using Regression Time Series and Econometrics, 8

forecasting procedures, 1

forecasting systems

    Algebraic Model, 276-278

    dispersion of demand, 297-300

    exponential smoothing, 284-287

        Horizontal Model, 287-288

        Seasonal Model, 289-293

        Trend Model, 288-290

        Trend Seasonal Model, 294

    gamma smoothing, 305

    Horizontal Exponential Smoothing Model, 301

    Logarithmic Models, 282-285

    Logistics Model, 281

    Regression Models, 278-280

    Seasonal Exponential Smoothing Model, 303

    seasonal profile forecasting, 346

    Trend Exponential Smoothing Model, 302-303

    Trigonometric Models, 280-281

forecasting VMI (vendor-managed inventory), 9-12

formulas

  EOQ (Economic Order Quantity), 355-356

  gamma smoothing, 305-308

FOURTE (Forecasting and Ordering Using Regression Time Series and Econometrics), 8

FP (Fixed Period Model), 179-185

  ordering strategy, 181

  variable demand, 183

FQ (Fixed Quantity Model), 179, 185-190

freight, scheduling, 346

freight forwarder program, DRP (distribution requirements planning), savings, 172

funnel program, 26

G

gaming industry, RFID (Radio Frequency Identity Tags), 58

gamma smoothing, 285, 305

  examples, 311-312

  versus exponential smoothing, 308-310

  inventory control metrics, VI (Volatility Index) = .08187, 321-322

  theory and formulas, 305-308

  TI, 312-313

    dispersion measurement, 314-316

    effects of increasing VI, 316-318

    inventory control metrics, 319-320

  VI (Volatility Index) = 1.0, 330-333

  VI (Volatility Index) = .20, 324-326

  VI (Volatility Index) = .50, 327-329

Gamma Smoothing Model, benchmarks, 322

GDS (Global Data Synchronization), 246

glass, Sweetwater, 384

Global Data Synchronization, 246

global temperatures, 373

GMROI (Gross Margin Return on Investment), 2

Go Green with Oracle Content Management, 261-272

gravity flow roller system, 67-68

green

  recycle, disposal, and hazardous metrics, ERP (Enterprise Resource Programs), 134

  transportation metrics, ERP (Enterprise Resource Programs), 134

  utilities metrics, ERP (Enterprise Resource Programs), 134

Green effect, EOQ (Economic Order Quantity), 366

green IT

  energy efficiency, 110-115

  energy usage, 109-110

  greenhouse gas emissions, 110

Green savings

  3PL (third-party logistics), 144-145

  ABCDE classification of inventory, 150

  central stocking, 157

  CPFR (Collaborative Planning, Forecasting, and Replenishment), 211-212

  customer portals, 105

  distribution portal, 109

  DRP (distribution requirements planning), 169, 171

    landfill savings, 170

    service-level savings, 170

    utility costs, 170

EDI (Advance Ship Notice, POs and invoices), 20-22

ERP (Enterprise Resource Programs), accounting controls, 131

Joint Order Allocation, 177

paper, 260

RF (Radio Frequency), WMS (Warehouse Management System), 47

substitution program, 152

TMS (Transportation Management System), 80-83

VMI Reduction of Inventory, 23-24

VPQ (Variable Period and Quantity Model), 198

WMS (Warehouse Management System), 38

green supply chain management, 376-378

Green Supply Chains, 376

Green value, TMS (Transportation Management System), 78-79

Green variable, supply chains, 10

greenhouse gas emissions, green IT, 110

Gross Margin Return on Investment, 2

GS1 (Global Standard 1), 247

GTIN numbers

data structures, 252-253

master data alignment, 250-251

H

hardware location, 113-114

Henry, Tom, 384

Horizontal Exponential Smoothing Model, 301

Horizontal Model, exponential smoothing, 287-288

hub-and-spoke arrangement, visual supply chain, 239

human resource management features, ERP (Enterprise Resource Programs), 127

HVAC (Heating, Ventilation, and Air Conditioning), 11

I

ice storage, Sweetwater, 387

ICT (information and communication technologies), 110

iMac, 4

implementing RFID (Radio Frequency Identity Tags), distribution industry case study, 68-70

Improve phase, Six Sigma, 390

Behavioral Health Hospital, 401-404

Improved Warehouse Worker Productivity, WMS (Warehouse Management System), 34-35

improving

Inventory Management, WMS (Warehouse Management System), 34

Transportation Performance, WMS (Warehouse Management System), 35-37

inbound freight, scheduling, 346

incentives, employees, 6

indirect cost savings, distribution industry case study, RFID (Radio Frequency Identity Tags), 74

individual item lead time, WMS (Warehouse Management System), 33

Industrial Revolution, consequences of, 369-373

information and communication technologies (ICT), 110

initialization, 300

Innovation Management, 4-5

installing RF systems, 224-225

insulation, Sweetwater, 385

Intergovernmental Panel on Climate Change (IPCC), 116

internal supply chains
  designing paperless environments with software, 255-258
  environmental facts, 255
  Mobius software, 258-259
  saving paper, 259
    Green Savings, 260
    Lean Savings, 259-260

intervals, forecast programs, 348

inventory
  Average Inventory, 162-163
  consigning, 11
  visual supply chain, 242

inventory control metrics
  gamma smoothing, TI, 319-320
  VI (Volatility Index) = .08187
    exponential smoothing, 320-321
    gamma smoothing, 321-322
  VI (Volatility Index) = 1.0
    exponential smoothing, 329-330
    gamma smoothing, 330-333
  VI (Volatility Index) = .20
    exponential smoothing, 323-324
    gamma smoothing, 324-326
  VI (Volatility Index) = .50
    exponential smoothing, 326-327
    gamma smoothing, 327-329

inventory knowledge, 64

inventory management, 147
  improving, 34
  WMS (Warehouse Management System), 29

inventory reduction, benefits of ERP (Enterprise Resource Programs), 129

invoices, 15
  EDI savings, 20-22

iPad, distribution portal, 107-108

IPCC (Intergovernmental Panel on Climate Change), 116

ISO (International Organization for Standardization), 133

IT Green Initiative, 110-115

IT green savings, distribution portal, 109

IT resources, sharing, 112

IT system redundancies, 112

item data accuracy, master data alignment, 245-246

Item Maintenance Transaction Set 888, 17

item synchronization, 247, 252-253
  data pools, 247
  data synchronization, 248-249

Items Price/Sales Catalog 832, 17

J

JIT (just-in-time), 10, 245, 354

Jobs, Steve, 4, 7

Joint Order Allocation, 173-176
  Green Savings, 177
  Lean Savings, 177

joint order system process, forecast programs, 351

just-in-time (JIT), 10, 245, 354

K

k factor, priority, 343
Keeling, C. David, 372
kilowatt-hours used, calculating, 118
knowledge management, 6-7

L

labor cost reductions, benefits
of ERP (Enterprise Resource
Programs), 130
landfill savings, DRP (distribution
requirements planning), 170
lead times, 349
Leadership in Energy and
Environmental Design. *See*
LEED (Leadership in Energy and
Environmental Design)
Leadership in Energy and
Environmental Design (LEED)
Platinum Certification,
Sweetwater, 384
Lean Green Supply Chain, 1
Lean Savings
3PL (third-party logistics), 143-144
ABCDE classification of inventory,
149-150
central stocking, 157
CPFR (Collaborative Planning,
Forecasting, and Replenishment),
210-211
customer portals, 104-105
DRP (distribution requirements
planning), 168-169, 171-172
EDI (Advance Ship Notice, POs,
and invoices), 20-22
ERP (Enterprise Resource
Programs), accounting
controls, 131
Joint Order Allocation, 177

paper, 259-260
promotional forecast system,
163-164
RF (Radio Frequency), WMS
(Warehouse Management
System), 46
substitution program, 151-152
TMS (Transportation Management
System), 93
VMI Reduction of Inventory, 22
VPQ (Variable Period and Quantity
Model), 197-198
WMS (Warehouse Management
System), 37-38
Lean Six Sigma, 389
LEED (Leadership in Energy and
Environmental Design), 375-376,
378-379
development, 379
LEED Certification, 380-381
LEED Green Building Rating
System, 380
licensing software, TMS
(Transportation Management
System), 77-78
lift by category, customer
portals, 101-102
lift by item, customer portals, 102
lift by month, customer portals, 102
light sensors, Sweetwater, 385
line accuracy, WMS (Warehouse
Management System), 32
line fill rate, WMS (Warehouse
Management System), 31
Logarithmic Models, 282-285
logistics industry, RFID (Radio
Frequency Identity Tags), 56
Logistics Model, 281
low-emitting materials,
Sweetwater, 387

Lowes, 11

LT (lead time), 180

  FQ (Fixed Quantity Model), 186

M

MAD (mean absolute deviation),
  280-281

  exponential smoothing, 294-297

  tracking signal, 298

manage stock, WMS (Warehouse
  Management System), 30

manage storage facilities, WMS
  (Warehouse Management
  System), 30

management information systems,
  forecast programs, 351

Managing by Walking Around, 6, 35

manual orders, TMS (Transportation
  Management System), 83

manufacturing, RFID (Radio
  Frequency Identity Tags), 58

manufacturing features, ERP
  (Enterprise Resource
  Programs), 127

master data alignment, 245

  GTIN numbers, 250-251

  item data accuracy, 245-246

material efficiency, 383

material handling, 215

material management, 122

Material Requirement
  Programs, 161-162

Material Safety Data Sheet
  (MSDS), 16

Mauna Loa CO_2, 371-372

mean absolute deviation
  (MAD), 280-281

Measure phase, Six Sigma, 390

  Behavioral Health Hospital, 395-397

mechanized takeaways, batch order
  summary sheets, 218-219

medical environment case studies,
  RFID (Radio Frequency Identity
  Tags), 60-62

  ROI, 62-63

  savings estimates, 62

Merchandising Optimizer, customer
  portals, 103

metrics, WMS (Warehouse
  Management System), 31-33

Microsoft SharePoint, 97, 114-115

  platform of services, 115

minimizing out-of-stocks, 150-151

Min/Max strategy, 350

Missouri Division of Processional
  Registration, Oracle Content
  Management, 268

Mobile Supply Chain, ERP
  (Enterprise Resource
  Programs), 124

Mobius software, 258-259

  saving paper, 259-260

MRP II (networked closed-loop
  manufacturing requirement
  planning), 9

MSDS (Material Safety Data
  Sheet), 16

MSKTD Associates, 384

Mulally, Allen, 7

N

ND (neighborhood
  development), 381

network optimization, third-party
  providers, 139-142

new items portal, 100

  distribution portal, 108

  savings, 100

New Product Merchandising Portal, customer portals, 105

number of back orders, WMS (Warehouse Management System), 33

O

occupant health and safety, 383

OI (Outliner Indicator), 343-344

On Device, 8

On Order Report, 106

on-demand, 7

on-device computing, ERP (Enterprise Resource Programs), 124

on-off power cycler devices, 112

on-order (OO), 181

onsite supplier (OSS), 10

onsite suppliers (OSS), third-party providers, 138-139

on-time delivery, WMS (Warehouse Management System), 33

open-to-buy system, forecast programs, 349

operational savings, customer portals, 106-107

Opportunity Management, 55

OQ, 181

Oracle Content Management, 217

"Go Green with Oracle Content Management," 261-272

order accuracy, WMS (Warehouse Management System), 32

order fill rate, WMS (Warehouse Management System), 31

order filling, RF (Radio Frequency), WMS (Warehouse Management System), 45-46

order fulfillment systems, batch order summary sheets, 222-224

order fulfillment technologies, 219-222

Order Fulfillment, WMS (Warehouse Management System), 29

order picking, 216

batch order picking, 217

WMS (Warehouse Management System), 36

order processing, WMS (Warehouse Management System), 31

order stocking, RF (WMS), 45

ordering strategy, FP (Fixed Period Model), 181

orders cycle time, WMS (Warehouse Management System), 32

order-to-cash cycle, CPFR (Collaborative Planning, Forecasting, and Replenishment), 206-207

Organizational Structure 210, 17

Organizational Structure 816, 16

OSHA (Occupational Safety and Health Administration), 16

OSS (onsite supplier), 10, 138-139

outdoor air delivery monitoring, Sweetwater, 388

out-of-stocks, minimizing, 150-151

P

packaging levels, UCC-12, 251

paper, 255

saving, 259

Green Savings, 260

Lean Savings, 259-260

Pareto charts, 397-394

Payment Order/Remittance Advice, 16

peddle run, visual supply chain, 240

pedigree tracking, pharmaceutical industry, 55

Pick to Light, 227-229

mechanics of, 229

plan-o-grams, 107

platform of services, SharePoint, 115

PLM (Product Life Cycle Management), 245

PMA (predetermined maximum available), 181

PO (purchase order), 14, 19-20

EDI savings, 20-22

Point of Sale Data Report, 106

postponement, WMS (Warehouse Management System), 31

power supplies, 113

Price Information 879, 16-17

price optimizer, customer portals, 102

Price/Sales Catalog, 16

priority, k factor, 343

Procter & Gamble KPIs Excel spreadsheet, ERP (Enterprise Resource Programs), 135

Product Life Cycle Management (PLM), 245

productivity enhancements, customer portals, 103-104

productivity metrics, Voice Pick, 233-237

profit-sharing program, Talent Management, 5

Promotion to Regular Usage (PRU), 160

Promotion to Stock Demand (PSD), 160

promotional forecast system, 159-163

Lean Savings, 163-164

promotional lift, 159

promotional use file, 161

provide connectivity to the enterprise, WMS (Warehouse Management System), 30

PRU (Promotion to Regular Usage), 160

PSD (Promotion to Stock Demand), 160

PUE (power usage effectiveness), 110

purchase orders. *See* PO (purchase order)

R

rack servers, 111

Radio Frequency. *See* RF (Radio Frequency)

Radio Frequency Identity Tags. *See* RFID (Radio Frequency Identity Tags)

Real Time Location Systems, 52

receive stock and returns/reverse logistics, WMS (Warehouse Management System), 30

Receiving Advice 861, 17

receiving processes, 225-226

Pick to Light, 227-229

RF picking system metrics, 227

RF productivity, 226

Voice Pick, 230-233

recycle, disposal, and hazardous metrics of green (ERP), 134

recycled content of materials, Sweetwater, 386

recycling, Sweetwater, 385

regional materials, Sweetwater, 386

regression analysis, forecast programs, 347

Regression Models, 278-280

renewable materials, Sweetwater, 384

replenishment policies, RFID (Radio Frequency Identity Tags), 57

resource management, creating world-class companies, 3-9

retaining employees, 5

RF (Radio Frequency), WMS (Warehouse Management System), 38-40

  applied analysis, 43-46

  directed putaway, 45

  Green Savings, 47

  improvements, 46

  Lean Savings, 46

  order filling, 45-46

  order stocking, 45

RF picking system metrics, receiving processes, 227

RF productivity

  receiving processes, 226

  stocking processes, 226

RF systems, installing, 224-225

RFID (Radio Frequency Identity Tags), 49

  advantages of, 51

  animal industry, 54

  apparel industry, 52-54

  Asset Life Cycle Management, 57

  auto industry, 55

  Autonomic Supply Chain Management, 59

  bullwhip effect, 57

  categories of real-time information, 51

  components of, 50

  cost of implementing, 49-50

  distribution industry case study, 63-70

    cost structure of RFID implementation, 69-71

    future recommendations, 74-75

    implementing RFID, 68-70

    ROI (return on investment), 70

    savings, 73-74

  gaming industry, 58

  growth of, 52

  healthcare and pharmaceutical industry, 55-56

  how it works, 50

  implementing, distribution industry case study, 68-70

  Jewelry Management Industry, 58

  logistics industry, 56

  manufacturing, 58

  medical environment case studies, 60-62

    ROI, 62-63

    savings estimates, 62

  replenishment policies, 57

  Supply Chain Management (SCM), 57

  WMS (Warehouse Management System), 56

RFID antennas and cabling, 50

RFID middleware, 50

RFID printer, 50

RFID reader, 50

RFID tags, 50

ROI (return on investment)

  distribution industry case study, RFID (Radio Frequency Identity Tags), 70

  medical environment case studies, RFID (Radio Frequency Identity Tags), 62-63

roof membrane, Sweetwater, 385

RTLS (Real Time Location Systems), 52

S

SAAS (Software as a Service), 7

safety stock (SS), 181

SAP, 133

savings

    certification programs, 26

    customer portals, 104-105

    distribution industry case study, RFID (Radio Frequency Identity Tags), 73-74

    EDI, 14-17

        Advance Ship Notice, 20-22

        invoices, 20-22

        PO (purchase order), 20-22

    freight forwarder program, 172

    medical environment case studies, RFID (Radio Frequency Identity Tags), 62

    new items portal, 100

    TMS (Transportation Management System), 94-95

    WMS (Warehouse Management System), 37-38

scalability and configurability, WMS (Warehouse Management System), 29

scan based trading programs, 16-17

SCE (Supply Chain Execution), 27

scheduling inbound freight, 346

SCM (Supply Chain Management), 27, 215

SCM (Supply Chain Management) features, ERP (Enterprise Resource Programs), 128-129

scorecarding, 24

SCP (Supply Chain Planning), 27

search for more productivity, SharePoint, 115

Seasonal Exponential Smoothing Model, 303, 333-338

Seasonal Gamma Smoothing, 333-338, 340-342

seasonal indexing, forecast programs, 350-351

Seasonal Model, exponential smoothing, 289-293

seasonal profile forecasting, 346

seasonal profiles, forecast programs, 350

servers

    blade servers, 114

    efficient servers, 111

    rack servers, 111

service-level factor, 357

service-level metrics, 345-346

service-level savings, DRP (distribution requirements planning), 170

SharePoint, 97, 114-115

    platform of services, 115

sharing IT resources, 112

Shaw Industries, 378

shelf life, 348

shelf life monitoring, WMS (Warehouse Management System), 29

Show Market Bulletins, automation, from vendor portals, 98-99

SIMS, 60

sites for collaboration, SharePoint, 115

Six Sigma, 389-390

    Behavioral Health Hospital, 390-391

        Analyze phase, 398-400

        Control phase, 405

        Define phase, 391-395

        Improve phase, 401-404

        Measure phase, 395-397

SKU, 154

software, licensing, TMS (Transportation Management System), 77-78

SOP (standard operating procedures), 12

sourcing visual supply chain, 242

special events, vendor portals, 101

special prices, vendor portals, 101

SSO (Specified Service Overall), 174

staff training, affinity analysis, 5

Standard Forwarding Company, Oracle Content Management, 266-267

standard operating procedures (SOP), 12

stock status, 180

stocking processes, 225-226
  Pick to Light, 227-229
  RF picking system metrics, 227
  RF productivity, 226
  Voice Pick, 230-233

storage devices, 112-113

Strategic Planning activity, CPFR (Collaborative Planning, Forecasting, and Replenishment), 202-203

substitution program, ABCDE classification of inventory, 150-151
  Green Savings, 152

Supply Chain Execution (SCE), 27

Supply Chain Management (SCM), 27
  RFID (Radio Frequency Identity Tags), 57

Supply Chain Planning (SCP), 27

supply chains, 2-14
  Green variable, 10

Surack, Chuck, 384

sustainability, 3

sustainable drive to green, ERP (Enterprise Resource Programs), 131-133

Swedish Medical, Oracle Content Management, 265-266

Sweetwater, 383-384
  building flushing, 387
  certified wood, 386-387
  commissioning of mechanical systems, 387
  construction-waste management, 386
  daylight, 385
  glass, 384
  ice storage, 387
  insulation, 385
  Leadership in Energy and Environmental Design (LEED) Platinum Certification, 384
  light sensors, 385
  low-emitting materials, 387
  outdoor air delivery monitoring, 388
  recycled content of materials, 386
  recycling, 385
  regional materials, 386
  renewable materials, 384
  roof membrane, 385
  tobacco smoke control, 388
  water use reduction, 386

system integration, WMS (Warehouse Management System), 28

T

Talent Management, 5
  profit-sharing program, 5

technological advancements, 6-7

technology, execution, 7-8

theories, gamma smoothing, 305-308

third-party providers, 137
   multimodal, 138
   network optimization, 139-142
   onsite suppliers (OSS), 138-139
TI, gamma smoothing, 312-313
   dispersion measurement, 314-316
   effects of increasing VI, 316-318
   inventory control metrics, 319-320
TMS (Transportation Management System), 28, 77
   ASN (Advance Ship Notice), 90
   automated forecast system, 83-90
   benefits of, 79-80
   economical routing, 80
   Green Savings, 80-83, 94
   Green value, 78-79
   Lean Savings, 93
   licensing software, 77-78
   manual orders, 83
   savings, 94-95
   vendors, 78
   visibility, 79
tobacco smoke control, Sweetwater, 388
trace and track, pharmaceutical industry, 56
Track and Trace, 166
tracking material flow, WMS (Warehouse Management System), 31
tracking signal, MAD (mean absolute deviation), 298
transaction sets, EDI, 14-17
   summary, 18
Transportation Carrier Shipment Status Message, 15
transportation costs, EOQ (Economic Order Quantity), 360

Transportation Management System. *See* TMS (Transportation Management System)
transportation metrics of green, ERP (Enterprise Resource Programs), 134
transportation performance, WMS (Warehouse Management System), 29
   improving, 35-37
transportation policies, visual supply chain, 242
Trend Exponential Smoothing Model, 302-303
Trend Model, exponential smoothing, 288-290
Trend Seasonal Model, exponential smoothing, 294
Trigonometric Models, 280-281
TS (tracking signal indicator), 344

U

UCC-12, packaging levels, 251
UCCnet, 247
utilities, calculating enterprise dollar cost of, 118
utilities metrics of green, ERP (Enterprise Resource Programs), 134
utility costs, DRP (distribution requirements planning), 170

V

Value Stream Mapping, 36
variable demand, FP (Fixed Period Model), 183
Variable Period and Quantity Model. *See* VPQ (Variable Period and Quantity Model)

variable pricing, customer portals, 102

variable-speed fans, 111-112

vendor lead time, WMS (Warehouse Management System), 33

vendor minimum, 174

vendor portals, B2B (business-to-business)

automation of Show Market Bulletins, 98-99

closeout and discontinued items, 100-101

new items portal, 100

new items portal, savings, 100

special events, 101

special prices, 101

vendor-management inventory, 9-12

vendors, TMS (Transportation Management System), 78

VI (Volatility Index), 153, 312

effects of increasing VI, gamma smoothing, 316-318

error measurements, 342-343

VI (Volatility Index) = .08187, inventory control metrics

exponential smoothing, 320-321

gamma smoothing, 321-322

VI (Volatility Index) = 1.0, inventory control metrics

exponential smoothing, 329-330

gamma smoothing, 330-333

VI (Volatility Index) = .20, inventory control metrics

exponential smoothing, 323-324

gamma smoothing, 324-326

VI (Volatility Index) = .50, inventory control metrics

exponential smoothing, 326-327

gamma smoothing, 327-329

VICS (Voluntary Interindustry Commerce Solutions Association), 42-43, 199

virtualization, 114

visibility, TMS (Transportation Management System), 79

visible supply chain, 239, 242-244

visual supply chain, 239-242

back-haul, 240

consolidation-points network, 240

dead run, 240

dynamic routing, 240

hub-and-spoke arrangement, 239

inventory, 242

peddle run, 240

sourcing, 242

transportation policies, 242

VMI (vendor-managed inventory), 9-12

VMI, EDI automation savings, 19-20

VMI partner document, 12

VMI productivity increase, 18

VMI reduction of inventory

Green Savings, 23-24

Leans Savings, 22

Voice Pick, 230-233

productivity metrics, 233-237

Voluntary Interindustry Commerce Solutions Association, 42-43, 199

VPQ (Variable Period and Quantity Model), 179, 190-197

Green Savings, 198

Lean Savings, 197-198

VSM (Value Stream Mapping), 36

W

Warehouse Management System. *See* WMS (Warehouse Management System)

Warehouse Productivity, WMS (Warehouse Management System), 29

water efficiency, 383

water use reduction, Sweetwater, 386

web-based platform, WMS (Warehouse Management System), 29

WebEDI (web-based EDI), 14-17

WMS (Warehouse Management System), 27-28

  cross docking, 30

  functionality of, 28-31

  Green Savings, 38

  improved warehouse worker productivity, 34-35

  inventory management, improving, 34

  Lean Savings, 37-38

  Managing by Walking Around, 35

  metrics, 31-33

  order picking, 36

  order processing, 31

  postponement, 31

  RF (Radio Frequency), 38-40

    applied analysis, 43-46

    directed putaway, 45

    Green Savings, 47

    improvements, 46

    Lean Savings, 46

    order filling, 45-46

    order stocking, 45

  RFID (Radio Frequency Identity Tags), 56

  savings, 37-38

  system integration, 28

  tracking material flow, 31

  Transportation Performance, improving, 35-37

  work planning, 31

work planning, WMS (Warehouse Management System), 31

world-class companies, creating

  EDI, savings, 14-17

  forecasting. *See* forecasting systems

  resource management, 3-9

Z

Z transform, 357

FINANCIAL TIMES

In an increasingly competitive world, it is quality
of thinking that gives an edge—an idea that opens new
doors, a technique that solves a problem, or an insight
that simply helps make sense of it all.

We work with leading authors in the various arenas
of business and finance to bring cutting-edge thinking
and best-learning practices to a global market.

It is our goal to create world-class print publications
and electronic products that give readers
knowledge and understanding that can then be
applied, whether studying or at work.

To find out more about our business
products, you can visit us at www.ftpress.com.